...ORS AWEIGH

...URBI

...AMELA BRITTON

...T · HENRY O'NEILL

. . . When your lonely heart
has learned its lesson
You'd be hers if only she
would call . . .

If I don't see her each day
I miss her
Gee, what a thrill,
Each time I kiss her.
I've got a terrible case
On Nancy with the laughing face . . .

FRANK SINATRA

my father

NANCY SINATRA

DOUBLEDAY & COMPANY, INC.
GARDEN CITY, NEW YORK
1985

Photographs on preceding pages:

"His face," said the sculptor Jo Davidson, "has a curious structure. Those cheekbones! Those bulges around the cheeks. That heavy lower lip…like a young Lincoln."

Tommy Dorsey & Co., (From left) Don Lotus, Clark Yocum, Phil Stevens, T.D., Buddy Rich, Frank Sinatra, Ziggy Elman, Jo Stafford, Chuck Lowry, John Huddleston. Sinatra hated those shoes—but Dorsey insisted.

Marquee, Golden Gate Theatre, San Francisco, 1946.

Anchors Aweigh poster.

From Here to Eternity, 1953. Center trio: Ernest Borgnine, Burt Lancaster, Frank Sinatra.

The Man, The Voice, The Chairman of the Board, in concert.

At the mike, recording.

Dean Martin and Frank Sinatra, friends

Far left: Vice President Lyndon B. Johnson. (Fourth from left) Senator Stuart Symington, then President John F. Kennedy, Frank Sinatra.

1983 Kennedy Center Honors award for Lifetime Achievement. From left: Virgil Thompson, Elia Kazan, Frank Sinatra, Katherine Dunham, James Stewart, Mrs. Reagan, and President Ronald Reagan.

Library of Congress Cataloging in Publication Data

Sinatra, Nancy.
   Frank Sinatra, My Father.

   1. Sinatra, Frank, 1915–   .   2. Singers—United States—Biography.   I. Title.
ML420.S565S6   1985   784.5′0092′4 [B]   85-6772
ISBN 0-385-18294-5

625566

CONTENTS

For you, Daddy—Love, Chicken

emember. Trying to remember. That's the hard part. We don't know at five years old that we might be praying for total recall at forty. One doesn't live a life as though there were a book in it.

It wasn't until last year that my dad gave me this wonderful advice: "You should keep a diary." Thanks, Pop, but that's for the next book. For this one, I have summoned up memories. Mine, my father's, the family's, his colleagues and friends. People who have refused to talk about Frank Sinatra for publication in the past have put their recollections in my trust. So this is, in part, a book of voices.

The overriding voice, obviously, is mine. It is a book that attempts to reveal the Frank Sinatra his daughter has lived with, worked with, heard about, and loved.

Thank heaven for all the wonderful memories I managed to find. And what about the forgotten moments? If they were important, wouldn't I have remembered them? Or did I not remember them because they didn't happen? Or will they crop up one at a time like water torture, like little nightmares, *after* this book is printed?

During the sixteen years, on and off, of research and recall, I came to the conclusion that Frank Sinatra has to be the most documented entertainer in history. The main problem is that seldom do any two sources agree on names, dates, and events. Therefore, given my faulty memory—and Frank Sinatra not being so great at that stuff, either—what the hell was going on?

My father is not much interested in looking backward, except for occasional evenings of reminiscence with a few close friends. He is embarrassed by excessive compliments, just as he is easily hurt by insensitivity or what he sees as disloyalty. He's also damned annoyed by inefficiency: "I'll do my job and you do yours."

He cherishes time with his friends and family: "I don't want to die because I won't see the people I love anymore."

He is a survivor. "Stay away from the dark thoughts, Chicken," he has always told me. Also—and this is one of the touchstones in my life—"Don't despair."

His blend of strength and softness has been the prevailing constant in my life. I remember his hands holding me while, as a child, I learned to swim, firm but gentle hands keeping me safe. I remember those same hands guiding me, balancing me, and then letting go, as I tried to ride a two-wheeler. I remember lunches with him at drive-ins, oil painting with him on the back porch, baseball games, where he taught me the rules. And I remember the bear hug he gave me recently when I told him how *much* I love him. I could feel the vibration of the sigh in his chest against my cheek. "Oohh," he said, "I'd turn the world upside down for you." In January '85, leaving after a visit with him in New York, I tiptoed into his bedroom at the Waldorf. He was asleep—under the covers, snuggled up like a little boy. Soft white snow drifted past the window across from his bed. This was my dad, nearing his seventieth birthday. Frank Sinatra, the most famous entertainer in the world. As I leaned down to kiss him goodbye I thought, "Please, God. Please don't let this be the last time I see him. Please take care of him, stay with him for me . . ." I kissed his cheek; I touched his face gently with my fingers, whispered, "I love you, Daddy," and tiptoed out again, knowing that part of me would be missing until the next time.

In my love for him, and with the feeling that no book has been able to present a true portrait of my father, I have been working, on and off, for those sixteen years, collecting memories, letters, photographs, and above all, talking with him. Just as "outside" sources were seldom able to agree on the exact nature of events in his life, so even among close friends and family there have been conflicts over dates, names, places, and what was said. Often, what began as rumor, and was printed and reprinted and broadcast as speculation and conjecture, would inevitably end up as "fact." That sort of sequence didn't help matters at all. With the exception of my father's own occasional writings, I have relied on little that has previously appeared in print. To come as close to the truth as possible, I sometimes resolved the disagreements by giving the benefit of the doubt to eye-witnesses other than my father. Perhaps people will believe the truth told by these voices. They were there . . .

After all, the people who were there, and The Man himself, are most apt to know what really happened—and why.

No book, including the best biography, manages to tell all. And I am not a biographer, I am a collector and an observer and a daughter. My hope is that, as a privileged person, as someone able to report from close to the interior of his life, I may be able to illuminate some truths, dissolve a few myths, and—as he celebrates his seventieth birthday this December—put into perspective the lives he has led. This is a love letter, but not a whitewash. My Dad doesn't need —and wouldn't want—that.

HE
THROWS
A
LONG
SHADOW

The day of his wedding in 1976 my sister Tina and I went to Dad with the traditional magnets of good fortune: Something borrowed. Something blue. Then, something old.

I had his identification bracelet from years earlier. "Here, Daddy," I said. "Wear this."

He shook his head. "Nah," he said, grumbling cheerfully. "I'm not going to wear that. I don't wear bracelets."

"But you have to wear something old, something new, something borrowed, something blue. And look, it has your name on it."

"I don't need it," he chuckled. "*I* know who I am."

Absolutely. But so few others do.

The Sinatra I know is a patriarch, a friend, a patriot, a musician, a businessman, a saloon singer, and so much more. He is a man with a public image built partly on fact and largely on myth. He is a man who embraces consistency, yet embodies contradiction. A man who treats the room to caviar and champagne and himself to a sandwich and Coca-Cola. A man who is strong in a crisis, but dissolves behind closed doors when it ends. Who likes to be alone—as long as he knows someone is near. Who is publicly the quintessential swinger, and privately old-fashioned, uncomfortable with "living together," secure with marriage.

To some, Sinatra epitomizes a Dead End kid never grown up, yet to others he evokes elegance and gentility. He is a perfectionist who is impatient with the process of perfecting. A compassionate friend and a fierce foe. A musical genius who doesn't really read music. A maverick who lives by rigid codes. A winner who feels connected to losers. The complexities run deep.

Yet, certain simple truths transcend all the layers. When asked why he was campaigning for Hubert Humphrey in 1968 Sinatra said, "Because he's a decent man and he cares about people. He cares about people that other people don't care about, and because I believe him and believe in him—and that's what a man ought to feel about his President."

Trying to define Frank Sinatra, a friend once said, is like trying to "analyze electricity." That was thirty years ago, and it holds true today. His celebrity is crowning its sixth decade. He is an original. An American original, who insists that the flag fly daily at his home, who reflects the throb of the nation's energy, the scope of its opportunity, the pride of its individuality, the zeal of its frontier integrity. He throws a long shadow.

I've lived in that shadow. And loved the warmth of the man who's cast it. We're not just father and daughter, with an easy, loving relationship, if there are such; we're joined at the hip. We *read* each other easily—even from a distance. I can predict his reaction to family news or to world news. I can go to the phone to call him and it'll ring and it'll be him. And it works in reverse. At 6:30 on the morning he was to have major surgery on his hand, already under sedation and not even aware that I was in the same town, he heard footsteps in the hospital corridor and called out, "Chicken?" He just knew it was me.

As the oldest of his three children, I knew him best when he lived with us. I was ten when he and my mother—Nancy Sr.—split in 1950. My brother, Frank Jr., was seven. Tina wasn't yet two. I don't remember as much as I would like of my experiences with him back then, but I observe him as grandfather with my two girls, A.J. and Amanda, and I know what he must have been like with me. He is so intuitive and so right in the way he handles them. He knows exactly what to do and, unlike many adults, he's never rude to the children. I said once that I wanted them to know him as Grandpa and not as Frank Sinatra. "I don't want their image of you to be a bow tie and a tux and black patent leather pumps." He agreed. He said he was aware of the potential problem, the unique situation.

Aware. Be aware. Be aware of everything around you. That's what he always told us. He didn't shelter us from the "outside world"—I went to public schools—but he knew the risks for kids of a celebrity and he wanted us on guard. When I was two, there was a threat to kidnap me. (Peter Pitchess, who would come back into our lives later, was an FBI man then and he posed as our gardener to protect me). When I was twenty-seven, a strange man came to my home and said he was my brother and if I didn't go to the door to see him he would blow my brains out; luckily, the police got to him before he got to me. Since I was a kid I've had nightmares about something happening to my dad.

Probably the biggest problem for a Sinatra kid is perspective. My brother has talked about the time a girl came up to him in a restaurant and said, "You're Frank Sinatra's son. Can I have one of your french fries?" Frankie looked at her, dumbfounded. "I want to keep it as a souvenir," she said.

"I was disgusted," Frankie said. "Is this what life is? Is this what being Frank Sinatra's son means? Giving a *potato* to a stranger as a keepsake? 'Look,' I told her. 'You think I'm someone special but I'm just like you.' I shook the ketchup bottle over the french fries . . . 'See. The ketchup won't come out. I have trouble with the ketchup bottles, too.'"

Frankie's had larger problems. Singing in Argentina in 1965, he was twenty-one years old and "scared to death." Later, at a press conference full of South American dignitaries, he was confronted by a girl: "All of a sudden she

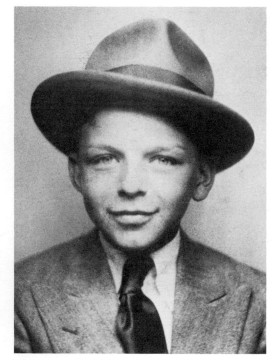

The taste for hats came early . . .

28

came up to me and said, 'This is for you!' And, whack!—she hit me in the eye. And there was a guy there with a camera, see. And the picture was printed around the world. The point being that this young girl was a fledgling ballerina or something and she wasn't making it and she had a manager who told her that Frank Sinatra's son was in town. 'All you have to do is go up and slap him and it will be in the papers and you'll get famous.' When I got back to the United States, a month later, my friends told me that it was on network news here: some girl had slapped Sinatra's son in South America because she didn't like the way his father treated women. That was the story as it was released up here. That kind of thing, it happens. A lot of guys who could never get to Sinatra get to me because I'm more accessible.

"I've had guys come to me and tell me they lent my father money forty years ago and would I give it to them. Once, when I was working way out on Long Island somewhere, a guy followed me back toward my motel room. He said my old man took a girl away from him in 1942. I said, 'Listen, if you cross over this threshold, into this room, I'll consider that burglary.' He charged in and I picked up an ashtray and hit him right on his head, and fractured his skull. The sheriff came and there was blood all over the floor and he said, 'Whose blood is that?' I said, 'His. He came into the room.' The sheriff said, 'Do you want to press charges against this guy?' I said, 'You'd better get him to a hospital.' And they took him away."

Frankie's never talked to Dad about those things. We try to protect him from news like that. "Not only that," Frankie has said, "it just wasn't of interest. Listen, he *knows.* He knows what's going to happen. He knew I was going to be susceptible to all that kind of crap when the time came. It was no secret."

"Didn't he try to prepare you for it?" someone once asked Frankie.

"No," Frankie said. "Nobody prepared *him* for it. He went out to see what the world would have. So his kid's going to have to make his own way, too. Now, he would protect the girls, he would protect his daughters, naturally, as any father would. But he said about me: 'My kid, if he gets a broken nose a couple of times, that ought to teach him to watch where he sticks his face.' "

Singing in Sinatra's shadow has been a burden for me as well as for Frankie. All those reviews, comparing me to my father. Ludicrous. To start with, you can't compare a female voice with a male voice. What's more, there's nobody in the *world* who has what Frank Sinatra has on a stage. Nobody else. Nobody has it. Why me?

After a time, I got fed up. It had been going on for twenty years. I read another review that again compared me with Dad, and I called the critic. I told her who I was and I said, "Okay, now don't get on the defensive. Keep a sense of humor about this call." She said, "Okay." And I said, "Listen. I want you to understand something. Nancy Sinatra will never be the man her father is."

She laughed. I laughed too, and said, "Write anything you want about my performance—you'll be doing me a favor if you give me suggestions. But *please,* no more comparisons. That's all I ask." She said, "I promise."

How can I—how could anyone—measure up to him? When Sinatra played New York's Paramount Theatre in the early 1940s—a skinny kid in his twenties, not long out of Hoboken, New Jersey—he caused the first generation gap. Frank Sinatra sang, teenage girls swooned, and their parents didn't get it.

Over the decades, the furor has grown. Listen to the brilliant opera star Robert Merrill: "You go through a stage door and out into a crowd with Frank and you can feel a certain tension. Many times Frank has said to me, 'God, I'd

And so did the smile.

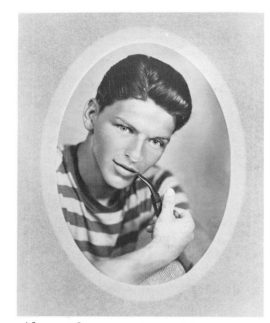

Above: The young hopeful in a Crosbyesque pose.
Below: One of the first glamour shots, used for answering fan mail.

love to walk on the Via Veneto, Rome. Just walk. Or Fifth Avenue. Or the Champs Élysées.' But he can't." After an event, as Merrill put it, "He needs people with him; he needs guards. My wife, Marion, and I left Carnegie Hall with him after a concert and there were hundreds of people waiting. And, as we left, they, this crowd—I don't know how to say it—but it was like a rainstorm, like a dark cloud. It just gathered and practically attacked us. And there was a limousine waiting there and Frank was behind us. He put his arms around Marion—he was concerned that she was going to get hurt. And he shoved us—actually, physically—into the car. We'd have been hurt. They mean well, but there's this tremendous adulation. People love him so, they forget he's a human being.

"I don't know anybody, maybe Presley in his day, who sets off this audience enthusiasm—I must touch you. I sang with Toscanini. Backstage, after a performance, people would come in and kiss his hands, his feet, wanted to touch him as though he wasn't real. But those were only a few people. With Frank, it's frightening."

The mystique starts, of course, with his music. Again, Robert Merrill: "Singers want to develop a style. They work at it, strive for it, sometimes they contrive it. Sinatra *instinctively* had a style. I mean, he was born with it. And it grew as he matured. Serious musicians regard him as an artist, a fine artist, a great American interpreter of our music. The beauty of Frank is that he is *word*-conscious and story-conscious and that's why he's so great. He's a storyteller—and a very compassionate man. He's sensitive—so automatically he's sensitive to his words, to the story that they tell. What you *are* comes out in your music."

Others agree. Arranger Gordon Jenkins told me how he and composer Jimmy Van Heusen "were listening to a playback of Frank singing Irving Berlin's 'All Alone.' 'All alone, I'm so all alone. There is no one else but you.' In tones of genuine woe. Van Heusen said, 'He *believes* it.'"

He does. "Throughout my career," my father once wrote, "if I have done anything, I have paid attention to every note and every word I sing—if I respect the song. If I cannot project this to a listener, I fail."

Irving Berlin: "Frank Sinatra is a songwriter's dream. No singer has done more for the songwriter. He knows his way around a song and does it his way, with tender, loving care."

He invests each song with a piece of his life.

Beyond the emotion, beyond the phrasing, it's so easy to recognize his voice. *Everybody* knows his voice. It is truly one of a kind. Mimics can't really capture the sound. I think it's the timbre, the structure of the throat, and the experience. There are singers who have it easier than Sinatra. They open their mouths and pleasing sounds come out without warm-up or preparation. Frank Sinatra works for every note, for every interval. He warms up, he rehearses, he studies. He does *not* sail through a concert; he strokes and kicks and breathes his way, treading water occasionally. At least once in a performance, more like three or four times, he catches a wave and, taking the audience with him, rides it all the way home. It's glorious.

Sam Weiss, a song plugger, worked with both my father and Bing Crosby. One day Sam arrived for a meeting with Bing and was confronted by an angry man from Bing's staff. "He said, 'What the hell is wrong with your friend Mr. Sinatra? *Tony Bennett* is the *greatest* singer in the world?' Apparently, Frank was quoted as saying that in a magazine. I figured he was annoyed that Frank didn't say that Bing Crosby was the greatest. So I took a chance and I said to

Bing, 'What are your thoughts on that?' And Bing said, 'There is only one guy that's the greatest singer in the whole world. His name is Sinatra. And nobody else.' "

The length of Sinatra's shadow is partly the result of charisma. Intensity. "Body language." Not only is he linked with songs, but with style. Instant identity. In the beginning, there were the floppy bow ties and the long, skinny body. ("I know the food here is lousy," the comedian Phil Silvers would say to him when they entertained at World War II army bases, "but *this* is ridiculous.") Later, there was his jauntiness—the raincoat draped over the shoulder, the hat at a cocky tilt, the expressions—ring-a-ding-ding—that spoke to the good times. Beyond that, in maturity, the maverick stance still. The lifelong Democrat turning to Nixon, to Reagan, "My Way."

Strength is at the core of his character. Mostly, strength of conviction. To him, for example, prejudice is abominable. A man of action, he has supported these beliefs accordingly. At my brother's christening, he was prepared to walk out until the priest, who originally had turned down my father's choice, agreed to allow a non-Catholic—Dad's close friend, Manie Sacks, a Jew—to be Frankie's godfather. In Palm Springs, according to Jack Benny, "He hit a fellow because the man had something to say against the Jews."

Be strong. Be true. We were talking once about Elvis Presley—Elvis and I were very close, and I felt a deep loss when he died. I couldn't accept it. I said, "Daddy, there's a connection between his death and the fact that he never got out in public. *You* managed, you've gone through the same thing he did." He said, "Oh, yes. You don't have to hide. You just keep moving." That's something I had never realized—keep moving, don't stop. A very important security precaution. Daddy added: "Elvis didn't grow musically."

I said, "His fans wouldn't *allow* him to."

He said, "Well, that's ridiculous. That means that he was a weak man."

Strength. "Don't tell me what to do," he once said. "Suggest." As his friend David Tebbett put it: "You *push* Frank and you can forget all about it—there's no chance in hell of his doing what you want." It's not that he's stubborn, he simply needs time to think it out.

An alternation of moods—high school serious and spread collar, spreading smile.

All part of his style. So are the good times. The long nights. The laughs. The extravagant life. Sheldon Keller, the comedy writer, told me of the time he worked on a Sinatra special: "The night before Frank was to tape, he was out drinking until four in the morning, leaving him with a raspy voice for the first two acts of the show. At one point during a break in the taping, he sat quietly in a chair murmuring and chastising himself: 'Drink, drink, drink. Smoke, smoke, smoke. Schmuck, schmuck, schmuck!' "

He picks up all the checks. He sends lavish gifts. It's only money. Gordon Jenkins: "We were working in Vegas. Frank had promised me some albums and called a bellboy to his dressing room and said, 'Go to my room, take the albums on the piano and bring them here.' He gave the boy the two keys.

"The boy came back with the keys and Frank gave him a one-hundred-dollar tip. I said, 'Hell, Frank, I would have done it for fifty.'

"Another time he was sitting at a table with some friends with his back to me. I came up behind him and said, 'Frank, it's Gordon. I am in a hell of a fix. I've left markers all over town and I'm stuck for thirty thousand.' I was kidding, but he never looked around, just reached in his pocket."

Sometimes the gifts take strange shapes, come in odd packages . . . Comedian Pat Henry worked for a while as my father's opening act. Pat: "You

The smile became the world's greatest grin—and by this stage it was difficult to say whether the teeth or the hat had become the endearing trademark.

John Bryson: "He has fought his way through a lifetime of adulation, loathing, criticism, riches, scandal, decline, triumph . . . to a point where . . . the man is some kind of folk hero." FS: "There are things I think I would have done if I had a chance again. I would have been a little more patient about getting out into the world . . . had more formal education . . . become an accomplished musician, in the sense that I would have studied formally . . ." Opposite, with Quincy Jones.

never know what's going to happen when you're with Frank. One day he came to New York, called me and said, 'Pat, have you got a passport?' I said, 'Why?' He said, 'In case we ever go to England. We may do something over there.' I said, 'Yeah, I got one.' He said, 'Well, come on, have dinner with me at Marino's. I'm having dinner with Kirk Kerkorian [owner of the MGM Grand Hotel] and the guys. Bring your passport. Let me see it.' Like an idiot, I go. I have thirty-seven dollars and a passport and I'm sitting there having dinner and Frank said, 'We're gonna go see Kirk's new plane; he's got a DC-9 and we're gonna go out and look at it at La Guardia.' So I said, 'Good.' Now we go out and he says, 'We're gonna give it a test run.' I said, 'Wonderful.' We get on the plane, we're giving it a test run, and soon it's two hours later. I say, 'How long are we gonna test this plane?' Frank says, 'Oh, I forgot to tell you—we're going to England.' I said, 'Are you *crazy?* I only got one suit to my name. What I'm wearing, that's all I've got.'

" 'So,' he says, 'we won't go to the same place twice.' "

He will give friends trips, gifts—mention admiration for something and you risk having him buy it for you the next day—and, most important, himself. "You sometimes feel like you have to run away from him," Burt Lancaster told me, "because if you say to Frank, 'I'm having a problem,' it becomes *his* problem. And sometimes maybe you'd rather try to work it out yourself."

But not always. Nancy Reagan: "When my husband was shot on March 30, 1981, your father was playing an engagement somewhere—I've forgotten where—perhaps in Vegas . . .

"Frank never called to say, 'Do you want me to come?' He just came. He shut down his show and just came. The next thing I knew, he was in Washington to be of support and help to me. It meant a great deal to me, and I'll always be grateful."

Sammy Davis, Jr.: "When I lost my eye in a car accident, the first place I went—because I *had* no place to go except the hotel room I was living in then—was to Palm Springs, to Frank. You can have a tendency, at a time like that, for self-pity: 'Oh, what am I going to do?' He cut it off by making me laugh. The jokes started when I was in the hospital and they continue today: An eye chart with an inscription: *'To Smokey. Practice. Practice.'* (He calls me Smokey because I smoke so much.) A gift: half a pair of binoculars, with the other half sawed off for Jilly Rizzo, whose bad eye is on the opposite side. The card: 'You guys should get together.' The only thing Sinatra ever said of a serious nature was, 'Don't worry about nothing'—and that's the *umbrella.*

"I had lost my equilibrium. He took me to the golf course and made me try to hit the ball. We would sit and he'd say, 'What did they teach you in the hospital? Did they give you this thing with pouring water?' And we'd go in the kitchen and he'd make me pour water in a glass. That kind of sensitivity is rare, rare.

"Another thing he does is anticipate *for* you. Meaning that by the time you get around to thinking about it, and go to say, 'Frank, there's something I—' he says, 'I've taken care of that.' And he knows exactly what you're talking about because that's the kind of investment he puts into a friendship."

On opening night at the Waldorf-Astoria's Empire Room some years ago, Tony Bennett received a call from Judy Garland, who was living in New York. Bennett: "She was hysterical. Someone was threatening her life and she needed immediate help.

"Because it was time for me to go on stage the only solution was to call Frank, who was appearing in Florida at the Fontainebleau. He had just recently

Nancy Sinatra: "I like the way Pete Hamill put it. 'Keep your eye on the high rollers . . . The passive among us are redeemed by the active; the timid by those whose lives are propelled by the sense of adventure . . .'"

completed Abby Mann's film *The Detective.* During the course of the filming Frank had met many New York City detectives and members of the Police Department who were great fans of his.

"I told Frank of Judy's terrible situation and he said he would call me back in fifteen minutes.

"In exactly ten minutes I had a call from Judy. 'I asked for help,' she said, 'but *this* is ridiculous.' I asked why.

" 'There are a thousand police in the street outside my brownstone . . . and about five hundred lawyers in my apartment!'

"In exactly fifteen minutes the promised call came from Frank. He said, 'That all right, kid?' "

Then, there is his charity. Beyond the benefits and public fund-raising he participates in are equally significant personal acts. Comedian Jack E. Leonard told me about the blank check my father gave him when Leonard was seriously ill and down on his luck. Gordon Jenkins told me that when he was disabled in a car crash, "Frank was the only one to offer financial help."

When my grandmother returned from a visit to Italy years ago, she told us about her audience with the Pope. He said to her, in Italian, "Your son is very close to God." She said, "Why, Father, what do you mean?" And he said, "Because he does God's work and he does not talk about it."

The shadow is lengthened further by the misrepresentations and the seeming contradictions. Sammy Davis, Jr., who's known him nearly forty years, has never seen my father throw a punch at anybody. Sammy: "He gets accused of more things, even when he wasn't there. It's like the James boys. A bank gets stuck up in Illinois and there were some white guys on horses, and the James boys did it, when they were never *in* Illinois.

"You know, I do remember when he *wanted* to punch someone. We were at this charity party, he's about ten sheets to the wind and the party's over, and he decided he was going to punch John Wayne out. We'd had a great time, and Duke had been over to our table, talking to Frank and I guess he'd been standing very close and Frank had said, 'You're *leaning* on me. You're leaning on me!' But that was hours before. And now, for no reason at all, Frank gets up and he says, 'You guys go to the car. I am going to punch that sonofabitch right in the mouth!' And there he goes, up the aisle . . . when he got to John Wayne, he began poking him with his finger. And Duke just looked at him and laughed. And the more Duke laughed, the more Frank poked. Duke finally just lifted him up, set him aside, and we all left.

"The next afternoon I told my wife, 'Honey, I'm going to see how Francis is.' So I got in the car and went to his house and his man, George, opens the door. He said, 'What's this I hear about the boss and John Wayne?' I said, 'What?' George said, 'I heard they got into a fight.'

"I said, 'Is Frank here at the house?'

" 'Yeah.'

"I said, 'He wouldn't *be* at the house if he fought John Wayne!'

"So out of the back came Frank, staggering to the bar. He said, 'I gotta get a Ramos gin fizz.' He gets it and he sits down, and I said, 'Hey, man! That was a good fight you guys had last night.' And he said, 'What fight?' We started to laugh, and that was the end of it. But the next thing I knew, less than forty-eight hours later, headlines in the paper: SINATRA AND WAYNE IN PARKING LOT BRAWL."

Volatile? Yes. Tells you what's on his mind? Yes. Temper? Yes. That's fact.

But recurring fistfights? Fiction, fiction, fiction. Well . . . maybe once in a while.

The worst fictions, though, involve, of course, the Mafia, the Mob. We'll come to those later. For the moment, all I want to say is that the allegations have distressed and depressed him. His artistry, his stature, his largesse, his tabloid reputation as tough guy, often disguise other aspects of the man, conceal the tenderness of the texture.

The movie director Richard Brooks, for one, perceives this.

Richard Brooks: "I remember him and Humphrey Bogart, Frank and Bogie, both of them, weeping over *A Star Is Born* with Freddie March, and wondering, 'Why are they crying? I'm moved, very moved by the picture, but why are they crying? And they cry every Christmas, every time they see the movie. Why? Something has touched their own personal experience. They're identifying with these two people. Very deeply. Which has to do with their own vulnerability.' So when I look at Frank Sinatra and he's standing there like he's got on a bulletproof vest, untouchable, remote, I don't *see* him that way. He's a very vulnerable man. He can be hurt easily."

An accurate impression. It is this vulnerability that sits at the center of Sinatra, that underscores his skills with a song and the puzzles in his personality. But why? Perhaps the answers can be found not only in his paternalism, his patriotism, his perfectionism, his temper, his ability to love, to hurt and be hurt, but deeper, in the fright of his birth, the mother who shaped him, and the mortality he has increasingly felt gnawing at the edges of his life, his legend, and his mystique.

Leo Rosten:
"In some way, however small and secret, each of us is a little mad . . . everyone is lonely at the bottom and cries to be understood. But we can never entirely understand someone else, and each of us remains part stranger even to those who love us . . . it is the weak who are cruel; gentleness is to be expected only from the strong . . . you can understand people better if you look at them—no matter how old or impressive they may be—as if they are children. For most of us never mature; we simply grow taller . . . the purpose in life is to matter—to count, to have it make some difference that we lived at all."

CHAPTER ONE
MARTY AND DOLLY

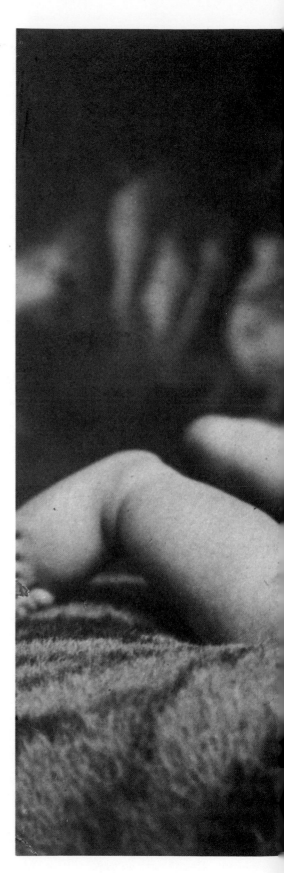

Give Me Your Tired, Your Poor

My father almost died the day he was born. He came into the world fighting for his life. He was thirteen and a half pounds at birth, a big baby lodged inside a tiny woman less than five feet tall. The doctor had trouble getting him out. The doctor tugged away with forceps, ripping the baby's ear, cheek and neck, and producing scars he would always carry. The newborn did not breathe. Thinking him dead, the doctor turned instead to treat the mother. The baby's grandmother scooped him up and held him under cold running water. *Life.*

Francis Albert Sinatra had won his first fight.

In his parents' cold-water flat that day, that experience, I believe, became a prevailing influence, a deeply personal tie to that invisible margin between being alive—or not. The new baby, in unthinkable pain, disconnected suddenly from his mother, desperate for breath. The struggle of the infant would shape the character and conduct of the boy and remain a motivating force in the man.

Perhaps in those few moments lie some of the forces behind the impatience, the steamroller ambition, his exhausting pace, extravagant style.

It was December 12, 1915. He was the son of Anthony Martin Sinatra, who had arrived as a child from Agrigento, Sicily, and Natalie Catherine Garavente from Genoa. They lived in Hoboken, New Jersey, a workingman's town across the Hudson River from New York City. It was a town of ethnic enclaves—Irish, Jewish, Italian—and ethnic frictions.

After arriving from Sicily with his wife and children, Dad's grandfather had worked at the American Pencil Company for eleven dollars a week. My dad told me about the consequences.

"He inhaled that dust for seventeen years and it wrecked his lungs. He couldn't do any better because he had nobody to teach him English. I remember my mother telling my father: 'If you don't bring him here to live with us, I'm going to take the boy and go.'"

The infant was injured at birth. FS: "My mother had the photographer take this photograph from the right because the wounds on the other side of my face and neck were still healing."

Nancy Sinatra: "My great-grandmother, Rose Garavente, holding my dad, 1915."

My dad's father started out as an apprentice in a cobbler's shop. He was known in his neighborhood, where everyone had a nickname, as "Tony the Shoemaker." He took up prizefighting and, because it was better in those days to have an Irish name than an Italian one (the Irish politicians controlled Hoboken), he adopted his manager's name and became known as "Marty O'Brien."

Marty did some work as an extra in the very early movies (nearby Fort Lee, New Jersey, was an early movie-making center). He labored as a boiler-maker in a shipyard and he ran a saloon, but most of his working years were with the Hoboken Fire Department. He was a good fireman, always first to arrive at the fires and he rose through the ranks to captain. He did the cooking at the firehouse.

Marty did have a wicked sense of humor. Once, when he was crossed by his pal, John the Florist, Marty slipped a strong laxative into John's drink. The laxative—Marty called it a "physic"—took hold quickly and John the Florist raced to the outhouse, which had been set aside for his exclusive use. He sat down and when he tried to stand up could not. The seat had been coated with heavy glue. "Get me out of here!" he kept screaming. Marty let him sit there, they say, pants down, stuck. There are endless family stories about playing jokes on each other.

The owner of another saloon owed Grandpa money. And for a long time. Finally, instead of giving Grandpa money, the man tried to pay him off with a horse. A horse not in the best of health. Dying, in fact. He delivered the horse to Grandpa and took off, leaving the animal to breathe its last few breaths. Later, in the dark, Grandpa walked the horse to the guy's saloon. He put the horse in the doorway and shot it. By the time the saloonkeeper arrived to open up, rigor mortis had set in. Business was off for a while, with a stiff horse blocking the doorway.

But Marty Sinatra was basically a gentle man. It was my grandmother, "Dolly," who was a strong and striking character.

Dolly and Marty met when they were kids, and Grandma's parents opposed the romance.

Cousin John Tredy: "Marty's parents were Sicilian, they were grape growers. Dolly's parents were Genovese, they were lithographers, and there was a class distinction between the families. But Dolly was a very aggressive girl, very strong-minded, and she did what she wanted to do."

Women weren't allowed at prize fights in those days, but when Grandpa fought Grandma's brother "Champ," she put on boy's clothes, tucked her hair up under a cap, and went. She was the first girl to get in to see a fight, she always insisted. There was no limit on rounds back then; you fought until somebody dropped. Marty and Champ fought forever: nobody fell down. And until the day my grandfather died, they argued over who had won.

Dolly and Marty eloped. They had a second ceremony later, after their families had acquiesced.

It was Dolly's determination, though, that helped shape my dad. There were many stories about her: that when he was a boy and had been naughty or acting up, she would chase him with a broomstick; that once, when he fell down a flight of stairs, she gave him holy hell as consolation and that the damage from Dolly threatened to be more severe than that from the fall; that he often went off to be alone, or sometimes to his cousin Buddy Garavente's house or to his Aunt Mary's for consolation (My father loves Aunt Mary dearly and speaks of her frequently. She is ninety-four.); that there was always friction between them

NS: "Marty and Dolly, my
grandparents, in their formal
wedding picture and later, on a
boat, with their son, Frankie."
Their favorite song began:
"You remind me of the girl who
used to go to school with me . . ."

because from the start he was as strong-minded as she was.

My father and I disagree about whether she was a tough cookie or not. He once said I make her sound like Ma Barker. I know she was formidable as well as wonderful and so, surely, did he. But he loved her then and he loves her now, as I do, and we differ in degree.

Frank Sinatra: "When I fell down the stairs, my mother was so scared she overreacted. If she whacked me, it was because of that. She didn't want me to hurt myself. She wanted me to be more careful." He never fell downstairs again.

Dolly once heard that Marty's sisters had made up a story about her having a boyfriend. She soon confronted them in their grocery store beneath their apartment. She knocked over olive barrels and pulled cans off the counter and the weights from the scales. So it seems clear that Dolly was not a lady to be trifled with. But as my father puts it:

"My mother wasn't tough; the *neighborhood* was tough. She was firm. She wanted me to be safe, to be a gentleman. She would have had me wear velvet pants, I think, except that in that neighborhood I would have gotten killed. The minute we could afford it, we moved from Monroe Street to an apartment on Park Avenue. The funny thing about it was that the guys in the new neighborhood were worse than the guys downtown. They were brighter, more insidious; well-mannered, with good clothes—and deadly." *They* were tough. Not knives and guns, but fists and stones.

"Sometimes my cousin, Sam Sinatra, would bring home a report card with better marks. That was no help. Stop showing it to her! I'd tell him." But he recalls with affection many other moments.

When Dad was three, Grandma worked as a chocolate dipper, covering the candies with chocolate and decorating them with identifying letters: *V* for vanilla cream, *M* for maple.

FS: "I remember my first visit to the candy store. She had a bucket of ice water and a vat of hot, fudgy chocolate. She dunked her hand in the icy water and then the hot chocolate, which stuck to her fingers. She then wrote the correct letter with the drippings from her fingertips. She gave me three pieces of chocolate. It was wonderful."

She was wonderful, too, in her own lively way. And so was Marty. My father spoke of him in 1985:

FS: "My father was a darling man, a quiet man. You know—he never *touched* me if I got in a jam. In spite of having been a professional boxer, he never laid a glove on me. My *mother* stayed in shape on me—she kept physically fit chasing me and whacking me around now and then.

"But he used to stare at me once in a while and I knew what was back of that stare.

"I don't think he could write more than his name. Nor could he read, not a hell of a lot, anyhow. If I'd get a letter that was funny, I wouldn't ask him to read it—we wouldn't do that to him, not embarrass him—but I'd read it to him or something interesting from the newspaper. He lived with the box in his last years; he loved just sitting there, looking at a television show. But he was a very quiet man, a lonely man. And *shy.* When I'd bring people over to the house in Fort Lee, years later, and we'd have a lot of people around the house, he'd cook for three days for us. And he wouldn't sit down. 'Come on, Dad,' I'd say, 'sit with us. These people have never met you.' 'No, no, no,' he'd say; 'you go ahead. I have to take care of things in the kitchen.' He was asthmatic and it bothered

NS: "Marty Sinatra, my fire-fighting grandfather, displays—proudly, I think—the hazards of his work to his wife, the doctor, and his son."

Opposite:
Firemen's picnic. Little Frankie is on the bottom row (right). Uncle Vincent is next to him.

him, especially if there were others in the room. You could hear him wheezing. If he had an attack, a coughing spell, he'd disappear—find a hole in the wall somewhere and be outside before you knew it.

"Oh, but he was a lovely, lovely man. I adored him. In some ways, the greatest man I ever knew in my life."

Grandma worked at various jobs including, in those early years, midwifery. Later, she became a committeewoman in Democratic party machine politics. As she developed political clout, her personality grew even more domineering. Dad told me that she once planned to run for mayor of Hoboken. Grandpa called him aside and said, "Listen, you've got to do something. Stop her. She's impossible to live with now."

Still, her influence helped Grandpa become a captain in the Fire Department. Her work helped bring in the money that allowed them to move from a tenement house to one of the better parts of town. But she wasn't home much. Grandma was always so involved elsewhere that when my dad came home from school, sometimes there was nothing to eat in the refrigerator. That wasn't a matter of money; she was off doing something else. So he'd wind up fixing himself mustard sandwiches.

Dad was an only child and often came home to an empty house. Not long after my oldest daughter, A.J., was born, he said, "I hope you'll consider having another baby. It was lonely for me. Very lonely." Loneliness is a part of him. It's always there—in his eyes.

Cousin John: "Aunt Dolly was always busy and I think Frankie was always underfoot a little bit. We used to go around the firehouse to see Frankie's father, and he'd throw us a nickel or dime. They used to give Frankie money, maybe to get him out of their way. They were always doing something. It wasn't a normal house like you would have with your children. It was different. They didn't have too much time for Frankie. He was always alone. He was warm, he wanted friendship. And that's why he always came around to our different homes.

"Frankie was really a soft kind of boy. You know, like his father, Marty. Marty was a pussycat, a real nice guy. Marty used to talk loud and rough, but he had a heart of gold. And he was very conscientious. He was a self-learned guy . . . Frank's got a lot of character like his mother. And he's got the other side like his father. When he was little, Frankie was the quietest boy of everybody. He and I used to sit in the corner and listen to the grownups. We never interfered."

Dad did not always like what he heard. As a boy, his passion for what came to be known as civil rights was triggered, he told me, by name-calling; kids in his neighborhood, he said, "calling each other ethnic names: nigger, wop, sheenie, dago, and all that kind of stuff.

"Something rubbed me the wrong way. And I'm not too sure that your grandmother wasn't a little bigoted about certain people, too. 'Cause I remember vaguely, I had a couple of falling-outs about it with her. Because she came from the old school; she was taught it by somebody else. I remember, from time to time—if I had a boy come into the house, or if I would go to other apartments in the tenement house to have supper with a big family, which I used to like to do—she would say to me, 'Is he Swedish or Jewish or what is he?' And I would say, 'What's the difference?' I was very young then. I may have been six or seven."

There were other influences too. Dad has small scars on his face that came as a result of his walking home through the "wrong" neighborhood: a kid

The King and Queen of the May Walk, Hoboken. NS: "My father's friend's name is unknown, which is just as well. He calls this 'The silliest picture I ever saw.'"

went into an ethnically different neighborhood at risk of being beaten up.

Just as it is today, street gangs protected their "turf," their territory. At one point, the neighborhood kids were calling him "Scarface." He decided to find the doctor who had given him the most severe scar at birth. When he did, he pounded on the door. Luckily for everyone, the doctor wasn't home. (Years later, the daughter of that doctor sent my father a wire, congratulating him on a performance or an award or a charitable act and he said, "Can you imagine what she'd say if she knew that I went after her dad when I was eleven years old?")

Once the Sinatras left the tenements, though, life was more pleasant. They moved to a house my mother has described as "lovely, on Garden Street in Hoboken, one of those tall, narrow buildings with several floors. There was a basement and three stories. It had a beautiful living room, a real dining room, and four bedrooms. Grandma and Grandpa's bedroom was on the second level and Frank's was up above. It was lovely, beautifully furnished, beautifully kept. Always."

My dad started at David E. Rue, Jr., High School in 1928, then moved on to A. J. Demarest High School in 1931. While in high school he had various jobs. In 1932, for eleven dollars a week, he delivered the *Jersey Observer,* a newspaper where his godfather, Frank Garrick, worked.

There was soon a little disagreement between them, something apparently about who was in charge. Since Frank Garrick *was* the circulation manager, he presumably had some right to think he was. In any case, the job didn't last. And it was just as well.

By then Frank Sinatra was beginning to sense what he wanted to do with his life. The ambition had come upon him slowly—no sudden sunburst. On the ramshackle radios of the 1920s he had listened to the crooner Russ Columbo and sung along. He had tried out his voice in school and found that people responded. He joined his high school glee club, he sang in the school band, and started to sing at parties. He liked the feeling and the applause. Gradually it came over him that he might want to sing for his living.

He quit high school in his senior year. In a nation deep in the Depression, even a family with two incomes, such as Marty and Dolly Sinatra's, was not about to indulge what seemed to be a whim.

FS: "What my father said was, do you want to get a regular job—a 'reggala' job—or do you wanna be a bum?" It was okay to leave school, Marty said, but young Frank had to get a real job—no music business.

"Back in the thirties I must have had fifteen jobs that had nothing to do with music." His father told him to go to Teijent and Lang, which later became Todd shipyards, and get into the shape-up, the daily lineup of people looking for work. The foreman—called the "Snapper"—was a friend of Grandpa's, had been his foreman.

"The Snapper ignored me for the first few days. He didn't know who I was. So my father called him and told him to look out for me. Dad gave me a union badge and I pinned it on my cap and went to shape up again. I was a kid with a baby face, and the other guys were older, with kids of their own. The Snapper spotted me and said, 'You Marty O'Brien's kid?' I said, 'That's right.' He told me I could have a job catching rivets. He took me over to the guy in charge. This guy had a cockney accent. He showed me where to stand and told me to hang onto the rope with one hand, and the metal catcher with the other. When I heard the words 'Comin' down' from over my head, I had to swing out and

The Big Wetting. FS: "One of my father's sisters, Dora, was married at an elaborate church event—a monsignor, a priest, a High Mass. I was the ring boy. The ceremony was long . . . very long . . . and I kept signaling my mother. But she wouldn't pay attention. So I wet my pants there at the altar."

catch the rivet, which was twelve inches long and white hot. Then he said I should 'Use the tong with the type' to pick up the rivet. I didn't know what he meant. I kept saying, 'What?' 'Use the tongs with the type,' he said. 'What?' He was getting mad. He went over and picked up these big tongs with *tape* wrapped around the handles and shoved them at me."

Frankie caught rivets, hanging over a four-story shaft, for three days until he swayed a little too far out. 'Comin' down.' And down it came, barely missing his shoulder. It crashed down to the bottom of the shaft. "It scared me so much I couldn't handle it. I had acrophobia and didn't know it. And I was hanging onto that rope and that burning hot rivet went by me like a bullet, singeing my shoulder. I got a different job."

He and his friend Danny Hannigan worked at Lyons and Carnahan Books ("From Primer to College") in the National Biscuit Company building on Sixteenth Street in New York City. They unloaded crates of books. First they took the crate apart, then they stacked the books on the lift, then they put the books *up* on the shelves. Next they read the new order to be filled and they took books down from the shelves, stacked them and built a crate around them. Then they took another crate apart. Books up . . . books down . . . build another crate. Until one day Frank said to Danny, "You know, this job is stupid." Danny had brothers and sisters, and his father wasn't well, so he felt he should stay. But Frank insisted there were better jobs.

The better job for the moment was back on the ships. The United Fruit Lines. Because my dad was skinny, about 115 pounds, he could get into places other guys couldn't. There were two hundred tubes in the condenser, which converted salt water to steam. They needed constant cleaning because of potential corrosion from the salt residue.

My dad's job was to crawl inside and unscrew the tubes, so they could be pulled out and cleaned and put back. Then he'd screw them back in again.

It was winter and there was ice in the water, and snowflakes as big as quarters. Some of the work was on the night shift. FS: "We were so cold that we would sneak around to the big coffeepot for some hot coffee to get warm. We got caught once by the guy above us. He had a Southern accent and he said to the Snapper, 'Ah don't lak what's goin' on around heah with you an' those dagos.' And, whack! the Snapper knocked him right in the river. Somebody dragged the guy out and defrosted him."

During that hardworking time, Frank entered and won a model-airplane-building contest, sponsored by Geisman's, a big, civic-minded clothing store. First prize was a short plane ride over New Jersey, and that was the beginning of his lifelong love affair with flying.

In the summer of 1934 he began another lifelong love affair.

Top right: One of Frankie's best moments with his mother was on a visit to the candy makers. Dolly Sinatra (bottom row, third from right) and her sister Josie (bottom row, far right) were chocolate dippers.

Bottom right: Echo Farms, the Catskills, 1923. FS: "One year we went up there for a little vacation. Old-fashioned boardinghouse and old-fashioned food. My mother bought me these clothes to go hiking. I've tried not to do much walking since." Dolly Sinatra, with the guitar.

Begin the Beguine

Francis Albert Sinatra met Nancy Carol Barbato while she was spending the summer in Long Branch, on the Jersey shore, and he was staying at his Aunt Josie's house across the road. Dad was nineteen. Mom was seventeen and just out of school.

The nation was still suffering in the Depression. Nancy's father, who was a plastering contractor, had built their house in a joint venture with his brother Ralph and sister Kate. It was a large house for that little town. They rented out two of the rooms to boarders, and the three of them, with their families, *big* families, shared the rest of the house.

The two teenagers, Frank and Nancy, noticed each other across the narrow street.

FS: "One of my relatives gave me a ukelele for my birthday or a Christmas present—it was worth about $2.95—and a book, with the fingering. And I learned to play it, just a few tunes."

Nancy Sr.: "Frank would have his ukelele and sometimes he'd sit on Josie's porch and sing. I knew his cousins Margie and Tony. One day I was on our porch giving myself a manicure. He said, 'How about mine?' I said okay, and he came over.

"It was a beautiful summer holiday. We walked along the boardwalk and went on the rides. My sister Julie worked the ice cream concession, and we would stop and chat with her. We went to dances at the casino and had picnics at the beach. It was lovely and romantic.

"Labor Day, everybody goes back to school. And I figured that would be the end of our little summer fling, forgetting that Hoboken is only a few miles away from Jersey City, where I lived. He called me and we continued going out. He would take buses to come to see me. When I was working and he wasn't I would give him the fare so that he could come over."

Dad remembers driving to pick up my mom for a date one night when he had an accident. Another car cut in front of him, causing him to swerve to the right, wrapping the passenger side of his car around a pole. "I was so lucky. If your mother had already been in the car she might have been killed."

Mom's father, my Grandpa Mike, as a plastering contractor, would give work to Dad and to Mom's brother Bart, who was about Dad's age. Early on, when they were first working for him, he'd pay them for a job, and then he'd have to undo everything they did, and do it over. According to Mom, they eventually got better and Grandpa Mike didn't have to undo it *all*.

FS: "At one point I said I wanted to be an engineer, to go to Stevens Institute in Hoboken, number two after MIT when I was a boy—a *great* school—because I loved the idea of bridges, tunnels, highways . . ." ("Apropos of nothing," he said in 1985, "they want to give me a honorary degree this May in engineering at Stevens.")

But he would sing in the shower, and sometimes Dolly would sing—or shout—back unflattering musical criticism and urged him to get that "reggala" job. My mother believes that "his mind was made up. We used to go to the most important part of town in Jersey City, Journal Square. They had theaters there, and we'd see movies and these different live acts. We saw Russ Columbo and Bing Crosby in his last vaudeville appearance. They were his idols. He had a burning desire to be like them."

FS: "I was a *big* fan of Bing's. But I never wanted to sing like him, because every kid on the block was boo-boo-boo-ing like Crosby. I wanted to be a different kind of singer. And my voice was up higher anyhow and I said, That's not for me. Bing was a troubador, the first real troubador that any of us had heard when we were fourteen or fifteen."

He made money wherever he could, at whatever jobs he could get, but singing remained at the center of his life, even if it had to be relegated to the periphery of his day. "I sang at social clubs and at roadhouses . . . sometimes for nothing or for a sandwich or cigarettes—all night for three packs. But I worked on one basic theory: stay alive, get as much practice as you can."

Borrowing some of the money from his parents, Frank Sinatra bought a small library of band arrangements for popular tunes and a portable sound system. This equipment gave him an edge over the other vocalists competing for one-nighters with local bands. He began to work more steadily, sometimes for as much as six dollars a night.

A trio in Hoboken—Jimmy Petrozelli ("Skelly"), Patty Principe ("Patty Prince") and Fred Tamburro ("Tamby")—liked to hang out in the saloon run by Marty and Dolly at Fourth and Jefferson streets. A radio program which had become a national institution, "Major Bowes and His Original Amateur Hour," conducted regular competitions. Before anyone could get on the show, there were tryouts. The show was a big thing. It was staged at New York's Capitol Theatre and aired on NBC radio. This led to a part in one of Bowes' touring companies.

"Round and round she goes," Bowes would intone in a remarkably flat voice, prefiguring the later Ed Sullivan, "and where she stops, nobody knows." The "she" was the wheel of fortune. A gong sounded to end long acts or dismiss hopeless ones and the audience voted. "Bowes was a hokey old man," said FS years later, smiling, "a grump, no sense of humor at all, and he had a brilliant apartment at the top of the Capitol."

The trio from Hoboken auditioned, and shortly thereafter Sinatra audi-

A man who would one day have a wonderful way with a lyric first tried his hand at writing them. His poem for the lovely Nancy:

*I don't care for moonlight
    on a country lane,
'less I've got companionship,
    pleasant to retain.
I don't care for moonlight
    out upon the sea,
'less I've got the proper kind
    of company with me.
I don't care for moonlight
    on a city street,
'less somebody close at hand
    is obviously sweet.
I don't care for moonlight
    anyplace, it's droll,
'less, well maybe, you would like
    to take a little stroll.*
—*Francis A. Sinatra (age nineteen)*

On Tour. The four in an amiable encounter with a pair of police on a pair of motorcycles. FS wrote on this photo he sent to Nancy: "The boys and I with a couple of 'Friends.' Santa Barbara, California, October 9, 1935."

The Hoboken Four (opposite), September 30, 1935, outside the Los Angeles Paramount Theatre. (Left to Right in white) Pat Principe, Fred Tamburro, FS, and James Petrozelli.

tioned on his own. "They won and I won. And when I was accepted, the old man said, 'They're going to be on the show a week from Sunday. Why don't we put you on together and we'll call it The Hoboken Four?' "

The newly augmented trio sang only two lines for Bowes and he said, "That's good enough."

On the show the Four sang "Shine" ("Shine away your blues-ies / Shine, start with your shoes-ies") and won with the biggest vote in the history of the Bowes amateur hour. The record was then said to be 31,000 votes; they received 40,000-plus and were now part of a unit in the Major's touring company.

They also made, as part of the deal, two short films, "moving pictures," directed by John Auer. FS: "I never did see them. Probably terrible . . ."

In any case, the pay was not terrible: $75 a week, which meant, "We were no longer amateurs. We were getting paid."

On tour, "We bought our own food and paid for our rooms and stayed at the best hotels. That was because outside, there was always a white banner, *Major Bowes' Amateurs Stopping Here.* The program was such a hit that people wanted to come see what we looked like, like animals in a cage. But one of the niceties was that people came backstage with cakes and homemade food, and women would say, 'You must miss your mother's cooking . . .' and all that kind of jazz and give us food like we were starving. It was sweet.

"In San Francisco, a guy about fifty came in and he said that he was born and brought up in Hoboken and he wanted to show us the town. And he was nice. So he took us to his house, we had a sandwich, met his family, and he showed us San Francisco. You see, that's the kind of power the *show* had."

Not all the Bowes units traveled in the same style, apparently.

A young singer named Robert Merrill was touring with another of Major Bowes's companies in that period. Merrill recalled, "We traveled like cattle, crammed together in trains. The Major was one of the stingiest men alive. Three or four of us in a room. I remember one hotel room—two dollars a night —had a little peephole in the door. I'd never seen that before. I inquired, and was told it had been a whorehouse."

Whatever the accommodations, after a time Sinatra began to tire of the tour. "That was the first time I had ever been away. I just wanted to go home. I missed my girl and I missed my family.

"And I think now that I also felt that I was going nowhere. I had auditioned as a solo and now I was part of a quartet but I was thinking solo, solo . . ."

So he left the tour and the Four became a trio again.

FS: "A musician friend of mine, a saxophone player, said, 'I hear they're going to audition at The Rustic Cabin where I'm working.' I asked him to intercede. And I went up and sang a few songs and got the job."

At The Cabin, "I did a little bit of everything. I never stopped. I showed people to tables, I sang with the band, I sang in between sets." The pay at the roadhouse in Englewood, New Jersey, was fifteen dollars a week, plus tips.

FS: "We had a blind piano player. Completely blind, with a shiny bald head. Between dance sets, I would push his little half-piano around. We'd go from table to table and he'd play and I'd sing. There was a dish on the piano. People would put coins in the dish.

"The piano player had a great ear. He always knew how much money was put in. But I used to tease him. Sometimes a person would hand me a coin and I wouldn't put it in the dish. He'd get very tense, thinking that it was paper money. Then later, when we'd split it up for the evening, I'd come clean and tell

him the truth, that it had only been a quarter or a half-dollar, whatever it was."

He scrambled. "But I didn't mind. Because I was learning. And we were on the air every night. The WNEW Dance Parade. That's what I wanted; I wanted to be heard. By people. No salary—they just picked up the orchestra. And people at home apparently danced to it. There were about fifteen clubs all around the area, each hooked up. It was great.

"I was running around, doing every sustaining [unsponsored] radio show I could get." He did as many as eighteen a week, even though no sponsor meant no pay. For example, he and a friend, guitarist Tony Mottola, landed a fifteen-minute, five-day-a-week radio show. Their theme song was "Blue Moon." They only made enough money for carfare—but they were working. And the experience was important.

The Rustic Cabin band was led by Harold Arden, who'd changed his name, understandably, from Harold Munchhausen or something of the sort. Then the post was taken over by Bill Henri, who'd changed *his* name from Henry Jacobs. Name changing was, of course, common then, sometimes forced, sometimes voluntary. Sinatra had already considered the name "Fred Trenton," in honor of his cousin Fred Treddy. When my father was about nine, Freddy had his own group, played the banjo, sang, and was thus the first professional entertainer in the family. The young Frank Sinatra went to watch his older cousin sing. Fred died of tuberculosis, aged twenty-eight.

The name changing, like Fred, was short-lived. It came about, as FS said:

". . . when I had a couple of jobs, including political rallies, where the candidate would come, and they'd have an orchestra and people would dance

50

The Major Bowes Theater of the Air, short film, 1935. The credits read: "The Big Minstrel Act includes Henry Stone, interlocutor; Petro and Prince, End Men; Buddy Fleck, Irene Mauseth, Donald Carroll, Alfred Richking, vocalists; Boris and Saul Matusevitch, accordionists; Arthur and Paul Monte, tap dancers; and Don Milo and his orchestra." Buried amid all that talent, not in the credits (front row, fourth from the right), was an unknown named Frank Sinatra.

and I sang. Some kid suggested that I ought to change my name, get a short name, something that people would remember . . .

"I said, 'What about Frankie Trent?' So I tried it and that lasted about two weeks [laughing]. We had flyers made, little paper advertisements, and distributed them, announcing Saturday night events at someplace like the Union Club in Hoboken, with such-and-such an orchestra and 'vocalist Frankie Trent.' And then my mother saw one.

" 'What's *this?*' she said. 'Get ridda' that. Don't you change your name. Your father finds out, he's gonna kick your ass.' " And, gentle man though Marty was, he might have.

"About that time I was also starting to see Nancy and she said, 'That's silly.' And so did my [second] cousin Ray, who worked in the NBC house orchestra. A long time before, I had written Ray and he had answered and said, 'Come over after the program one night, I'll keep the producer in the booth, and the director. Bring a piano player and do a few tunes. If they like you, maybe they'll sign you.' Well, back then I wasn't ready yet. I was very bad and I knew it. So I thanked Ray. I also mentioned the name changing. He said, 'Are you *kiddin'?* That's the most beautiful name in the world—it's so musical.'

"Okay. So I kept it."

Ray's name was Sinatra, too.

Generally, Dad drove from Jersey City to Englewood with other musicians, often in the company of Harry Schuchman, the saxophone player who had helped him get the audition:

"Frank had this red Chrysler, I'll never forget it. This was around 1937, right after the Depression. I kept saying to myself, 'This kid, how can he afford this kind of car?' "

It was his Dad's car.

Even at that time women were responsive. Or, as Schuchman put it, "He had more broads around than you ever saw. I used to sit there and watch the gals with your father and I'd think to myself, 'What do they see in him? He's such a skinny little guy.' But when he opened his mouth, you knew. He had that charisma that went right out to every gal in the room, I don't care if she was ten or a hundred."

He had the temper, too.

Schuchman: "They used to play cards in the back room, in between sets. Your father played cards and I'll tell you this: When he lost, he would take the whole deck of cards and throw it out the window. He'd say, 'Get these goddamn cards outta here!'

"He had to be a winner, and if he didn't win, he felt it was *wrong.* He had this drive, always had this drive to better himself.

"I remember he got a portable record player—which in those days was quite a thing. I'll never forget this. He had a record of Rimsky-Korsakov's *Scheherazade,* and he used to sit there and I'd tell him, 'That's the oboe. Now here's a violin.' He knew a lot about dance music and bands, but I think that was the first time he ever really got into symphonic music to know the different instruments of the orchestra."

Nancy Sinatra Sr.: "He was always striving to be better. Learning. Hoping to get on with a bigger band. He knew The Rustic Cabin was only a stepping-stone."

He took multiple jobs, singing at the Cabin at night and on radio during the day. For seventy-five cents a show, he worked fifteen minutes daily at radio

Bill Henri and His Headliners, The Rustic Cabin, a roadhouse in New Jersey, summer, 1938. Leader, Henry Jacobs ("Bill Henri"); first trumpet, John Buccini; second trumpet, Sal Reo; tenor sax, Harry Schuchman; first sax, Jack Zerk; third sax, Harry Zinquist; drums, Don Rigney; bass, John Martucci; piano, Henry Lapidus; vocalist, Frank Sinatra.

station WAAT in Jersey City. Another time, for seventy cents a week, he did shows with another young singer, Dinah Shore, in New York.

On February 4, 1939, Francis Albert Sinatra and Nancy Carol Barbato were married. She was making twenty-five dollars a week as a secretary and he'd been given a raise at the Cabin to twenty-five dollars a week. That was enough to live on, but not enough for a trip. So the young couple had a "pretend honeymoon" in their very own apartment on Audubon Avenue in Jersey City. My mother has recalled it as being wonderful. They fixed up the little place together. "Frank was very handy. He put up towel racks and after I made the curtains, he hung them. We really had fun in our first home." Life couldn't have been easy, but they had assets—they were young and they were in love. Frank Sinatra: "In Nancy I found beauty, warmth and understanding; being with her was my only escape from what seemed to be a grim world."

The day before the wedding, Frank Sinatra made a demo called "Our Love," with the Frank Manne orchestra. Soon, he hoped, he would be making the real thing. He left their apartment every morning and raced around all day, hustling between cities and jobs. His ambition was to join a prominent band.

FS: "In those days, working with a big band was the end of the rainbow for any singer who wanted to make it." He heard that the respected trumpet player Harry James was leaving Benny Goodman to start a band of his own. Nancy got a fifteen-dollar advance on her salary so he could have publicity pictures taken to give to Harry James.

Harry Schuchman: "I remember that day. He had the pictures taken, but couldn't get to Harry. So he got someone to lay them on his agent's desk."

James heard him on the radio, then came to the Rustic Cabin. Dad sang "Begin the Beguine." The band leader liked what he heard and he liked what he saw. James hired him.

The man named Sinatra was in the big time.

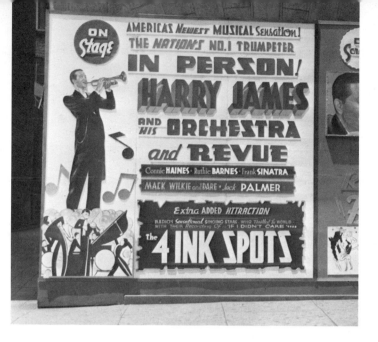

CHAPTER TWO
THE ROAD

All or Nothing at All

The Big Bands and American music. They're synonymous. Frank Sinatra and American music. They're synonymous. The two had to get together. Together they made history. Or so it seems to me.

FS: "When I started singing at The Rustic Cabin, that was for experience. I wanted to keep doing that to get better and better. On my night off, Monday, I would go to wherever there was a big band playing around New York and I'd just stand at the bandstand, like kids used to do. And I saw all the good bands and then I saw Dorsey. I thought to myself, That's the band to be with because he features his artists so well.

"So did Harry. He had arrangements done up for me as though it was my orchestra, not his. Rather than the orchestra doing the first chorus, and then the vocalist doing the second chorus and back to the orchestra, he used a lot of arrangements where the orchestra played half a chorus and I'd finish the whole song. He was a sensational guy.

"A big band in those days meant ten men or more. Fortunately, my own career got under way just in time for me to take advantage of the opportunities the big bands offered . . . Whether you were an instrumentalist or a vocalist, working in a band was an important part of growing up, musically and as a human being. It was a career builder, a seat of learning, a sort of cross-country college that taught you about collaboration, brotherhood, and sharing rough times. There is no teacher like experience, of course. And singing in a band is like lifting weights. You're conditioning yourself."

The education came at a price. And that price was the life you led on the road. Sinatra had been with the Harry James band for only a short time when they went on the road for several months. Those were the days of slow trains and boring buses and exhausting car caravans, city to city. There was fun and camaraderie, sure, but, as always, for some, loneliness. And often, surprises you didn't need.

Nancy and Frank Sinatra (left) in Jersey City, expecting their first child. Daughter-to-be Nancy Jr.: "That's me under the hat. As I know now, it's understandable that he'd record the soliloquy from Carousel *as often as he did":*

Gotta get ready before she comes
I gotta make certain that she
Won't be brought up in slums
With a lot of bums like me.
She's got to be sheltered
  and fed and dressed
In the best that money can buy.
I never knew how to get money
But I'll try, by God, I'll try.
I'll go out and make it,
Or steal it, or take it, or die.

With Harry James. His first big break, his first big band. FS: "This is the New York World's Fair, one of the early jobs I played. A matinee job, we played in the afternoons, not at night. The singer was named Marge, an Italian girl from Newark." The Fountain Lake bandshell, August 22, 1939.

The Harry James Band, the Steel Pier, Atlantic City, New Jersey, 1939. Top row, from left: Claude Lakey, Jack "Jumbo" Gardner, Bill Luther. Middle row: Jack Schaeffer, Thurman "Jug" Teague, Drew Page, Russ Brown, Claude Bowen, Red Kent. Front row: Ralph Hawkins, Truett Jones, Connie Haines, Harry James, Frank Sinatra, Dave Matthews, Jack Palmer.

The James band in a partying mood, after a one-nighter in Rome, New York. What with the business and the trains, and given the slenderness of the leader and the male singer, they needed a square meal. FS: "You know, if it's possible, Harry was thinner than I was. He really was a rail."

FS: "When it comes to professional experience, there's nothing to beat those one-nighter tours, when you rotate between five places around the clock —the bus, your hotel room, the greasy-spoon restaurant, the dressing room (if any), and the bandstand. Then back on the bus to the next night's gig, maybe four hundred miles away or more."

His young wife went along. The band traveled in separate cars, joining up in major cities. They had a nice stay in Chicago. I've always enjoyed Chicago but didn't know why, because I'd never spent any real time there. A few hours between trains. Walks by the lake. Marshall Field's. The Pump Room. Dinner at Hefner's. Lunch with Irv Kupcinet. One day not too long ago, I said to Mom, "Chicago's my favorite city, but I don't know why." She said, "Maybe it's because you 'happened' there." . . . My kind of town, Chicago is . . .

Then it was on to Los Angeles, a place Mom was really looking forward to.

Nancy Sr.: "My parents had always been intrigued with California. They had all these books with pictures of California homes, they talked about it a lot, and I was intrigued too. When I got here, I fell in love with it immediately. Four of us—Frank and I, the drummer and the arranger, got a big apartment. It was all beautiful."

Except. The band was booked into a fancy place, Victor Hugo's, but, in the words of Harry James, "They didn't care for us, and refused to pay us." As the band scrambled to find some paying work, money ran short. One day, according to Harry, "the whole band chipped in to buy spaghetti and the makings for your mom to cook for us. Spaghetti never tasted so good."

Another day, the arranger's mother sent him a tin of cookies, with a dollar tucked inside. Nancy Sr.: "I was able to fix a beautiful meal for four— spinach, mashed potatoes, hamburger. With a dollar."

She went out collecting empty Coke bottles, for their deposit value. One night she expressed a wish for a ham sandwich and a piece of apple pie. Frank disappeared. When he returned with the food—he had taken the empty soda bottles and cashed them in—he put it down on the table, looked at his room-mates, and said, "Don't touch this. This is for Nancy."

There was no argument. Because (among other reasons) by then the secret was out. As Harry James wrote me: "The only bright note in that seem-ingly desperate time was the happy news from your mother that you were on the way."

Nancy Sr.: "A couple of months of this and we were getting worried. Because I was pregnant and we had to make payments on this new car we had— they were about to take our car away from us—and we didn't want to write to the family about it and worry *them.* But we managed because somebody always came up with a few dollars. I was living on onion sandwiches—fried-onion sandwiches—for a long time."

On balance, though, Frank Sinatra's move to the James band had been a good one. He had been hired, Harry said, because "I liked Frank's way of talking a lyric." In August 1939, Harry recorded "All or Nothing at All," with vocal refrain by Frank Sinatra. It didn't sell. In July, Frank had appeared with the James Band at the Roseland Ballroom on Broadway and received his first review —one line in *Metronome,* written by George T. Simon. He liked "the very pleasing vocals of Frank Sinatra whose easy phrasing is especially commend-able." That same month, with the band, Frank Sinatra made his first commer-cially released records, singing "From the Bottom of My Heart " and "Melancholy Mood."

He loved the band and he loved Harry James. When Harry died in July 1983, Dad told me, "He made it all possible for us."

As much by not holding him back as by hiring him. There were more prominent bands than Harry's, and Frank Sinatra had his eye on them. In particular, there were Glenn Miller's band and Goodman's and Dorsey's, and Tommy Dorsey's was a showcase for singers.

Before James contacted him, Sinatra had been planning to sign on with a band run by Bob Chester; they'd rehearsed together and Chester had had arrangements written for him. One day in New York when Dad was with the James band, "the rumor came through the grapevine," according to Harry Schuchman, who had joined the Chester band, "that Frank was going to come by that night to sing with us. The reason was that Tommy Dorsey, a friend of Bob Chester's, was going to be at our show. Frank showed up and was sitting at a table with your mother and my wife Helen when Tommy walked in. Frank whispered to Nancy and Helen, 'Listen to this, Tom,' then got up from the table, went to the bandstand, and told Bob what song to play. It was an audition for Tommy, whether or not Tommy knew it. Frank knew where he was going and where he *wanted* to go."

Dorsey was a tough, argumentative guy. Originally, he'd had a band with his brother, Jimmy—the Dorsey Brothers—but they fought constantly. As my brother, Frank, said, "Finally they had a parting of the ways, with Tommy leaving to form his own band. Nearly twenty years later, in the 1950s, they got back together again for a record date. Tommy said, 'Where am I going to stand in the studio to play? Where do you want me to stand?' And Jimmy said, 'What do you mean? All this time, Mac'—Jimmy used to call Tommy 'Mac'—'and you don't know where you're going to stand? We've been together all these years and you don't know where to stand?' And Tommy folded up his trombone and was halfway out of the studio when suddenly he came back.

" 'Wait a minute!' he said, '*I* left in '37. *You* leave this time.' "

I'm told that Tommy could cause storms, and in 1939, following a series of arguments between them, he made a move that cost him Jack Leonard, his key male vocalist.

Jack Leonard: "Tommy came down real hard on a couple of trumpet players who were buddies of mine. We had been working hard, about twenty hours straight, and I just walked out. I didn't have an argument, with him. I never said a word, I just walked. I was coming to the defense of a couple of friends of mine in the band. I walked out and I never went back."

Ironically, Jack Leonard's girl friend had played the James-Sinatra recording of "All or Nothing at All" for him and Jack loved it. In turn, he had played it for Dorsey. Leonard, who loved the "purity" of Sinatra's voice, had helped get FS his chance.

Dorsey offered the job to Sinatra. "I was so excited that I called Nancy at home in New Jersey and told her what had happened. She knew that this was my dream and after she expressed her happiness she said, 'That means you'll be getting more money.'

"I said, 'I never even talked money.'

"She said, 'What do you mean, you didn't talk money?'

"I said, 'I don't know, I was just so happy to get the job.' " Well, as it turned out, it was $100 a week on a long-term contract. Just how long and how binding, my dad would discover later.

Night and day under the hide of me there's an oh such a hungry yearning burning inside of me . . .

He was already bound to a two-year contract with James. But Harry was ready to dissolve it with a handshake because, he said, "I think that's what you want. And just be sure that he's paying you a lot more than I'm paying." FS: "That's because Tommy's band was like the Miller band, they were known as rich bands. They got more work and made more money."

So James wouldn't stand in the way; all he asked was that he be given time to find a replacement. That turned out to be the talented Dick Haymes. While waiting for Sinatra, Dorsey hired Allan De Witt as Jack Leonard's immediate but temporary replacement.

Even with his ambition, Sinatra had mixed feelings about the move.

FS: "It happened in Buffalo. We were in Buffalo's Shea Theatre, like Shea Stadium, and it was 1940, in January, bitter cold but in *summertime* it's cold up there. Listen to who was on the bill. The picture playing was *Balalaika* with Nelson Eddy and Ilona Massey, and on stage was the Harry James Orchestra, with vocalists Frank Sinatra and Connie Haines. Also Burt Lancaster and Nick Cravat, a little guy who used to do stunts with Burt, and Red Skelton. *That* was the bill. And by 1943, just about everybody on that stage had become a star, a major star. Skelton was signed by MGM, James was signed by MGM, I was signed by RKO and then went to MGM, and Connie became the lead vocalist for another big orchestra.

"That was the last gig I had with James and I was going home to spend some time with Nancy and she was to meet me at the train the next morning and the band was going to Hartford to do a one-nighter. Now it sounds kind of hokey but you can see the scene this begins to make. It was rather like *Death of a Salesman* in the snow as I stood there with my two bags and the bus was pulling away and I had lived with those guys and they were fun and I stood there like a schmuck and I'm in tears as I see the red lights going away. And the snow's coming down and I figure to myself I ain't never gonna make it, and I'll never get home and it'll be terrible, I'm going to die up here in the Buffalo snow. Well, that's what happened that night, and I think it makes a picture."

Frank Sinatra joined the Tommy Dorsey band in January 1940. The band manager sent a ticket.

FS: "I took the train from Grand Central Station to Chicago and then one to Rockford, Illinois, where the band was playing. It was like going from one school to another. I was timid. I was going to meet a whole new group of people. I had known Tommy a bit because on the road, bands cross paths from time to time. But I was really kind of frightened. I was nervous but I faked a couple of tunes and I knew the lyrics of some songs so that we did all right with the audience, a group of kids—it was a holiday prom or something like that—but apart from Jo Stafford, I didn't get a very warm welcome. I was cold-shouldered by that whole band.

"I think they were just saying, Well, let's see what he can do. They loved Jack Leonard and I did, too—as a vocalist. It took some time. You see, they had grown up together as a band. After the Dorsey brothers split, Tommy had a Dixieland band. Which was not the style. Dixie was going out and Goodman was coming in from Chicago and was killing everybody, because it was swing, the day of swing. But before I joined Tommy he had hired Sy Oliver, who was becoming a famous arranger, and Bill Finegan, who later had the great Sauter-Finegan orchestra."

The Dorsey Band, headed by "the sentimental gentleman," was indeed

She may be waiting just anticipating things she may never possess while she's without them try a little tenderness.

an all-star team of talent—with musicians Ziggy Elman, Bunny Berigan, Buddy Rich, Joe Bushkin; arrangers Oliver, Axel Stordahl, Paul Weston; singers Jo Stafford and the Pied Pipers. Joining that band was like joining the 1927 New York Yankees with Babe Ruth, Lou Gehrig, and the rest of Murderers' Row: a rookie had a lot to live up to. Sinatra came to his Dorsey debut under considerable pressure.

His new colleagues were skeptical. Sitting on the bandstand when Sinatra walked on stage for the first time, what Jo Stafford perceived was a "very young, slim figure with more hair than he needed. We were all sort of sitting back—like, 'Oh yeah, who are you?' Then he began to sing." After four bars, Stafford thought, "Wow! *This* is an absolutely new, unique sound."

"Nobody had ever sounded like that," Stafford recalled years later. "In those days most male singers' biggest thing was to try and sound as much like Bing as possible. Well, he didn't sound anything like Bing. He didn't sound like anybody else that I had ever heard. I was mightily impressed."

Maybe Jo was, and her nice husband, John Huddleston, but not everybody. FS: "A lot of guys just didn't bother with me and so I said the hell with it. Then, as I got better and better over six months or so, and began to develop and delineate a method of long phraseology, they began to take notice. Something was happening. Something strange, maybe, but Tommy loved it, because that's the way he played. Tommy's was a tremendous orchestra. What artists he had—maybe the best band ever."

But it took time. Meanwhile, life on the road had its compensations.

Jo Stafford: "We traveled a lot by bus, and, well, a band bus is madness. Absolutely madness! It was arranged like on a bandstand. On a bandstand, if you have strings, the strings are in front, and they're fairly calm people who behave themselves. Next are the saxophones, who can get a *little* rowdy—not *too* much —then come the trombones, who get fairly raunchy, and then the trumpet players, who are out of control. And that's exactly the way the bus worked. Starting in the front it's fairly calm, but as you worked back, you came to your saxophone players, then the trombone players, then the trumpet section. Your father was in the back—with the rhythm section. The rhythm section could be real evil. I was in the back too, in the last seat, with Buddy's drums; I made my bed with his bass drum—that was where my feet went.

"Oh, the tragedies of the road. One time, in Ohio, we were on a long jaunt and the bus broke down in some little residential town. Just a little street, with houses, and families, and it was like five thirty, six o'clock in the morning. And the bus couldn't be fixed, so they were going to have to send a bus from Cleveland to pick us up, and we sat and we sat and we sat, and now the crazies start getting cabin fever and didn't know what to do. Finally, Buddy got out his drums and set them up and a couple of the guys got some horns and at seven o'clock in the morning, this little town in Ohio was graced with a jam session . . . which I'm not sure they were really prepared for.

"Another thing your father will remember is our bus driver. His last name was 'King' and he went out of New York with us on this three-week road trip. He went out a very neat man, with his little leather tie and his billed cap on. But that's not the way he came back. The guys in the band almost drove him crazy because he kept getting lost. We would have a short trip to make and we'd think, 'Now we're going to get to actually get in the bed and lie horizontal and sleep.' And King would get lost and the band would keep getting madder and madder, until finally, one night—it was in the South some place—it was raining

The "rich bands" went by plane. (Front row) FS and Don Lotus, on the way to a Dorsey date. (Second row) Ray Linn and Heinie Beau (FS: "Where you from?" Beau: "Fond du Lac, Wisconsin." FS: "You're kiddin. Nobody comes from a place like that.") (Third row) Jo Stafford and her husband, John Huddleston. (Last row, right) Ziggy Elman.

and we came to this bridge and the water was torrential. King stopped and said, 'We're going to have to test this bridge to see if it will carry the bus.' And somebody said, 'How do you think we're going to do *that?*' And he said, 'Well, several of us will just have to walk across this bridge.' I can't *repeat* the response, but finally they all said, 'King—you're the perfect tester—out you go!' And he went.

"Once, King got lost trying to get us to Altoona, Pennsylvania. That was one of our worst nights. I'm not sure you should want to get to Altoona but we did and we got thoroughly lost, were about six hours late, at which point the guys in the band made a sign which they put on the side of the bus: *'Altoona or bust!'* Coming back home toward New York the guys were so mad at him they threw all his maps out the window and he couldn't even find New York City. Ever after that, when anybody was bugging us, we had three words. We used them in all situations . . . 'Straight ahead, driver. Straight ahead, driver.' That was 'the road'—the ever-loving road."

The road could be fun and the road could be depressing. Ruth Cosgrove, who would become Milton Berle's wife, was a teenager dating Buddy Rich in those days and later a close and permanent friend of my father's. Ruth Berle: "I remember very clearly Frank telling me how lonely it was on the road, how lonely it was to spend Christmas, Thanksgiving away from his family . . . the fact that he had to be in Minneapolis on Christmas and be alone or be with the guys."

Mom no longer traveled with him. She had stopped in her last months of pregnancy. And after I was born—on June 8, 1940—she had to stay home with me. The day I was born, my father was off singing with the band. When he heard the news, Jo Stafford told me, "he was so excited that all he did all night was talk about his new baby girl."

But he hadn't been there for the birth. Already, I was being prepared for having to share him with the rest of the world. It was the start of what became one of the themes of my life: A father who was always going away. My father was always saying goodbye.

In November 1940, he went to the West Coast—to appear with the Dorsey band in his first movie, *Las Vegas Nights.* With Jo Stafford and the Pipers, he recorded "I'll Never Smile Again," their first record to reach number one on the charts, and every time I heard it, my mom told me, I would cry. Although the words meant nothing to me, I knew the voice belonged to my daddy.

But where was he? Not inside that funny box. And why couldn't I see him?

 ## On the Street of Dreams

In 1941 a *Billboard* poll named Sinatra the Most Outstanding Male Band Vocalist in the United States. His fame was growing—and so were his voice and his technique. His diction was flawless. *Love,* not *luv; your,* not *yore.* He worked at it constantly. He worked at all aspects of his music. He wanted to be the best ever.

FS: "It was in early 1940 that I really began developing a style of my own. Tommy didn't work much with me. He devoted his time to the musicians and

Hasbrouck Heights, New Jersey. FS: "I should send a copy of this book to Iacocca and say, 'See! I was driving Chryslers before you even got involved.'" So was the author.

The Dorsey band and dancers. The small figure toward the right rear, telling jokes with the great piano man Joe Bushkin, both being ignored by Buddy Rich on drums, said: "I used to sit up at the back. Not down front. I didn't like sitting with the singers." At the microphone, The Pied Pipers.

arrangements, so that left me on my own to experiment. The thing that influenced me most was the way Tommy played his trombone. He would take a musical phrase and play it all the way through seemingly without breathing, for eight, ten, maybe sixteen bars.

"How in the hell did he do it? I used to sit behind him on the bandstand and watch, trying to see him sneak a breath. But I never saw the bellows move in his back. His jacket didn't even move. I used to edge my chair to the side a little, and peek around to watch him. Finally, after a while, I discovered that he had a 'sneak pinhole' in the corner of his mouth—not an actual hole, but a tiny place he left open where he was breathing. In the middle of a phrase, while the tone was still being carried through the trombone, he'd go *shhhhh* and take a quick breath and play another four bars with that breath. Why couldn't a singer do that too? Fascinated, I began listening to other soloists. I bought every Jascha Heifetz record I could find and listened to him play the violin hour after hour. His constant bowing, where you never heard a break, carried the melody line straight on through, just like Dorsey's trombone.

"It was my idea to make my voice work in the same way as a trombone or violin—not sounding like them, but 'playing' the voice like those instruments. The first thing I needed was extraordinary breath control, which I didn't have. I began swimming every chance I got in public pools—taking laps under water and thinking song lyrics to myself as I swam, holding my breath."

This was not easy because of a perforated eardrum, a defect caused by the forceps that had torn his head during birth. It was painful, but he did it.

"I worked out on the track at the Stevens Institute in Hoboken, running one lap, trotting the next. Pretty soon I had good breath control, but that still wasn't the whole answer. I still had to learn to sneak a breath without being too obvious. It was easier for Dorsey to do it through his 'pinhole' while he played the trombone. He could control the inhalation better because the horn's mouthpiece was covering most of his mouth. Try it and see, and sing at the same time.

"Instead of singing only two bars or four bars of music at a time—like most of the other guys around—I was able to sing six bars, and in some songs eight bars, without taking a visible or audible breath. This gave the melody a flowing, unbroken quality and that—if anything—was what made me sound different. It wasn't the voice alone; in fact, my voice was always a little too high, I thought, and not as good in natural quality as some of the competition."

Jo Stafford: "Frank is a perfectionist about his work. That was one of the things I really enjoyed about working with him, because musically I like it perfect too. So did Tommy. Tommy was a taskmaster only insofar as your work was concerned. It was not like the Glenn Miller Band. We used to call them 'the Boy Scouts.' Tommy only cared about your performance and your work. As long as you did that well, that was it. An honest mistake—a clarinet squeak, or somebody forgetting a word, a real, honest mistake—he understood that and there was no problem. Carelessness? Then you got it—on your head." Dorsey's tough professional standards became the model for those Frank Sinatra would live by and demand of people who worked with, and for, him.

Dorsey dished it out but he could take it, too—even from the kid. Songwriter Sammy Cahn: "I remember when the Dorsey band with Frank, and Ziggy and Buddy and Stafford and all the rest were at the Palladium in Hollywood. Tommy came late. Frank took over as the conductor and when Tommy came in, Frank really read him off. Tommy, funny enough, was really put down for being late and he tried to apologize to Frank who'd have none of it."

Indeed, Tommy Dorsey and Frank Sinatra didn't always agree on things. Presidential speech writer and television producer Paul Keyes was a seventeen-year-old high school student in Portland, Maine, when the Dorsey band played a one-nighter at Ricker Gardens in the spring of 1941. Following the dance, the members of the band walked to Howard Johnson's restaurant for a late supper. With his autograph book, Keyes approached Dorsey in Howard Johnson's, not realizing he was violating the privacy of a section of the restaurant Tommy had ordered closed off to anybody but band members.

Paul Keyes: "Mr. Dorsey was, to say the least, unfriendly, and had me physically removed from the premises. A few minutes later I saw Frank Sinatra leave the private room and I followed him to the men's room to get his autograph. He was most friendly and signed my book ('What's your name, kid?') to me personally. I mentioned that I wanted to get the autographs of the rest of the orchestra but that Mr. Dorsey had thrown me out of the room. 'Come with me, kid.' Frank took me into the room and introduced me warmly to Ziggy Elman, Connie Haines, Jo Stafford, Buddy Rich, and all of the members of the orchestra with: 'This is my friend, Paul. Write something nice to him in his autograph book.' After he had introduced me to everybody in the orchestra, he took me over to Tommy. 'Tommy, this is my friend Paul, and I want you to write something nice in his book. He's a good kid.' Mr. Dorsey, recognizing me but not batting an eye, did as Frank requested and signed my book. Frank then invited me to pull up a chair and have a bite with the band."

Frank Sinatra cared about the fans, particularly the "kids." More than twenty years later he talked about one particular memory of those days: "It had been snowing all day, and we got to this high school and there were these kids

Overleaf: The Tommy Dorsey Orchestra, 1942. Trumpets: Ziggy Elman, Jimmy Zito, Jim Blake, Ray Linn. Trombones: George Arus, Dave Jacobs, Jim Skiles. Saxes: Fred Stulce, Heinie Beau, Don Lodice, Vince Yocum, Harry Schuchman. Leader: Tommy Dorsey. Vocalists: Chuck Lowry, Jo Stafford, Frank Sinatra, John Huddleston. Drums: Buddy Rich. Guitar: Clark Yocum. Piano: Milton Raskin. Harp: Ruth Hill. Bass: Phil Stephens. Violins: Lenny Posner, Raoul Paliaken, Bill Ehrenkrantz, Al Beller, Cy Miroff, Bernie Linterow. Violas: Sam Ross, Lenny Atkins. Cello: George Ricci.

standing in the snow; the kids had been waiting all day. Well, there was a chance the concert might have to be canceled. But it wasn't; the show went on and all these kids got in and the band played not only until eleven, but until four o'clock in the morning."

He still remembered what a warm moment that had been—putting on a show for those kids who had been lined up in the snow.

We lived in a nice apartment on Bergen Avenue in Jersey City, and, with the band on the road, my mother and I were alone there a lot. In December 1941, the United States went to war and, from the ensuing year, though I only turned two, I have one vivid image: the blackouts. The curtains drawn. The lights turned off. And Mom and I sitting on the floor, holding each other in the darkness. Daddy was busy, I guess. He was, it seemed, a voice on the radio most of the time, or a picture in the newspaper.

But when he was home, I was happy.

My mother saw to it that we led a normal life. I remember visiting Grandma and Grandpa Barbato. Their house was three stories tall and on the top floor was the prettiest black and white tile bathroom. The house was warm and friendly. I could smell the good Neapolitan sauces cooking in the kitchen. Grandpa Mike made his own wine, and Jenny taught me how to put butter on a Uneeda Biscuit. There were aunts (five) and uncles (three) all over the place, and opera played constantly.

Visiting Marty and Dolly was fun, too. Grandpa was very funny, and they were both good cooks. Grandpa's food was Sicilian style and Grandma's was Genovese—a little lighter, with a French flavor. The furniture in their parlor always had plastic on it that stuck to the backs of my legs. Grandma had a button box and we played with the pretty buttons for hours. But in my opinion the most fun was at Marty's saloon.

"Bampa," I would say, my diction a little lacking, "go da *soon,* pease?" And though Dolly would have a fit, we'd often go off, Grandpa and I, to the "soon."

I guess I was destined to be a saloon singer's daughter.

My father wanted to do military service. He was drafted and my mom packed his stuff and he went off. Goodbye again. Mom figured she wouldn't see him for a long time—at least until after basic training. But he was rejected because of that punctured eardrum. Several times, he tried to enlist.

Ruth Berle: "He wanted so desperately to go into the service. I remember sitting with him in one of the New York hotels—the Astor or the Pennsylvania. He was enraged. He had been turned down again that day. He had tried everything to get into the service. And he had this thing that he still has, this patriotism.

"I joined the Army—the WACs. It made an enormous impression on him and he always kept in touch. The day I got my commission, he sent me flowers, in Des Moines, Iowa. I'll never forget this WAC second lieutenant, who had been my commanding officer in OCS, who I'd been terrified of. She was awestruck. She said, 'Frank Sinatra!' And I thought, 'Jesus, I was so afraid of this schmuck, and now she's kissing my ass. I can't believe it. Why didn't I know it earlier? I wouldn't have had to work so hard.'"

Not everyone was as impressed by him, though.

George Burns: "Your father was singing with Tommy Dorsey's band, and Gracie Allen and I were doing a half-hour radio show in which we always used a singer.

The band did so much overtime in making the movie Las Vegas Nights *that the studio, as a form of compensation, said they would have each person's portrait made. Dorsey, never one to lose an opportunity, said, "Let's have a composite done for publicity." As the writers John Martland and Alan Dell observed: "Frank appears to have got along well with Dorsey. They were remarkably alike in many ways. Both were quick-tempered, ambitious, and musically*

"Anyway, we were offered Frank Sinatra for two hundred and fifty dollars a week, and at the same time we were offered an act called The Smoothies (two fellows and a girl) also for two hundred and fifty dollars. Well, being a showman and always thinking, I hired The Smoothies. I said to myself, why should I take this kid Sinatra for two hundred and fifty dollars when I can get three people for the same money?

"All right, a man is entitled to a mistake. Don't forget, later on I did discover people like Jed Newmann, Elsie Thackeray, and that all-time great, Willard Moody. So you see, things have a way of evening themselves out. You win some, you lose some."

In 1942, though still a member of the Dorsey band, Frank Sinatra recorded his first solo songs, with Axel Stordahl as his arranger and conductor. His ambitions again began to grow.

Sammy Cahn: "I vividly remember sitting with him one night, and he leaned in and said with the kind of intensity that can only come from great talent: 'I am going to be the biggest singer there ever was.' I looked at him and said, 'There is no way anything can get in your way!' He reached over, grabbed my arm and said, 'You *do* believe me, then.' Boy, did I *believe!*"

Cahn and Axel Stordahl were rooming in a musicians' hotel in Hollywood, the Castle Argyle: "One night the phone rang, and Frank told us he wanted to leave Tommy—and he wanted Axel to get ready to move in with him. We looked at each other."

FS: "When I went to leave, Tommy made it impossible. I remember that it was in the month of September, in Washington, D.C. I went into the dressing room and told Tommy that I wanted to leave the orchestra and he kind of smiled. What for? he said. You know you're doing great with the band and we got a lot of arrangements for you. I said I understand that but I just want to go out on my own. He said, I don't think so.

"I said okay, but I'm going to leave. He said, You've got a contract. I said, I had a contract with Harry but Harry took the contract and tore it up and wished me luck. And I added, I'll give you one year's notice. This time next year, I'm leaving.

"Actually, I loved and admired him. He was a taskmaster and a brilliant musician and I liked it because he made everybody toe the line. He was also a man who detested the idea that a member of the orchestra would leave. Now, a musician gives a bandleader two weeks' notice and then he can leave. He cannot, however, leave the orchestra and not show up and *then* send a message that he has quit. Then the band leader can call the musicians' union and they bring him up on charges. So if he gives two weeks' notice he walks away and can go to another orchestra. In those days, Artie Shaw was stealing from Jimmy Dorsey and everybody was swapping musicians. Tommy hated that. He wanted the band to be set. I could understand that because the orchestra was drilled like a platoon. And when new men arrived, it meant rehearsing and getting the guy to fit in and so Dorsey just resented the idea of my leaving. From the time I told him, he wouldn't talk to me. I'd say, Tom, let's talk, please, but he was angry for months. And soon I said, I want to talk to you about somebody replacing me.

"What was funny, but not very, is that when I left Harry I recommended Dick Haymes and I told Tommy now that I could probably get Haymes. As a matter of fact, Dick did replace me. (When I saw Harry two years later, he said, Jesus, every time I train a singer you come along and steal him from me.) But Tommy was just so resentful and angry that I said the hell with it, while he was

uncompromising. Both had large egos. With Dorsey, FS moved out from being just a band singer who did the vocal refrain to one who pressed to do solo sides, who was "soon threatening to become more important than the band behind him . . ." Dorsey allowed the solo records (arranged and conducted by Axel Stordahl) which resulted in the first obvious "separation" of vocalist and band.

The young singer had a voice and a vision. Nancy Sinatra (NS): "His first recording of 'All or Nothing at All' is still young, sweet, and strong. I can understand what the fuss was about. My God. He was something." He was beginning to think of moving out—and moving on. He was thinking "solo, solo, solo . . ."

still claiming I had signed a piece of paper.

"Well, it was a ratty piece of paper. It called for me to pay him one third of my earnings for as long as I was in the entertainment business."

Sinatra started working some on his own anyhow, without leaving the band, doing weekends in Providence and such, and he got an agent and was studying vocal technique with John Quinlan in New York when a man named Manie Sacks—

"—came into my life, one of the nicest people God ever made in this world. He was a man who never could say No. He told me that Bill Bailey would like me to do some sustaining shows and I said that's fine with me because it's more exposure. And I did those for six months or a year. In the interim, Manie said, What are you going to do about the Dorsey thing because we're getting letters from his manager, saying that they expect to get one third of your salary?"

That's when one of the irresponsible stories about Sinatra got its start. Over the years, all sorts of silly accounts have been told of how he extricated himself from the punitive, unfair Dorsey deal—and the stories are as punishing and unfair as the contract was.

FS: "It began to come out of the ground that my mother went to Tommy or that the racket guys went to Tommy and convinced him that he should let me go. And that's so far afield it's scary. It's *incredible*.

"Manie said, 'I think we'd better get a lawyer. I think we ought to see Medina.' I said, 'Who is he?' And Manie said, 'He's one of the greatest lawyers in America.' He was Tom Dewey's lawyer and a lawyer for big companies. We got an appointment and went to see him and I didn't even have a copy of the contract. But we described it. He said, Well, that seems awfully tough to me, and he expressed his understanding of why we would want to get out of it. But—and these are not his exact words—he said something like 'This is not quite my métier. I wouldn't know exactly how to handle this; I have been a corporate lawyer for so many years.' So we thanked him and went out."

(Later, as Justice Harold Medina, that lawyer became famous for accomplishments beyond corporate law.)

"So a couple of weeks went by and Manie said to me, I've got the guy. His name is Henry Jaffe and he is Dinah Shore's lawyer and mentor. Fine. So we got up there in the Newsweek building and little Henry is sitting there behind a big cigar. The following ensued:

"He contacted Dorsey and Dorsey had his manager speak to him and say that he didn't want to talk, he wanted his money. Now, Henry Jaffe was, I believe, the legal secretary of AFRA, the American Federation of Radio Artists. Tommy, mind you, was playing many remotes from hotels. At eleven o'clock at night, you heard all the dance bands and I have a hunch that Henry said to Tommy, Do you like broadcasting on NBC? And Tommy said, Yes, he liked it a lot. Well, said Henry, how about we talk about Frank Sinatra and we'll see what kind of deal we can make—if you want to continue on radio.

"And I understand that then there was a meeting. It wasn't quite satisfactory. I found out later that Henry went next to Jules Stein at MCA. I was being handled by the agents Rockwell-O'Keefe and was beginning to catch on. Henry said to Stein, Would you like to manage Frank Sinatra? Stein said, By all means, but I understand he's with another agent. Henry said, I'll handle that part. He spelled out the rest.

"He convinced Jules Stein to give Tommy Dorsey about $75,000 and to give him more play dates on the road. My end of it was like $25,000.

"Anyhow, *that's* how I got out of the Dorsey contract. No gangster called anyone. (Sonofabitch, I've been with that thing for so many years . . .)"

The Hearst papers and others who disagreed with Sinatra's support for F.D.R. would later use this episode against him, starting the allegations about his connections with "The Mob." Reporters at odds with his liberal politics—it seems hard to believe today—would embroider the event.

As for Henry Jaffe? FS: "I thought he knew what to do with a client. Anyone who could con Jules Stein that way . . . I retained him as an attorney for many years."

He made the break in September 1942. He'd been thinking of the move since he'd played New York's Paramount Theatre with the Dorsey band and experienced the first fierce adulation of the fans.

What was it about him?

FS: "I think my appeal was due to the fact that there hadn't been a troubador around for ten or twenty years, from the time that Bing had broken in and went on to radio and movies. And he, strangely enough, had appealed primarily to older people, middle-aged people. When I came on the scene and people began noticing me at the Paramount, I think the kids were looking for somebody to cheer for. Also, the war had just started. They were looking for somebody who represented those gone in their life.

"I began to realize that there must be something to all this commotion. I didn't know exactly what it was, but I figured I had something that must be important. So I decided to try it alone, without a band.

"The other reason was that I had been thinking. The number one guy in the world was obviously Crosby. Nobody was going to touch him because he really was the best. Still, I thought, at some future time there has to be a number two. And a number three and so on. When Russ Columbo was killed in that terrible accident—he was accidentally shot with a souvenir pirate pistol or something; they didn't know it was loaded and the shot ricocheted off his agent's desk and killed him—he was the runner-up under Crosby. I was thinking and dreaming about growing and moving up. And in traveling from city to city, I got to know Bob Eberly, whose singing was wonderful—boy, he was a good singer! Fine quality and wonderful intonation. And Como was equally good and I got to know him. But when I began to see the reaction from the kids wherever we appeared, I thought further about going on my own. It began to dawn on me that if I didn't get out and go as a soloist before Bob Eberly or Perry Como, I would have to fight even harder to displace those guys and be number two. I had heard through the bandstand grapevine that Eberly might break off from Jimmy Dorsey, might be striking out on his own. If he got out ahead of me, I'd be in trouble."

What were the dimensions of the "commotion" when Dorsey's band played the Paramount?

Jo Stafford: "When the stage went down into the pit, the audience was right there, on top of you. In those days the girl singers were always wearing flowers in their hair, and it used to be downright dangerous when the pit went down. Just the fact that I knew Frank Sinatra and sat next to him on the bandstand was enough for them to snatch my hair out! They would grab for those flowers, for my earrings, for anything! So when the bandstand went down, I had to get way in the back, so that they wouldn't tear something off me."

But the real hysteria had only begun.

Not everything was pure progress. FS: "I had just started to make it. I was appearing at the Paramount and I had just discovered art. One day, I was at the Museum of Modern Art and I just couldn't believe it . . . all those paintings. A girl whispered to her mother, 'Mama, I think that's Frank Sinatra' . . . Her mother answered, 'What's <u>he</u> doing in a place like this?' I just had to leave."

And it was years before he could bring himself to go back.

CHAPTER THREE
ON HIS OWN

Night and Day

When Frank Sinatra and Tommy Dorsey split up in September of 1942, they bid farewell on the radio. It was sad, I'm told. FS introduced his replacement, Dick Haymes. But—onward and upward, and he had nearly three months to get ready. One of the first things he did was to sign Hank Sanicola as his manager. There was a lot to do in preparation for his first solo stand at the Paramount. The term "solo" is not really accurate since he was booked in with headliner Benny Goodman and his band. He was, however, hired separately and paid by the Paramount, which meant an increase in earnings.

While rehearsing his new act, Sinatra stayed active in radio. He did "Reflections" on CBS, and in October 1942 he began a show on WABC called "Frank Sinatra Sings." (He did that show for four months.)

Thoroughly rehearsed and completely prepared, Sinatra opened at the Paramount Theatre in New York's Times Square on December 30, 1942. Well—he *thought* he was prepared. As it turned out, nobody was. A famous comedian was one of those swept up by the surprise.

Jack Benny: "I was in New York City doing a radio show, and Bob Weitman, who ran the Paramount, came to me and asked if just before I do my radio show, I could come over to the Paramount for the debut of Frank Sinatra. I said *who?* He said, 'Frank Sinatra, and Benny Goodman's Orchestra is also playing and Benny Goodman will introduce you, and you will introduce Frank Sinatra.' So I said, 'Well, who the hell is Frank Sinatra?' and he said to me, 'You mean to tell me that you have never heard of Frank Sinatra?' I said, 'No.' He said, 'Well, he is the hottest thing in the country right now.' I said, 'I'm sorry, but I never heard of him. But, Bob, I'll do this for you and Benny Goodman and Sinatra too if it is any help.' So I go there. I'm backstage with Benny Goodman, waiting to be introduced, and Bob Weitman was there, and they introduced me to this skinny little kid called Frank Sinatra. I shook hands with him and said hello, and he said, 'Hello, Mr. Benny.' Now, it's time for the introductions, and

first Benny Goodman went on and did his act, and then he says, 'Now, ladies and gentlemen, to introduce our honored guest, we have Jack Benny.' So I walked out on a little ramp and got a very fine reception, you know, I thought it was nice. I certainly didn't think Sinatra would get much of anything 'cause I never heard of him. So, they introduce me and I did two or three jokes and they laughed and then I realized there were a lot of young people out there, proba- bly waiting for Sinatra, so I introduced Frank Sinatra as if he were one of my closest friends—you know, I made a big thing of it and I had to make all of this up, 'cause I didn't know who he was—and then I said, 'Well, anyway, ladies and gentlemen, here he is, Frank Sinatra'—and I thought the goddamned building was going to cave in. I never heard such a commotion with people running down to the stage, screaming and nearly knocking me off the ramp. All this for a fellow I never heard of."

The first time he heard the reception, Sinatra, too, was startled: "The sound that greeted me was absolutely deafening. It was a tremendous roar. Five thousand kids, stamping, yelling, screaming, applauding. I was scared stiff. I couldn't move a muscle. Benny Goodman froze, too. He was so scared he turned around, looked at the audience, and said, 'What the hell is that?' I burst out laughing."

Bob Weitman: "There were about five thousand people in the theatre at the time, and all five thousand were of one voice, 'F-R-A-N-K-I-E-E-E-E-E!' The young, the old—as one person—got up and danced in the aisles and jumped on the stage. The loge and the balcony swayed. One of the managers came over to me and said, 'The balcony is rocking—what do we do?' We struck up the National Anthem."

The engagement ran for four weeks. "Frankie!" "The Voice!" His nick- names and his legend began to take shape. He hired a press agent, George B. Evans, who capitalized on the hysteria. Sinatra's fans were mostly young girls. In acknowledgment of the ankle-length socks they wore, usually with saddle shoes, they were united with a snappy label: *bobby-soxers.* In acknowledgment of those who fairly fainted away at the sound or sight of Sinatra, there was another: *swooners.*

The adulation was all too real. Singers had created excitement in the past —opera tenors, Rudy Vallee, crooners Russ Columbo and Bing Crosby—but nothing like this. Describing it in *The New Yorker,* author E. J. Kahn, Jr., noted that "Girls have plucked hairs from his head and, at somewhat less trouble to him, have collected clippings of his hair from the floors of barbershops. One Sinatra fan carries around in a locket what she insists is a Sinatra hangnail . . . 'I shiver all the way up and down my spine when you sing,' a girl wrote Sinatra, 'just like I did when I had scarlet fever.' 'After the fourth time I fell out of a chair and bumped my head,' said another, 'I decided to sit on the floor in the begin- ning when I listen to you.' . . . As a rule, any public appearance by Sinatra is a guarantee of at least a modest riot . . . when Sinatra was to appear in a Boston armory, the management had the seats bolted to the floor . . . The Paramount

The phenomenon erupts, now that he is on his own. Here, the famed bobby-soxers express their mingled cries of pleasure and pain at the Paramount Theatre, New York City. Wrote jazz critic Barry Ulanov: "I simply don't understand why this adoring public won't stem their roaring adulation long enough to listen to the skeleton of their dreams."

Outside the Paramount, pandemonium. The girl kissing the photograph of "The Sigh Guy" (alternately, "The Sultan of Swoon") was underscoring not only her emotions but Time *magazine's report: "Not since the days of Rudolph Valentino has American womanhood made such unabashed public love to an entertainer." Most of the adoring were identifiable not only by their socks but by their saddle shoes.*

is the shrine of their disorder . . . many of his fans literally consider the theatre their home and spend the day in it, occupying a seat through half a dozen shows for the price of one ticket." Fans of both men, Kahn reported, could become rather heated when arguing the relative skills of Sinatra and his chief rival in musical popularity polls, Bing Crosby. An "admirer of Sinatra," Kahn wrote, "had to be taken to the hospital after her roommate, a Crosby fan, had stabbed her with an ice-pick during a debate."

Fans began to invade our home. We had moved from our Bergen Street apartment in Jersey City to a house in Hasbrouck Heights, New Jersey. Nancy Sr.: "The fans would come out there all the time. There was no wall around the property. No privacy. I'd go into my bedroom and all of a sudden, I'd see somebody's face in the window. It scared me. They'd sit out there on the lawn for hours. We tried asking them to go home but they wouldn't leave. And I'd feel so sorry for them I would send out doughnuts and something for them to drink."

My mother made the soft, floppy bow ties that were becoming a trademark. "I had a terrible time keeping him in ties. Fans would yank them off him for souvenirs. I made them by the dozens."

Until his press agent's office took over, Mom was in charge of his fan mail. "I sent out hundreds of pictures. And I used to do all the writing. I would sign his name—copy his signature because he didn't have time for that. My sisters would help by addressing the envelopes. We'd do it a couple of hours a night.

"It was exciting and it was a lot of work. It was constant work. Frank worked *very, very* hard. He'd come home so tired, he'd just flop. And I'd think, 'Whatever happens, it's going to be worth it because he's giving his *all.*'"

He did six shows a day at the Paramount, beginning at 11 A.M. Richie Lisella was Dad's assistant road manager: "Sometimes he'd box for relaxation between shows, in a rehearsal hall upstairs. He'd come back on stage and he'd recognize some of the same faces in the audience. He'd say, 'I know you kids are out of school, you're here six shows.' So he'd send me out to get a lot of sandwiches for them—thirty, forty sandwiches at a time. I used to get them at Walgreen's Drugstore. Almost forty years later I walked into the bus station in

New York and I saw, working there, the girl who used to be behind the counter at Walgreen's. She said, 'I don't believe it. The Paramount Theatre. You used to buy all those turkey sandwiches.'

"Outside the Paramount the lines started at eleven o'clock at night for a show eleven o'clock in the morning. They'd be there all night. When they saw him they'd get wild. I saw fans run under the horses of mounted policemen. I saw them turn over a car."

In the Paramount days, Sinatra occasionally would ask another young singer to fill in for him.

Perry Como: "He'd say, 'Do you want to sing a couple of shows for me?' Can you imagine me walking on to the Paramount stage? It was like putting your head in a damn guillotine. I'll never forget the first time. I walked out like an idiot. They don't know who I am. 'What the hell are *you* doing,' they say. And I said, 'Hey, wait a minute! I don't have to *do* this, you know.' I was young and Italian. I said, 'Frank called. He's not feeling well, so I'm going to sing a few songs. If you want it, fine. If you don't, I'll get out of here. No big deal.' "

Perry Como was to become his own big deal, with his own beautiful voice.

In 1943 Marjorie Diven was put in charge of coordinating and corresponding with the Frank Sinatra fan clubs. She soon drew up her perception of a typical fan: "She's a fourteen-year-old girl living in a small town. She never gets to see anybody except her family, who haven't much money, and her schoolmates. She's lonely. On the way home from school, she stops at a drugstore for an ice-cream soda and picks up a movie magazine. She reads about Frank's life and it sounds wonderful . . . She writes him a letter. She imagines he gets about six or seven letters a day, and she visualizes him at his breakfast table, with her letter propped against the toaster. She calculates how long it will take for his answer to her to come back. When the time arrives and she hears the postman coming, she runs down the lane to her mailbox, one of those wobbly rural boxes. She keeps this up for three weeks, while her family makes fun of her. It's the thought of that fourteen-year-old girl running down that lane to that wobbly mailbox that makes me sympathetic to the fans."

He couldn't get out of a building after he entered it. Stopping in Little Italy for a pizza, he was there for only a few moments—and then had to leave through a basement window, to avoid the crowd that had instantly congregated. On the way out, and having had no time for dessert, he had passed a pastry tray and, just like old times, pocketed a few for later.

Marjorie Diven's description lends support to Dad's own analysis of his appeal back then: "Psychologists tried to go into the reasons with all sorts of deep theories. I could have told them why. Perfectly simple: it was the war years, and there was a great loneliness. And I was the boy in every corner drugstore, the boy who'd gone off, drafted to the war. That was all."

Not quite. Indeed, at 5'10 1/2" and 138 pounds, with a 29-inch waist, he had the look of the kid in the drugstore. But, there was also that special voice with its splendid purity. And, for those kids able to see him in performance, there was the shock of the blue eyes with some kind of loneliness behind the twinkle. The stance, the lean body, echoing the microphone, and the broad-shouldered jacket, making him a triangle. The quivering lower lip. The expressive hands. The sweet speaking voice. The shyness. The *vulnerability*. Every girl wanted to take care of him. The needy, hungry quality. Every girl wanted to feed him.

Comic-book biographies were artifacts of the time, sentimental and unreliable slush, early evidence, although amiable, of some of the silly stories that would swirl around him thereafter.

MICKEY NIEVES ANN BACHMAN GLORIA KAHN DOLORES McMULLEN JEAN DRAKE

CONNIE GUY

LYNN ELLOVICH

DOT NIX

JOAN FOX

Ellen Coughlin

Jean Lee

CAROL REHMAN

JANET WOLFENSTEIN

JOAN MILLER

BEVERLY BUSH

When he left a hotel, they'd follow him. When he left a city, they'd phone ahead and alert others and that fan club would go to the airport, demonstrating how fan *and* fanatic *are similar in spirit. Once, he stopped in a restaurant in New York's Little Italy. A little boy spotted him, and called for reinforcements. When FS tried to leave, he was forced to use a basement window. But not without first picking up a few freshly baked pastries.*

So the fans went nuts. But he did not. He worked hard to keep his perspective. Once, he told me, when he was working his way up, he met Al Jolson. Sinatra was so excited. He said hello and put out his hand. And Jolson put his own hand in his pocket and pulled out some kind of financial statement and he said, "You think you can do as good as this, kid?" Never shook his hand. And the young singer was crushed.

The Sinatra style would be different.

Peggy Lee: "When he first became such a smashing success at the Paramount Theatre, I was singing with the Benny Goodman Orchestra. We did many shows a day. During that engagement I was the victim of ptomaine poisoning passed on by a liverwurst sandwich from a nearby food counter. It was severe enough to last for two or three days, although it seemed like forever. For all but one show I staggered on to the stage to do my little part and would almost crawl back to my dressing room. During all that time I had one of the nicest male nurses any girl could ask for. Your father. With all of the excitement that was going on in his life (you could hear the bobby-soxers screaming all the way up to the fifth floor, which is where the dressing rooms were) he would come in after each of his performances to see what he could do for my comfort. He brought me blankets. He brought me a radio to play softly and when I was finally able to take any kind of nourishment, he brought me hot tea and cups of broth with crackers and encouraging words."

FS was already good at surprising his friends, showing up unexpectedly.

Jo Stafford: "I was still with the Pipers and we were playing a theatre in New Jersey and he was playing someplace in New York, probably the Paramount. At our last show, we were just finishing our act—getting ready to go off —and during the applause for the last number, we heard a roar go up—just a roar—and we didn't know *what* happened. We looked, and on the stage strolled Frank. We did, 'I'll Never Smile Again,' and, of course, the house came down."

One of the fans was fairly well known himself. After meeting Franklin Delano Roosevelt, Sinatra said: "There's the greatest guy alive today—and here's this little guy from Hoboken, shaking his hand."

The Song Is You

Sometimes Mom took me to the Paramount to see Daddy. I spent a lot of time in "Uncle" Bob Weitman's office, sitting on his lap, drawing at his desk. And they'd take me backstage to listen to Daddy sing. I'd have a good time until they started "I'll never smile again, until I smile at you . . ." And then my tears would come. What *was* it about that song?

In September 1943, Freeman Gosden, costar of the radio show "Amos 'n' Andy," had his twelve-year-old daughter, Virginia, rushed to the hospital with a severe throat infection.

Gosden: "After consultation among three doctors, it was decided that the infection required surgery. They all agreed that the abscess was coming to a head, but they should wait before operating. It was also decided that in order to help her morale, she should be returned home, which was done.

"Her mother had passed away in 1942, but with the aid of the nurses and the constant visits from the doctors, we were doing as well as could be expected. However, her temperature started up. It reached a dangerously high degree and stayed there. We all started to seriously worry. Things looked very bad. The doctors again requested that I do everything possible to keep her spirits up.

"I learned that my good friend Dave Sarnoff, then Chairman of the Board of RCA, had just arrived in town, and I also heard that the very popular singer Frank Sinatra was on the same plane with him. Virginia, like millions of other kids, was an avid Sinatra fan. I called Dave and asked if by chance he had met Frank on the plane. He said he had a long visit with him coming across the country and he also told me that he seemed to be a very nice young boy. When I told Dave what I had in mind, he advised me to call him, which I did.

"At this point, Virginia's illness was serious. I thought a visit from her idol would help and the doctors agreed. I called Sinatra, identified myself and told him the situation. His reply I shall never forget. 'I'll be there in twenty minutes.' Virginia seemed to brighten at the thought of his coming and I heard her quietly ask the nurse to fix her hair a little. Frank arrived and spent almost forty-five minutes sitting on the side of her bed, telling her about everything she wanted to hear—how he started in show business, what his ambitions were, the songs he liked to sing best, etc. I noticed she was brighter. She actually seemed to improve right before my eyes. Frank kissed her cheek and before leaving, he made a promise: He would think of her every day.

ONE NIGHT ONLY
SAT. AUG. 14 9:00 P.M.
FRANK SINATRA
with the L.A. Philharmonic Orchestra
HOLLYWOOD BOWL
ONE NIGHT ONLY
SAT. AUG. 14 9:00 P.M.

Overleaf: The Paramount, October 1944. New York police turn out in force, prepared now for the next onslaught of affection.

England, February 1950. He was known there, briefly, as "The Ambassador of Miserablism." His admirers heard in his songs, or felt in the pain of their love, delicious misery.

"About four hours later, a messenger arrived. Sinatra had gone to the studios where the famous Lucky Strike Orchestra was in session. He had made her a special record. First on the record was the very warm message from Frank starting with 'My Dear Virginia,' and very sweetly he told her how important it was for her to get well, he would see her soon, and so forth and then, remembering what he had promised her just before leaving her bedside, the orchestra started softly fading in behind his talking with its introduction and Frank sang the very popular song of that era to Virginia, 'Sunday, Monday, or Always.'

"A few days later, my daughter went through the operation. The incision had to be made from the outside, and it was successful. One of her first requests after surgery was to play the record on the little turntable we had put by her bedside."

In January 1943, Sinatra did his second Paramount appearance as a solo performer, this time with Johnny Long's band.

The Lucky Strike Orchestra, with whom Sinatra had recorded his song for Virginia Gosden, played each week on a radio program that had become an American institution, "Your Hit Parade." Working with research that included sales of records, sales of sheet music, and the number of times songs were played on jukeboxes, the hit parade disclosed and ranked the most popular songs in the country. With even the cast and crew sworn to keep the results secret until airtime, all week people waited eagerly for "the countdown," during which they'd learn the ratings and hear the songs sung by the top talent in America. In 1943 Frank Sinatra became part of that talent. He became a regular on "Your Hit Parade," along with Eileen Barton and Beryl Davis.

As his popularity increased, Sinatra met more and more famous people. Just after being introduced to the President of the United States, Franklin Delano Roosevelt, who was in a wheelchair, F.D.R. summoned him—"Psst, Frank"—to stoop down. So the singer leaned over, put his ear close to the President's face, and F.D.R. whispered in his ear: "I promise not to tell anyone. What's number one this Saturday?"

On another occasion, the President invited my father to the White House for tea. F.D.R. remarked, teasing, "You know, fainting, which was once so prevalent, has become a lost art among the ladies. I'm glad you have revived it."

But FS found it all more impressive than funny. Sinatra thought, after their first meeting, *There's the greatest guy alive today—and here's a little guy from Hoboken, shaking his hand.*

The following year, the little guy from Hoboken would produce—with his wife—another little guy, Franklin Wayne Emanuel Sinatra, nine pounds. My brother was named for the President and for Manie Sacks, not the father.

In 1943, Frank Sinatra not only joined "Your Hit Parade," but also—beginning with an appearance at New York's Rio Bomba Club—launched a nightclub act. This was different. The pacing and selection of songs were very important. And it was here, at last, that the society folks, at least the nightclubbing set, got to see him in action.

Manie Sacks, the head of Columbia Records, had heard Sinatra sing with the Dorsey band in 1941, and told him he was talented. "Would you record me as a soloist?" Manie was asked. "Any time you're ready," was the answer.

FS had been ready in 1942, but he was still affiliated with RCA (through his contract with Dorsey) and so Manie and Columbia had to wait.

In January of '42, Frank Sinatra and Axel Stordahl had made some recordings for RCA's subsidiary label, Bluebird, which were notable because they featured a string section, a woodwind section, easy rhythm, and no brass. Using Axel's poetic orchestrations they had created a much more intimate sound: "Night and Day," "Lamplighter's Serenade," "The Night We Called It a Day," "The Song Is You." The string section was very important to FS. By the time he had left the Dorsey band, Tommy had a string section which he had inherited from Artie Shaw, who had enlisted in the Navy, and Frank had felt its power.

"Isn't she feeling well, or is that Frank Sinatra?"

These lovely young British women at the London Palladium could hardly have passed for miserable. Several show their enthusiasm by (1) open-mouthed adoration and (2) dressing like their hero.

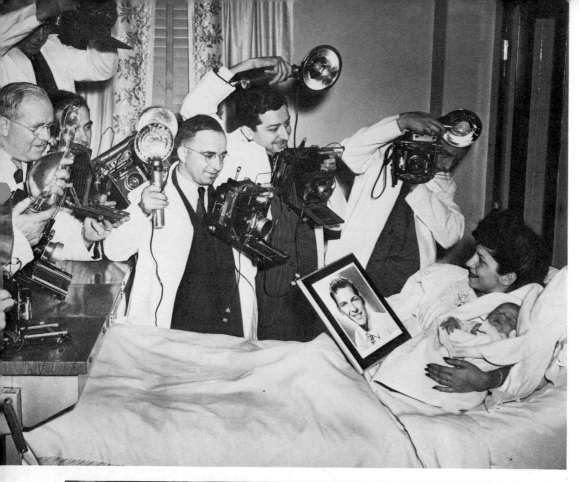

Top, left: Nancy Sinatra presents their second child, Franklin Wayne Emanuel Sinatra, at the Margaret Hague hospital, Jersey City.

Intense adoration became on occasion an uncontrollable crush. Below, Sinatra's press agent, George Evans (shown over his right shoulder), who should be happy, is as concerned as the cops. The understandably frightened faces of the young people and the police show how group admiration can turn into unintended mob violence. The singer's longtime associate Jack Entratter is the large man on his left.

FS: "If James had had strings at the time I was with the band, I'd never have left him. Because, in 1940, Tommy didn't have strings . . . I was always crazy about strings for a vocal background." Following Sinatra's session for Bluebird, Harry Meyerson, the A & R chief, had said, "Frank was not like a band vocalist at all. He came in self-assured, slugging. He knew exactly what he wanted. He knew he was good."

Axel Stordahl: "I think this was the turning point of his career. I think he began to think then what he might do on his own."

In 1943 Columbia was finally able to sign Sinatra to its label and wanted him to rerecord "All or Nothing at All," but the musicians' union—headed by James C. Petrillo—was on a strike that didn't end until Armistice Day, 1944. So they rereleased the Harry James 1939 version. The rest is popular music history. It became a classic.

With the success of his records, Sinatra, with conductor Morris Stoloff, packed the Hollywood Bowl for a live appearance in August, 1943. He was awed by the reaction of the fans.

Frank Sinatra: "They converged on our car and practically picked it up. There must have been five thousand kids jammed up behind the forty or fifty people mashed against the car. It was exciting—but it scares the wits out of you, too."

It was Manie Sacks, of course, who—with the encouragement of CBS's William S. Paley—had signed Sinatra to the Columbia label. Manie also had helped him get an agent—MCA—and the "Hit Parade" slot. And it was Manie, and a team led by Henry Jaffe, assisted by agents Frank Cooper and Norman Weiss, who had helped Sinatra break free from Dorsey.

There was a special bond between Manie and Dad, a bond observed often by Manie's nephew, the television executive Herman Rush: "Friends were having dinner with Manie and Frank one night and one remarked, 'Gosh, you two look alike! Don't people ever get you two mixed up?' 'Sure,' said Frank, 'it happens all the time. We were doing a benefit in Philadelphia, Manie's home town. After the show I saw people flocking around him, asking for *my* autograph. That always embarrassed Manie; he never knows what to say or do, or whose name to sign, his or mine. He began to look around like a cornered rabbit and spied me. He signaled for me to get him off the spot so I walked over to where the kids were getting *our* autograph. I slapped Manie on the back and said, 'Hiya, Frank—how's your throat?' And I just left him there, blushing and cursing and signing.' "

The confusion was understandable. Beyond the similarity of appearance, Manie Sacks—with his own big heart—projected something of what was evolving as the Sinatra style.

And the fervor and fever were evolving—erupting—as well. FS played the Paramount again in May '43, and in October of '44 with Raymond Paige and his orchestra. On Columbus Day, Mayor La Guardia gave his annual speech to a smaller crowd than FS had waiting in line at the Paramount. It was bedlam. Tens of thousands of girls, many of whom had waited since the night before, caused a major riot that began at noon and lasted till late that night. Policemen finally had to drag the kids away. Many of the girls inside the theatre refused to leave their seats after the show, so the police pried them loose to make way for the next wave. There has been nothing since "The Columbus Day Riot" to equal this hysteria since—including the phenomenally popular Elvis and the Beatles.

Here, at the Hollywood Bowl, he might well have been singing about his new son.

I wonder what he'll think of me I guess he'll call me the old man I guess he'll think I can lick every other fella's father Well, I can.

CHAPTER FOUR
HAPPINESS IS . . .

The Things We Did
Last Summer

In the spring of 1944, Mom and little Frankie and I took the Twentieth Century Limited to Chicago and the Super Chief on to Pasadena, just outside Los Angeles. My dad had chosen and purchased a house for us and we couldn't wait to see it.

We settled into our new home at 10051 Valley Spring Lane on Toluca Lake in the San Fernando Valley. I was so happy in that big pink house. We were a real family. I learned to roller skate there, and ride my bike. I had a friend named Joanne Fulton who lived across the street, and actor Bill Goodwin's daughter, Jill, and bandleader Jan Savitt's girls, Devi and JoAnn, used to come over to play.

It was a beautiful life, with few goodbyes. We had a kayak and a Penguin sailboat and a rowboat and a big raft. We used to catch our dinner in the lake—trout—and, of course, we were always swimming. Dad and I swam across the lake to a neighbor's dock one day, and as we were climbing out of the water, I slipped and hit my face on the dock. There was some blood and I was terrified, but my Dad was cool. He reached down and scooped up my two front teeth. That night I had a neat visit from the tooth fairy. Fifty cents.

One Fourth of July, my parents invited everyone who lived around the lake to sit outside at sunset for our fireworks show. My brother and I were in charge of the music, a record player with marching-band records. And Mom did the decorating—lots of red, white, and blue. And Dad, of course, did the fireworks. He had two big cartons of them out on the raft. And on the newly erected flagpole he nailed the pinwheels. He had on his white pants and his striped shirt and he wore his yachting hat and his brand new wrist watch. He looked so handsome.

All the neighbors were out with their picnic baskets, and the people whose homes were around the bend rowed their boats nearby so they could see.

Looking out from their new dining room, little Nancy, Frank, little Frank, and Nancy Sinatra have a happy view of the future. Their house on Toluca Lake in the San Fernando Valley, North Hollywood, was across from Universal Studios. Nearby was a large and handsome country club which Sinatra would not join because they would not admit Jews. Instead, he became the first non-Jewish member of Hillcrest Country Club.

At dusk, Dad pushed the raft away from our dock and dropped anchor about halfway across the lake. He pointed to Frankie and me on our grassy hill—that was our cue to start the music—and he raised the flag. The marching band played and the people stood up and saluted and Dad opened the cartons of fireworks. We were breathless, Frankie and I, hands over hearts, hearts, mouths, and eyes wide open, as we watched Dad set a match to the first pinwheel . . . and it started to spin and the bright sparks went flying around and some of them set the next pinwheel off and some of them landed in one of the boxes. Suddenly Dad's well-choreographed program exploded. All at once. Roman candles shot up and rockets flew and everything got smoky. Our father disappeared to the strains of "The Stars and Stripes Forever." I ran down the hill screaming, "Daddy! Daddy!" And pretty soon, there he was, pulling himself out of the water, with his brand-new, not very waterproof watch. And, he was still wearing his hat. The people in the boats put the fire out with lake water. What a Fourth!

Our house became headquarters for friends—Sammy Cahn, Phil Silvers, Don McGuire, Axel, Jack Benny and Mary, George Burns and Gracie—and for an annual New Year's party for two hundred guests that featured entertainment by some of Hollywood's most famous names. I never saw *one* of those shows because Frankie and I were always shipped off to Grandma Barbato's new house, which Grandpa Mike built when they, too, moved West. The shows consisted of songs, jokes, and skits. Sammy Cahn wrote parodies of lots of songs of the day—strictly R-rated, as were most of the jokes and skits, too.

My parents were smart this time and bought a house with a wall around it for privacy. But it seemed to be impossible to escape the phone . . . until my father figured out a way. He used the raft. There in the middle of the lake, he and Axel and Don played cards in a sanctuary free of telephone calls.

They would hang out at Palm Springs, too, at the Lone Palm Hotel, when Frank wanted to get away from everything. Soon we built a house in Palm Springs. It was a lovely house with a circular drive, fronted by two tall, skinny palm trees. My brother's room had bunk beds and my room had white wallpaper with pink, blue, and yellow butterflies. We had a pool shaped like a grand piano. Dad taught Frankie how to swim there; he had him hang onto a big, empty popcorn tin and kick. We kept an army jeep at the house. Daddy would take Frankie and me out—I can't say riding—bumping and swerving. There was only one paved road in Palm Springs then.

One day, Mom and Frankie and I drove to Palm Springs with Sam Weiss, the song plugger. Daddy had been on the road, and we were going to spend some time with him at our house on Alejo Road.

On this trip, the plan was for Sam to drive us down, for us to see Daddy for a couple of days, and then for Sam to drive us home, leaving our parents alone. They didn't get to spend time alone very often. When I realized I was being sent away, I couldn't stand it. I cried and cried—not a tantrum, not angry, but afraid of leaving my mom; I had never been without her.

I couldn't stop crying. Frankie, never lacking emotion, caught it, and we both cried and cried. Daddy, out of pity, or in a desperate attempt to save his sanity, eventually said to Mom, "I guess you'd better go with them." So Mom packed us up, put us in the car with Sam, and climbed in the back seat next to her spoiled brat of a daughter. When we were out of sight of the two skinny palm trees and Daddy, Mom started to cry softly. She tried to hide her tears behind dark glasses. Now, I had never seen my mother cry before—I mean,

mothers don't cry, *children* cry. It's not a mother's job.

I was shocked and frightened. I didn't know what to do. I was afraid to say anything. So I shut up, and Frankie shut up, and Sam was disgusted with both of us. It took four hours to drive from Palm Springs to L.A. in those days—now it only takes two—but it *seemed* like twelve.

When we got home to Toluca Lake, we were met by our governess, Georgie Hardwick, who had been the governess to the Crosby boys. We'd had a few other governesses—Whitey, Kathleen, Dolores, Mamie—but Georgie was the toughest. She was great. And in this situation, expecting to see only two very small people walk through the door *sans* mother, she flashed me a look I'll never forget. From that day on, without lectures, without words, Georgie quietly, gently, transformed me into an unspoiled child.

Memories from those years on the lake:

Although I went to public schools, I was a "Hollywood" kid. As a little girl, I once attended a party at the home of Atwater Kent. There were rides—a merry-go-round, a Ferris wheel; there were clowns and magicians; there were hot dogs and cotton candy, and games and prizes and elephants. It was really bizarre. All the little guests with their governesses. White gloves, lots of ruffled organdy and black patent leather on the little rich kids. I don't know how we survived that stuff, it was such wretched excess.

Once my friends Maureen, Babbie, Lindy, Julie, and I decided to raise money for the March of Dimes. So we put on a production of Cinderella. We had hoped to sell a lot of tickets and make a fortune for the cause, but as it turned out, Jane Wyman (Maureen's mom), Anne Shirley (Julie's mom), Betty Furness (Babbie's mom), Edy Wasserman (Lindy's mom) and Nancy Sinatra (my mom)

It was a lovely time, summed up in retrospect by "The Things We Did Last Summer" . . . The juniors were storing up memories of a time that was to be no more.

(Below) The man who made it possible and who would, not long after, leave it, loved to use this raft for isolated games of poker with pals. One Fourth of July fireworks demonstration on the raft ended with everything in smoke and him in the lake.

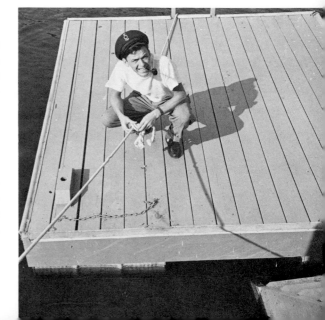

were the only customers. We may have donated only fifty cents to the March of Dimes, but we had a guest list to rival a Hollywood premiere . . .

Whose little girl are you? Most of my friends were civilians. Nice, regular kids from school: Jane, Binnie, Beth, Kathy, Linda, Val—all great kids. But on the Hollywood side of my life were Maureen Reagan, Ronald's kid; Lindy Wasserman, Lew's kid; Julie Payne, John's kid; Babbie Green, Johnny's kid, and so on. They were great kids, too. I had two sets of friends, and saw the best and worst of both kinds of life . . .

One time, when my dad came in after work at the studio, Frankie and I were already in our beds. I was shocked to see his arm in a sling. He and Mom tiptoed into my room and kissed me goodnight. I didn't want to hurt Daddy's feelings, so I didn't mention his big white bandage. I'm sure they had an explanation all planned, anticipating my reaction (I was seven years old, and I *was* frightened). But instead, as they quietly left the room, I heard Dad whisper, "I guess she didn't see it." I cried myself to sleep. Dad had chipped his elbow while filming a scene, but I never asked about it, and he didn't force an explanation on me. He believed in telling children only as much as they want to hear. I follow the same rule with my children, and it works. "Don't ask me a question unless you want to hear a truthful answer . . ."

One night around midnight, sometime near Christmas, Daddy woke me. "Chicken, wake up. Come out on the deck." He helped me put on my robe and slippers and led me outside to see—of all things—*snow*. It was snowing in Los Angeles, and he wanted to share that rarity with me . . .

Universal Studios was very near our house, right next door to the Lakeside Country Club. One day a fire started in the studio and burned up the whole back lot. My daddy and I watched the thick black smoke together for hours and hours. Its ashes covered our house and all the flowers and trees were sooty. Dad was very sad, I remember, as we watched those dreams and all that work and memories flame into dust . . .

Higher and Higher

Higher and Higher was Frank Sinatra's first important film. He played himself, and his sweetness was evident. The songs he sang were beautifully orchestrated (by Axel): "A Lovely Way to Spend an Evening," "I Couldn't Sleep a Wink Last Night" (which was nominated for an Academy Award), "The Music Stopped," and more. His voice was young but sure, and hearing these songs today melts my heart. The film was a showcase vehicle for him and the title described the direction of his career.

Step Lively followed in 1944. His first screen kiss! The movie was a zany version of the play *Room Service*. FS played a singing playwright. Once again, though, his songs were the highlights, especially "As Long as There's Music." And again, Axel did the charts.

Among his short subjects from this period is one I really love: *The All Star Bond Rally*. It was one of many films made by the U.S. Treasury Department to encourage people to buy war bonds. Dad sings "Saturday Night (Is the Loneliest Night of the Week)" with Harry James and Betty Grable sings and marches to "I'll Be Marching to a Love Song." This is a fascinating look at our country's show folk "at war." Bob Hope, Bing Crosby, Harpo Marx, Fibber McGee and

I'm not much to look at nothin' to see Just glad I'm living and lucky to be I got a woman, crazy for me She's funny that way.

NS: "My father sang this song for my mother—sang it to her, recorded it for her, addressed it to her when she was in the audience. I think of them still when I hear it. It remains one of his favorite songs."

Wartime. FS: "The Hollywood Canteen. All those uniforms . . . on Cahuenga Boulevard where all the movie actresses went . . . to serve coffee and drinks and doughnuts and all that stuff." NS: "Here, he's with Ginger Rogers and, I think, Fibber McGee of radio fame, doing their number for the boys."

Molly—they're all here in this little film.

Frank Sinatra's finest hour at RKO was his own personal project, and must be seen to be appreciated. *The House I Live In* (1945) is as special as the people involved: Producer Frank Ross *(The Robe, Of Mice and Men);* Director Mervyn LeRoy *(The Wizard of Oz, Little Caesar);* Music Director Axel Stordahl; and the man who wrote the sensitive, original screenplay, which dealt with religious intolerance and extolled patriotism, was Albert Maltz. Sinatra and Maltz fought and won the battle to get this small but powerful film made. Ross, LeRoy and Sinatra took no salary and film profits were donated to various juvenile organizations.

FS's views on intolerance became well known. William Paley knew of Dad's interest in civil rights and arranged for him to do a lecture tour. He visited campuses, including a Midwestern school where there had been some incidents, to try to convince the kids that prejudice was senseless. When singing "Ol' Man River," he refused to use the traditional line, "Darkies all work on the Mississippi," using, instead, "Here we all work on the Mississippi." He received commendations from, among others, the Bureau for Inter-cultural Education, and the National Conference of Christians and Jews. He was given the American Unity Award for "advancing the cause of better Americanism." All of which naturally led the conservative press to insinuate that he was a communist.

My first Sinatra lesson about intolerance came one day when I was eight years old. Dad and I were sitting in the sun in the backyard overlooking the lake. He was reading a magazine and on the cover was Albert Einstein. I looked at the picture and giggled. Dad said, "What's so funny, sweetheart?" I said, "He looks so Jewish." (I don't know where I had picked up such stuff—maybe at school.) Well, my father's face . . . I had never seen him angry before. He glared at me and he said loudly, "Nobody *looks* anything—remember that." He never mentioned it again. I, obviously, never forgot it.

A fine writer wrote about "the courage" it took for Frank Sinatra "to be an honest citizen." Norman Corwin: "You may not think that takes much courage. It's something you do every time you vote and pay taxes. But it's different with an artist whose fortune happens to be his voice—his appeal to the public . . . In 1944, during the presidential campaign, I produced a big, all network Election Eve broadcast for our late president (Franklin Delano Roosevelt) . . . A famous comedian had agreed to be on the broadcast. In doing so he would have had to come out publicly for the man in whom he believed . . . His advisers urged him not to take a stand. They told him, in effect: 'Think of the people in your audience who have already made up their minds to vote the other way . . . They may resent you . . . Maybe your pictures and personal appearances will do bad business. You may lose half your income.' He was influenced by these advisers, and he never appeared . . . In the same campaign Frank fought tooth and nail for the candidate of his choice. He electioneered for F.D.R. all over the country. He made speeches and sang, and never worried for a minute whether any of his fans differed with his politics . . . Since those days, Frank has served an even greater cause, a non-partisan cause, and served it unsparingly . . . He had been preaching unity—the unity of all peoples . . . It would be easy for Frank to rest on his laurels, or to use his fantastically great fame strictly as a source of income. But he is a citizen above all else. Being that, he is, as all good citizens automatically become, a patriot."

Orson Welles remembers an earlier incident when Sinatra was not shy about putting his principles on the line. Welles: "We drove to his uncle's house

Sinatra became a spokesman for decency and equality. He took an Albert Maltz story to studio heads and it became an Oscar-winning short film on fairness and tolerance. Above, a scene from The House I Live In, *1945. FS: "Look fellas, religion makes no difference except to a Nazi or somebody as stupid. Why, people all over the world worship God in different ways . . . Do you know what this wonderful country is made of? It's made up of a hundred different kinds of people, and a hundred different ways of talking, and a hundred different ways of going to church. But they're all American ways . . . My dad came from Italy, but I'm an American. Should I hate your father cause he came from Ireland or France or Russia? Wouldn't I be a first-class fathead?"*

for calamari and on the way back we stopped for coffee. Our driver, as it happened, was a black man and the guy in the diner wouldn't serve him. Your dad reached across the counter and grabbed this nine-foot giant by the front of his shirt and said, *'You're serving coffee for three.'* After a beat, the man said, 'Yes.' No sporting event here. It was a mosquito vs. a gorilla. FS made the score with sheer force of character."

In 1945 FS made his last forties Paramount appearance, with Jan Savitt and his band. That same year, while still under contract to RKO, Sinatra sang "Ol' Man River" at a benefit for a home for the Jewish aged in Los Angeles. One of the people who bought tickets for his wife's favorite charity was Louis B. Mayer. L.B. was visibly moved by the Sinatra rendition of the Jerome Kern classic.

FS: "I knew his face but I'd never met him. But I could see tears running down, I could see the tears in his eyes. I guess the song, and the way I sang it, made him cry. So L.B. turned to Eddie Mannix, an aide, and said, 'I want that boy.' Let me tell you something: He was a giant. When he said, 'I want that boy,' he got that boy."

t MGM Metro-Goldwyn-Mayer

the Frank Sinatra–Gene Kelly partnership began, sustained through the years and in three milestone movies. At a ceremony honoring Gene years later, FS recalled their early days.

FS: "We became a team only because he had the patience of Job, and he had the fortitude not to punch me in the mouth because I was so impatient. Movie-making took a lot of time, and I couldn't understand why . . . He just managed to calm me when it was important to calm me, because we were doing something that we wanted to do. We loved doing it, and I loved it. And we made some fun movies together. He taught me everything I know. I couldn't walk, let alone dance. I was a guy who got up and hung onto a microphone—with both arms together, and a bad tuxedo, brown shoes . . . And all of a sudden I was a 'star.' And one of the reasons why I became a 'star' was Gene Kelly."

Gene Kelly: "During those days of the forties, Francis Albert was the idol of American womanhood, not just the young girls, but the old as well. Working with him a lot, I got pushed into many of the frenzied mob scenes where the crowds went berserk just to be near him, and, if possible, touch him. Well, being his partner, I often had to pay the price and get *my* clothes torn, and flee with him to limousines with motors running to help us escape whole of limb. We, his cronies, became accustomed to this procedure, but never let up ribbing him about his strange effect on the female sex. I guess I kidded him the most . . . One night at my home during a long session of jokes, games, singing and music, my infant daughter started to bawl blue murder. My wife tried to quiet her, but to no avail. She was determined to make a scene . . . Frank, as a last resort, reached out and took her in his arms, and started to sing to her. Her face turned from rage to wonderment—she opened her big eyes and stared at him—and smiled—and smiled—and at the end of a chorus and a half, she was blissfully asleep, still smiling. I never kidded your father again about his effect on women."

He has always been gentle with children, a real softie. Recently, he reminded me of the time he took me to get my tonsils out. FS: "You looked at me when I got you to the hospital and you looked at the building, and then you looked at me again, and I couldn't stand it. I backed up and went home and said to Mother, '*You* take her to the hospital.' And I went to New York."

That's my pop.

On my fifth birthday, my dad took several of my friends and me to Lew Wasserman's office at MCA. I always loved going there. It was a pretty two-story building, white with green shutters, on the corner of Little Santa Monica and Rexford Drive in Beverly Hills. It looks exactly the same today, though it is now the home of Litton Industries. Uncle Lew's office (he was the head of MCA) was beautiful. Very masculine with a big desk and great big leather chairs. In his big screening room, my friends and I climbed into even bigger chairs and saw our first movie, *Anchors Aweigh.*

The year before, when *Anchors Aweigh* was being filmed, something wonderful and characteristic had happened.

Sammy Cahn: "Joe Pasternak called Frank in and asked his advice on who might do the score—Kern, Gershwin, Rodgers and Hart? Frank said casually, 'Sammy Cahn.' You can't imagine the stunned reaction: *Sammy Cahn? Who is he?*

"Well, MGM wasn't ready yet to let young Sinatra pick the writers for this million-dollar production, and the first of the many Sinatra scenes started! It came to such an impasse that Lew Wasserman of MCA came to me and said, 'Unless Frank gives in, he will lose the picture.' Would I talk to Frank? I, of course, went to Frank and said, 'Frank, you've done me more honor than I can handle. Why don't you pass this one, and there will be others.' He looked at me and said, 'If you're not there Monday I'm not there Monday.' Any night you happen to catch *Anchors Aweigh* you will notice it says: *Songs by Sammy Cahn and Jule Styne.*"

During this period, Gene Kelly wasn't the only one who taught FS about making movies. George Sidney, who had directed *Anchors Aweigh*, was a no-

Gathering in the Oscar for **The House I Live In,** *FS shares the stage with the actor (later senator) who presented it, George Murphy, and the winsome young actress Peggy Ann Garner. He could not have known how long it would be before he'd again hold another Oscar or how important the next one would be to his life, career, and spirits.*

Opposite: One of the great teams is born, brought together to do a movie called Anchors Aweigh. *FS: "When I arrived at MGM, I was a nobody in movies. And because I didn't think I was as talented as some of the people, I went through periods of depression and I'd get terribly embarrassed. After all, what was I then? A crooner . . . But Gene [Kelly] saw me through. I was born with a couple of left feet and it was Gene who got me to dance . . . Apart from being a great artist, he's a born teacher. I enjoyed his company in spite of his insane insistence on hard work . . . rehearsing routines for as long as eight weeks. Eight weeks!* You can shoot a whole picture in that time." *But nobody ever shot pictures better of their kind than MGM and the two sailors.*

Overleaf: The classic group portrait. MGM's roster of stars, at the Silver Jubilee, 1949. Left to right, Top Row: *Alexis Smith, Ann Sothern, J. Carroll Naish, Dean Stockwell, Lewis Stone, Clinton Sundberg, Robert Taylor, Audrey Totter, Spencer Tracy, Esther Williams, Keenan Wynn.* Second Row: *Peter Lawford, Ann Miller, Ricardo Montalban, Jules Munshin, George Murphy, Reginald Owen, Walter Pidgeon, Jane Powell, Ginger Rogers, Frank Sinatra, Red Skelton.* Third Row: *Katharine Hepburn, John Hodiak, Claude Jarman, Jr., Van Johnson, Jennifer Jones, Louis Jourdan, Howard Keel, Gene Kelly, Christopher Kent (Alf Kjellin), Angela Lansbury, Mario Lanza, Janet Leigh.* Fourth Row: *Gloria DeHaven, Tom Drake, Jimmy Durante, Vera Ellen, Errol Flynn, Clark Gable, Ava Gardner, Judy Garland, Betty Garrett, Edmund Gwenn, Kathryn Grayson, Van Heflin.* Fifth Row: *Lionel Barrymore, June Allyson, Leon Ames, Fred Astaire, Edward Arnold, Mary Astor, Ethel Barrymore, Spring Byington, James Craig, Arlene Dahl, and Lassie.*

nonsense guy who didn't believe in wasting time. And my father was becoming known, with Gene and others, as a man who liked to get it right on the first take.

George Sidney: "It took the cameraman about twelve minutes to light a scene, and after that he'd be playing around for another thirty, lighting the walls. You know the expression, follow the money, follow the star? No wall ever won an Academy Award . . .

"Sinatra didn't originate the whole thing of getting it in one or two takes. Spencer Tracy . . . with Spence you'd do it in one or two takes and that was it. Look, Frank knows he's good, and he goes on, and he gives it, and he lets go . . . It's like anything . . . like rehearsing when you're blowing a trumpet. If you know the conductor's gonna keep on rehearsing it, you're not gonna hit that high C, you're gonna lay off. But if you know: this is the money . . . then, off you go!

"Gable was the same way. At one minute to nine, he was in front of the camera. If he was supposed to have a hat on and be carrying a glove and a flower, he was ready to go, and God help you if you weren't ready . . . If the girl was late, he would scream and yell. And if she was late by two or three minutes, he'd be up at the front office. And that, I think, is part of being an artist."

. . . And a professional. That's one of the things I learned from my dad.

The MGM years, those earliest days in L.A., were my happiest as a child. Everything was so nice. I wasn't yet fully aware that my dad was heading for something beyond stardom, that he was special and that I was, therefore, special too; some sort of minor celebrity myself. My birth had been announced with headlines and photographs. I wasn't yet conscious of the fact that we were constantly being scrutinized, reported on, and sometimes lied about in the press. Ignorance, said someone who wasn't, is bliss, and I was a blissful kid. My parents kept certain realities from me and I lived in a radio world of "Grand Central Station" and "Let's Pretend." TV wasn't yet a presence and the nightly news did not dominate each evening. There was little to frighten a seven-year-old except her own fantasies and fears.

My brother and I had been lucky, so far. But Tina was on the way, and for my young sister, life would be much different. My life was about to change, too, and drastically.

On tour for the USO often meant being on the water as well as on the road. (Or in the air. The crew of one plane named it "The Voice.") In Italy, Sinatra and his buddy Phil Silvers (far right) are doing their duty, with Silvers telling the military how the war should have been won.

CHAPTER FIVE
THE
LONG
GOODBYE

Give Me Five Minutes More

"The President is dead," the radio announcer said. I was only four, but there is no misunderstanding those four words. F.D.R.—gone. Harry Truman. Hiroshima and Nagasaki. The times were changing. The bobby-soxers were growing up, and Frank Sinatra was on top. And he was doing his part, touring for the USO, and was beginning to adjust to the loss of President Roosevelt.

His first film under his new contract at MGM was *Till the Clouds Roll By.* He was a special guest star, and sang "Ol' Man River." When I watch it now, I know why L.B. cried. It's a shining moment.

Some of his notable 78 rpm recordings in '44 and '45 are part of that time —"Embraceable You," "Why Shouldn't I," "She's Funny That Way," "Put Your Dreams Away" (his theme song), "The House I Live In," "Someone to Watch Over Me," "Try a Little Tenderness," "Nancy" which was written about me when I was five years old by Phil Silvers and Jimmy Van Heusen . . . there were more. My favorite was the two-part "Soliloquy" from *Carousel.*

Radio was still going strong. Frank Sinatra went from "Your Hit Parade," which was sponsored by Lucky Strike cigarettes ("LSMFT—Lucky Strike Means Fine Tobacco"), to "Songs by Sinatra," sponsored by Old Gold cigarettes ("Try a treat instead of a treatment"). The Old Gold show aired for two years. It featured FS, The Pied Pipers (now with June Hutton), and Axel (who had married June). Guest stars included: the Crosby Boys, Peggy Lee, Dinah Shore, Jane Powell, and Burns and Allen. Dad also guested on other people's shows: Bob Hope's, Danny Kaye's, "Music for Millions," and a lot of Armed Forces Radio shows. In 1947, Frank Sinatra went back to "Your Hit Parade." This time he costarred with Doris Day. In 1949, Lucky Strike started a new show called "Light Up Time," which FS did for three years with Dorothy Kirsten. By his early thirties, he had come a long way.

Along the way, lasting friendships had begun, and now that he had some clout, he tried to put it to good use. Back in the Rio Bomba days, he had met

another young singer, Dean Martin. They'd spent little time together, but they had an instant rapport and FS kept trying to help Dean get a break. He was always on the lookout.

Dean Martin: "Every time he found a part, he called. I was in Cleveland. He said, 'I have a part for you in a picture.' I said, 'No, thanks. It's the last time I'm telling you: You got there the hard way, I'm gonna get there.' But he continued to call. 'I got a part for you, you idiot.' I said it again: 'I'll get there, I'll *get* there.' He said, 'I know you'll get there, but you'll get there faster if you do what I say.'"

In 1947, Frank Sinatra was going back on stage in New York, to headline at the Capitol Theatre. There was a trio that interested him, and so—in Toots Shor's restaurant, when he agreed to do the Capitol gig—he asked Sidney Fairmont, who ran the theatre, to locate them.

The act was the Will Mastin Trio—Sammy Davis, Jr., his uncle, Will, and his dad.

Sammy: "Sidney Fairmont told me that Frank said to him, 'It's a dancing act. The kid in it. See if you can find him.'

" 'What's their name?' Sid says.

" 'I don't know. He works with his dad and his uncle. Or two uncles. Something like that. Find him.'

" 'You can *imagine* what I had to go through to get you here,' Sid told me, 'because Frank didn't want any of the leading dancing acts, he wanted *you*.'

"Their man finds us. We're making three hundred and fifty dollars a week, and I'm living in Harlem. We went to our agent and the agent said, 'This has got to be a mistake, but Sidney Fairmont wants to talk to you.' My Uncle Will did all the business for the act. So we went to Mr. Fairmont and I stayed outside. My uncle came out of the meeting and he said, 'You know that singer you're always talking about? You play his records.'

"I said, 'Frank Sinatra?'

" 'Well, he's coming into the Capitol; you're going to work with him.'

"I went, 'What?' We had worked with Mickey Rooney once and so Will said, 'Probably Mickey talked to him and told him about us.' Then Will said, 'He's giving us twelve hundred and fifty dollars a week. It's *his* show.'

"Frank was giving us *twelve hundred and fifty dollars* a week! We had never seen that much money in our lives.

"Our first rehearsal, and in walks Frank, with the coat over his shoulder. He said, 'Good afternoon, everybody.' And he walked over to me and said, 'My name is Frank Sinatra.' I said, 'I know . . . I know, I was the kid in the army who used to go to see you do your radio show.'

Left: "Your Hit Parade," an immensely popular radio show, had its own succession of stars. Sinatra went from "Your Hit Parade," sponsored by Lucky Strike cigarettes, to his own show, sponsored by Old Gold. He went back to "Your Hit Parade," then on to a new show, "Light Up Time," with Dorothy Kirsten (on his left), a Metropolitan Opera Star.

"He said, 'Wait a minute! Are you the one that I used to give tickets to in Hollywood? You had on an army uniform. You used to come and catch "The Old Gold Show"?' I said, 'Yessir, I am.' He said, 'Hey! So you're the kid!'

"Frank said, 'Do the act for me once. Run it out.' So we did this thing, and Frank must have said to himself that the only way these people are going to get away with this is if I introduce them.' So, in the show, Frank himself does the opening. He comes out, sings a couple of songs, then he'd say, 'Ladies and gentlemen. Now I'm going to get the show started. Here's some cats that dance up a storm—and keep your eye on the little guy in the middle—*personal* friend of mine.' Well, that's *all!*"

The next year was 1948. We got our first TV set. It was a great big clunker with a very small screen. Frankie and I watched Channel 5, KTLA, so we named the set "Mr. Kitla." Our favorite programs were "Hopalong Cassidy" (we called him Dragalong Catastrophe), and "Time for Beanie" with Beanie, the lead puppet, and Cecil, the seasick sea serpent, and Captain Huffenpuff and Dishonest John—*hissss!* Later our favorite became—smokin' rockets—"Space Patrol." Mr. Kitla wasn't the only new addition to our family. At last Dad was actually able to be in town when one of his children was born.

Nancy Sr.: "We were at the house in Toluca Lake, playing charades. I said to Jule Styne's wife Ethel, 'I don't feel good, I think I'd better go upstairs.' We

Armed Forces Radio drew its complement of stars, including some of Hollywood's most famous and talented children. **Back Row: Gary Crosby, Peggy Ann Garner, Elizabeth Taylor, Roddy McDowall, FS. Front Row: Lindsay Crosby, Margaret O'Brien, Nancy Sinatra, Dennis Crosby, Philip Crosby.**

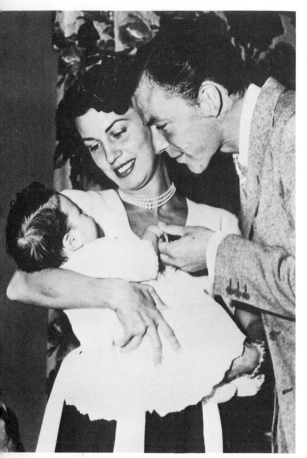

Debut: The coming-out-party photograph, recording the birth of Christina (Tina) Sinatra. The expectant father ran all the red lights on Sunset Boulevard between his house and Cedars of Lebanon Hospital. Said her sister, Nancy Sinatra: "My birth cost Dad about forty bucks and Tina's was supposed to reflect Pop's income. My father offered a deal, a compromise, but the benign doctor said, in effect, 'I can't charge the poor people much so I have to hit on you rich guys.' We all agree she was worth it."

kept timing the pains. I said, 'You know, this is going to be very fast, I think.' Frank kept coming up to see how I was doing. Finally I said, 'I think I have to go in.' It was about two in the morning—they were still playing charades. He drove me to the hospital. He went through red lights and he had a good time."

Later that same day, Dad and I were sitting on our grassy hill by the lake, listening to the radio. The announcer said, "Frank Sinatra got a terrific Father's Day present today—a brand-new baby girl." We said, "Yippee!"

I'll never forget the day Dad brought Mom and Christina home. There she was, this tiny stranger, my baby sister, all wrapped up in a yellow blanket. Dad had a new little girl, Frankie and I had a new partner in crime. Oh boy!

But Tina didn't get to know life the way I had known it. She didn't get to know Daddy as I knew him. She got a bad deal.

Over the next year and a half, our lives turned around. We moved away from the lake to 320 North Carolwood Drive, on the west side. Our house sat on about three acres. We had a pool, a badminton court, a big fishpond, a separate play yard, a beautiful rose garden, and an orchard. Tangerines, lemons, avocados . . . it was something. We hadn't been there long when terrible things began to happen.

One night Dad was appearing at the Copacabana in New York and when he opened his mouth to sing—

FS: "Nothing came out—absolutely nothing—just dust. I was never so panic-stricken in my whole life. I remember looking at the audience, there was a blizzard outside, about seventy people in the place—and they knew something serious had happened. There was absolute silence—stunning, absolute silence. I looked at them, and they looked at me, and I looked at Skitch Henderson, who was playing the piano. His face was ghastly white. Finally I turned to the audience and whispered into the microphone, 'Good night,' and walked off the floor."

A vocal-cord hemorrhage had caused bleeding in his throat. That could be—and was—cured.

There was another problem, though, one that was, as it turned out, incurable.

Don't Worry 'Bout Me

As far as I know, Dad didn't tell me that this time he wasn't coming home. And Mom said nothing. They let me think he was just going on another trip.

But this trip was different. This was the long goodbye we had rehearsed so often, but the one I could never completely accept. My brother was to suffer, too. And my sister and her father said goodbye before she could say hello.

Tina Sinatra: "When he left home, I was a baby, so I wasn't accustomed to a man in the house, a father. I didn't feel the wrench; I didn't know him. Conversely, I had to deal with this very nice man coming through our lives from time to time. It was always—certainly—a special occasion. But there was a point where you realized that everything had to be just so. You know, we had to get cleaned and washed and combed and groomed and it wasn't comfortable. And he would come and go and come and go. And I didn't know where to *find* him. But I think I've gotten off a lot easier than others. I never had the feelings of what I'm told all children go through, where the child feels as much to blame—he's left *me,* not *you,* Mommy. What I did feel was that when he was around, I was different. I couldn't figure out why. Who is "he" that I should change? I used to feel nervous when I was going to see him. I had anxiety."

The separation was, of course, roughest on my mother. I would see her faint into her plate at dinner from the stress. Sometimes it was heart palpitations, sometimes a cold, sometimes fatigue. Until then, she had never been sick. I used to think it was the food, you know. Maybe she wasn't eating right. She was in pain. And, though I wasn't aware of it, her pain was exacerbated by the scandal. She was deeply in love and terribly hurt. I would hear her crying quietly at night while I was going to sleep. She would never show it in front of us, *never,* but my room was next to hers and I would tiptoe out and I'd listen at the door and she'd be crying. Sometimes I would go in to her and just put my arms around her. And sometimes I would just go away, thinking, "Mind your own business. Daddy's just on the road again."

I harbored so many questions. I was only nine years old. Why didn't he come home? Did *I* do anything wrong? Doesn't Daddy love us anymore? Why is Mommy crying? What can *I* do to help? It's strange, I know, but I didn't *ask* any of the questions. Maybe I was afraid of the answers. However, a few months later I came face to face with them. One day while I was playing dress-up in Mom's dressing room, I climbed up on a chair to get a shoe box off a shelf and knocked to the floor a stack of magazines that Mom had hidden in her closet. I sat down in the midst of the pile. They were movie magazines like *Photoplay* and *Modern Screen,* and they were filled with pictures of Dad and a pretty lady named Ava Gardner and Mom and Frankie and Baby Tina and me. There were also pictures of Dad with other ladies. I remember Marilyn Maxwell and Lana Turner. I was devastated—just like Mom. After all, as Tina said—and I know Daddy felt this—he had left me, too.

The following story illustrates a day in the life of a visiting father: One day we heard that Dad was coming to visit us at Carolwood Drive, and Frankie and I were all gussied up in our white blazers with brass buttons, with our hair slicked back (mine was in braids). We were playing with our Lionel electric train set while we waited—and we got into a fight. It must have been something important, because Frankie threw the train engine at me. It hit me just under my eye—and that engine (made of steel) was *heavy.* I got so mad I punched him in the nose. He ran crying to Mom, who put his face in the sink to catch the drippings. After she mopped him up, she came after me to let me have it for punching my baby brother—and saw my bleeding eye. She just threw her hands up, frustrated, unable to say anything. There's Frankie crying and bleeding, and Nancy crying and bleeding, and the doorbell is ringing. My dad was greeted by a calm scene, two kids with tears and blood dripping all over their white blazers and shoes.

My mother's funny. For many years, as she's remarked, the public image of her is that of a fat little Italian lady in the kitchen in an apron, with a spoon in her hand. And she's so different from that, so lovely. She has more genuine glamour in an inch of her than in all the starlets and stars put together.

One of the things that will endear a person to me faster than anything—probably *the* thing—is if the person asks me about my mother. It was always, "How's your father?" and "Oh, you're Frank's daughter."

After the split, many of the people who professed to be my mother's

As a girl, Nancy saw in some movie magazines "pictures of Dad and a pretty lady named Ava Gardner . . ." When they met, the young girl "couldn't stop staring."

friends disappeared. Mom tried to keep us stabilized during the months of scandal. The teasing from the kids at school . . . the pieces in the paper. Mores were different then. People were supposed to stay married. But after a time, I think she felt she was destroying Dad's life by not giving him his freedom, and that this thing with Ava was more than just another casual affair. She also had her pride. And although, in her heart, as a good Catholic, she knew she would always be his wife, she let Dad go and got a divorce. Nancy Barbato Sinatra survived the pain and the notoriety and surfaced with her dignity intact.

Eventually, inevitably, I would meet this other woman. The first time we met, there was no preparation. It was meant to be matter-of-fact.

They were living in a house in Coldwater Canyon. My father came by to pick me up and as we were driving away, he said: "I want to stop by and show you my house."

"Okay," I said.

When we went in, there was a woman upstairs at her dressing table, brushing her shoulder-length hair.

Daddy said, "Chicken, this is Ava."

I said, "Hi, how do you do?" or whatever, just as I had been taught, and that was that.

Except that instead of feeling pain or resentment or anger, what I saw knocked my little socks off. I could imagine a bit of what my father felt. And he was clearly swept away.

My heart melted just looking at her. I was only a kid. I didn't *know* about beauty—that awesome kind of beauty . . . she was just the most beautiful creature I had ever seen in my life. I couldn't stop staring at her.

My sister, Tina, looks a little like Ava did in those days. My sister is an exquisite girl. But Ava had a reckless look about her. She didn't bother with her hair or makeup—it was sort of haphazard. No matter. Her hair was naturally curly. On my first weekend with them in Palm Springs she was wearing her hair short. She would dive into the pool, looking like a goddess on the diving board, swim a few lengths, throw on a terry robe, come inside, kneel down in front of the wall heater, turn on the fan, dry her hair with a shake and a few rubs with her fingers, and be a goddess again. No makeup, perfect skin, and a wonderful voice.

She spoke in whispers. She'd grown up in the Deep South, but there was no trace of an accent when I met her. Dad said that she'd worked very hard to get rid of it so she could be in the movies. She had the magnetism that few stars possess.

Ava gave me my first lipstick. It was called Tangee Natural and in the stick it was an orange neon color, but on your lips it took on the tone of your pigmentation. If your lips were pale, it turned them very pale pink. If they were deeper, it would turn a deeper color. I wish they still made it today—Ava's makeup secret and my first.

At last, in my preteenage wisdom, I had some understanding of why Daddy had left us. A few years ago, though, when I asked him if, given the choice again, he would have left, he said "No."

My memories of life with Ava are funny, blurry images of the Coldwater Canyon house, visits to Ava's sister, Bappie, dinners in restaurants, car rides, weekends in Palm Springs, their dog "Rags," a spunky Welsh Corgi who made us all laugh. Happy moments. Ava was loose and "up." However, the underlying

The leaves began to fade
Like promises we made.
How could a love that seemed
so right go wrong?
The things we did last summer
I'll remember all winter long.

mood of my memories is loneliness, sadness. Because, for me, everything was always temporary. I got to the point where I almost didn't want to see my dad, because I hated having to leave him each time. I got used to being near him again and I liked being near him, but then I would lose him again.

Put Your Dreams Away

Paralleling Sinatra's changing life, the music business was changing too. The Big Bands began to fade. Rock and roll wasn't here yet, but gimmick songs were. "Goodnight, Irene," "Bim Bam Baby," and "One Finger Melody" (his first forty-five rpm single), were just three of FS's novelty records. Wisely, he stayed with the good stuff, too: "London by Night," "April in Paris," "I'm a Fool to Want You " (which he co-wrote), "I Hear a Rhapsody," "Why Try to Change Me Now."

Yet change was inescapable.

Frank Sinatra, Jr.: "In terms of Pop's era, what happened was that his old-style records—Sinatra singing good music with good arrangements—was not working anymore. Meantime, the power structure in the record business was changing too. Dad's experience was that if you were a bandleader or a solo singer, *you* had control over what you recorded. Now, the word was, 'Butt out. Don't make waves.' The A & R man—Artists and Repertoire—was in charge. At Columbia now, that was Mitch Miller. He told Pop to record a song using a washboard. Pop said, 'Mitch, really? A *wash*board??' The song was 'Tennessee Newsboy.' Pop recorded it."

In movies, FS had followed *Anchors Aweigh* with *It Happened in Brooklyn* (1947), which had the notable tunes "Time After Time" and "It's the Same Old Dream." He and Jimmy Durante were good together. Then he bounced between RKO, for *The Miracle of the Bells,* and MGM, for *The Kissing Bandit* (a film he jokes about to this day). In 1949 MGM released two Sinatra-Kelly films. *Take Me Out to the Ball Game* was a good musical with a great cast, including Esther Williams. "O'Brien, to Ryan, to Goldberg," with Frank, Gene, and Jules Munshin, is fun.

But the great one followed. Gene directed *On the Town* with Stanley Donen. Betty Comden and Adolph Green wrote it. Three sailors on leave in New York meet three pretty girls. What else does a movie musical need? "New York, New York, a hell of a town. The Bronx is up and the Battery's down . . ." FS and Betty Garrett do one of the niftiest duets ever, "Come Up to My Place," and Ann Miller dances around a dinosaur to a tune called "Primitive Man." I love this movie. So do my kids, by the way—and so, I think, does half the world.

Mitch Miller had Dad do a record with Dagmar, a tall, supremely busty woman who played a dumb or at least deadpan blonde. The "tune" was titled "Mama Will Bark" and FS told Frankie Jr., "I growled and barked on the record." Recalling the commercial wisdom of it, he added, "The only good business it did was with dogs."

Double Dynamite (1951) at RKO, with Groucho, was to have been called "It's Only Money." It's a happy little movie, but it didn't do very well, as art or as money invested.

In 1952 FS made *Meet Danny Wilson.* Dad is really good in this, his first dramatic role. He sings some lovely songs: "I've Got a Crush on You," "She's

Funny That Way." The movie had a good cast, with a good team, but this one didn't do too well either.

Despite the box-office figures, each of these films was a valuable learning experience, and things were frequently fun on the sets.

In the 1948 film *The Miracle of the Bells,* FS played a priest, Father Paul. One day, as they were shooting it, his old friend George "Bullets" Durgom—who'd worked as a record promoter and advance man for the Dorsey band—came to the set. Bullets's mother was with him, an elderly, foreign-born woman who knew nothing about movies or records but for years had heard her son talk of this man Sinatra, whom she was now going to meet. Bullets introduced her to Dad, who had just walked off the set in his costume. So *that's* who this Frank Sinatra was—a priest. Bullets Durgom: "She was impressed. She ran over, knelt down and kissed his ring. And Frank, God bless him, he didn't want to embarrass her, so he never told her he wasn't a priest. He carried it off."

Frank Sinatra's "home life" was split among Palm Springs, Los Angeles, an apartment on Central Park South in New York, and in 1952 the Sands Hotel in Las Vegas.

Meanwhile his family was digging in on Carolwood Drive. Bomber Shapiro, Frankie, and I were the only kids on our street. We really *owned* that street. (Tina was a toddler.) It was our territory and we took full advantage of it. We lived in a small, exclusive neighborhood between Beverly Hills and Bel Air called Holmby Hills. They didn't believe much in having children, the folks in Holmby Hills—at least it seemed that way to the big three—Bomber and Frankie and me.

We got home from school at three-thirty, and we'd grab something to eat and take off. Some days we'd just play out in the front yard. Football or baseball —we played both with the same rubber ball. Other days would be for collecting bugs, which we kept (but not for very long, unfortunately) in a kitchen matchbox lined with lettuce leaves.

Our absolutely, positively favorite thing was tormenting the neighbors. And boy, did we have neighbors. You could drop names like water bombs: Robert Ryan lived across the street, next door to Bomber. Loretta Young lived one house down from us. Up the street lived the man who built Westwood, and next to him—our hero because he took us for rides in his train—lived Walt Disney. Beyond Mr. Disney's house, our street curved around at the base of two canyons—Beverly Glen and Benedict—and that was the area we assaulted most frequently.

Armed with rubber knives, and with our paper sacks full of raisins and chips for sustenance, we would make our way up unexplored driveways, ready to launch an attack on any foe. Of course, no one dared to interfere with the big three except an occasional dog, and we would make mincemeat of him (not literally, of course) in no time flat, sometimes by running for our lives. Boy, were we some team.

By the end of the afternoon, we usually had conquered several more yards of land to add to our territory. Then, with a number of shaggy, four-legged prisoners of war, we'd march home to the fort—Mom and Mrs. Shapiro—exhausted, filthy, and happy. The next morning, we'd be on the curb on Bomber's side of the street, waiting docilely for our school bus, pretending to be students.

I grew up very fast. It seemed like overnight . . . what with the divorce, and going from Emerson Junior High to University High, and getting my period, and then my learner's permit and driver's license, and an engagement ring, and a diaphragm . . . But life was never quite as dangerous, never again the adventure that it was when we were hiking through those canyons, Bomber and Frankie and me.

In the real world, a fledgling industry was beginning to prove itself more than just a fluke. The tube . . . Uncle Miltie . . . "Dragnet" . . . in-home entertainment was catching on. In 1950 FS made his first television appearance with Beatrice Lillie and Bob Hope in "The Star-Spangled Revue" on NBC. Later that same year he began "The Frank Sinatra Show" which was to run through April of '52. The show followed the soon-to-become-standard variety format, with lots of songs and different guests every week.

For those who didn't yet own a television set, the radio still carried many hours of The Voice. "Light Up Time" had ended, but Frank was doing guest spots with Bob Hope and Jack Benny, several shows for the BBC, and he began

Rags and Riches

Phil Silvers: "I had come to Hollywood after years in burlesque. But my career stopped. I was getting a gang of money under my MGM contract but could not seem to get into a picture. In frustration, I became a party entertainer. When I was invited to a home, the first thing I would look for was the piano, and during this time I developed routines . . . In burlesque, my buddy and best friend was Rags Ragland. He had done similar routines with me.

"These were the war years, and Frank, at the height of his career, was asked to go overseas to entertain our armed forces. I got a call from Frank's manager. Would I go with him? I did, and taught him the Rags routines—Frank loves comedy. We toured North Africa and Italy . . . and we were a smash. Talk about women reacting to Frank's singing—you should have heard the armed

two new radio programs of his own: "The Rocky Fortune Show" (which was drama) and "To Be Perfectly Frank" (which was, of course, music).

So, though many people reported otherwise, the "failure" of Frank Sinatra's career during this period didn't quite occur. His career was different. Relatively, it *was* at a low, compared to the crooner-swooner era. But he never stopped working.

Or having fun. The time was a rare one. When Mayer saw and heard him sing, he had passed the word. FS: "I was sitting in the makeup chair at RKO when Joe Nolan, a nice guy who was in charge of production, came in and said to me, You'd better get your bag packed. You've been traded. I said, What is this, a ball club or something? He said that Mayer wanted me and he had me. I went from $25,000 a picture to $130,000 a picture.

"Now if you were at Metro, they signed you and you got paid every week. But it was almost like the rule of the NFL—if you didn't do a picture, you were on suspension until the end of the picture. Then they'd give you another script

---

forces, the men.

"Back in Hollywood, I got a call from the guy who ran the Copacabana in New York. He said what a wonderful thing it would be for Rags and me, now that we were both in pictures, to play the Copa together. We agreed.

"But Rags became seriously ill. It was tough to get into hospitals in those days; Frank arranged to get him into Cedars. He was never to leave alive. I tried to cancel the Copa, and of course got 'the show must go on' routine. They offered me both salaries and I went. After six sleepless nights, and arranging for Rags's funeral, I arrived in New York to open at the Copa devoid of emotion and material, since most of the routines had to be done with Rags.

". . . Opening night at the Copa. I was sitting in the dressing room. The club was jammed with professionals. This was a form of requiem, for they all knew Rags, and I imagine had some indication of what this night meant to me emotionally. I sat there wondering what to do, what to go on with—it had all been planned with Rags, but now I was on my own. Then the door . . . and a voice said, 'Hi, what do we open with?'

"I blinked—thought I had flipped. Standing in the doorway was Frank Sinatra, who I knew was in the middle of making a picture in Hollywood.

"I know Frank—you don't thank him—you don't say, 'Gee, Frank, you came.' You play it cool. So, I said, 'Well, I'll do a few minutes first, and when I touch my tie you appear and we'll do our routines. You know them all.'

"I can't tell you the reaction when he came out and stood with me and I looked at him and said, 'Scram, kid, I work alone.' And then the standard jokes like, 'I know there is a food shortage, but this is ridiculous,' and 'The blood bank is two blocks up the street,' etc. We proceeded to do an hour and three quarters of material and at our conclusion received an ovation.

"Still, I was subject to tears, but I had to say something about Rags. I also knew that if I spoke I would cry and I didn't think that belonged in a nightclub. I managed to say, 'May I take a bow for Rags?' at which point emotion overtook me and I rushed off the floor to the dressing room in tears. I sat there and said to myself, 'Why did I have to spoil this evening with an outburst?' Suddenly I noticed there wasn't a sound in the Copa, which is usually a bedlam after a show . . . not a sound. I opened the dressing-room door and peeked out, and without a single exception, everybody, including most of the waiters, had their head bowed; and if they were not crying, they were deep in remorse. I thought: This is Rags's requiem.

"As I said earlier, gratitude embarrassed Frank. I looked for him to thank him for this expression of love and complete friendship, but he was gone—back to Hollywood, where he had caused a two-day delay because of this gesture. I had no opportunity to thank him then; it is redundant to thank him now. But this is Sinatra. You don't thank him. You just lean back and accept it."

Louis Burton Mayer, movie mogul. His capacity for star- and movie-making was legendary.

FS loved MGM, its treatment of stars, its vast facilities, including the commissary. "They made the best chicken soup in the world. And L.B. had a chef who made it just the way he liked it. Until one day when L.B. went on vacation and bought, expensively, two songbirds. L.B. left them at the studio, assuming they would be taken to his house for his aviary. That day, at lunch, the chef beamed on him and said: 'I think you're going to like today's soup very much. I made it with the new birds you brought. Very tender, very tasty.' L.B. blanched, then reddened. He said: 'You did what?' "

and if you took it, fine, and if you didn't take it, they didn't kick you out, you just didn't get paid for a time. But you didn't want for anything. Instead of chintzy little dressing rooms, theirs were beautiful, made of cedar, with settees and coffeemakers and a record player. But no telephone, because it could spoil a scene if the phone started ringing in the middle of it. But I said, I have to have a phone. I love the telephone. I don't love it when it rings and rings and nobody answers, but I needed one because I was beginning to get into other businesses, too. So we came up with an idea of how to solve it. We silenced the bell and put on a light. I did a lot of other things, and usually the minute I said I'd like something, Bang, it was done. I was his boy until I made a wisecrack later, but for a long time there was nothing better.

"It was almost like a womb. Everything was done for you. If an actor was signed and had to move out from the East, and he wanted to buy a house for his family, they would lay out the money and deduct a little each week.

"Some of us used to sit at a long table in the studio commissary. In those days, the cameramen sat at one and the publicity men at another and the writers and so on, segregated, and we sat at a bunch of little square tables put together. But at such a long table, we couldn't talk to each other. I was getting teased unmercifully by Judy Garland and Gene Kelly and Van Johnson and Junie Allyson and Julie Munshin and they'd say, 'And what did you have Mr. Mayer do for you today?' I'd tell them to get off my back but they'd see me coming up and say, Here comes The Star. One day Judy said, Listen, you have so many connections here in this goddamn studio, why don't you get a big round table like they have at Hillcrest (a country club) where all the comics sit, so that we could talk? She was kidding.

"When I finished lunch and Gene and I went back to the set, I was in a sailor suit—I was never *out* of a sailor suit until I did *Some Came Running*, the Jim Jones book, when I got into a soldier suit. But I got out because the character was mustered out and put on civilian clothes. I called the head of carpentry. Listen, I said, could you make me a table, a big round table, by tomorrow morning—for lunch? 'Sure,' he said, 'where do you want it?'

"I said, in the corner of the commissary farthest from the door. So he built a table, and it was beautifully done: thick oak with one big, fat graceful leg in the middle so there was nothing to get in the way of human legs and chairs and it seated about fourteen people.

"And I couldn't wait to see their faces the next morning and that was beautiful, too. Look at this! Holy ——! Judy was saying, and screaming and laughing. She had the most wonderful laugh, a wonderful sound, and when she laughed her whole body laughed and we all laughed with her. Carve your initials in it, I said.

"It was warm and happy and I miss it today. There's no such thing anymore. Mayer was a genius. I don't think he knew the front of a camera from the back but he knew people and when he booked people, I don't think he ever missed. They became major stars. He had good people working under him and the best of everything around him. Even when I wasn't working for a few days, I'd get up a little later and then go there for lunch and everybody would say, *We don't get to sleep late . . .*"

At MGM, my dad's relationship with Louis B. Mayer had always been an odd one. Mayer had been so taken with FS's singing at the benefit that he sort of adopted him. He really loved him, and the feeling was mutual.

L.B. would call FS in occasionally for chats. In order to get to L.B.'s office, you had to go through Ida's office. Ida, L.B.'s secretary, was like an army sergeant. Dad told me that every time he went into her office and the door closed behind him, he thought he would never get out. It was like being trapped. Ida would push a button, and the door to L.B.'s office would open, and L.B. would be sitting way the hell down the other end of the room.

To FS, who loved L.B. but was slightly nervous in his presence, it seemed like a ten-mile trek across that room. And he said that as he made the walk down, he could see little L.B.'s legs dangling under the desk. Finally, he would sit down opposite him and L.B., without preliminaries, would say something like: "So? Does Kate Hepburn have to get up on the platform with that Communist or not?"

And Dad would start to respond, "Well, I don't know. It's just a . . ."

"SHADDUP!" L.B. would bark.

The next time L.B. would call him in for a chat, the studio head would again begin out of the blue: "So? Van Johnson has to buy a convertible with a metal thing up here so when he gets in a wreck it has to hit him and open his head or what?"

And Dad would say, "Well, maybe he didn't have . . ."

"SHADDUP!"

That was the type of "chat" they had, time after time. L.B. would do the talking; FS would just sit there, usually costumed in a sailor suit, feeling very close to his boss—more like family.

When Harry Rapf, a close friend and studio associate of L.B.'s died, L.B. called Dad in and said, "So? Would you think that other people would go to this funeral? Why am I the only one at the funeral? What happened? What is this? *I am the only one at the funeral!!!*"

And Dad said, "Maybe they should have sent out an announcement or something."

"SHADDUP! AND GETOUT!"

Another warm little chat concluded.

Word circulated around the studio that L.B. was about to divorce his wife; he was dating the singer and actress Ginny Simms. L.B. had a stable of horses—racehorses and riding horses—and liked to ride on weekends. While he was out riding one day, the horse threw L.B., who broke several bones and ended up in a cast from his knees to his chest.

Dad and Gene Kelly were working on a movie when they heard about the accident. Dad said, "He didn't fall off a horse, he fell off Ginny Simms." Very flip, very silly, a cruel remark.

And Gene said, "You stupid dago bastard—when are you going to learn to keep your mouth shut?" Dad said, "You're right, Shanty, I'm sorry." Gene knew how sensitive L.B. was about everything. You'd think my dad would have known, after those chats.

Weeks went by and L.B. got out of the cast. When he came back to work, he called Dad in for another chat. This time, the walk toward the desk seemed more than ever like the Last Mile.

"So? I hear you been making jokes about my lady friend."

"Yeah, oh, I wish I could take that back. I'm so sorry. I wish I'd *never* said anything so stupid." Dad was mortified. He would never intentionally hurt this lovely man.

And L.B. said, "That's not a very nice thing to do." Then he added, "I want you to leave here, and I don't ever want you to come back again."

FS: "Here, at MGM, I was in a sailor suit . . . I was never out of a sailor suit." L.B. Mayer's little "chats" with his young star would end in disaster after a wisecrack.

© PHILIPPE HALSMAN, 1954

CHAPTER SIX
SURVIVAL

Just One of Those Things

My father no longer had the security of his three major contracts.

Frank Sinatra's latest movies had not done well. And his records were not selling well, either. In 1952 Columbia dropped him. And so did his talent agency, MCA. He didn't have a movie studio, an agent, or a record label. This left him looking for new homes.

Frank Jr.: "His old friend Manie Sacks had been lured away from Columbia, and was the head of RCA Victor. Manie called a meeting with his entire staff, the whole A & R Department, the Marketing Department, the Distributing Department, everybody at RCA Victor, New York. He said, 'We want to sign Sinatra. What can you do with him? Can you move him?'

"Three days later the staff reported back, 'Manie, we can't do it. There's nothing we can do with Sinatra.' Manie, in turn, reported this to Dad. Manie said it was the hardest thing he ever had to tell him. 'The guys don't think they can move you. Not interested. I could force it and get you on the label with us, but I'd rather you went somewhere else than have you come on with these guys who think, in all honesty, they can't do it.' Pop assured Manie that he understood."

In the whirlpool of all this, his relationship with Ava was suffering. They had been married in November, 1951. Artist Paul Clemens, a good friend of both, puts it this way:

"The woman is suddenly in demand and the man is not. It's difficult in a household to accommodate to that. And with Frank and Ava, there was tension even before that. There was always tension. My wife and I spent a weekend with them in Palm Springs. It was fun, but lots of tension. I remember we went to the Racquet Club and Frank stopped at the bar to say hello to the owner, actor Charlie Farrell. There were people milling around, and among them were attractive girls who were pleased to meet Frank. We walked ahead and sat down at the table and Frank said, 'I'll be right along.' Well, Ava took about five or six

If we'd thought a bit
of the end of it
when we started painting the town,
we'd have been aware
that our love affair
was too hot not to cool down . . .

minutes of this, and all of a sudden she said, 'I'm leaving.' When Ava says, 'I'm leaving,' that's an open-ended itinerary because she's a woman of means and temperament. She could mean back to the house, or into L.A. She could mean London or Acapulco. So I said, 'I'll drive you home.' Not *merely* to see that she got home, so that we knew where she was, but also to secure our transportation, because we had all come there in one car. When I returned to the Racquet Club and told Frank what I did, I remember he said, 'Good thinking.

"When we got home later, Frank disappeared and we had a nightcap and went to bed. About three-thirty in the morning there was a rap on our door and there was Frank, fully dressed, *not* in desert clothes but in a long, dark blue coat like a London Burberry. He'd had a few drinks, and he'd reached that point where some people you'd say were drunk, but with Frank it only made him a little more punctilious—his posture was very erect, his speech was *more* articulate and his manners were more courtly.

"He said, 'Paul, I hate to wake you at this hour of the night, but I'm going into town and I didn't want you to wake in the morning and find that I was gone without saying goodbye.'

"Well, I could only assume it was because of an argument with Ava. And I said, 'Frank, how are you going to get to the airport? Could I drive you and then bring the car back?' And he said, 'Yeah, that's a good idea, sure. Come as you are.' I had on a robe and pajamas and slippers . . . He said, 'We've got to run over and pick up Jimmy Van Heusen, he's going to fly me in.' So we go to pick up Jimmy, who got in the back. Frank was driving and the fog was getting denser and denser by the foot as we moved toward the airport. When we got there, we were greeted by a policeman at the gate who peered in, recognized Frank and said, 'How do you do, Mr. Sinatra? If you want to get in the airport, I'm sorry, but it's closed. Nothing going out or in.' Frank said, 'You're sure?' The officer said, 'Look.' And Frank turned and looked at Jimmy, and Jimmy looked at me, and Frank was content that we were not going to get off. So we turned around and went back, dropped Jimmy off, and drove back to the house; Frank was feeling somewhat better about returning to the house. He obviously had made a point of his departure, but God had intervened and he had no choice—he had to return to the house. He was not returning hat-in-hand or penitent—it was an act of nature, so he was reconciled to it himself. So we got in the house and I went back to bed. Frank disappeared and in the morning we had scrambled eggs and caviar for breakfast and there was peace in the desert again."

But only for a while. The odds were against Frank Sinatra and Ava Gardner. It was a stacked deck. Her career was thriving, and his, for the time being, was not. And they were both so passionate about everything, so much alike. It wasn't fair, really. It was as much unfortunate timing as anything else. But they had each other for a little while and they enriched each other's lives.

The passion, the tumult, the pain of parting, changed Dad's way of living and working. Sammy Davis told me that this was ". . . a very quiet, morose time. And I think he solved it—whatever he was going through—by keeping it all inside of him and filing it, putting it aside to use later in his art." Sammy's point is well made. Just listen to "In the Wee Small Hours" or "Only the Lonely." Frank Sinatra put that pain to good use.

Tina Sinatra: "Dad . . . He would come and go and come and go and I didn't know where to find him . . ."

I don't know what brought about the actual breakup, although I've heard many stories. It doesn't really matter. The end result was the same.

I do know that their careers, which by necessity involved constant traveling, pushed them into a long-distance relationship. They relied on telephone lines to connect them a good deal of the time and, whenever possible, airplanes to bring them together for brief visits on locations.

Though the final divorce came later, in 1955, the end might have been the long moment when Dad flew to Naples for a concert, expecting his wife to join him there.

Ava did not appear.

Perhaps, at the end of it, the fact was that they simply couldn't stay together because they couldn't bear to be apart.

Ultimately, it was healthier for them to pursue separate lives. All I do know is that Dad was so *sad* . . . He had a body full of sighs. And it took a long time for him to begin to live again . . . A long time. "What a period of time that was," he said. "It was all Mondays."

I knew when I hugged him I was helping to heal the wound—but a hug from a daughter was only a Band-Aid, not a cure.

Many years later, when my first marriage ended, I went home to my mother's house. In her bed, crying and feeling frightened and sorry for myself, I thought it was the end of the world. Dad came in that first night and he said, "I know you're sad. I know you're unhappy, and I know you're miserable. But I can only tell you that it will pass, and I'm glad you're not alone. You have me and Mom and your sister and brother. I had to go through it alone."

Ava never married again.

Whenever word of their troubles got out, the press was on Dad again, kicking him when he was down, poking into the private corners of his life. Some of the "friends" from the good times disappeared. Real, challenging work wasn't available.

Yet a few things stayed the same. One who observed them was good friend Dorothy Manners, a woman who worked for the columnist Louella Parsons and took over her column after Louella died.

Dorothy Manners: "Never did he lose that presence, that sense of being in charge of things. I remember, I was giving a little dinner in Chinatown— Jimmy Van Heusen, Frank, and a few other friends. I went to pay the check and the man told me, 'Mr. Sinatra's taken care of it.' Later, we went to the Cocoanut Grove and he picked up *that* check. And he was broke. He had owned a piece of property in back of Saks, in Beverly Hills. Louis B. Mayer bought it from him. Frank wanted $125,000, or at least $100,000. L.B. gave him $75,000, cash on the spot. It's worth millions today. Millions."

Cartoonist Al Capp: "Frank Sinatra was the first great public figure I ever wrote about. I called him Hal Fascinatra. I remember my news syndicate was so worried about what his reaction might be, and we were all surprised when he telephoned and told me how thrilled he was with it . . . He always made it a point to send me champagne whenever he happened to see me in a restaurant. In those years when he was so broke, I ran into him in a restaurant. Sure enough, the bottle of champagne was sent over as usual."

The financial obligation uppermost in his mind, "the thing that worried him the most," Dorothy Manners told me, "was you kids and Nancy out at the house in Holmby Hills.

FS: "What a period of time that was. It was all Mondays . . ."

Nancy: "It was a dark enough time to lead him to deep despair—even to contemplate and approach the edge of suicide. It is impossible to know whether it was the loss of this love; or the loss of all the love and luck and work that his life had known before this very 'down' hour; or what complex of motives moved him to the brink. Others may speculate

on what could cause any human being to consider ending his own life. We have to respect the eternal privacy which means that we can never know.

"Later, he would counsel me not to despair, that despair can lead to terrible things. And later, I learned, he credited Jackie Gleason with being the man, the friend, who saw him through it."

"His main thing was to pay that mortgage. It was a big load for him to carry because that was a big house and a lot of property. I think the only thing that would have done him in would have been if his family had been forced to move out of that house. He was dead set and determined to do it. And he did!

"But it was a tough time. He went to a recording studio once and there were kids outside taunting him: 'We love Eddie Fisher! We love Eddie Fisher.' And Frank said, 'I like him, too.' That was tough."

When my Dad said he liked Eddie Fisher too, he meant it; his was no flip or sarcastic remark. That is a side of him that I know and want to share—the sweetness.

In April 1952 he went to Hawaii to do a series of concerts and spent a great deal of time in the company of his friend Buck Buchwach, a Honolulu newspaperman.

Buchwach: "Frank made a few appearances in Honolulu and then, to assist a struggling promoter, flew to the island of Kauai to do weekend shows at the Kauai County Fair. It was raining and the dilapidated tent was leaking during the first performance. He walked onstage and raindrops hit his traveling tux. 'For just one second,' he told me, 'considering the whole situation, I wondered if the show really did have to go on. Then I peeked out at the audience. There were a few hundred, tops. They weren't wearing fancy clothes or expensive jewelry. They wore color-splattered aloha shirts, jeans, mumus, and such. Homey. And their warmth and friendliness circulated throughout that tent; it smacked me in the face. When two little brown-skinned young girls later gave me a couple of handmade leis and little kisses, I almost broke down.'

"Before the final show at the Kauai County Fair, your father and I talked for a few minutes in a car outside the show tent. Frank took out a cigarette, and quietly puffed spirals of smoke. Though outside it was still raining, he had changed at his nearby hotel into his finest dress tuxedo, a magnificent shirt, his patent leather shoes, and his favorite ring. He went on and sang, song after song, hit after hit, maybe twenty. I was stunned. It was, merely, fantastic; it was one thousand percent for several hundred small-town ticket holders with big hearts and hands that grew red from clapping.

"Afterward, Frank had tears in his eyes. 'Buck, I sang the best I know how,' he said. 'Those people deserved it. It's a night I'll never forget.'"

That night Frank Sinatra made a prediction. "Tonight," he told Buck Buchwach, "marks the first night on the way back. I can feel it in every bone."

From Here to Eternity

va was making important films: *Mogambo* with Clark Gable and *The Great Sinner* with Gregory Peck. For many reasons, Dad desperately needed an important movie. Columbia Pictures was about to film James Jones's bestselling novel *From Here to Eternity.* When he had read the novel, my father said to his friend Robert Weitman, "Rob, there is a part in here that I must play."

It was the part of an army private, a feisty underdog described by *Time* magazine as "the roistering, ill-starred little Italian named Maggio." It was a part that Frank Sinatra could identify with, that he would likely have played for nothing.

But he had little chance of getting it. He had no reputation as a dramatic

NS: *"When my father read James Jones's* From Here to Eternity *he said, 'For the first time in my life I was reading something I really had to do. I just felt it—I just knew I could do it, and I just couldn't get it out of my head.'"*

actor. Even though he had received good notices on some earlier roles, he was fighting his crooner image—and he was not good box office.

Paul Clemens: "Harry Cohn was studio head at Colúmbia. A relentlessly tough man. Harry's wife, Joan, was a good friend of mine. I had just broken up with my wife, and Joan Cohn, who liked to paint, said to me, 'I'm not painting these days. Why don't you use my studio?' So I moved in there, in this converted coach house next to their house, and I noticed that out at poolside every day

Harry Cohn and the producer Buddy Adler were working on something. I was doing some sketches of Ava. And from the pool Harry could see her coming and going. One day he said, 'You know Ava pretty well, Paul?' I said, 'Well, I've known her, yes, for several years.' He said, 'Could you bring her to dinner here?' I said, 'Well, I could ask her, Harry.' Ava was kind of lonely in town—Frank was away working—and not happy with her circumstances, and she had met Joan Cohn and liked her. So when I asked her if she would like to come to dinner at the Cohns', she accepted.

"Ava knew that what Buddy Adler and Harry were working on around poolside was the script of *From Here to Eternity.* And at the Cohns' that night Ava said, 'You know who's right for that part of Maggio, don't you? That sonofabitch of a husband of mine. He's perfect for it.' (She didn't say it with any rancor; that's the way she would talk.) And Joan said, 'My God, you're right!'

"During dinner it was obvious that Harry wanted to sell Ava on a project. He had a bunch of second-unit footage on something called *Joseph and His Brethren,* which was shot in Egypt. It was good footage, but it was footage in search of a picture. Ava wanted nothing to do with it. Instead, she put in a few words for Frank, and hoped that Joan Cohn would carry the ball."

Ava had to leave for Africa to begin filming *Mogambo.* Frank, still trying to hold his marriage together, went with her.

Joan Cohn did indeed carry the ball. A week later Frank Sinatra received a telegram from his agent, Bert Allenberg, telling him to come home. On November 14, 1952, Frank did his screen test for Maggio in Hollywood.

Burt Lancaster: "It was Monty [Montgomery Clift] who watched the filming of one of Frank's close-ups and said, 'He's going to win the Academy Award.' . . . That's what Monty felt . . ."

PHIL STERN/GLOBE PHOTOS

Joan Cohn said: "Harry called me at home one day and told me to come to the Columbia lot. He sat me down—just the two of us—in a projection room —and he ran the two screen tests. Not once, not twice, but three times. One, then the other, one, then the other. I sat there and watched them three times. Then Harry turned to me and I said, 'Well, you've got a nice Jewish boy and you've got a nice Italian boy, Harry. What's your problem?' "

Harry made the ethnically accurate choice.

Frank Sinatra: "When I heard that Eli Wallach was testing for the part, I thought I was dead. He was such a good performer. In November, I did the Texaco Star Theatre with Milton Berle, shopped for Ava's Christmas presents in New York, and went to Montreal for a nightclub date. Harry Cohn called me there."

Frank Sinatra was Angelo Maggio.

The stars of the film were Burt Lancaster, Deborah Kerr, Montgomery Clift, and Donna Reed. The director was Fred Zinnemann. In April 1953, they flew to Hawaii to begin filming.

Burt Lancaster: "Deborah Kerr and me and Frank and Monty are sitting up in the front. And he and Monty are drunk. Monty, poor Monty, was this kind of a drinker—he'd chug-a-lug one martini and conk out. And Frank was, I believe, having a few problems, and so, when we arrived, these two bums were unconscious. They were gone! Deborah and I had to wake them up . . . This is the way they arrived, and Harry Cohn is down there with the press and everything.

"Well, we got through that, and now we start to do the picture. Every night, after work, we would meet in Frank's room. In those days your father wore the funny little double-breasted suits—very dapper, with the gold cuff links and so forth. Didn't have any money, but always dapper and always very generous. He had a gold lighter—a Dunhill lighter—and I said, 'Gee, that's a pretty lighter.' 'It's yours,' he said. 'But, Frank—I don't *use* a lighter. I *lose* them all the time, so I use matches.' 'You gotta take it!' I had to take it or he was going to hit me. And, of course, I lost the lighter.

"Anyway, he had a refrigerator in his room and he would open it and there would be these iced glasses. And he would now prepare the martinis. He'd put on a waiter's white apron, and serve the martinis with some snacks while we were getting ready to go to an eight o'clock dinner. We'd sit and chat about the day's work and he would try his nightly call to Ava, who was in Spain. In those days in Spain, if you lived *next door* to your friends, you couldn't get them on the telephone, let alone trying to get them on the phone from Hawaii. He never got through. Not one night. When you finished your martini, he would take the glass away from you and open up the icebox and get a fresh cold glass and by eight o'clock, he and Monty would be unconscious. I mean, *really* unconscious. Every night.

"So Deborah and I would take your father's clothes off and put him to bed. Then I would take Monty on my shoulder and we would carry him down to *his* room, take *his* clothes off, and dump *him* in bed. And then she and I and the Zinnemanns would go out and have dinner. We did that every single night and, to this day, Frank calls me 'Mother.' On my birthday, I can be in Istanbul or Scotland or God knows where, and a telegram arrives, saying 'Dear Mother— Happy Birthday. Brother Francis.'

"We became very good friends. And he and Monty were good friends.

Your father, as you know, has a hot temper and one night when we'd come back to Los Angeles, we were doing a scene at the Columbia Ranch. It's thirty-eight degrees, which is cold. Especially at night—one or two in the morning. And we had these big ash cans with fires in them and the crew is walking around with burlap bags wrapped over their feet, and Monty and Frank and I are in these lightweight suntans. [Army uniforms.] We're doing the scene where I'm sitting in the road with Monty and at the end of the scene in comes Frank, who has been beaten up by Borgnine, and he dies in Monty's arms.

"So we were in suntans. And it was cold. The crew gave us coffee and they laced it with brandy. After about two sips Monty was unconscious. And they had to call off the shooting for an hour or two. Monty got up, we walked him around, and then Frank and I went with him to a little tent and he lay down on a cot. A man comes rushing into the tent. His name was Jack Fier and he was the Head of Production for Columbia, working under Harry Cohn. He was a famous character who always carried a whip in his hand, a very imperious kind of a guy. And immediately he began to holler at Monty: 'You can't do this. You've got to let us know if you're sick. I'll get an ambulance—take you to a hospital. Got a lot of insurance.' And Frank immediately gets up and goes over to hit Fier and I grabbed Frank and said, 'Put it down, now, take it easy.' And then Fier said, 'I don't mean to make any disturbance, but I've got to know about this. If you're sick, we've got to get a doctor. If you're not going to be able to go on with the show . . .' And Frank is ready to go again and I'm calming Frank down and suddenly this quiet voice said, 'Mr. Fier, I'll have to ask you to leave.' And we turned around and it's Monty. And Fier says, 'Well, I mean, er . . .' He didn't know how to deal with this sort of nonviolent approach to things. He said, 'Look, I'm sure it's not your *fault*, but we're going to lose money.' Monty says, 'Mr. Fier, I'll have to ask you to leave.' Whereupon Fier, not knowing what to do, just slaps himself with his whip, turns around and says, 'Well, all right.' And off he goes. And I look at Monty and Monty turns to Frank and me, and Monty says, 'That's the bravest thing I've ever done in my life.' Whereupon your father starts to cry and I start to cry. Your father goes over and takes Monty in his arms and kisses him. That was Monty.

"It was Monty who, when watching the filming, saw the rushes of one of Frank's close-ups and said, 'He's going to win the Academy Award.' Your Father's fervor, his anger, his bitterness had something to do with the character of 'Maggio,' but also with what he had gone through in the last number of years: a sense of defeat, and the whole world crashing in on him, his marriage to Ava going to pieces—all of these things caused this ferment in him, and they all came out in that performance. You knew that this was a raging little man who was, at the same time, a *good* human being. And that's what Monty *felt* was going to happen.

Monty was right.

The night of the 1954 Academy Awards was my mother's birthday. She invited my father to dinner. We gave him a tiny gold Oscar mounted on a disc the size of a quarter. He'd have his Oscar from us, no matter what the Academy's decision. Mom asked us what we wanted engraved on it. We chose, *Dad, all our love from here to eternity.*

In speaking of that night, my father said, "When I walked up there to receive the Oscar, one of the brightest memories flashed . . . Those two leis I got from the little Hawaiian girls at the Kauai County Fair . . .

"From that moment, everything seemed to go right for me."

FS with actress Donna Reed. Nancy: "Dad literally ran *down the aisle, took his Oscar for acting, looked at the orchestra, and said, grinning: 'I see a lot of the guys in the band here that I recognize. But nobody's asked me to sing.' I had never* seen *him so happy."*

Frankie (Frank Sinatra, Jr.) was only ten years old when he saw From Here to Eternity. *Remembering the fight scene and the bully, played by Ernest Borgnine, Frankie turned to his father after the Oscar ceremonies and said, "You know, Dad, when I see that man, Fatso, I'm gonna kill him!" "No, son, you don't kill him," FS said, "you* kiss *him. He helped me win the Academy Award."*

123

CHAPTER SEVEN
CAPITOL

Got the World on a String

Upon leaving Columbia Records, where he'd produced such fine sides as "I Could Write a Book," "I Hear a Rhapsody," "The Birth of the Blues" and my 1952 favorite—"Why Try to Change Me Now," my father and Axel Stordahl moved to Capitol Records. Their first session was a good one, and a single, "I'm Walking Behind You," was the result. Whenever Dad did a recording session, he sent me a set of rough dubs—test records made of lightweight acetate. I was proud that he was interested in my opinion. When he sent me the dubs from that first session at Capitol, I liked "I'm Walking Behind You" a lot. I called him up to tell him so, but I also felt obliged to mention an Eddie Fisher version I had heard on radio. Dad told me not to worry about it. As it happened, both versions sold well, with the edge going to Fisher. But Pop was gaining ground. I could tell by the records, and the reactions of my friends at school.

At Capitol, producer Voyle Gilmore took FS under his wing. In addition to having Dad continue his work with Axel, Gilmore wanted to team him with trumpet player Billy May because of Billy's humorous style.

Billy May: "I had a moderate amount of success on records and found myself in the band business. When I got the call to work with Frank, I was with my band in Florida and couldn't do the gig. But I told Gilmore to feel free to let somebody else do the charts in the Billy May style."

For Dad's first session, Heinie Beau had given the May touch to "My Lean Baby." For the second session, Gilmore hired the young trombonist-arranger Nelson Riddle, who'd had some hits which included "Mona Lisa" for Nat King Cole and "Quiet Village" for Les Baxter. Nelson did the arrangements for Dad's "South of the Border" and "I Love You" *a la* Billy May, but completed the set with arrangements in his own style. It was the beginning of a musical partnership that would span decades and carry them through over ninety recording sessions together.

Nelson's orchestrations seemed to extract not necessarily a better, but a

In a Capitol Records studio, Frank Sinatra looks into the booth, listening to a playback, searching, as always, for perfection.

different voice from FS. Together they developed a stronger, more sophisticated Sinatra sound. Their first session produced "I've Got the World on a String" and "Don't Worry 'Bout Me." Their next pairing blew everything wide open. "Anytime, Anywhere" backed with "From Here to Eternity" became a hit. Another superb side, "My One and Only Love," also came out of that session. This song is perhaps *the* most difficult popular song to sing. The intervals are extremely tricky, and FS performed them beautifully. These songs, though ballads, had a different feel.

Frank Jr.: "Nelson began to pump a little more power into the sound. Instead of sounding like that silky smooth crooner of the forties, now Pop was putting more energy into it, belting a little more. His voice lowered, too, got better, lost some of its sweetness. His whole attitude was becoming a little more hip now. The curly-haired, bow-tied image was gone. Now there was the long tie—and the hat."

Soon came the album titles that evoked a lifestyle: "Swing Easy!" "Songs for Swingin' Lovers!" "A Swingin' Affair!" And the single "Young at Heart." In 1954 *Billboard* picked Sinatra as the top male singer, "Young at Heart" as the year's best record, and "Swing Easy" as the best LP. *Metronome* named him "Singer of the Year" . . . It was a time for "A Foggy Day," "I Get a Kick Out of You," "They Can't Take That Away from Me," "Day In, Day Out," "All of Me," "The Christmas Waltz," and "It Was Just One of Those Things."

In 1955 Dad and Nelson did my favorite album, *In the Wee Small Hours.* This includes the incredibly poignant interpretations of "I'll Be Around," "I Get Along Without You Very Well," "When Your Lover Has Gone."

A technical development—a new format—was a factor, after the music itself.

Stan Cornyn, later an executive with Warner records: "The day of the long-playing ten-inch eight-song album had arrived. A new record-listening habit was created. People listened long rather than fast . . . The long-playing novelty—put one on and forget record changers forever!—became the Sinatra medium . . . He was building up, album by album, a body of poetic interpretation, preserved on records, such as no artist before him had done. For all his crashing self-assertion, through his art he was suggesting that man is still only a child, frightened and whimpering in the dark."

Nelson and Dad got together again on a new work, "Songs for Swingin' Lovers." Frank Jr.: "They'd been told how many songs to put on the album, and they were following instructions. They were supposed to finish the album on Friday night. Thursday, in the middle of the night, the A & R department called Sinatra and said, 'We need three more songs for "Swingin' Lovers." ' He says, 'This is a helluva time to tell me.' He called Nelson, who was living out in Malibu, and woke him up. Told Nelson they need three more arrangements.

"The next night, coming in from Malibu for the final date, Nelson's wife was driving and he was in the back seat with a flashlight, still writing out the parts. One of those arrangements was for 'I've Got You Under My Skin.'

"At the studio Nelson got up and started to conduct. Nelson Riddle is the kind of a guy, well, a volcano would go up next to him, he'd say, 'How about that?' Absolutely unflappable. Now, Nelson conducted the set, and after they'd rehearsed 'I've Got You Under My Skin,' everybody just sat there. It was an old song, been recorded a thousand times, not a new song, right? An old song . . . but all the women had tears in their eyes and the whole orchestra, when they were done playing, stood up and applauded. For Nelson Riddle. This doesn't happen. But Nelson, he just stood there with cigarette ashes on him and said, 'Yeah, how about that?' "

The record became a Sinatra classic.

"The album was completed that Friday and was being shipped to the stores the next *Monday.* That's how much in demand it was. That's how hot Pop was—all the kids, they'd put on Sinatra's 'Swingin' Lovers' and play it. I can remember Dad saying, 'Gee.' You know, all the teenagers, Nancy's friends, are saying, 'Hey, *that* kid's old man is *it.*' "

That was true. At last Dad had driven through that dense well of teenage indifference. He was discovered by a new generation.

It was, for me, an exciting time musically. I was in junior high. Rhythm and blues. Rock and roll. Elvis. The Everlys. Chuck Berry. I was still studying classical piano. Debussy. Mendelssohn. Liszt. And sitting in on Sinatra sessions. My father, for God's sake! Can you imagine what this was like? FS and some of the most exciting orchestrating in American history. It was not only an intensely interesting learning experience, but a great time. FS was always up for them, and the musicians responded with like enthusiasm. It became a status thing, doing a Sinatra gig.

In 1956, as in 1952, FS campaigned for Adlai Stevenson. There were lots of pretty girls and parties. His life was getting better—to put it mildly. It was, in fact, a heady time for all of us.

With his Academy Award and his Capitol hits, he was more prominent than ever. *Time* put him on its cover in 1955, observing that "last week, still four months shy of forty, he was well away on a second career that promises to be if anything, more brilliant than the first . . . In the movies, Frank Sinatra is currently more in demand than any other performer . . . On the nightclub and variety circuit, Frank has a rating that stands second to none in pull or payoff . . ." And in records and television, the magazine reported, he was right at the top, too.

Australian tour, 1955. A privileged time for Nancy Sinatra, a chance to be with her father and to see more of the world. The two-week tour was a success. What happened between daughter and father took much longer to heal.

The Fall

he year of the *Time* cover story I was fourteen and I had a new sample of that life at the top. My dad had signed on for a concert tour of Australia, and he invited me to go along. It was exciting. He was going to be mine for a whole three weeks.

My mom bought me some new clothes and made me a traveling suit in a comfortable navy-checked fabric for the thirty-six-hour flight. My first road trip —halfway around the world. There was a whole troupe of us: FS, myself, comedian Frank D'Amor, singer Ann McCormack, guitarist Al Viola, drummer Max Albright, pianist Bill Miller, and saxophonist Bud Shank.

We landed in Honolulu and were greeted by hula girls, leis, and suitably balmy trade winds. It was romantic, and though I had a boyfriend at school, I was still in love with my father. We spent one night at the Surf Rider Hotel after a great dinner at Canliss, a restaurant owned by a friend of Dad's. We didn't want to leave Hawaii, which, in 1955, was still paradise. We flew in a BOAC big-bellied Stratocruiser for the rest of the trip. FS and company spent much of the flight in the belly of the big plane, because that's where the bar was. There were jam sessions and jokes, and I had the time of my life. After a stop in Fiji, there

was a quick refueling stop on Canton Island that was a little weird. The landing was okay, but the take-off . . . The big plane, with a full load, started at one end of the runway, which was one edge of the island, and lumbered all the way down to the other end of the runway, which was also the other edge of the island. That's how small Canton is. When we finally lifted off, we dropped down *toward* the ocean—just like taking off from an aircraft carrier, when the bottom falls out.

The Australians gave Sinatra a warm, enthusiastic welcome. The audiences were big and very receptive, but the press assaulted him. It was as if they had been laying for him! He was criticized because—can you believe it?—"nobody swooned." He even was blamed for setting off a false fire alarm. This was my first exposure to the cruelty, inadvertent or intentional, of the press. I hated it. But nothing was going to spoil my vacation with my dad. I had him all to myself.

Melbourne was cosmopolitan—but Sidney was poetic. A harbor and

beaches that looked like a Potthast canvas. We went boating and learned to use a harpoon. The coastline was plagued by sharks, and all small boats were on alert. FS speared one. Headlines!

I was keeping a diary of the trip and writing letters home every day. One afternoon I ran out of hotel stationery in my bedroom, and I went into Dad's room looking for some. I opened the desk drawer. Inside was some intimate ladies' apparel.

I knew he had been seeing one of the girls in the show, but I didn't know she had been with him next door.

For the rest of the trip, I was destroyed. It was awful. I was suddenly deeply sad. I stopped writing in my little diary. I just didn't care.

He had cheated on me. And right on schedule, for it was time to begin again the long, painful process of separation. My father's freedom of expression once again had jarred someone close to him. But this time, it was me. My mom had gone out on dates, and with some mighty nice men, but if they'd spent the

"I believe in a team of people," FS told John Bryson. ". . . four heads are better than one. I want the best strength I can have behind me . . ." Sinatra, known for his way with a melody, his beautifully enunciated and felt reading of a lyric, is meticulous too about giving credit to the superlative composers, lyricists, arrangers, musicians, producers, and directors with whom he has worked.

night I didn't know about it. I had never thought about it at all until Dad forced me to.

Until then, and for a time thereafter, I had a blurry view of marriage or of any male/female relationship. My divining rod, for years, would not point clearly to the right man—until Hugh Lambert came along. I was always searching for my father or in reaction to him.

For me at fourteen, it was an important lesson, a good example. Even though I didn't realize it then, it was time for me to grow up. To leave the "oasis" of childhood. To be subject to what Dr. William Appleton has described in his book *Fathers and Daughters* as the "Theory of the Fall of Father."

Because no man can remain an ideal hero forever to his little girl, every father must fall. The degree and timing of his descent profoundly influence the level of maturity his daughter achieves. The timing and severity of father's fall evoke responses ranging from naïveté to compassionate acceptance to shocked insecurity. Men who pretend to be perfect encourage their offspring to remain childlike in their expectations of themselves and others. Those who fall suddenly and excessively, especially when their daughters are too young, can scar them badly, leaving the woman afraid to trust men as lovers or at work, and with badly shaken self-esteem. The trauma can be overcome, but it takes a long time. When a man reveals his humanity to his daughter in a gradual and caring way when she is old enough to stand it, he actively prepares her for adulthood. By abandoning his role as her hero, he aids her in leaving him.

My hero had aided me in leaving him all right, and I was badly shaken, but I wasn't scarred. My father's fall was perfectly timed. Ultimately, my response would be "compassionate acceptance." But for a long time I was just angry. We still talked, but he had to make all the efforts and phone calls.

I never spoke with him about the episode. That was a mistake. I should have said something right away. My mother finally asked me what was wrong and I told her. I'm sure she explained it to Dad. I couldn't. Back then, in 1955, it just hurt.

All the Way

FS was building a new house in the desert. Palm Springs was growing up, too. A few years before, we had needed our jeep to manage the dirt roads, sand dunes, and tumbleweeds. Now all the streets were paved and the town was jumping—with night spots: the Doll House, Chi-Chi, Ruby's Dunes, as well as the Fun in the Sun Candy Store. Nathanson's little market, "Jerry's," was dwarfed by supermarkets and department stores. New houses and hotels meant more people, and so, in his quest for privacy, Dad had purchased a piece of land on the other side of Palm Springs, on the edge of a tiny town called Cathedral City. The land was part of a country-club development and offered golfing and a clubhouse with a dining room. Our house was built on the seventeenth fairway. It was a cozy two-bedroom home with a tiny kitchen and dining area, and a nice living room. Dad had a swimming pool off the living room and master bedroom. We made several trips to see the progress of the construction. The pool area was always a problem because it was adjacent to the golf course and everyone could look in. And sometimes golfers actually walked in. One clown drove a golf cart right into the pool. There was a lot more work to be done, but FS wanted to do things slowly and stay financially sound.

Watching things grow is one of Dad's passions. We had made many trips

PHIL STERN/GLOBE PHOTOS

Given a choice, I would choose
to have a magic wand
*   that I could use*
to draw a melody
*   from that enchanted maze*
of brass and keys and wood
*   and wind and steel.*
And I would stand there, big
*   and brave,*
and quietly say, Gentlemen,
*   play for me . . .*
Play for me . . .

At the Capitol Towers studios in Los Angeles (left) the man without much formal musical education conducts a session for "Tone Poems of Color," the first album recorded at the new Tower.

to Las Vegas to see the Sands Hotel being built. That was exciting too, but the real building began after the construction was completed, when the showroom was open for business. Danny Thomas opened the Copa Room at the Sands in 1952.

Soon, the Sands was *the* place. Jack Entratter, Nick Kelly, Carl Cohen, they were quite a team. They knew what talent to book, what food to serve. They also knew how to be generous, and they weren't afraid to be. There were always free drinks for the gamblers ("The house would like to buy you a drink.") On special occasions there were bags of silver dollars for guests. There was the Chuck Wagon—all you can eat for a dollar. There was an easygoing feeling that doesn't exist anymore. Of course, thirty-dollar plane rides don't exist anymore either. Or fifteen-dollar rooms.

Dean, Sammy, Danny Thomas, Jerry Lewis, Red Skelton—the whole roster was exciting. The casual mood prevailed. From building to building. No ties, no codes. Each building was named for a racetrack: Churchill Downs, Hollywood Park, Hialeah. Dad had an apartment there that would be our Las Vegas home for many years.

And it was a new home. Dad was the hottest attraction in a hot town.

The songs being sung by Frank Sinatra at the Sands marked, I believe, the pinnacle of his recording career to date . . . "You Make Me Feel So Young," "How About You," "I Won't Dance," "I Wish I Were in Love Again," "Baby Won't You Please Come Home"—these from the albums. Remarkable singles were "Learnin' the Blues," "How Little We Know," "Hey, Jealous Lover," "Witchcraft," "Tell Her You Love Her," and "All the Way."

Many Sinatra classic recordings jumped out of his movies and TV shows: "Love and Marriage" from *Our Town* (CBS 1955); "The Tender Trap," title song (1955); "Wait For Me," from *Johnny Concho;* "You're Sensational," from *High Society;* "I Could Write a Book," "There's a Small Hotel," and absolutely—sorry, Lena—"The Lady Is a Tramp," all from *Pal Joey.*

FS rerecorded some of his forties favorites: "I Couldn't Sleep a Wink Last Night," "Oh, Look at Me Now," "I'm a Fool to Want You," which critic George T. Simon called "the most emotional side of Frank I have ever heard." He sang it for Ava . . .

One more important note was the theme album. The invitations to— "Come Fly with Me," "Come Dance with Me." And to have "A Jolly Christmas." "Where Are You?" followed by the devastating "Only the Lonely."

The mid-fifties was an enormously active period for Dad as a movie actor as well as a singer. He worked with a range of strong, interesting people, and often there was friction and sparks.

He did *Young at Heart* with Doris Day, and they disagreed about the script's ending, and about her husband's presence on the set (he was her agent), and about when to start work. (She liked to start early, he thought noon was a nice time.) He did *Guys and Dolls* with Marlon Brando and went into it feeling that the picture would be a lot stronger if he, not Brando, had played Sky Masterson, the more vocal singing role; and if singers, not movie stars, had played the other leads in the musical; and if more attention had been paid to the great score. Sinatra and Brando: one a Method actor, searching for motivation and perfection in take after take, the other an instinctual actor, who revved himself to do his very best on the first take.

Henry Silva was an actor FS didn't know but admired. Their first meeting was in two cars, waiting for a light to change on Sunset Boulevard. Sinatra called

Bing Crosby on Frank Sinatra:
"A talent like that comes along once in a lifetime . . .
Why in my *lifetime?"*

Frank Sinatra on Bing Crosby:
"He was the father of my career . . . the idol of my youth . . . and the dear, dear friend of my maturity."

Comedian Joe E. Lewis was not a notorious teetotaler. He was, instead, very fond of Scotch whisky. FS remembers one occasion when both men found themselves, perhaps to their surprise, in Paris, where Joe had great difficulty with the language. One day, Joe E. came lurching in, narrowly missing most of the furniture and just slightly off vertical, to say, "I've finally met somebody who speaks English." "Who?" Frank asked. "A cat," Lewis offered. "It said, 'Meow.'"

across to the startled Silva: "Hi, Henry, I like your work." And drove away. (And later hired him for parts in his movies.) Henry Silva: "Frank always wanted to do his best. And he felt that, for him, the *first* take was always his best. He'd been told that. And when you work with him, he sets the tone. With him, you know it's first take. Even if you don't think you can do it, you pull it out of yourself. You say, 'I gotta give it to this guy.' I'd get myself up, like a horse getting out of the starting gate and—I'd trained for it mentally—the gun goes off and you go!"

If there was friction, there was also mutual respect. Silva was at a friend's house one day when Brando walked in: "Brando had just made the picture with Frank and started talking about him. He got very quiet and seemed to be very, very far away and all of a sudden he sat back, and Brando, the great actor, said—you could barely hear him—'Boy, to be able to sing like that.'"

Doris said later that "Despite Frank's sure and rather cocky exterior, I always felt there was a sad vulnerability about him." Once, when she was sniffling after an emotional scene, someone attempted to throw a box of Kleenex to her and it was as if he had thrown it at her. It hit her forehead and when Frank looked up, he sprang at the man who had flipped the box. "Don't ever do that! You don't throw things at a lady, understand? Over the years," Doris said, "whenever I pull a Kleenex out of a box, I think of Frank."

Sinatra worked on *The Man with the Golden Arm* in 1955, too, playing a heroin addict who writhes through cold-turkey withdrawal. It was demanding, a torturing piece of work, the only role he *really* wanted to play, almost *needed* to play, since Maggio—and it earned him another Academy Award nomination. Critic Arthur Knight called him "an actor of rare ability" who gave "a truly virtuoso performance . . . He brings to the character much that has not been written into the script, a shade of sweetness, a sense of edgy indestructibility that actually creates the appeal and intrinsic interest of the role." Dad hadn't been sure he deserved an Oscar for "Eternity," but he felt he did now; his friend Ernest Borgnine won instead, for *Marty*.

The next year, 1956, while he was filming *High Society*, Dad took me to lunch. Halfway through, a petite girl wearing blue jeans and a babushka came over to chat. She was in the movie, too. She was pale and pretty with a gentle voice—and Dad called her "Gracie." He called her Gracie until the day she died, even after Grace Kelly became "Her Serene Highness, Princess Grace of Monaco" to almost everyone else.

Bing Crosby was their costar in *High Society* and, during a break from filming, Bing and Jimmy Van Heusen went to visit Dad in Las Vegas, where he was fulfilling a singing engagement. Bing Crosby: "Jimmy was a dear and valued friend of Frank's and a tosspot of considerable reputation. Frank was playing the Sands Hotel, and we were told he was on the verge of a complete physical collapse, a condition induced by a great deal of hard work, some late nights, some all-nights, no sleep or rest, and a great deal of sauce. Jimmy and I went over that night to see Frank backstage, and I offered to go on for him so he could give his throat a rest and recover. 'No, thanks,' he croaked grandly. 'I can handle it all right. But, Bing, there's something I want to talk to you about. Can you meet me at Luigi's after the show?' I, of course, agreed, and when he showed up, we took a booth in the corner and ordered some drinks. 'What did you want to talk to me about?' I queried. 'Bing,' he said, 'we've got to do something about Van Heusen. He's not taking very good care of himself!' . . . I wanted to say, 'Why don't we limber up on you.'"

The Joker Is Wild, in which Dad portrayed the comedian Joe E. Lewis, was filmed in 1956. A close friendship developed and he and Joe E. began working the Sands together. The memory of the two of them standing onstage at separate lecterns, wearing eyeglasses down low on the tips of their noses, reading from William Shakespeare, is one I cherish. Dad read nicely, pronounced words properly. Joe E. garbled everything with his guttural slurring. He was pixilated. Definitely pixilated. I remember Dad telling me how important it was to keep Joe interested in food. To keep him eating. "When in doubt, Chicken, give him a corned beef on rye or a hot dog, he'll always eat that." But no sweets; we had to keep him away from sweets.

Joe E. Lewis: "I was having a sweet dessert in the restaurant one day when Frank said to me, 'Joe, you are not supposed to eat that—you're diabetic.' 'Don't worry about me,' I said, 'I'm very calorie-conscious. I won't even shake hands with Sugar Ray Robinson!'"

Nightclubs, movies, records. Director George Sidney: "Frank was finishing up *Joker* at Paramount. And I went over there to talk to him. He's recording, and he's making pictures, and he's running the world. You know, he's doing everything. I said, 'Frank, tell me something. How do you do all these things?' And he looked at me and he said, 'Very simple. One thing at a time.' And that was it. Concentration. Amazing concentration. People think he's all over the place, but he's the most orderly person the world's ever known. People do not understand it."

Sammy Davis, Jr.: "I was doing a gig at this nightclub in L.A., Ciro's. And Frank would bring all the heavyweights to see us. Then he started taking me around, introducing me to Gary Cooper, Judy Garland—all those people. He'd call me up: 'Come on, I'll take you to dinner.' Then, later, we'd go up to Betty and Bogie's house.

"I was the only young black person that traveled in that sort of circle. Frank and I would talk about prejudiced people and you know how he is. He'd say, 'Aah, they're all full of shit!' And that's the end of that. That's all he'd ever say: 'Pay no attention to that.'"

He never expanded on it with words, according to Sammy, which doesn't surprise me, because when Daddy does, he gets livid. But he did it with action, making sure that Sammy was accepted wherever they went.

Sammy: "Now I go through many things a day and meet many kinds of people and I can handle it all because of that learning experience, early in my life, with Frank. He took me around. He *forced* me to learn how to deal with different types of people. Now, can you imagine me, a guy making three hundred and fifty dollars a week, sitting up shooting dice in a house in Hollywood with thousands on the line, Frank saying, 'Sam, shoot for me!' Now they're shooting *thousands* of dollars here! You know—five thousand dollars—and I got lucky one night and won, like twelve thousand dollars for him. Frank says, 'That's enough!' And he said, 'Here!' Just peeled some bills off and gave them to me and said to the driver he had at the time: 'Run Sam home. Look after him and come back and get me.' So I said my goodnights and when I got home I checked and there was like three thousand dollars in my pocket—money I'd crumpled up in my hand. He just *gave* it to me.

"I wanted to be like him so bad."

It was a prolific time. A powerful time. His music, his films, a mountain of work—had made him powerful. Many people wanted to be like him, live the life he seemed to exemplify. The Capitol years were definitely, in many ways, the ultimate years.

Of his mentor, the enormously versatile and prodigious performer Sammy Davis, Jr., said: "I wanted to be like him so bad . . ."

CHAPTER EIGHT
GROWING UP

Like Father . . .

I t wasn't easy, being a child of Frank Sinatra. So much to live up to. So many people competing for him. My brother had a particularly tough time. To get attention, he was always the clown. If they found anything wrong in the neighborhood, the cops would come to our house, because my brother and his friends were always clowning. Nothing drastic, but if the police, say, found something painted on a tree, our house was their first stop. I came home from school once and found two policemen in our living room talking to Mom and Dad. They were all seated around our square coffee table looking mighty serious. Some street lights had been shot out with a BB gun. Frankie, of course, was the prime suspect.

Then one night my brother got into real trouble. He was roaming around and ran into some gang kids he knew. They were laying for an enemy gang and he stayed with them. The police broke it up and took them in for violating a Los Angeles municipal curfew ordinance: they were twelve and thirteen years old —too young to be out after 10 P.M. without an adult.

My mother woke me at about 2 A.M. She said, "Will you come with me, please? I've got to get your brother out of jail."

My parents were rightfully concerned. And they made most major decisions about us together. After those first years of pain, Mom was able to be with Dad again. She was ahead of her time. There was little or no joint custody then. The woman took the kids, the man saw them on weekends, and that was it. For us, Mom dealt Daddy in. They were able to be friends. They still are.

They decided that Frankie should go to a boarding school. He had been living in a house with three females—four including the housekeeper—and they felt it was important that he experience a daily environment with men as well as women. They found an excellent co-ed school with a lot of male teachers and boys Frankie's age. It was located in Idyllwild, up in the mountains just above my father's house in Palm Springs. Dad or someone in his trust would

Nancy Sinatra: "George Sidney took this photograph in 1957 when FS was the man everybody wanted to be—tops in the polls, on the charts, and just about everywhere. Pete Hamill wrote these lines later, which seem to me perfectly to set the spirit, catch the mood."

"Take the chance, roll the dice, push your talent, love who you want to love, taste the wine, listen to the music, dance the dance.

"If you're knocked down, get up. Losing is nothing, for we all lose everything at the end.

"But we never win at all if we don't enter the fray."

Jack Benny: "At dinner, I happened to mention to Frank that I had a dozen beautiful gold watches and none of them kept good time, possibly because I never wound them. Three days later, I got this handsome Timex from Frank, who says it will run for a year and then you merely have to change the battery, which just costs a dollar.

"I can't wait until the year is up. I'm gonna send back the watch with a note and make him spend the dollar, saying that if you're gonna get me a present, I want the whole present . . ."

always be close by if there were an emergency.

For a while, Frankie was lonely and hurt. He said Mom and Dad had pushed him out, that they didn't want him. It wasn't until he was older that he thanked them for recognizing the danger he'd been in of becoming a statistic, one of those people whose lives have been wrecked by the pressures of being "Hollywood Kids." Soon he adjusted and made the best of it. He grew musically at the Desert Sun School, too. He started his own little band and when we visited they performed for us. His classical piano training served him well. They were good.

I was attending a Los Angeles public school—University High—with a blend of rich kids, poor kids, eggheads, cheerleaders, gang guys, lettermen, a few Jewish princesses, many WASPs, blacks, Latinos, Asiatics. I never wore good clothes to school. My cashmere sweaters stayed in my drawer, not because I was afraid of ruining them, but because I didn't want the other kids, the ones with less than we had, to feel bad. I tried to be just like everybody else—but it didn't always work out.

The YMCA and YWCA had a program in our high school called Hi-Y Tri-Y clubs. You joined one of several Tri-Y clubs and stayed with it through your high-school years. My Tri-Y was called the Tierres. Every year, aside from our volunteer work, we took part in a competition called "The Song Banquet." Each club presented a three-minute musical routine, with original lyrics, about school life and the Y.

I was song chairman of the Tierres. I was studying classical music and had a strong musical foundation to begin with, and every year, at our grade level, the Tierres won first place. One time, we did a particularly intricate routine based on Edvard Grieg's Concerto in A minor. I had taught the Tierres three- and four-part harmony and lyrics "Boom—Boom Boom Boom . . . Let's count our blessings, all that we possess, not wordly riches, but love and hap-pi-ness . . ." The judges gave us first prize and the parents of the kids in the other clubs said, in effect, "Hold it. They couldn't have done that Grieg thing by themselves. They must have had professional help. I mean, look at their song chairman. Look who her father is." You know, as if—give me a break—I wasn't capable of putting "Boom Boom Boom" to a concerto all by myself. And no matter that my dad hadn't even been in town for weeks.

Little by little, we were learning the price of fame by proxy, the struggle to find our own identity. In her own way my sister probably had the healthiest attitude. Tina Sinatra: "I was nine or ten before I realized he was *somebody*. I don't know why. I knew he was famous, but, still, I always wondered why people stared at me when I was with him. And I finally asked and he said, 'They're *not* staring at you, they're staring at *me*.' "

Tina was nine in 1957. It was a year with some sadness for FS; his good friend Humphrey Bogart died on January 14, and Dad, who was working at the Copa, could not do his show: "I'm afraid I won't be coherent." But mostly, it was a year of joy. His career was continuing to flourish. It was a time of bookings at the Sands Hotel, many of his finest Capitol recordings, exciting films, and TV and radio work. Even with the volume of engagements in those Fabulous Fifties, Sinatra managed a full social and personal life, rich with friends and his children and good times. It was a period of energy and tumult and rough edges and gemlike performances shaped and polished to an illuminating, sometimes blinding, brilliance.

Frank Jr.: "I can remember when 'Come Fly with Me' was released in

December of 1957 . . . waking up after this album had been shipped to the disc jockeys in L.A. and—during traffic hour, which is the biggest sales time on radio—I can remember the morning disc jockey at the top station in town playing the *whole* side of this album and saying, 'We'll be back with the second side of this new Sinatra album after this commercial.' Played the whole side of one album—and during traffic hour! *Nobody* did that."

Sinatra continued to work with Nelson Riddle, too. Frank Jr.: "In 1958 they did 'Only the Lonely,' which, for my money, is the greatest blues album that was ever made. This album should be available in drugstores by prescription only—because this is *death*, this record. Photographer John Engstead, who shot our family portraits, used to have records playing in the background when he was photographing people. When we went to his studio one year, he had 'Only the Lonely' sitting on the pile. I said, 'Do you use that?' 'No,' he said, 'I can't play that record anymore. I'd tell people to smile and nobody wanted to *smile* when this record was on.'"

Dad also began recording with Gordon Jenkins. Frank Jr.: "I asked him why he always changed arrangers. 'To get a different sound,' he said. 'Just to get a different sound on different records.'"

"Billy is driving," my father once said, "Nelson has depth, and with Gordon, it's all so beautifully simple that to me it's like being back in the womb."

It was excellent balance, excellent change of pace. Frank Jr.: "There are some singers who don't know how to pick a good orchestrator. There's one thing that Sinatra has, especially when it comes to music: taste. In picking arrangers. In picking songs. Some people are very good singers and pick the dumbest goddamn songs in the world. Other people are bad singers and they pick the greatest songs you ever heard in your life. Pop has both the taste to pick it and the tools to cut it."

As with Axel in the forties, with each of his key arrangers in the fifties, Sinatra gave and received respect. Nelson Riddle: "The man himself somehow draws everything out of you. And I always felt that my rather placid disposition had a beneficial effect on him. I was able to calm him down sometimes. He would start snapping at somebody and I would say—I don't know where the hell I got the nerve (I was in my early thirties then)—I'd say, 'Come on, pal, what's the point of doing that?' He'd give me a hard look, then he'd stop. I wish he'd had somebody around lots of those times when he wasn't in control. He could have done without that. He always felt like a fighter. He always felt combative against the world. He felt for some reason that the world was out to get him and he was gonna show 'em. I don't think he ever stopped that."

Billy May and Nelson were quite different. Frank Jr.: "Billy, in those days, was so funny. People would ask me, 'What's Billy May like?' I'd say, 'If Oliver Hardy had been an arranger he'd have been Billy May.' Billy used to come in wearing blue jeans and the trademark tennis shoes, and a Hawaiian shirt. He was crazy, but you couldn't get mad at him because he was so *funny.*"

The last song they were recording one night was "The Road to Mandalay." They went through it, and when they did "And the dawn comes up like thunder—*Bong!*—outta China . . . 'cross the bay," percussionist Lou Singer hit the gong cue with gusto.

Billy May: "That gong was big, like the one on the J. Arthur Rank movie logo. And when Lou hit it, it rang and rang. When Frank heard it the first time he said, 'Yeah! Let me hear it again.' *BONNGGG* . . . He said, 'Yeah, Billy.

Jackie Gleason and FS have been friends since the forties when they drove Toots Shor nuts signing his name to tabs, adding tips as big as endowments. Later, they did bits on each other's TV shows, "rehearsing" by phone, working from a few cues. Gleason once saw Sinatra in the shower and told him he looked like a "tuning fork."

Let's end it with the gong—and let the mother ring!' "

"And the dawn comes up like thunder—*BONG!*" That's the way they left it, wordlessly.

Frank Jr.: "Billy May *loved* him, Billy May adores Pop—all the arrangers do, because whatever they write he can sing . . . He also stays out of their way. 'Respect the date,' he always says, 'respect the date—it's his date.' He means that the arranger, it's his date. The arranger of the orchestra who writes for every instrument, including the singer, is like the director in a movie. He says, 'Jump!' You say 'How high?' When Pop and Billy worked on one album, they went into the booth to sit down and listen to the playback. The producer got up out of his chair and said, 'Frank?' Pop said, 'No, let Billy sit there—it's his date.' "

In terms of enjoying the good times, Dad and Billy were compatible, too. Billy May: "One time, we were doing some records at Capitol, and it was his birthday. I didn't know it was his birthday—nobody did—so we booked the date that day. And he came in—he'd been out celebrating before that—and we ran a thing down and I could tell he wasn't really into it at all. And I said, 'Is the lead-sheet o.k.? Can you read it all right?' And he said, 'I can't even *see* it.' So with that, he gave up and he invited the whole band up to his house for a party."

Guitarist Tony Mottola: "There is great mutual respect between Frank and musicians. In New York in the late 1950s I was doing a three-a-week TV show starring Perry Como. One day at rehearsal we were told Perry had laryngitis and could not do the show. Frank was in town at that time, I think on his way to Europe on holiday. The producer called Frank and asked if he would do the show for Perry. Frank said yes. The conductor, Mitch Ayres, was told that Frank was coming but had no charts [arrangements] with him, so Mitch had two of Perry's arrangers standing by to write some charts for Frank. When Frank walked in, he said, 'What was Perry doing on the show tonight?' Told there were arrangers standing by to write whatever he wanted to do, Frank said, 'No, we'll do whatever Perry had programmed. I'll use his charts.' And on the show that night he did just that. He made things so comfortable and pleasant for everyone."

Tony first knew Dad when they were teenagers appearing on radio station WAAT in Jersey City: "When people ask me, 'What is Frank Sinatra really like?' I tell them to me he is no different in one regard than he was when I knew him as a young kid. If he is your friend you could never have one more loyal."

And he expects loyalty in return. Sammy Davis, Jr.: "When a friend disappoints him, doesn't rally around him, does something morally wrong—by *his* standard of morality—that's it, man, Goodbye."

Once Dad thought that he'd been betrayed, somehow, by Bullets Durgom (the man whose mother thought FS was a priest). Bullets had managed Jackie Gleason in the fifties. When Gleason was not available for a show FS wanted him to appear in, no one explained that prior contractual commitments were impossible to break, although Gleason innocently had promised to do the show. "Next thing, *I'm* being blamed that Jackie can't go on." And so, as Bullets put it, "Frank refused to talk to me. For a few years."

But when they finally did get together, Bullets offered his refound friend a little advice. "Frank always believes what he hears. You can turn Frank against anybody you want. So I said, 'Frank, somebody tells you something, why don't you check it out? He can make an enemy out of a friend in a minute.' So now, it's okay between us."

"Respect the date. It's his date," i.e., the arranger's. (Left) FS, Jr. (Middle) Irving "Sarge" Weiss, with FS for forty years, a music man for all seasons. Record date—"Come Blow Your Horn."

1958. Sinatra once asked Dean Martin to come up to Lake Tahoe and work for a week. That was the arrangement: no talk of money, contracts, etc. After the date, both men were due in Las Vegas. Martin, known to be nervous about flying, asked, approaching the airport, "What kind of plane you got now?" Sinatra said, "See that big white plane there?" Martin nodded and FS said, "That's not it." Instead, FS's plane was "the little red French fighter jet," he had named the Interim *(while he waited for a bigger plane on order). In addition to making a marvelous contribution to Martin's fear-of-flying, it added to his intense claustrophobia. The cockpit of the* Interim *was tiny. Martin: "The pilot presses a button and this top glass slides over my head . . . Here's the pilot in front of me this far. I said, 'Where's the bar?' and Frank reaches down, gets a bottle of J&B, says 'Here.'*

"We're up about thirty-five thousand feet and Frank hands me a check. For a lot of money. 'Why didn't you give me this check down on the ground?' 'Because,' he said, 'you wouldn't have gotten on the plane, that's why."

Producer Howard Koch: "I learned never to talk to Frank on the phone about something important, because I never knew who was with him that might be egging him on or coloring his thinking. I was very careful never to settle anything unless we were together. And I know another thing, too: When he has his shoulders up, it's best not to get into any new discussions about projects, because he's going to be negative."

Koch understood. In the fifties, FS formed several movie production companies. With his ability to read people, he picked Howard Koch to head them. Howard later became president of Paramount.

With friends, he speaks in shorthand; certain things go unspoken, assumed. Sammy Davis, Jr.: "When I have a problem, Frank's conversations with me will go something like this: 'Are you okay, Smokey?' 'Yeah, I'm okay.' 'You're sure?' 'Yeah, I'm sure.' That simple and you know he's offering help."

As a teenager, I tried to be a good reflection on my dad. I was an A student and never had any serious problems—nothing that would cause bad press or even rumors. Of course, my mother deserves the lion's share of credit for raising all of us, but Pop was always there too, and if I needed to talk, I'd call and say "Daddy, I've got to discuss something." He'd say simply, "Shoot." I would spill it and he would listen and then give me a quick, thoughtful resolution. I never came away from a talk feeling unsettled or in limbo. He was decisive. That is a wonderful quality: right or wrong—make a decision. Don't leave yourself or anyone else stranded.

But you have to know how to read him.

Sammy Cahn: "Jimmy Van Heusen, Lillian Small, and I wrote the song, 'All the Way,' for his movie, *The Joker Is Wild.* We went up to Vegas to sing it to him and were told he would hear it before breakfast, which meant four in the afternoon. We were seated in the living room and the door opened and out he came looking like *all* the Dorian Grays. He looked at me, grimaced and said, 'You before breakfast—*yichhh!*' I looked back at him and said, 'Hey, from where I'm standing I'm not sure who is being punished more.' Van Heusen gave me an intro and we sang 'All the Way.' He listened, and when I had sung the last word and note, he turned and said, 'Let's eat.' We had a marvelous meal and we left. When we got outside, Lillian Small had tears in her eyes. 'How could he not like that song?' she moaned. I said, 'What song didn't he like?' She said, 'The song you just sang.' I said, 'Oh, he loved it!' 'How do you know?' she said. I said, 'He loves them all.' "

The song won an Academy Award.

The fact is, he assumes professionals will do their jobs well. Do your job poorly, you hear from him. Do it well, he usually says nothing. That's Dad's style. Do it right. "I'm a bottom-line guy," he says. Be professional. Don't waste time.

And be on time. He's compulsive about that. I remember following him, in my car, to a record session one night just after I got my license. I was a teenager, very proud that I could drive, and I wanted him to be proud of the way I drove the car. He was driving fast, but I was taking my time, stopping before the crosswalks, looking both ways. I was doing everything by the book, and I didn't know I was driving him crazy. I thought, "Why is he going so fast and then slamming on his brakes? Gee, that's strange, I wonder if there's something wrong with his *car?*" When we got to the studio, he said, "What the hell were you doing? I'm late." He wasn't late, he was right on the button of eight o'clock. I had forgotten he likes to arrive ten minutes early.

He's a man of action. The actress Eleanor Parker: *"Hole in the Head* was shot in the late fall of 1958, and mixed with the hard work and excitement of making what we all were sure would be an excellent picture was the hard work and excitement of Christmas and Christmas shopping. In conversations on the set about children and toys, I remembered that a favorite of all my kids was a toy pinball machine which had long since been sent on its way to toyland Valhalla . . . I was determined to move upward and onward: a real, store-bought professional superflasher of a pinball machine. But how? Well, never fear—Frank Sinatra is here! The machines are manufactured in Chicago and readily available by means of a catalog which would be brought to me at once, if not sooner. Action. What a relief. All I had to do was wait for the catalog, place my order. However, waiting for the catalog became an ordeal. Each passing day brought a reminder from me that time was getting short and each reminder was met with the cool assurance. He would bring the book the next day. Finally I was forced to the conclusion that the conversation was charming, but the pinball machine was TILT.

"A week before Christmas, the doorbell rang. I opened the door and there—fully grown and gaily bedecked with a patchwork of color papers and ribbons—was the machine, a gift from Santa Sinatra, whose card complained, *I couldn't get the catalog so here's the machine instead. I wanted to surprise you for Christmas but you're such a nag!"*

Actress Lee Remick: "My ex-husband was directing a television special with Frank. Working on it, Bill stayed up all night for something like four nights in a row. He fell asleep at the wheel of his car, got into an accident, and it was life and death. I was working on a movie in Tennessee and they called me, so my mother and I flew out to L.A. . . . We checked into the Beverly Hills Hotel and stayed there a week until they told me my husband was going to live. I had to go back to finish the movie, so I went to the desk of the hotel to take care of the bill. It had been taken care of. By Frank. Which I didn't understand, because I don't

Overleaf: The splendid head above the surge of seersucker belongs to composer and music master Jimmy Van Heusen. His "first formal job" for FS was Our Town. *To Nancy: "When the time came to run through the score for him, I went to your home. Conditions there made it slightly difficult to hear the seven songs for the first time [including "Love and Marriage"] . . . Tina and Frankie Jr. and you were all over his lap and your mother was in the kitchen getting some beautiful food ready and with the clatter of plates and kids underfoot it was not easy to impress him with my clever cantatas . . . Those were the lean years for him but there was nothing lean about his love for his family . . . and I watched it all, first with impatience because my cadenzas got clobbered but later with the great wish that I were as lucky as he . . ."*

143

believe I'd ever even *met* Frank at this point, and if I *had,* it was very briefly."

Bob Weitman: "In the fifties, Frank and Ed Sullivan were feuding. I was then with CBS. Ed Sullivan was putting on a show at the Maguire Air Force Base and on his way home after the show was in an automobile wreck and was near death. In the true tradition of our show business, where 'the show must go on,' I had received a call from Frank Stanton, who was the president of CBS. He said, 'Bob, do we cancel the show for next Sunday? What do you think we ought to do?' Frank at that time was doing a show on ABC. I talked to Frank and just said to him, 'The fellow that you are feuding with is in the hospital at death's door. What would you think of appearing on his show on another network?'

"And as only Frank could say, 'Where is Ed? What time do you want me?' He called Ed Sullivan, who was in an oxygen tent in a hospital. Sylvia Sullivan, his wife, answered the phone. Ed Sullivan was enormously touched by a fellow who was feuding him, an adversary, who was now going to host his show."

In 1958 Manie Sacks was dying of leukemia.

Herman Rush: "The doctor had issued standing orders—'No visitors,' but one afternoon the rule was broken by a young man on the thin side who stopped by the hospital, unannounced, to see Manie. 'Just say Frank Sinatra's calling.' Unexpected, unannounced, Sinatra had suddenly closed down production of *Kings Go Forth,* a movie he was starring in, covered the cost of a two-day shutdown personally, and had flown to Philadelphia to see Manie."

When Uncle Manie died, my father cried. He said, "When I holler for help, he ain't gonna be there anymore. There's a little bit of Manie in everything good that has ever happened to me."

The Sands

During this sadness, and the pressures of all Dad's work, there was a great need for relief, in many cases comic. Most of the joking took place at the Sands. Las Vegas was attracting worldwide attention and Sinatra remained the town's hottest draw.

Jack Benny: "Frank was playing the Sands, and I was in the audience and he knew I was out there, and the place was jammed, and he said, 'Ladies and gentlemen, I have a very dear friend in the audience' and he gives this very big buildup—and then he says, 'My friend, Jack Benny is in the audience.' I took a bow and said, 'Frank, can I say something?' He said, 'Certainly, go ahead.' I said, 'This place is so packed I thought *I* was playing here.' He fell on the floor laughing."

Jack Benny *always* broke up my father—made him laugh harder than anyone before or since. And, believe me, there's been lots of laughter in his life —especially in those Las Vegas days. There had to be, with people like Sammy Davis, Jr., and Dean Martin usually on the scene. Dean, in fact, is the funniest man I know. Once, Dad played a trick on him, told Dean that he had great seats for an important Dodger game and then took him up to the last row of the top tier. "I couldn't see anything," Dean told me. "From up there, it was a rumor. The game was a *rumor.*"

(On top of that, Dad had told Dean to bet the Dodgers. He did and they lost.)

There were lots of laughs in those late fifties and little sleep. Henry Silva:

"He never slept much; we were working on a movie. I said to him one morning, 'Frank, how much sleep did you get last night?' He said, 'I went to bed at six and got up at seven-thirty.'"

He's been like that most of his life: reads or talks on the telephone much of the night. Has breakfast with the early risers like Spencer Tracy (who would always lecture him about not sleeping) when his nighttime company can't stay up anymore. Silva: "He'd invite me to the house. At four in the morning, I'd get my jacket. 'Where you going?' he'd say. I'd say, 'Frank, it's four o'clock. I gotta get up soon.' I'd be there with Dean, Sammy, Leo Durocher. He didn't want anyone to leave. He'd actually get sad."

It was a wacky time.

Kirk Douglas: "In the wee hours of the morning, and after more than a few drinks, Frank insisted on waking up the manager of the Sands, Carl Cohen, a very nice Jewish man. Frank became obstreperous, an argument ensued, Carl Cohen punched Frank in the mouth and knocked him down.

"Most people avoided ever referring to this embarrassing episode. I couldn't resist, and asked Frank, 'What happened—did you and Carl Cohen have a fight in Las Vegas?' Frank was in an embarrassing situation and, to me, that is the test of a man. Frank paused, looked at me with his steely blue eyes, and said, 'Yes.' Then a twinkle came to his eyes and he added, 'Kirk, I learned one thing. Never fight a Jew in the desert.'"

Pianist Bill Miller: "At the Sands, he was doing a number with just me, just piano alone, and for some unknown reason, the sustaining pedal went out, and it clunked to the floor, and your Dad heard that and kept right on singing. And then the piano began to creak, and he heard *that*, and he kinda looked back, but he kept singing. And finally the right leg of the piano began to give, and all I could do was hold it up with my right knee till we finished the tune. It was a ballad, everything was quiet. We barely finished the tune, and I had to hop away from the piano because my leg was tired from holding up the entire piano and I knew it was gonna fall, and I had to get out of the way, so I hopped away and the piano toppled over, and Frank—remember, he'd kept singing all the while—finally he acknowledges it. The piano topples and he turns around to me and said, 'You having a little trouble back there?' Then he turns to the audience and says, 'Look at this: twenty-million-dollar hotel, dollar ninety-eight piano.'"

His discipline in hysterically funny, even slapstick, situations always amazes me. It's his concentration.

He always had style and he added stature. Henry Silva: "He invited me to a party, and every major star in Hollywood was there. And when Frank arrived, the sound went down, I don't know how many decibels. Happened all the time. The energy dropped and everybody focused on him. Whether they looked at him or not, the focus was on him."

I know what Henry is talking about. It is as if everybody takes a deep breath. And then, when the beat is over, the voices get louder—as if everybody

Soviet Premier and Mrs. Nikita Khrushchev visiting the set of Can-Can *in 1959. Khrushchev called the can-can dance number "immoral." * Newsweek *reported that advance ticket sales were bigger than those for* Ben-Hur, *adding, ". . . being condemned by Khrushchev may be an even bigger commercial than being banned in Boston."*

Above: Two phenomena, 1960, one once called "The Voice," the other, "The Pelvis." Nancy Sinatra found that the two men shared the same passion for the underdog. On the night Presley's daughter was born, he called Nancy at about 3 A.M. After the good news, she said, "You sound so sad." "I am sad," Elvis said. "I'm thinking of all the other babies born tonight. Especially the black ones, who have nothing to start with—and wondering what their future will be. I think I should have stayed in the church and become a preacher." Nancy told him that he had reached many more people with his music than from a pulpit.

is auditioning. I think this embarrasses Dad even now.

As I grew older, I became part of that life. When I graduated from high school, I enrolled in college—at USC. I loved school except for one problem familiar to so many students—the subjects that I wanted to take had so many prerequisites that I had to take two years of garbage in order to get to my major. I wanted music appreciation, but I ended up dissecting frogs and wondering what I was doing in college. I left school in my first semester to pursue a career as a singer. My father was deeply disappointed. He really wanted me to have the education he never had. But he gave me a job and a chance.

I was going to sneak into show business—on national television before millions of people on Frank Sinatra's special to welcome Elvis Presley back from the army. Elvis was to be discharged in January of 1960. I was in New York taking crash courses in voice, dance, and drama when two phone calls came. The first was from my boyfriend, singer Tommy Sands, who asked me to come home to Los Angeles and marry him. The second was from my father, singer Frank Sinatra, who asked me to go to Fort Dix to meet Elvis Presley's plane.

Going to Fort Dix was easy. At about ten on a snowy January morning, Elvis became a civilian. FS had asked me to take EP a welcome-home present and I did. On the advice of Elvis's manager, Colonel Tom Parker, I had picked out two ruffled tuxedo shirts and now presented them to Elvis along with Frank's regards. And Tommy's. Tommy and Elvis had been friends as kids and both had been managed by Tom Parker until the colonel, realizing what was about to happen with Elvis, decided Tommy should have another manager who could give him more attention.

The plan was for me to go from Fort Dix to New York's Idlewild Airport and home. Tommy was to meet me at the plane in L.A., with my mother—and an engagement ring. The weather didn't cooperate; the snow turned into a blizzard. Henri Giné, Dad's New York road manager, David Gershenson, Dad's New York public relations representative, Bob Smoren, Dad's New York driver, and Dad's L.A. daughter were stranded on the New Jersey Turnpike for ten hours. It was nearly 9 P.M. when we reached Weehawken, New Jersey. We went to 37 King Avenue, to Marty and Dolly's instead of to New York. Grandma said, "Where the hell have you been, for chrissake? I called the governor and he had the goddam state militia out looking for you." Then she sat us all down to the four-course meal she and Marty and Uncle Vincent had spent all day preparing. They knew I would come to them.

The next day I left for home. I boarded the plane at 9 A.M. The snow had stopped, but the weather was still so wicked that after each takeoff and landing the runway had to be de-iced. It took seven hours before my flight finally left.

I had told FS on the phone about my pending engagement, "Daddy, I have something to tell you." "Shoot." "I want to marry Tommy." "Are you sure about this?" "Yes." "Does he make you happy?" "Yes." "Okay, Chicken. If this is what you want." He didn't interfere or lecture on the hazards of being married to a singer. We both, of course, realized the obvious parallels. But, this was Hollywood, folks, and I was definitely a Hollywood kid—my feet firmly rooted in celluloid, in glorious Technicolor.

On September 11, 1960, I became Mrs. Thomas Adrian Sands. Frank Sinatra gave me away with tears in his eyes. Just before he walked with me down the aisle, he presented me with a pair of star-shaped diamond earrings, "to match the stars in your eyes." But this time I was leaving him. It was a new kind of goodbye.

CHAPTER NINE
THE
SUMMIT

Come Fly with Me

hey called themselves "the Summit." When they worked together, it was a summit meeting indeed, a gathering—within the entertainment world—of the top. Frank and Dean and Sammy. Joey Bishop. Peter Lawford. And whoever else from the upper ranks of show business—Bing Crosby, Milton Berle, Don Rickles, Judy Garland, Shirley MacLaine—happened to be around at that time and in that place.

The early sixties was their time and Las Vegas was their place. They made movies there and played nightclubs there and set a tone of arrogance and confidence, of energy and expectation that spoke to and for many of their generation.

They were in their forties, mostly—part of the generation now taking its turn at power, the generation that was forging, in politics, the New Frontier. And the man who, of course, best embodied all this was their friend.

John Kennedy had come into Dad's life some years before. Dad had met him when he was a senator, just after he married Jacqueline Bouvier. Dad remembers sitting around with some of that group during the Democratic Convention of 1956 and, the instant the '56 ticket was determined, hearing Bobby Kennedy say, "Okay. That's it. Now we go to work for the next one." For the 1960 Presidential election. Four years later. Not a minute to waste. FS was impressed.

Whenever J.F.K. or another person of prominence sat in the audience, Dad gave a colleague the honor of introducing him or her to the crowd. One time Dean Martin would do it, another time Sammy, and so on. I remember the night Dean said to a room that was full of extra excitement and some kind of tangible glow: "There's a senator here tonight and this senator is running for

They called themselves the Summit. And they had fun. Here, Dean Martin takes the fall and FS, Sammy Davis, Jr., Peter Lawford, Joey Bishop, and guest summiteer Buddy Lester (right) share the gag.

President or something and we play golf together, we go fishing together, and he's one of my best buddies" and he turned to FS and said, "What the hell *is* his name?" and John Kennedy started laughing . . .

It was a zany, irreverent bunch. They could say anything to each other, no offense, anything for a laugh, because they knew what was in their hearts. Billy May: "I was at Frank's house once, and Peter Lawford comes in with Pat. So, Frank—he's a gracious host—goes over to greet her. And Dean goes with him. And Sammy is across the room and he hollers at the top of his lungs: 'Get those dagos away from the President's sister.' "

Their racial and ethnic gags were awful and wonderful. No one was safe. FS said to Sammy on one occasion when the lights were low, "You better keep smiling, Smokey, so we can see where you are," but on another he forecast a future where "We're gonna' grow colored cotton and hire white pickers."

Dean: "One night Sammy came out on stage and did his dancing and he jumped on the piano and sat there. Sammy was through, but he wouldn't get off —just sat there on the piano. And Frank had to sing. So I just walked over and— Sammy only weighs about 110 pounds—I picked him up and I walked over to the mike and I said, 'I want to thank the NAACP for this wonderful trophy.' "

Poor Sammy. They had these stools they sat on up on the stage. They sawed the legs off his, made him sit on this little stool. Out on the putting green, they'd use regular golf clubs and make him use a miniature putter. Sammy: "We used to go to the steam room every day, and we all had these white robes, with our names on back. I came in one day and my robe's not there. I said, 'Where's my robe?' The attendant said, 'I'm sorry, Mr. Davis, but we had to get rid of your robe.' I said, 'Why did you get rid of my robe, man?' He said, 'Well, Mr. Sinatra told me to get you a new robe.' So he gets up and he gives me a brown robe, brown towels, and brown soap. 'Mr. Sinatra said you can't use the white soap or the white towels.' Frank comes out from behind a curtain: 'What the hell's going on out here?' I said, 'This is your idea of funny, huh?' And we all cracked up."

They were so wonderfully silly. Dad was singing the sentimental song "It Was a Very Good Year." As he sang the sweet lyric "When I was seventeen . . ." Dean Martin sang through an offstage mike, "You were a pain in the ass." Dean: "Frank broke up. Couldn't sing for two minutes." Dad quieted down, the room quieted, and everybody was back in the mood of the mellow ballad. Thirty-two bars, almost two minutes later, Dad was singing softly again, "When I was thirty-five . . ."

"You were still a pain in the ass," Dean yelled.

Jack Benny had taught Dad an important lesson. "I always open my show with three sure jokes," Jack had said. "Jokes I've used before. Sure shots. Never with untried material." Dad learned to do the same. He always opened with three sure shots—songs familiar to the audience as well as to him. This became a cardinal rule. One night, Dean came out to open one of their shows and instead of singing the songs he was supposed to do, he sang the three songs with which Sinatra planned to open. "Did them in the same key, too," he bragged later. Meanwhile, my father was in the steam room, out of earshot—as Dean knew— and when he appeared afterward to do his numbers, he sang them beautifully— but the applause was weak. Dean: "They're thinking, 'Hey, so what, not these songs again'—and Frank doesn't know what's going on." So much for cardinal rules.

That's the way it went, all the time, when they were at their summit together.

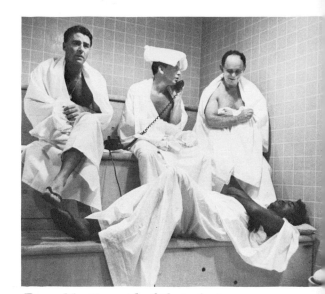

Dean Martin said of their first appearance in Las Vegas together: "We're in the steam room and Sammy came running in and said, 'Guess what?' I said, 'What is this, a knock-knock? What guess what?' He said, 'The room is filled.' Now, the Sands only held 325 people. We all thought it was so great. Yet here we were, five of the biggest people in the business, in our prime. We could have had 32,000 people. But filling the room? We never took anything for granted. None of us ever thought we were the greatest thing that ever happened. That's what's wrong with some performers today . . . They start at the top . . . Somebody gets a hit record. There's no way to go but down . . . You got to start at the bottom like we did. We all started at the bottom."

Peter Lawford: "I couldn't wait to get to work. Everybody was flowing on the same wavelength. It was so much fun. We would do two shows at night, get to bed at four-thirty or five, get up again at seven or eight, and go to work on a movie. We'd come back, go to the steam room, get something to eat, and start all over again—two shows. They were taking bets we'd all end up in a box."

Sammy: "It was like a team. The only thing missing was the marching band. You *had* to be in that steam room. Better not show up late. That was where everything began."

Dean: "We got Rickles in the steam room. He began mouthing off, abusing us. I held the door open while Frank was talking to him, and then I grabbed the towel he had around him, and Frank shoved him out. I closed the door, and there he was—outside with no clothes."

At one point, they were living in Vegas, doing two shows a night, and making a movie way out in the desert during the day. Dean: "Frank and I used to fly there in a helicopter, forty minutes. We did it two days and Frank looks at me and he says, 'This is boring.' So I said, 'What do you want me to do, throw you out?' He said, 'Something different!' I said, 'Forget about it, tomorrow it'll be different.' So I got up a little earlier than usual, I went to a gun store, I got two .22's. When we got on the helicopter—he didn't know I had them—I gave him one, a loaded .22. I said, 'Here, I guess you'll want to sit on the outside now. We can shoot some rabbits.' And time just flew by, he was shooting at anything, dust, as long as he had something to do. I started shooting across his face. He said, 'You're a little close there, dago.' Hell, I didn't want him to be bored, right?

"I mean, Frank and I are brothers, right? Blood brothers. We cut the top of our thumbs and we became brothers. He wanted to cut the wrist. I said, 'What, are you, *crazy?* No, here's good enough.' To me, he's always been my brother. We're alike."

They could kid around and call each other names in fun, but outsiders who did it with malice were in trouble. Dean: "Frank and I were at the Polo Lounge. We were with six other people, mindin' our business, and we were a little loud. When we were goin' out the door, there is a couple of guys, and one of 'em says, 'There goes the two loud dagos.' Well, Frank got there one split second ahead of me, and he hit one guy, I hit the other, picked 'em up and threw 'em against the wall. The cops came. We said we didn't know who did it and walked out."

Billy May: "Here's what Dean told the cops. Some civilian got floored and the cops were questioning Dean about what happened. 'I dunno,' says Dean. 'I just looked around and saw this guy laying there, passed out, and since that's usually *me*, I didn't pay any attention.' "

Sammy: "You've never seen such nuttiness in your life. Especially in Vegas. And it was mostly innocent fun, as compared to what people were thinking. We traveled as a group, man. And people couldn't get over it: 'Here comes Frank and Sam and Dean.' We'd go to a restaurant. Or into the lounge. And every night Frank would turn to me and say, 'We're all *men* sitting here; where are all the broads?'

"Sometimes he'd say, 'Smokey, I don't see nobody pretty here!' So one night I got dancers—chorus girls. I called up some friends and I said, 'I want ten from the Stardust.' Then, I called for ten from the Frontier. I said, 'They're all going to meet Frank Sinatra and Dean Martin.' While our show was going on, I had a big table set up in the lounge. We walked into the lounge that night, here sat all these girls, man! Oh, there must have been twenty, twenty-five. Frank

1960. To the Summit at the Sands, for much the same reasons— laughter, music, enjoyment, relaxation—came another man, a senator, on his way to a higher summit.

155

My funny Valentine
sweet comic Valentine
you make me smile
with my heart . . .

A haunting photograph of Marilyn Monroe, seated ringside.

said, 'You're crazy!' I said, 'Let me introduce you.'

"So all the girls were sitting around, and Frank was being Mr. Social. By four-thirty, almost everybody was gone. And I got a chick, but every time *I* tried to make a move out of there, Frank would say, 'Hey, where are you going, Smokey? Sit down! Listen—come here! You remember this story—when we—' And it was six o'clock in the morning and my girl was gone and he was still telling me stories. Just the two of us. Then, finally, we're walking back to his suite. It was broad daylight, just me and Frank and the security guys from the hotel, and walking back I said to him, 'I hope you're satisfied. There must have been twenty-five girls there.' 'Yeah,' he said, smiling. So I said, 'Then why am I alone with you?' "

Yet, for all the revelry, there was a reputation that grew beyond common sense. Few people knew the real story about most of his drinking. At a party once, he had a drink in his hand and he told me, "You take a couple of sips and you put it down in one corner and you walk away and they give you another drink and they think you're drinking a lot. It's important. They think you're as relaxed as they are, but you don't have to drink." He wasn't saying, "This is what *you* should do, Nancy." He was saying, "This is what *I* do." And I remember thinking, "Oh, is that how he does it?"

When he was in pain, or in need of comic relief, he could get good and

Martin said: "I have a partner now. Frank. I wake up in the morning and I don't worry about where I'm working; I worry about where he's working. And if I'm working with him." Then Dean explains, helpfully, "You see, Frank never had a partner before because nobody likes him."

They were all partners, of a sort, and headquarters was the steam room, which brought out their worst in practical jokes, their candid confessions, and the residue of the nights before. Occasionally, on stage, they were joined by a favorite female pal— Shirley MacLaine, Judy Garland —but it was basically a male club. An actress once said, "Frank is a very attentive man. But I don't understand him. He takes me out, then seems to spend most of the evening talking to the guys."

drunk . . . usually with a couple of friends to share his misery or mirth. But socially, in that goldfish bowl, he didn't. He would never be drunk. And we're speaking of the sixties now, when the other guys could really get stoned, when the *world* was getting stoned. He could always sing well; was always alert for work. He used to have fun—but always controlled. He could keep late hours because he never slept much. I've always felt he's had trouble sleeping because he just doesn't want to waste that precious time.

So, there was exaggeration—particularly about the drinking and the romances. Sammy: "Shirley MacLaine used to hang out with us. Crazy Shirley. She was one of the *guys!* None of us ever hit on Shirley. She said once, 'Here I was, surrounded by the most attractive men in the world, and they made me feel like a *boy!*' "

They ruled Las Vegas. Late at night, Dad and Dean and Sam used to go out in the casino and deal. The dealers would just step aside and these crazy guys would get behind the table and let everybody win. You know, turn up both their cards, so anybody would know whether to hit or not. If the dealer had twenty showing—that is, if Sinatra had twenty showing—and you had nineteen, he'd just keep hitting you until you got two aces or a deuce and then he'd take the extra cards away and say, "Okay, you've got twenty-one." And pay you with the House's money.

And, in one sense, why not? He and his friends were pulling in the people who played at the tables and the machines and put the money in the House's bank.

Grandma loved to play the slot machines. And she did *not* like to lose. So they'd rig a machine for her. Put it out of order to everyone else, then kind of dance Grandma to the right machine where she'd hit jackpot after jackpot.

"Summit" was exactly the right word, a summit of high spirits and high rolling and high living and laughter and song. When Tommy and I were married at the Sands, the bellmen kept stuffing envelopes under our door all night— gifts of money from the staff and the high rollers.

Sammy: "Oh, those were glory days. If we're together now for more than two or three hours, whatever the evening is we wind up relating some incident, something about that period. Because that Camelot time—that was a special time."

The Emperor

My father has dear friends who are not Presidents or performers.

One member of the gang was Michael Romanoff. Michael was their "emperor." Though born not in Russia but in Brooklyn, and not Romanoff but Gergenson, he adopted a royal Russian identity and bestowed gifts of land or water on his subjects, Frank, Sam, Dean, Jimmy Van Heusen. If Dad did something especially well, Michael would say, "Well done, old boy," and make him a gift of the Ural Mountains.

If FS did something to displease the emperor, Michael would take the gifts back. Michael and his wife Gloria were part of the intimate circle of friends Dad loved. He was the proprietor of Romanoff's Restaurant in Beverly Hills and was unique. A darling man, with great style. Gentle, kind and so homely he was beautiful. Many years older than FS, he became something of a father figure. I think until Grandpa moved out to California it was a toss-up as to who took his place in Dad's life, Michael or Bert Allenberg, Dad's agent. In any event, between Michael and Gloria and Bert and Millie Allenberg, Dad had a place to go—to relax and to talk things over.

FS had Michael with him whenever possible. Europe, Las Vegas, New York. Michael went to Miami Beach for the filming of *Tony Rome* and ended up with a featured role in the movie. He was a welcome guest in my mother's home and he taught my brother to play chess.

On one trip from L.A. to London and back, Sinatra and Dean Martin began their longest-running gag. They picked Michael up, as Dad said, "dressed in his London clothes with bowler and umbrella—very natty. We stole his cigarettes in the car and fixed the pack." Fixing the pack meant breaking the cigarettes in two without disrupting the cellophane. They would do it from the bottom of the pack and tape it carefully back together. And when Michael went for a smoke, he'd pull out a piece of a Chesterfield and stick the little stub in his mouth and do a very slow burn which would put the Katzenjammer kids (FS and Dean) completely away.

They fixed the cigarettes on the airplane. They had phoned ahead to the Savoy Hotel in London and had the packs fixed in the suite. They did the same thing with each restaurant. Wherever they went, the dandified Michael ended up with cigarette stubs. They told him that Chesterfield must have something against him and tried very hard not to laugh as that sweet man carefully opened each "new" pack.

They were in London to do *The Road to Hong Kong* as a favor to Bing Crosby, and when the cameo was finished they decided to do a little shopping. Michael took them to a tie shop and asked them to choose what they wanted. The store made the ties to order; all they had to do was pick out any fabrics they liked. Dad and Dean declined with thanks but Michael ordered six ties.

Later, back at the hotel, Michael was taking a nap when the ties were delivered. So Dad and Dean seized the opportunity to "improve" the ties. They cut most of the threads in the seam that joins both ends of the ties—the part that goes under the collar in the back. When Michael came out of his room for cocktails FS said offhandedly, "Your ties were delivered, old boy. They're in the package on the table." Michael said, "Thank you. I give you the Volga River," and took one out, asked the guys if it went as splendidly with his trousers as he thought, and put it around his neck. He began to slide it under his collar as a man does by pulling back and forth on each end and—rrip—he had half a tie in each hand. He did a take and Dean, who was leaning against the wall, began to wilt from holding back the laughter. Dad flashed him a *"Not now!"* look and Michael went on to the next tie. Same thing. Next natty tie, same thing, in two parts. The following day Michael and friends went back to the store and faced the poor salesman. Dad said, "Michael was so angry he threw the ties right in the guy's face." The clerk was terribly distressed and insisted the ties were fine when they left the shop. They had been carefully inspected. There comes a pause. Michael asked Dean and Dad who could have played such a nasty trick. They said Vic Damone, who was working in London at the time.

Meanwhile, Michael was still going along with the cigarette gag. His last stronghold was his own cigarette case, which he guarded closely. The night they left for home, Michael had a few drinks and Dean managed to pinch his gold case and slip it to Frank who fixed the contents so that when they got on the plane, Michael couldn't smoke there either, unless he developed a taste for fragments.

At London's Heathrow Airport the three turned toward the first-class lounge.

"I'm sorry, sir," said the hostess, "but your seats are in coach." Dean said, "I didn't sit in the back when I was a bum, are you crazy? Sit back there with all the guys in the white shirts?" Frank said, "Neither do I. What are you talking about?" The girl said, "It says here that you called and asked that we change your tickets. Your seats are in the back." Whack! Michael slammed his umbrella on the counter, causing airport security to rally round. "What do you mean? My friends and I never travel any other way but first class." Whack! "I'm so sorry," said the girl, "but you did call, Mr. Sinatra." Dad and Dean looked at each other and said, "Vic" . . . Vic Damone could imitate Frank's voice. Vic *had* done this trick.

In New York, Dad called ahead about the cigarettes to "21"—same business. When they arrived they were met at the steps by writer Harry Kurnitz who, when he saw Romanoff, promptly threw himself face down in the snow in a gesture of respect. Michael calmly stepped over him, pronouncing Kurnitz "A good subject," and strolled into the restaurant. Dad said it was one of the funniest sights he ever saw.

All the cigarette packs in our New York apartment, Suite 2500 in the Waldorf Towers, were fixed. By this time Michael was looking forward to his wife and his home and a return to some semblance of sanity. When they arrived at the Romanoffs' house in Beverly Hills Michael got out wearily and the guys said, "Hey, old boy, where are your manners? Aren't you going to invite us in for a drink?" Mannerly Michael, tired as he was, said, "Of course."

Gloria greeted them warmly and served up cocktails while Michael, confident and secure in the sanctity of his own home, picked up a new, sealed pack of Chesterfields from the bar, sat back, relaxed at last, and pulled a cigarette from the pack—only to end up with another stub. He looked at the little half cigarette in his fingers . . . looked at Frank . . . looked at Dean . . . slowly turned to his wife with a look that said, *"Et tu,* Gloria?"

Soon after their return home, Vic Damone went to Romanoff's for dinner. Michael had him thrown out.

Some of the best parties were at the house of Rosalind Russell and her husband, the producer Frederick Brisson. Rosie, as Dad called her, was a lovely lady and a great hostess and her home reflected the warmth she felt for her friends. The Brisson bar was a cozy beige hangout . . . One Brisson wedding anniversary was especially memorable. After a luscious dinner, laved in aquavit (served in glasses that would not stand up, so you had to polish off the drink before you put the glass down on its side, or forever hold it), the guests went into the darkened living room and sat down. Each guest was blindfolded and issued brown paper sacks filled with strange-feeling stuff. Then we were told to open the bags. The idea of the game was to make a hat out of the contents of the bag, and the best hat would win. The bags were full of feathers, tinfoil, ribbons, pieces of tulle and chiffon, satin, beads, sequins, paper clips, and Scotch tape. The giggling and the language of this kindergarten group was raucous enough, but when time was called, the lights were turned on and all the guests were told to wear their creations. It was a surrealist fantasy—Kirk Douglas in red feathers, Bill Goetz in beaded mesh with a pink bow; all would have challenged Lilly Daché, but my dad's was the simplest and most elegant solution. Leaving all the materials and frills and baubles on his lap, he wore the paper sack on his head.

"The Emperor," Michael Romanoff, with one of his loyal subjects, poolside at Sinatra's Palm Springs place. Said subject made Romanoff the butt of a long-running gag. (See text.)

CHAPTER TEN
DISCRIMINATION

What Is America to Me?

ammy Davis, Jr., is part of our family. Sam and I and Frankie and Tina and Dad went to the opening of Disneyland together. Sam and I and Frankie and Tina and Dad went to Atlantic City together. A birthday in the Sinatra family, Sam was there. A wedding, Sam was there. A funeral, Sam was there.

Sammy was a part of us. The color of his skin was never an issue.

It was, though, with other people. And sometimes surprisingly so. When John Kennedy was elected President, Dad produced and starred in the Inaugural Gala. Laurence Olivier performed, and Bette Davis, Leonard Bernstein, Milton Berle, Gene Kelly, Jimmy Durante, Juliet Prowse. But although there were blacks in the show, Harry Belafonte, Sidney Poitier, Ella Fitzgerald among them, Sammy Davis was not. He was planning to marry a famous white actress and the politicians, Sam later told me, "thought that was a little too controversial for the time."

Sammy Davis, Jr.: "Peter Lawford called me on the phone. He said, 'Sam, I know you understand these things. They've got those rednecks down there and, well, The Man thinks it would just smack of . . .' 'The Man?' 'The President, yes.' I said, 'Hey, don't worry about it, man.' I never mentioned it, never brought it up with Frank."

Frank knew. He has confirmed the facts for me. He has told me it was one of the few times he ever felt at such a loss. In the past he'd always been able to help Sammy. In the years when blacks had not been allowed to live or gamble in the major Las Vegas hotels, when Sam had to stand behind a white friend who would place his bets, Dad had been able to protest, had helped bring about change. But now he could do nothing.

Las Vegas, 1960. The wedding of the actress May Britt and
Sammy Davis, Jr. Frank Sinatra, best man; Shirley Rhodes (right,
wife of Sammy's conductor, George Rhodes), matron of honor.
Sammy is, for all the Sinatras, a member of the family.

Sam was crushed. He adored J.F.K. Shortly after Sam received that embarrassing phone call, I had an experience that helped illuminate my own small understanding of how hurt he must have felt.

My husband Tommy and I made a trip to Nashville for a recording date. We flew there in Dad's plane. FS was always security-conscious, so to look after us he sent along his houseman, George Jacobs, a kind, friendly man.

Arriving in Nashville, we went to our hotel. We had made reservations well in advance and didn't have to wait in line. The desk clerk saw us approach and quickly welcomed us: "Mr. and Mrs. Sands, one double, and Mr. George Jacobs, one single." Tommy said the information was correct and the clerk gave him the room keys.

George was still outside, dealing with the luggage. We went to our room and waited for him. The phone rang and the desk clerk asked Tommy to come down. I went too. George was at the desk. The clerk said, "I'm sorry, but Mr. Jacobs can't stay here." I didn't know what he meant, but Tommy, who was born in Louisiana, did. So did George. I said, "Why can't he stay here?" It really didn't hit me, I swear. I was so stupid. The clerk said, "This hotel is for white people only."

I was never so shocked. The word "prejudice" had never connected before. Never gone from my head to my guts. It wasn't just the icy reality, it was the blatant disregard for another person's feelings. This sonofabitch was so matter-of-fact, so *cool* about it.

George was sweet, saying, "Don't worry, Nan, I'll stay someplace else."

"If *you* stay someplace else," I said, *"I* stay someplace else." Tommy agreed and told the bellman to take the bags and get us a taxi. Meanwhile Joe

Big night, big snowstorm. With Jacqueline Kennedy at the J.F.K. Inaugural Gala, which FS had organized and produced. Said J.F.K., "We're all indebted to a great friend, Frank Sinatra. Long before he could sing he was pulling in votes in a New Jersey precinct . . . Tonight, we saw excellence."

Performers against prejudice have a chance to set the example. (Here, FS, Sammy Davis, Jr., and Rosalind Russell.) Said Sinatra in 1968: ". . . I don't know why we can't grow up. It took us long enough to get past the stage where we were calling Italians 'wops' and 'dagos' but if we don't drop this 'nigger' thing we just won't be around much longer."

Cool, the clerk, is saying, "I don't think any of the Negro hotels will allow you to stay, Mrs. Sands."

I was determined that we would all stay in the same hotel. I called Dad from a pay phone and he told me that, since it was late, maybe we should spend the night there, let George find another place, and he would make some calls in the morning. I figured he meant to the governor of Tennessee. But I was *so mad* I would have none of it. FS said, "Okay, do what you have to do."

We went to the other side of town. The cab driver took us to what he felt was the best "Negro hotel." It was run-down, dilapidated. But we were together.

Just for a while, I had felt the effects of racial prejudice—the anger, the humiliation. I never looked at Sam the same way after that. Not because of his color but because of his *dignity* in enduring and rising above that rot.

As part of our family, Sam spent a great deal of time over the years sharing meals at my grandparents' home. A true Italian meal can last several hours, and Sunday dinner at Marty and Dolly's house usually consisted of as many as nine courses. First an antipasto—marinated olives, roasted red peppers, mozzarella cheese sliced with tomatoes, potatoes and red onions, eggplant parmigiana, marinated garbanzo beans, anchovies, mushrooms. Then a starter course—shrimp scampi with garlic butter, or clams, or calamari, accompanied by a raw vegetable tray. Next a pasta course—spaghetti or ziti or mostaccioli, homemade cavitelli or homemade gnocchi, or perhaps ravioli or canneloni or fettucine. A meat course—beefsteak, pork, or veal, possibly meatballs and homemade sausage, or a real treat, braciole, veal pounded thin and spread with herbs and pine nuts, then rolled like crepes and cooked in tomato sauce. Still another course—cooked greens, usually bitter, like escarole or *broccoli di rapa,* with a little olive oil and garlic. Then chicken—cacciatore style or with a white wine and herb sauce. And finally a cold, crunchy green salad, followed by dessert and espresso with anisette or sambuca.

Each course would be accompanied by an appropriate wine and followed by a rest or break, which was always filled with great conversation. The time spent at the table was warm and happy and guests shared in the warmth that radiates from Italian families, shared the camaraderie and the passions of Italians.

Italians *love* food. Italians *love* music. Italians *love* Italians. There's a lot of hugging among Italians—I grew up with so much *hugging.* And Italian men embrace other men, warmly and without restraint. The love and loyalty in an Italian family is so pervasive, so important.

In the early 1960s the place where I—and my father—felt this sense of family strongly was at Cal-Neva, a lodge and gambling casino in Lake Tahoe, on the California-Nevada border. Dad was an owner of Cal-Neva, pronounced Kal-Neeva. He designed it to accommodate his dreams.

Uncle Ruby—his trusted friend Irwin Rubinstein of Ruby's Dunes Restaurant in Palm Springs—ran the dining room, and another dear friend, Skinny D'Amato, of the 500 Club in Atlantic City, ran the showroom. Cal-Neva was a place to go, a place to work, a place to be together. We all needed time with Dad and the lake offered us a quiet, peaceful time with him.

Like Dad, Cal-Neva was unpretentious yet glamorous, homey yet exciting. It reflected his ideas, even his favorite colors—beige, orange, brown. Everything and everyone in the place was hand-picked by Frank Sinatra. To say that

Dolly Sinatra, mother of FS, still rising to an occasion, characteristically. Having told her story, she sits down to applause from family and friends and a hug from her grandson, Frankie.

"Dinner at Marty and Dolly's," writes the author of her grandparents, "lasted several hours and nine courses. Italians love food. Italians love music. Italians love Italians. Maybe that's why I grew up with so much hugging . . . and so much laughter."

he had worked hard to make Cal-Neva a success would not begin to approximate his effort. But it was worth it—a dream come true, a Sinatraland with bright lights, music, gambling. It offered night life and razzle-dazzle juxtaposed with natural things: clear water, clean air, giant trees, outdoor sports, and the purple mountains.

I remember endless views of the lake. I remember how well Tommy sang there, in the high altitude. I remember my mother's smiles. She came up there a lot, and that was so important to me. We could all be together again up there. Even though my father's romances were with others, he and Mom did spend time together at Cal-Neva. I loved seeing that, reinforcing my dream that perhaps there was a chance for a reconciliation. God, we were all so happy there.

And then. And then in 1963 we were threatened with the loss of Cal-Neva. The threats were born of discrimination. Not as overt as the discrimination against Sam, or George Jacobs. Subtler, but discrimination nevertheless.

The buzz word was "Mafia." The mob. For years, people—particularly some of the right-wing press—had been making allegations about Frank Sinatra's "ties to organized crime." Investigating those "ties," some law enforcement officers from Nevada once came to Los Angeles County Sheriff Peter Pitchess for help.

Peter Pitchess: "I told them, 'I have probably spent more time investigating Frank Sinatra than any other man or organization. First, because I was active in the intelligence section of the FBI when I was an agent; then as sheriff; then because Mr. Sinatra is my personal friend and I *had* to find out to protect my career. And let me tell you something: You might just as well go home because you're not going to confirm any of those things.' "

Had Frank Sinatra been with mob guys? Sure. And so had all the singers who played the saloons and clubs when he was coming up, and he had known the old ward heelers, too. Many of the bootleggers, men who ran the speakeasies during Prohibition, had remained in the nightclub business after drinking became legal. And many had remained linked with people who operated outside the law, in big and small cities around America, including, when the action moved there, Vegas and Reno in Nevada. Some, I hasten to add, were not Italian but Jewish or Irish. A lot of Americans made their living and earned their first fortunes that way.

After Prohibition, many of the speaks became legitimate jazz clubs. "Swing Alley," Fifty-second Street between Sixth and Seventh avenues, was the mecca in New York. Dad remembers late night trips to Leon and Eddy's, Kelly's Stables, Tony's Wife (where he loved to listen to Mabel Mercer), 3 Deuces, Club 18, Onyx Club, and The Famous Door (owned by Lennie Hayton, run by Dad's old friend Sam Weiss, and so named because all of the famous patrons signed the door as they entered!). Through the postwar days, the people who owned the speaks tended to own the clubs. The guys who operated the speakeasies were qualified to run nightclubs. They knew the rules. They were also, most of them, in their own way, bighearted.

If a performer who worked the club circuit was down and out, a place like Mr. Kelly's in Chicago would give him a job. Then when the guy was back on his feet, and in some cases a star, he would go back and play Mr. Kelly's for $150 a week or for nothing to return the favor. That's the way it worked.

Even I had known those people all my life. That was the simple fact of being on or around the club circuit. I'd hear those names and I'd say to myself,

"Oh, my God. This one's just been questioned in a murder. This one's under investigation for tax evasion." And they're sitting with you, talking about their families—their wives and their kids and their grandchildren.

Frank Sinatra, Jr.: "I was singing in some dive in the Midwest once, a converted old movie theater with a rickety old stairway in the back. And I'm in this funky dressing room when an FBI agent I know comes up, with his children, for autographs. I sign and he goes down the stairs with his children and coming up the stairs with *his* grandchildren is this man who's number one in the town, *really* the Godfather. And they're waving to each other on the stairs. I'm standing there in the doorway with my tuxedo on and I say, 'I don't believe this. I thought you guys were bitter enemies.' And the young FBI agent looks at the old man and he says, 'That's only during business hours. How are you?'

"The old man says he's fine.

" 'Good,' the FBI guy says. 'I'll see you in court.'

"Nancy, I've worked for organized crime figures all my life. In nightclubs. In Vegas. Me and everybody else."

Ask Dean Martin, ask Danny Thomas, ask Jerry Lewis, ask anyone who came up on the club circuit and you'll be told without hesitation that crime figures were on the scene. And that these crime figures, going back to bootlegging days, have not been exclusively Italian. But put a vowel at the end of a performer's name and there's suspicion that he is not merely on the periphery of that criminal element, but part of it. And *that* is discrimination.

Because Sinatra has been king of the hill among Italian performers he has suffered the most from this prejudice.

In the bestselling novel *The Godfather*, the author creates a character, a singer, who is "owned" by the mob. The press and some of the public assumed the character *had* to be Frank Sinatra. Well, my father *is* a character, all right, and the Mario Puzo fiction is based on facts. But the facts pertain to another performer.

My father was a victim of old prejudices in September 1963, when the Nevada gaming commission tried to take away his license to operate a gambling casino, a license he needed if he was to make a success of his Cal-Neva Lodge.

They came after him on the grounds that the Chicago crime boss, Sam Giancana, had been at Cal-Neva—a violation of Nevada law since Giancana, as a known criminal, was blacklisted from all gambling establishments. In his newspaper column Hank Greenspun, publisher of the Las Vegas *Sun* and a tough investigator of the mob, reacted to the investigation with disbelief:

"I will not attempt to characterize the ridiculousness of the move to revoke singer Frank Sinatra's gaming license at Lake Tahoe but I do object to the efforts of the control board to make fools of the public.

"Frank Sinatra is not a hoodlum, has never been accused of such and has not been identified by anyone as a member of any crime syndicate in the country . . .

"The gaming members know or should know that Giancana appears wherever Phyllis McGuire of the singing McGuire Sisters plays . . .

"In short, the fellow was visiting his girl as he has done hundreds of times in Las Vegas . . .

"It might be suggested to the gaming control board that there might be some operators in the gaming business who also might have associations with known hoodlums. It might even be suggested that some licensees are known hoodlums.

Dorothy (Dot) Uhlemann, executive secretary to Sinatra. FS: "I love and admire the best secretaries, by whatever title, for all the flak they get, for all the good they do. I'm not an executive in the usual nine-to-five sense; I'm more a five-to-nine man, or a little later, given the nature of my work. For years I've been blessed by Dot, who is warm, sweet, a detective, a people-finder, and who is never upset—one of the formidable qualities in any woman or man. I envy people who are gentle, I suppose, because gentleness has never been my strongest suit. (Though sometimes I try a little tenderness . . .)

"We have a fine young woman in our office, too, Lori Anderson, and I'm reminded of how secretaries are sometimes the least-appreciated people on the scene. The unfeeling boss gives his computer more respect . . .

"Trying to explain Dorothy is like trying to explain every leaf in a tulip, and what makes each color more beautiful than the other."

"And these are not talented entertainers that we are talking about but actual killers.

"So with all the horrible record of criminal associations that many members of the gaming industry have and which have not been severed, the only person chosen as a sacrifice to gaming rectitude is Frank Sinatra."

At the time of the investigation Dad was negotiating to sell Reprise, the record company he'd founded three years before, to Warner Brothers. The Reprise deal was potentially very profitable for him. Cal-Neva, in the meantime, had not been doing too well financially. Open only on weekends once summer ended, the lodge was dependent on strong summer revenue and the 1963 summer season had not been too successful.

Dad had a conversation with the Nevada State Gaming Board in which he asked them to not interfere with the last opportunity to make some money for the summer season, knowing that he would only be open on weekends from then on.

Dad's attorney, Milton (Mickey) Rudin: "When that request was refused, the conversation went from civil to something that was considered rather strong language. This resulted in disciplinary proceedings being brought against Cal-Neva and your father, threatening the loss of the gambling license. They raised the question that Sam Giancana had visited Cal-Neva sometime in the early part of August. We were prepared to prove that your father did not know that Sam Giancana was there, had not invited Sam Giancana, and that in fact he [Giancana] had not stayed at Cal-Neva Lodge. We made full preparations to oppose the disciplinary proceedings and, even if we lost at the administrative level, to take an appeal, because this was clearly an unfair situation."

While these proceedings were pending, Mickey Rudin got a call from Jack Warner, the head of Warner Brothers. Warner insisted that Rudin come down to see him immediately. He told Mickey that if Dad was going to become associated with Warner Brothers and be listed as an executive, Warner did not want all of the newspaper publicity concerning Nevada and the Giancana incident. Warner said, "I know it's all bullshit about Giancana, but I'm tired of the image of Las Vegas. I like having Frank as a partner, but if he's going to become involved in Warner Brothers Pictures and own a third of Warner Brothers Records, I think he should not go on with this hearing."

Warner made it quite clear that if Dad did not surrender his license and thereby end the proceedings, the deal was to be called off. Warner's ultimatum left no room for discussion. And although he was all "warmed up to oppose the revocation of the license," ready to contest it and prove they were wrong, Mickey went to their lawyer in Nevada and said, "Reverse paths, turn in the license. I can't make both deals."

My father, a passionate man, was unable to fight back.

Dad authorized Mickey to surrender the license. He never went to a hearing—just terminated the license. But a deeper reason he did not fight back, Dad told me, was not because of Warner Brothers, but because the investigation was potentially embarrassing to his friend President Kennedy. He cared more about Kennedy than he did about proving he was right.

The President's brother, U.S. Attorney General Robert Kennedy, was overseeing a serious fight against organized crime. Ultimately, Bobby Kennedy waged a successful war against "corruption in Nevada's gaming industry." But like an antibiotic, he destroyed a lot of the good life as well as the bad. Frank Sinatra was the single most visible figure in Nevada in those days, so he took

Nancy Sinatra: "He admired Jack Kennedy, as we all did, worked for him in the 1960 campaign, raised money for him. And made him laugh.

"Henry Silva, an actor friend, remembers the time when J.F.K. was sitting at a table at the Sands and a busboy, moved by the moment, shouted out a toast—'To the next President of the United States.' "

Silva: "The thing that really got me was that Kennedy said, in a quiet voice, 'I hope so.' Like a little boy. It was so real. 'Cause there's a little child in all of us and he allowed that to come through. It was really a moment of magic."

Nancy: "It was all magic. For this patriotic American dreamer, it was the ultimate compliment that the President of the United States was his friend."

Sinatra (here shown in "the Kennedy room") made plans for a new visit from the recently inaugurated John Kennedy. The visit never took place. The plaque marks an earlier visit. Said Frank, when Kennedy was gone: "For a brief moment, he was the brightest star in our lives. I loved him."

most of the flak. He took it because he was Sinatra. He survived it because he was *innocent.* It's that obvious and just that simple.

But he paid an insurmountably high price for being Sinatra. He lost his license, he lost his dream, Cal-Neva, he suffered the pain of public criticism. He never lost his self-respect because he was innocent: he'd been used.

What hurt me most was that I couldn't share his pain. He has always tried to protect us from *all* pain, so it figured that he would keep me a safe distance from his. Still, I hadn't felt this inadequate since the breakup of his marriage to Ava when I was only a kid and unable to help. In my mind, he never recovered from not being able to fight to save Cal-Neva—and his reputation.

One of the keys to my father's personality is his ability—perhaps his need—to express his feelings, at the time, to the right person. In burying his desire to make this a fight to the finish (even though it would have hurt him financially), he buried a lot of anger. He wasn't used to harboring ill-feelings forever, and it is this result of the Cal-Neva incident which he bore from then on. The press, of course, had a field day. Or week or month.

Suddenly a new element was forced into his core—one with which he had great difficulty. It took away what was left of naïve beliefs; it encouraged him to carry a grudge. It made him defensive. Up until then, his problems with the press, family, friends had been solved or resolved one at a time. From this point on, general statements were made—Frank Sinatra versus the American press—instead of small, separate disputes with individuals. The mythical war began. But he had made his choice. He never blamed anyone else. But for once, he didn't get mad and he couldn't get even . . .

He just hurt. The idea that as long as he was right he couldn't be touched no longer held. There was more vulnerability in his life now, and a push, perhaps, closer to the line between skepticism and pessimism.

But he could not, he would not, allow his own self-interests to hurt John Kennedy. His love for Kennedy was so strong. J.F.K. was his friend. For the patriotic American dreamer, this was the ultimate compliment: the President of the United States was his *friend.* During the 1960 campaign, J.F.K. had stayed at our Palm Springs home and afterward Dad had put a gold plaque on the door of the little guest room: "John Fitzgerald Kennedy Slept Here."

A short time before the Cal-Neva investigation, J.F.K. announced plans for another visit to Palm Springs. Dad had been working with an architect, expanding the house. With the President coming, FS added a pair of two-bedroom cottages out by the pool. In the main house he built a big dining room with a cathedral ceiling, made the tiny kitchen into a butler's pantry and added an industrial-type kitchen. He turned the little guest room into a library but left the J.F.K. plaque on the door. He pushed the living room and bar walls out a few feet and brought in giant boulders and cactus plants to shield the pool area from the adjacent golf course. He redecorated everything except his own bedroom, which seemed small now compared to the rest of the house. He painted and papered and carpeted and draped. Some of this, much of this, he would have done anyhow but with the understanding that he would be entertaining J.F.K., he had a cement landing pad for a helicopter constructed. (The most reliable and authoritative account of this episode is in the book by Kenneth P. O'Donnell and David F. Powers, *Johnny, We Hardly Knew Ye.)*

O'Donnell had asked the Secret Service to select a place with the necessary and best security. My father's place was more or less open, but Bing's house backed up into a mountain and was ideal for their purposes. O'Donnell said that when a change of plans was announced, he heard that Peter Lawford was "hysterical" because the President had promised to stay with Sinatra and when Lawford called O'Donnell, he said, "Don't you realize Crosby is a *Republican?*" To which O'Donnell replied, "I don't care if he's a Red Chinaman—the Secret Service likes his place better than Sinatra's."

Later, it was reported, O'Donnell says, that the Attorney General had advised against staying at my dad's place "because of associations with known criminals." Instead, Robert Kennedy had called O'Donnell to urge staying at the Sinatra family residence, but even that didn't work.

The President came to Palm Springs. And stayed at Bing Crosby's house. He phoned Dad from Bing's. It was a disappointment in Dad's life. But he never stopped loving and supporting Jack Kennedy. He thought J.F.K. was great for the country, great for the world. In November 1963, on the day the President was murdered, Dad was filming a scene for his movie *Robin and the Seven Hoods*. The company was on location in a cemetery, not far, ironically, from a gravestone bearing the name Kennedy. When the news of the assassination was brought to Dad, he began to walk. And walk. He said, "Get me the White House." He talked on the phone to someone at the White House, then came back and said, "Let's shoot this thing, 'cause I don't want to come back here anymore."

After that he disappeared. I couldn't reach him for those three dark days. He had gone home to Palm Springs and locked himself away—in his bedroom, the only part of the house that was still the same as when his friend, the President, once had visited him.

Nancy believes that the loss of the Cal-Neva Lodge at Lake Tahoe, California (architect David Jacobson, Jr.'s, rendering) meant a new sadness for her father, coming as it did on the heels (word carefully chosen) of renewed charges about "links to organized crime." Other links were more to the point: the sale of his Reprise Records company to Warner Brothers and his friendship with J.F.K. Caught in a bind of loyalties and business, Sinatra couldn't fight back. Said one observer of the "legal" proceedings: Sinatra has been "the victim of printer's ink."

CHAPTER ELEVEN
HAPPY BIRTHDAY

Kidnap

President Kennedy died in Dallas on November 22, 1963. Sixteen days later on December 8, 1963, my brother was appearing with Sam Donahue and "The Tommy Dorsey Band" at Harrah's Club in Lake Tahoe. Frankie and his friend, trumpet player John Foss, were having dinner before the show in Frankie's room—No. 417—at the lodge where Harrah's entertainers stayed. Shortly after nine o'clock there was a knock on the door. "Who is it?" asked Frankie.

"I have a delivery for Mr. Sinatra—a package."

Frankie opened the door to find a .38 revolver pointed at him. Two men in ski parkas pushed their way into his room and told Frankie and John Foss to lie face down on the floor with their hands behind their backs. The men taped John and Frankie's hands, blindfolded them, and took their wallets. Then the men untaped Frankie's hands and told him to stand up and put on a coat and shoes. As he was getting into his coat he heard one of the men say to John, "Don't make any noise for ten minutes. If we don't make it to Sacramento, there will be trouble." Then my brother was dragged out into the darkness.

Snow had been falling all day. High winds had knocked down many of the tall Sierra trees. It was a dreadful night, a blizzard. Under his coat my brother wore only a T-shirt, trousers and loafers—no socks. Freezing, he was shoved into the back seat of a car and made to lie down. They drove off into the storm.

When John Foss was able to undo his taped wrists, he phoned the police. A dispatcher for the Nevada State Highway Patrol sent a message to the FBI: "According to the Douglas County Sheriff's Office, Frank Sinatra, Jr., was kidnapped at Harrah's Club Lodge about half an hour ago. Two men are involved. They have him in a car. Roadblocks are being established."

The message was received at FBI Headquarters in Washington, D.C., and forwarded to FBI Chief J. Edgar Hoover and Attorney General Robert F.

Left: "Frankie opened the door to find a .38 revolver pointed at him."

Top: Frank used to cut the hair of his son, achieving a bowl-like look that was in no way as glamorous as the bowls where each would sing in time. But these were loving acts anyhow, despite the fact that, says the author, "as a barber, he was a splendid singer."

Kennedy.

The car carrying Frankie quickly came upon a roadblock. The driver removed Frankie's blindfold and ordered him to pretend he was asleep. Frankie did not believe that John Foss had had sufficient time to break free and notify the police. He thought the roadblock had been set up to make certain that cars were equipped with tire chains. Hearing the kidnappers threaten to shoot if any policeman gave them trouble, Frankie kept very still and did as he had been told. When the car passed through the roadblock, his blindfold was restored and he was forced to swallow two sleeping pills.

My mother was at home in Bel Air, having a relaxing Sunday night, when the phone call came from Frankie's manager, Tino Barzie, who had the room next door to 417. My sister heard Mom gasp. Tina: "After she hung up the phone, she began pacing up and down in disbelief." Mom somehow composed herself enough to make two phone calls. The first was to Dad in Palm Springs, the second to me in New Orleans.

There were other calls. One to Bobby Kennedy. He said, "Yeah, we're onto it. I've got two hundred and forty-eight men on it. There'll be more by tonight."

Next, Dad called Mickey Rudin and chartered a plane to Reno where at midnight he met Charles W. Bates, the special agent in charge of the San Francisco office of the FBI. By then the FBI had agents at Mom's house and had already put taps on her phones.

At the Mapes Hotel in Reno, Dad received some telephone advice from FBI Chief J. Edgar Hoover: "Just keep your mouth shut, Frank. Don't talk to anyone but law officers . . ." He also received a call from Bobby Kennedy—a more personal call, one father to another.

I was in my room at the Roosevelt Hotel in New Orleans watching TV, while Tommy was singing in his show downstairs when Mom called. She told me to sit down because she had bad news. (I feel sorry for anyone who ever hears those words out of nowhere.) As I listened to her voice: "Brother . . . kidnapped . . . Dad . . . Reno . . ." She sounded faraway and calm. She told me three FBI men were staying in her house and she had to get off the line, in case the kidnappers tried to contact her. Kidnappers. FBI. These are words you never want to have crash into your life. I called the backstage extension and left word for my husband to call me as soon as he got offstage. My first thought was to pack and go home on the next plane, but then I grew frightened: What if it's a conspiracy? My life's been threatened before . . . people have threatened to kidnap me before . . . What should I do? And what about Tommy. He loves Frankie, too. If they hurt my brother, my husband will be here alone . . .

I really didn't know what to do. I also didn't know that FBI men already had arrived at the hotel to guard me. When Tommy came upstairs, we decided I shouldn't be moving around. I should stay put and await instructions.

In New Jersey, Grandma and Grandpa heard the horrible news from their son.

The kidnap car was traveling toward Los Angeles while we waited—in California, Nevada, Louisiana, and New Jersey—for the kidnappers to make contact. We waited nearly seventeen hours.

Dad had been joined in Reno by Mickey Rudin, Jack Entratter of the Sands Hotel, and Dean Elson, special agent in charge of the FBI in Nevada. Dean Elson: "Sinatra would have gone anywhere, paid any amount, risked everything; all he wanted was his son back alive."

At 4:45 P.M., December 9, my father received the first phone call from one of the kidnappers. The FBI taped it:

"Is this Frank Sinatra?"

"Speaking. This is Frank Sinatra Senior."

"It doesn't sound like Sinatra."

"Well it is. This is Frank Sinatra."

"Can you be available at 9 A.M. tomorrow morning?"

"Yes, I can."

"Okay. Your son is in good shape, don't worry about him. See if you can do something about the roadblocks."

The next morning, after another sleepless night, Dad received the second call.

"Hello."

"Sinatra?"

"Yeah."

A new voice: "Hello, Dad?"

"Frankie?"

"Yeah."

"How are you, son?"

"All right."

"Are you warm enough?"

No response.

"You on the other end of the phone there . . . You on the other end there?"

"Yeah."

"You want to talk to me about making a deal—You want to resolve this thing?"

"Yeah I do, but I can't do it right now, Frank."

"Why not?"

"Gotta wait till around two o'clock."

"Well, do you have any idea what you want?"

"Oh, naturally we want money."

"Well, just tell me about how much you want."

"Well, I can't tell you that now."

"I don't understand why you can't give me an idea so we can begin to get some stuff ready for you."

"Well, that's what I'm afraid of. I don't want you to have too much time to get ready."

"Well, I gotta have some time."

"I know. But you see, don't—don't rile me. You're making me nervous. I'll call you back about two o'clock."

"Well, can you call before that?"

"I don't think so. I gotta hang up now."

"Can I talk to Frankie again?"

. . . dial tone . . .

The next call ordered Dad to go to Ron's Service Station in Carson City. By the time Dad and Dean Elson arrived, station attendant Don McStay had already received four calls for Frank Sinatra—and figured one of the owner's friends was playing some kind of joke. The attendant was asked to leave the room while Dad answered the next phone call, which explained the ransom demand. When they left, Elson told the attendant not to mention to *anyone*

Nancy says: "Again, Carousel *says it for them and, I think, for all fathers and sons . . ."*

He might be a champ
of the heavyweights
or a fella who sells you glue
or President of the United States
that'd be all right too . . .

what had happened, and McStay gave his word. He thought to himself, "I hope I didn't blow anything by getting annoyed with the caller."

In Beverly Hills, Al Hart, a close family friend and president of the City National Bank, had been alerted and was ready. The kidnappers demanded $240,000 in small used bills. All day, until dark, Al Hart and his people photographed each bill and made it ready for the drop. One of the FBI people said, "What are we going to put this money in, a paper bag?" The bills weighed twenty-three pounds. Al Hart said, "Go buy a valise." The man went to a department store, J. W. Robinson's, which remained open until nine P.M., then returned and said he didn't have enough money to buy the $56 bag. Al Hart took some of the ransom money and gave it to him. They later put $239,985 into the new valise.

Daddy was instructed to go to Los Angeles to await the next call. Mom, Tina, and Daddy, with other family members and several FBI agents, waited together in Mom's house. At 9:26 P.M. Dad was instructed to go to a gas station in Beverly Hills. There, another phone call ordered him to have a courier bring the money to a phone booth in L.A. International Airport at 11 P.M. and to use the name Patrick Henry.

Dad asked J. Edgar Hoover to send an FBI courier who would stay cool and not get Frankie in trouble. The agent went to the designated phone and waited. "Patrick Henry? . . . This is John Adams." The courier was directed to a gas station, where he was to ask for a road map. "We'll be looking you over at the gas station. Hang around for five minutes and . . . drive north on Sepulveda . . . Stop at the gas station at Sepulveda and Olympic."

At the gas station the FBI man was told that Frankie was going to be let go "four hours after you drop the money and get lost." The agent asked if he could "speak to Frank Jr." He was told, "No," because "he's not here, he's someplace else." And then the agent was told to go to still another gas station, where the next call came. He was instructed to put the money between two school buses parked at the station, and then check into a hotel. He did so, after 10 P.M., December 10.

My brother was being held captive by a third man in a small house in the San Fernando Valley. He was cold and tired and frightened. By the night of the drop, he had had it. The original two kidnappers had gone off to collect the money while the third man guarded Frankie. After receiving a phone call at 10 P.M. the man said, "We got the money but we got a problem. One of the guys got scared and ran. I think I better not let you go." Frankie said, "You let me go or I'll kill you. If you want to stop me you'll have to kill me. One of us is going to die."

The next four hours seemed like ten to my family. Mom, Dad, and Tina—Frankie called her "Squeaky"—in California, Tommy and I in New Orleans, Grandma and Grandpa in New Jersey, were hoping and praying that my brother, only nineteen years old with his whole life ahead of him, would be returned to us. Most kidnap victims are never seen again. I was in panic: "Frankie, my friend, my nemesis, my baby brother, my partner in crime. Where are you? I forgive you for hitting me with the train engine. I forgive you for all the times you were a pain. I even forgive you for pulling all the books off the shelves in the library. Just come home."

Marty and Dolly absolutely adored their grandson. He was their favorite. He could do no wrong. He represented immortality to them. He would carry on their name, their traditions. Grandma always called him "my boy" and vowed

Frank Sinatra, Jr.: "I've studied with Frank Sinatra, although he doesn't know I've studied with him . . . I've been following him around all my life . . ."

Asked what kind of advice he has given his son, FS answered in part: "The press? This will get laughs but I mean it: Be honest and courteous and fair and hope the press reciprocates. I don't mean the entertainer should be subservient, but he should be frank and square—he'll need members of the press all his life. All of us have. In spite of my so-called problems, I've had a damned good press. Frankie should trust individual members until he finds that he can't."

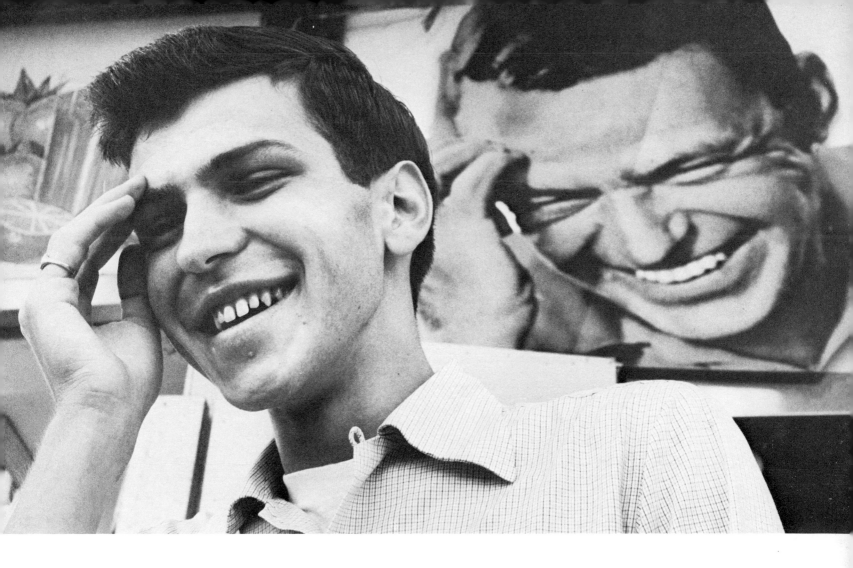

to leave him all her possessions. Now she never stopped praying for him. Her rosary beads were never out of her hands.

"Squeaky" and Frankie were very close. He was her *big* brother—for the most part, the only visible, constant male in Tina's life. She was still just a little girl, only fifteen. She needed her big brother. He was the one who, when she was a child and locked herself in the bathroom, climbed up on the roof and through the window to get her out to safety. He was her hero. She was so frightened for him.

When Frank Sinatra, Jr., was very small, his daddy would sing this song to him: "Sweetest little fella, everybody knows . . . Don't know what to call him, but he's mighty lak a rose . . ." He used to trim Frankie's hair personally. He was so proud of his boy. For his part, Frankie worshipped his dad. He spent hours locked in his bedroom playing Dad's records over and over. He emulated his father's generosity—always wanting to treat everyone. "He's so like me it's frightening," Dad said when Frankie was nine. "If I stand in front of the fireplace with my hands behind my back, he does the same thing. He composes his own music and sings too. When I do a TV show, he quotes everything I said the next time I see him." He wanted his son home.

And Mom. She'd carried him for nine months, nursed him for nearly two years. A mother's love: Guiding. Teaching. Nurturing. Worrying. Caring. Giving. She was bumping into furniture now, unable to concentrate or finish a sentence. God, bring him home.

At 2 A.M., four hours after the ransom was paid, Daddy went to get his son. If he was afraid the kidnappers wouldn't keep their word—and he must have been, just like the rest of us—he did not show it to his family. He held Tina's face in his hands and said firmly, "I'm going to bring your brother home." And to Mom, with even greater conviction, "I'm going to bring him *home.*" They clung together for a moment, sharing whatever it is parents share at a time like that, and then he left on the most important errand of his life and went looking for his boy. He got in his car as instructed—alone.

Frankie, meanwhile, had suggested to the man guarding him that perhaps the two other kidnappers were not coming back with the money. Perhaps they were leaving him to take the rap. That had persuaded the man to drive Frankie to the designated drop-off point in Los Angeles—but now, approaching the drop-off point, the man became apprehensive. Afraid someone had given him away, he told Frankie he was going to take him back to Canoga Park. Frankie assured him that Frank Sinatra would not have told anyone.

At 2:35 A.M. Daddy returned to the house—alone. Tina: "Do you know what Dad's face looked like? I've never seen a face look like that." He thought the criminals had taken the money and not let Frankie go.

The man driving Frankie had let him go, after the designated time, at the drop-off point on the San Diego Freeway at the Mulholland Drive exit. Terrified that the man might come back, Frankie pulled down his blindfold and ran for cover. He picked up a big rock and stuck it in his pocket; it was the only thing he could find in the desolate spot that resembled a weapon. He didn't see his father's car, so he decided he'd better walk toward Bel Air. Once off the freeway, he heard a car engine screaming up the hill and ducked behind a hedge out of range of the headlights. It was a bronze Ford sedan with men wearing overcoats and hats. By the time he realized they must have been FBI men, they were gone. He saw a morning paper in someone's driveway. It was dated December 11, 1963—one day before his father's birthday.

Another car came by, this time very slowly, but Frankie hid again. He was so scared. Then, realizing it was a car from the private security service, the Bel Air Patrol, he shouted, "Hey." The car stopped and Frankie identified himself and asked to be driven to his mother's home. The security man, George C. Jones, knew where it was because Mom's was one of the houses on his route. Shivering with cold from his two-mile walk, Frankie asked Jones to turn on the heat. He still had no socks, and had lost weight. He was skinny, hungry, exhausted, terrified, and freezing. But alive.

Because he had seen press people crowding Mom's driveway for three days, Jones stopped the car near the Bel Air Patrol office and said he was concerned about getting Frankie through the reporters and photographers. My brother said, "Suppose I get in the trunk. Then if we can't get through, we can come back to the office and do something else." Jones agreed.

George C. Jones: "Nobody knew I had the boy in the trunk. I drove on up to the home, passed the cars, the newspaper people, all the officers, into the parking area in front of the house." He then backed the trunk of the car to within a few feet of the front door and told Frankie he was going to get Mom or Dad. "I went to the door and knocked. Two men opened the door and I recognized Mrs. Sinatra standing inside. I looked at her and said, 'Mrs. Sinatra, I have your boy in the trunk of my car—and he is all right.' She gasped. She just stood there looking at me. Mr. Sinatra came to the door. I told him the same thing, that Frankie was okay, and in my trunk. He didn't smile. All he said was

The kidnapping. Backed up by Guy McElwaine, Mr. Sinatra, anguish and concern written on the famous face, talks to reporters, tells them that a ransom has been paid.

'Let's get that trunk open.' Then Mr. and Mrs. Sinatra and five or six other people came out and I unlocked the trunk—and there was Frankie."

Frankie remembers seeing Dad's shoes first, then legs, chest, and face. He climbed out and said, "Hi, Mom. Hi, Dad." They put their arms around him and began hugging and kissing him. They invited patrolman Jones to come in. He later said, "I sure was tickled to see that boy come up to the car—and happier still when he went into his own house." Our prayers were answered, Frankie was home. Happy birthday, Dad.

Soon, Bobby Kennedy called. He spoke to Dad and then to Frankie: "Are you all right, son?"

"Yes, sir."

"Let me talk to one of my men." Elson took the phone and was told to "implement the ramrod." With Frankie safely home, the FBI began a full-scale search for the kidnappers.

Next, J. Edgar Hoover called as he wrote to me later.

J. Edgar Hoover: "I told your father how pleased I was that Frank Jr. had been safely returned. I recall pointing out to him that although he would now be besieged by inquiries from the news media, we still had numerous productive leads to pursue and would be able to do so only if the case received a minimum of publicity. Your father, of course, cooperated in every possible way. Within a short time, our investigation was completed and early on the morning of December 14th, I had the pleasure of telephoning your father again to inform him that the kidnappers were in custody."

My brother broke open the case. Frank Sinatra, Jr.: "When the agents came to interview me the night I got away from those bastards, they told me to

Frank Jr., the ordeal also visible in his face and that of his mother and sister Tina (to his left), speaks to the press following his release.

His father's advice about the press backfired with a few of the reporters and columnists, as the charge of "Hoax" was put into the air. Subsequent stories referred to "The Sinatra trial." Young Frankie's trials were not then—or now—over.

179

remember every little thing. I said, 'When they led me into the house I tripped on a piece of weather stripping at the door, on the ground.' I told them about hearing little airplanes overhead. I told them the make of the car: 'A Plymouth, a Plymouth station wagon.' My aunt used to have one and I remembered the sound of the back door; this one had the same sound. One of the guys led me around because I was blindfolded, and I could feel his hands. I told the Bureau, 'The man who has this hand works with harsh chemicals. He's a mechanic, a carpenter or a painter 'cause it's like alligator scales inside his hand.' Turned out he was a painter. The FBI used all this stuff to break the case."

My brother was questioned for several hours by Dean Elson and the other FBI men who were at Mom's house. When he finally went to sleep, it was in Tina's room. His kid sister kept peeking at him as he slept, making sure he was really there—that she wasn't dreaming.

As soon as I knew Frankie was safe, I flew home. We had a tearful, laughing reunion. The night we got the news that the kidnappers were in custody, we opened a magnum of champagne. My mother, who doesn't drink, drank most of it. She was so happy she didn't even have a headache the next day.

The ordeal took its toll on my father. The lack of sleep. Little food. The dramatic temperature changes. Flying in the stormy skies. He had been distraught, even desperate—two things he had never been before. He handled each moment as it came. Even the worst one—when he'd gone to pick up his son and he wasn't there. I can't bear, even now, the image of him driving back to Mom's, alone in the car.

Afterward, his body reacted. He got sick. He went home to Palm Springs to recover. He spent the time healing. Reflecting. While mourners filed past the Eternal Flame at Arlington, while our country was still in shock, while Bobby and the other Kennedys were trying to pick up the torn pieces of their lives, my father was trying to understand all these shattering events. It was all so emotionally draining—Jack, Frankie, Cal-Neva . . . overwhelming.

At Christmastime Dad received a note from a friend. In the midst of her own grief, she had taken time to write. Jacqueline Kennedy echoed his own thoughts when she wrote that 1963 had been a terrible year, and the only good thing about it was that Frankie was safe.

The Real Crime

At the trial of the three men who had kidnapped my brother, two of the attorneys for the defense created the idea that it had all been a hoax. Having been planted in the minds of the press, this became the central theme of most reporting. I know that intelligent people understood, because of the evidence presented at the trial, that this was ridiculous. And I know that many news people are intelligent. So I can only assume that the cruel headlines were just to get at Target A—Francis Albert Sinatra.

When the suggestion was planted that the "hoax" had been created for publicity purposes, my father said only, "This family needs publicity like it needs peritonitis."

Portions of the press even began to refer to it as "the Sinatra trial." I heard a local newsman say that on TV and I phoned him, I was so furious. He

Nancy Sinatra and her brother (right) in rehearsal for a Smothers Brothers TV show. NS: "My father understands that it's not easy being a Sinatra kid, whatever the privileges. And perhaps it's especially uneasy being a son. My brother is apt to be candid and his sense of humor is off the nearest wall. But there are clues. He told Megan Rosenfeld of the Washington Post, 'I want to look at things without distortion. It reminds me of a line in Becket when the king says, "Why must you destroy all my illusions?" And he answers, "Because you should have none, my prince."'

"My brother and sister and I grew up thinking naïvely that the world lived as we did—with, as he said, 'a car in every driveway.' But life has shown otherwise. When he sings 'The Tender Trap' or 'That's Life,' songs identified with Dad, and gets extra applause, he says, smiling, to the audience, 'I can see where your loyalties lie.' And he calls himself the 'Avis' of the Sinatra household.

"Some of these comments are fun, and some are close to the bone, but he also says, as if in echo of the old man, 'If you can't handle the bad times, you can't handle the good ones.'"

made it sound as if my brother was the one on trial and not his abductors—that Frankie was the criminal instead of the victim. One isolated incident would have been tolerable, but the same attitude spread to the rest of the world. In England, the TV show "That Was the Week That Was" did a scathing, unfunny satire, which cost them later when FS won a lawsuit against them.

The defense attorneys tried to keep recalling my father to the witness stand, because every time Sinatra took the stand the courtroom would be packed and the publicity would heat up again. Judge East finally told the defense that they would not be permitted to subpoena Sinatra Sr. again.

The trial lasted four weeks. Judge William G. East retired the jury saying, "I must comment: there is no direct evidence in this case by Frank Sinatra Jr. or persons in his behalf that prearrangements were made for his abduction."

The federal jury dismissed the hoax business in less than forty minutes, and after several hours returned a verdict of guilty on all six counts. Two of the men received life sentences and the third, the man who let my brother go, was sentenced to seventy-five years.

Within months of the sentencing, my mother and father received a letter from a chaplain at the prison where two of the three had been sent. He asked that my parents forgive the two men; that they regretted causing my parents suffering and anxiety during the kidnapping, ". . . as well as perhaps some embarrassment during the trial."

Perhaps some embarrassment? I didn't know what to make of such a statement. But FS did.

He replied that he presumed a purpose of the letter was "that we take some action to express our forgiveness in order to alleviate the punishment" the court had imposed. He resented the implication that this had been a case of Sinatra vs. the defendants rather than The People of the United States vs. the accused. He said the use of the words "perhaps some embarrassment" caused him to wonder whether the defendants even afterward fully understood that by permitting their counsel to make opening statements in court about a hoax, and by doing the same thing outside with the press, they had caused the Sinatra family considerable anguish.

The conduct of the defendants during the trial had affected the way the press reported the case "and suspicion was created in the minds of many people as to the honesty and truthfulness of our son." Nothing had been done by the kidnappers since the trial to remove that suspicion. Not only were they insensitive to the harm done by the hoax claim, he went on, but such a charge meant that both the Department of Justice and the FBI were either parties to a hoax or "too stupid to realize" they were being taken in.

His words were as strong as his feelings. "In my opinion," he wrote, "my son has either gotten over the effects of the kidnapping or will easily get over (them) since he is a strong person; however, unless something affirmative is done by the defendants, the cloud of suspicion which hangs over his head will continue to affect adversely his life and career."

The cloud did exactly that. Frankie's reputation was ruined for a long time. Even people in the audience at his shows heckled him. It was awful. My brother, who had been well on his way to success, suffered a terrible blow from the publicity. In career terms, it was peritonitis.

Once more, some of the media people had aimed their arrows at Frank Sinatra. But they had missed. This time they hit his son.

Robert Francis Kennedy and Francis Albert Sinatra. The capture of the kidnappers was brought about in part by the intervention of Robert Kennedy, then Attorney General of the U.S.A. FS: "The top cop. He helped me. He made one of the first calls, he and John Edgar Hoover." "We've got over two hundred agents on it." Kennedy told FS, "and there will be more." "We'll get those clowns," said Hoover.

CHAPTER TWELVE
RING-A-DING-DING

ne thing had been salvaged.

The sale of Dad's record company, Reprise, to Warner Brothers gave him big money, real security for the first time in his life. He'd made lots of money in his life and given away lots, but nothing like this. The sale gave him a high corporate position, attractive quarters (they designed an L-shaped one-story building for him), and it was thought for a while that Frank Sinatra might take over as head of the studio when Jack Warner retired. FS was reminded of Rudyard Kipling, who wrote: "If you . . . meet with triumph and disaster . . . treat those two impostors just the same."

Frank Sinatra had started his own record company in self-defense against the new technology that was becoming the vogue in the business: overdubbing, multiple tracks, the sterility of studios dominated by machines, not energized by live audiences. It was important for FS to have control of his dates, to fight off the technicians who wanted to overproduce, and to maintain, instead, the life and spontaneity of his work.

Frank Sinatra: "I adore making records. I'd rather do that than almost anything else. You can never do anything in life quite on your own—you don't live on your own little island. Making a record is as near as you can get to it—although, of course, the arranger and the orchestra play an enormous part. But once you're on that record singing, it's you and you alone. If it's bad and gets criticized, it's you who's to blame—no one else. If it's good, it's also you. I myself can't work well except under pressure. If there's too much time available, I don't like it—not enough stimulus. And I'll never record before eight o'clock in the evening. The voice is more relaxed then."

It was 1965 and he was headed for fifty. Life *photographer John Dominis and writer Tommy Thompson caught it. Frank Sinatra said it. "You gotta love living, baby. Dying's a pain in the ass."*

Nancy: "In 1967, Sarge Weiss brought a duet to the attention of FS, who said: "Let's tack it onto the end of the [Antonio Carlos] Jobim date." So, the A-team stepped aside and I came in with my little B-team and we recorded it with my father. We did the song in two takes (we would have done it in one except that my dad got silly, endlessly sounding his S's for fun, like Daffy Duck.) Mo Ostin, President of Reprise, bet him $2 that the song would fail. During the playback in the booth FS said, 'That's going to be Number One.' That song was 'Something Stupid.' It became number one, sold several million —and it still sells. Disc jockeys loved to call it 'the incest song.' "

For Frank Sinatra, the second-best place to be is on stage with an audience in front of you and a band behind you. The first and best place to be is in a recording studio, surrounded by sound, surrounded by the band. There is an excitement about a live session that happens nowhere else. It's the anticipation —what will the chart sound like?—and the actual process of recording—and the playback! Being able to listen to what you've done immediately after you've done it. No waiting or worrying: if it's wrong, fix it, then and there. The sharing is an important part of a session. Engineers, producers, musicians, singers, all hearing the results of their labors—each person listening for his own contribution. Is it good? Are there any "clams"? Each one respecting the other's integrity, and if someone needs another take, he usually gets it.

It's really too bad that most producers today don't know—or allow themselves the chance to know—what it's like to record a live date. It is, speaking from experience, the best way to capture the spirit of the artists. Most critics, when comparing albums of the fifties and early sixties with later recordings, forget that a lot of the earlier magic came from *live* sessions. The energy level is higher. Everybody's there, playing at the same time, not in sections, dribs and drabs.

It is uncomfortable for someone who is accustomed to that energy to stand alone in a studio and sing to a playback heard through a headset. To begin with, you should be able to hear the music through your nose and your mouth and your skin—not just through your ears. In a live session your pitch is better, much more accurate. It's the difference between singing to a record or in front of a live band.

Frank Sinatra thrived on working with bands. With jazz arranger Johnny Mandel he recorded the first Reprise album, *Ring-a-Ding-Ding.* With Billy May he did *Swing Along with Me;* with Sy Oliver he did *I Remember Tommy,* a tribute to Dorsey. And with Don Costa he did the milestone *Sinatra and Strings.*

Frank Sinatra, Jr.: *"Sinatra and Strings* opened up a whole new era. The orchestras were getting bigger. Pop wanted that bigger, lush string sound.

"They assembled the huge orchestra for one date. The old man walked in that night for the first take, 'Hey, hey, ring-a-ding-ding,' and he was playing with his hat and everything, and he saw the concertmaster, Felix Slatkin, slumped over in his chair. Felix had his violin still in its case across his lap. He was sweating. He looked up and said, 'Frank, I don't feel good.' My old man turned around and looked at Costa with all the music and the *fifty* musicians. But the concertmaster didn't feel good. So Dad turned around to Hank Sanicola and he said, 'Hank, pay everybody off.' And he got up on the conductor's podium and said—tap, tap—'Everybody, good evening. Turn in your W-4 forms, we're not recording tonight. Come back tomorrow night at eight.' Pushed the whole album session back one day. Slatkin was not well, and he was not going to record without the concertmaster. Paid everybody off and sent them home. Got to do it right."

Sinatra always did it right. The Reprise records were more than considerable successes. His stature continued to grow. Frank Jr.: "One day Ray Charles was recording in a studio near Dad's. On a ten-minute break they brought Ray in to visit with Sinatra. A guy took a picture. The following week, one of the record trade magazines ran the picture of the two of them. The caption said, 'The recording industry as it stands today.' "

There was not always such awe. At one session they ended up without an

A & R man present. Frank Jr.: "So my old man went to Felix Slatkin and said, 'Felix, who are we going to get to A & R from the booth? This is all intricate orchestration.' Felix said, 'Let's put Eleanor in.' And my father said, 'Beautiful!' There were six cellists on hand. Eleanor Slatkin was one of them. Felix went to his wife, who is a fine musician, and talked to her. Eleanor got up from her chair and put her cello back into its case. Instead of six cellos, they'd record with five. She rolled up her sleeves and went into the booth, and she was a *tyrant*. 'Just a minute boys,' she'd say through the P.A. system. 'Shhh! Quiet, boys, Mommy's talking!' And she'd yell, 'You idiot!' and come bounding out of the booth at the musicians. My old man would say, 'But Eleanor—' She'd say, 'Shut up!' And he'd say, 'Yes, ma'am.' And they'd start up and she'd stop and say, 'Sorry, Francis— you can do *better* than that.' And she produced a beautifully balanced album."

Life was sometimes sillier and often just as serious on the movie sets. The results were a lot of laughter and a number of first-rate films.

Sammy Davis, Jr.: "It was all so nuts. We were making one movie and Frank was suddenly told, 'This movie is too long.' So Frank grabbed the script, pulled out a fistful of pages and tore them up. 'There,' he said, 'it's shorter now.' "

They did the Summit movies—*Ocean's Eleven, Sergeants Three, Robin and the Seven Hoods.* And, in addition to these romps at the summit, he also did more substantial work: *Von Ryan's Express, Come Blow Your Horn, The Manchurian Candidate, The Detective.*

Speaking of Sinatra's acting, Humphrey Bogart once said, "Frank's a hell of a guy. He tries to live his own life. If he could only stay away from the broads and devote some time to develop himself as an actor, he'd be one of the best in the business."

More and more in his films of the sixties, FS began to "develop himself." As a professional, I gained more and more respect for his ability to translate his insights about life to the screen characters he portrayed. As a woman, I fell in love with him over and over again with each new film. As a daughter, I was proud.

His sixties films were shot at various locations. In addition to his great pal Jilly, he liked to have around certain actors who were his cronies—Henry Silva, Dick Bakalyan ("Dickie B."), Brad Dexter. They could get rather rowdy. "You travel with your dad," Dickie B. once told me, "you see every jail in the world."

Dick Bakalyan: "In Cortina, I made the mistake of going to bed early. Frank said, 'No, no. We must stay up.' I said, '*You* stay up. I'm going to bed.' I went. The next day, while I was at work, they broke into my room, threw all my clothes out the window."

Dad bought Dickie B. a new wardrobe, and the adventure continued.

Dickie B.: "One day at this villa in Rome, Jilly blew up Brad Dexter's shoes. Brad had wanted some new shoes and he was talking about it and we got tired of hearing about it. And at the right moment your Dad said, 'Look out there!' On the patio Jilly set off some cherry bombs in the shoes and they blew twenty feet in the air. We were hysterical.

"We go to Portofino to this yacht, and Brad comes up to your Dad and says, 'Listen, I'm going to get even with Jilly about my shoes. I'm going to get him off the boat in the water and when I give you the signal, blow up his shoes.' Your Dad says, 'Great idea.' Brad gets Jilly in the water and gives the signal and your father says, 'Give me *Brad's* shoes.' He lights the cherry bomb and Brad is in the water saying, 'Hey, Jilly! Look what they're doing to your—*Hey!* Those

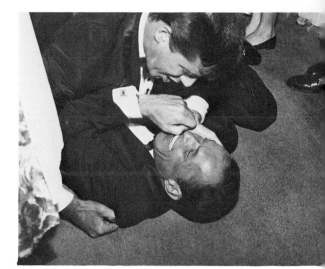

Jerry Lewis: "On stage, I did my impression of Sinatra and it was terrific because I weighed a hundred and eleven pounds wearing Flagg Brothers shoes that weighed fifteen pounds each and were as thick as Carmen Miranda's feet. So I was beyond emaciation and midway through the song a doctor would come out and give me a shot in the arm so that I could finish.

"He called me one evening and said, 'What are you doing, Jew?' And I said, 'Nothing in particular, Wop.' He said to meet him the next morning and 'Bring your tools.' We flew to Rockford, Illinois, got to this coliseum seating about twenty thousand. Your Dad had hired a thirty-piece orchestra. We did the show about 8:30 p.m., brought in a hundred and three thousand dollars, and flew back to Los Angeles around four in the morning. This performance was for one fireman who had died, and his family. He said, 'Thanks, you're a good friend.' And I said, 'Thank you. You're a good man, Frank.'"

NS: "What Jerry doesn't say is that he's always there for Pop."

*The Power Lunch, Warner Brothers,
1965. In Sinatra's office, after the
sale of his Reprise Records to Warner,
Frank and Jack Warner (right,
clockwise) lunch with FS's lawyer-
agent-friend, Milton "Mickey" Rudin
and Walter McEwen of Warner Bros.
Sinatra calls Rudin "the Judge,"
invests him with considerable responsibility (so much so that for a
time they would not fly together) and
for years has had no other agent.*

Sinatra and others on the subject:

Richard Condon, author: "Frank once told me that the only way to negotiate a dispute, figuratively, was to kick the disputant in the ankle and, as he hopped on one foot, belt him soundly across the chops."

FS: "Women? I've never met a man in my life who could give another man advice about women . . . I'm supposed to have a Ph.D. on the subject but I've flunked more often than not. I'm very fond of women; I admire them. But, like all men, I don't understand them.

"Sex? There's not enough quantity and certainly not enough quality . . . [to reporters] If I'd had as many affairs as you fellows claim, I'd be speaking to you today from a jar in the Harvard Medical School."

FS: "Money? It doesn't thrill me. Never has . . . You gotta' spend it. Move it around."

are *my* shoes!!' BOOM! And they floated in Portofino harbor.

"Always something. I was always learning something. I remember once in Portofino, we were having a few drinks and the guy brought the bill. It was for eighty-something dollars—for like four drinks. And I started to get on the guy about it. And your dad said, 'Cool it. Back off. Forget it.' And I didn't understand that and I got up and walked out of the restaurant. I didn't understand. Until he explained to me that people do that everywhere he goes. You give them an argument and then they get a lot of press.

"This guy was looking for a hassle. He was looking for the argument so that he would get some press in his place—Sinatra was there and an argument developed. So I learned something. Forget it.

"In Rome, these paparazzi guys, they were bananas, they'd drive him crazy. But he never hit one. Oh, no! *I* went over a table after one, though, and there was a picture of it in a magazine."

Sinatra and his buddies traveled around for nightclub appearances, too.

Joey Bishop: "I remember on one occasion, we had checked into the Fontainebleau Hotel in Miami Beach. Frank, Sammy, and Peter were up on the fifteenth floor, which were the penthouses, and they gave me a room on the seventh floor. Frank wanted to rehearse something, so he said to Sammy, 'Run down the hall and get Joey.' Sammy said, 'He's on the seventh floor.' And Frank said, 'They didn't give him a suite?' And he got on the phone and said, 'If Joey Bishop isn't in a suite on the fifteenth floor in five minutes, we'll be out of this hotel and there'll be no show.' I don't know what's going on. All of a sudden six bellhops run into my room. I thought the hotel was on fire. They took the drawers, they took my clothes. I said, 'What are you doing?' They said, 'We got to have you out of here in five minutes. Frank's orders.' "

Joey had occasion to see several sides of Frank Sinatra. "One time we were having dinner and some guy came by and took a potato out of your father's plate. And Frank said, 'Hey pal, are you hungry?' The guy says, 'Yeah.' Frank said, 'Sit down.' And he gave him his dinner. I thought for sure there was gonna be trouble from the guys surrounding your father, but Frank says, 'Jeez, relax, the man's hungry.' "

Eventually, Joey and Dad had a falling out. According to Joey, there were a couple of misunderstandings and Dad stopped talking to him. Joey Bishop: "I was a scapegoat."

Perhaps so. But Joey made a mistake many people, myself included, make in disputes with Frank Sinatra. Joey did not confront him directly. Joey did not explain the situation to him directly. He did not argue it out with him. Instead, Joey moved unprotesting out of Daddy's life.

You've *got* to face Frank Sinatra. Tell him the truth. Battle it out. Yes, he'll get mad. And so will you. But you'll come to some conclusion. You can't be so in awe of him that you're awed right out of a relationship.

People say he walks down a path and leaves havoc in his wake. I say that the people who can't keep up create that havoc. His friend the producer George Schlatter has taken it further: "There have been times when Frank has walked through a situation and left bodies strewn about. He may have given some of them a little shove, but half of those people bumped into *each other;* they were knocked down by *each other.* Particularly in cases when people are blaming each other for whatever problems may exist."

Sometimes people think he's angry at them because of incidents and outbursts he's long ago forgotten. Sometimes problems have lingered for years because people couldn't understand that instead of running away from his anger, instead of abandoning the situation, all they had to do in the first place was keep the communication open. You've got to have the guts to face his—or anybody's—dark side. Frank Sinatra is patient and tolerant. But if you push it or don't heed a warning, look out. He can be a hothead—like a child sometimes. But he gets it off his chest and gets on with his life and, most of the time, unless there's been some deep, substantive wound, it's over and done with right there.

Right and wrong, clearly defined.

That dark side is part of his honesty. There's no sneaky side to him. As Flip Wilson says, "What you see is what you get." And even if what you get is an explosion, that's healthy. If a person doesn't allow his dark side to surface, he's probably not in control of it.

Sammy Davis, Jr.: "Any time I've seen him be rude, and this is the God's honest truth, Nan, the cat deserved it. But where I will put up with what the cat did, or Dean will, Frank won't. He'll say it right to you, 'Don't *do* that,' because that's his rule, and if he has told you 'Don't come over here,' you come sneaking in, well, *me*, I'd go 'Hey, didn't I say? Come on, get outta here!' But Frank gets *very upset* about that because he has this line of right and wrong, and it's important to him. Like this guy came up at a dinner and said, 'I'd like to take one picture, if I could.' Frank said, 'All right—take one.' And the guy started taking a series of pictures. Frank said, 'Hey! Hey, that's enough already! You asked for *one*.' It's that basic."

Motion picture executive Richard Zanuck: "Despite his complexities, your father, more than anything else, is *real* . . . I've honestly never met anyone quite so real, and in this respect he is a totally unique personality, living in an all-too-real world inhabited for the most part by unreal people who are afraid to face the truth about their problems, their lives, and particularly about themselves as individuals. The great difference between Frank and the rest of us is that he is able to see himself, judge himself and others, judge life as it *really* is, and not as we would like it to be . . . And it is obvious that in doing so he becomes his own toughest critic.

"These are, perhaps, parts of his persistent problems with the lower orders of the press. He has a tendency to tell the truth and yet to be sensitive to the feelings of others, to keep it light and yet to be basically serious, and he must have naïvely expected this from others, including those with cameras, microphones, and recorders. As his own critic, he doesn't need cheap shots.

"This quality of his makes Frank rather frightening to many who have been associated with him," said Dick Zanuck. When one looks at Frank, one can't help but see the truth about oneself mirrored in the expression on his face. He knows where you're at, where he's at, and where it's all at—and this of course makes life around Frank rather tense most of the time, primarily because we are not conditioned to face ourselves down—something that Frank insisted upon and mastered a long time ago.

"There have been countless words written about Frank in the past and surely a lot more will come—but whatever they say about him, be it on the one hand that he is a complex, perplexing but loyal and generous man, or, on the other hand, that he is a son of a bitch, the thing *I know* about him is that he's a *real*, complex, perplexing, loyal and generous man, and if he is in fact a son of a bitch, he's a *true* one and not a pretender. Whatever he is, all of us can only guess; *Frank knows.*"

In response to my letter asking for *his* letter, Dick Zanuck wrote:

On one of his tours for charity, writes Nancy Sinatra, "a little blind girl asked Dad, 'What color is the wind?' She couldn't see the tears in his eyes as he answered, 'No one knows because the wind moves too fast.'"

"I think," says a friend, "you can never judge anything that has to do with Frank as of the moment or the month . . . you have to wait, like wine, to see the maturity . . ."

Noël Coward, introducing The Man: "Never once a breach of taste; never once the wrong move."

I've seen that face before
That face in the mirror.
I know that face,
I've seen that face before
I knew that dopey guy
when he didn't know
*   how to tie his tie,*
He stood right there
*   and he had hair galore!*

The man in the looking glass,
Who can he be, the man
*   in the looking glass*
Can he possibly be me?
Where's our young Romeo,
the lad who used to sigh
Who's the middle-aged Lothario,
with the twinkle in his eye?

He seems so much wiser now,
Less lonely—but then
could be he's only
*   pretending again.*
Man in the looking glass,
*   smiling away*
How's your sacroiliac today?

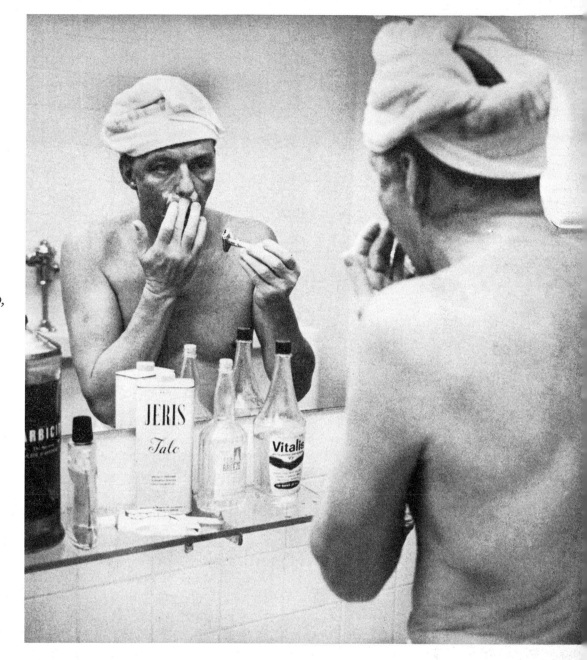

"They fly in his plane, eat his food, drink his whiskey, get fantastic gifts, are entertained internationally; and with all the friends, he has always been a complete loner." (A close companion, quoted by John Bryson.)

"At the risk of being rude, Nancy, or perhaps I'm telling you something you already know, Frank will be the one least impressed by reading what others think of him. It's just not his kind of thing."

There are distinguished echoes. Cary Grant: "Frank Sinatra is a unique man, utterly without hypocrisy. It's unusual for most people, and almost frightening to some, to be faced with honesty." Danny Kaye: "There are only two people I have met in my life—one is Katharine Hepburn and one is Frank Sinatra—from whom I've never left a conversation saying, 'I wonder what they meant by that.' You know exactly what they meant because they said exactly what they felt."

CHAPTER THIRTEEN
BOOTS

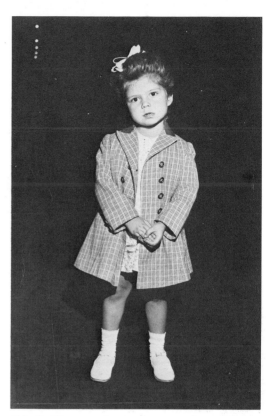

Little Nancy showed an early instinct for stylish boots— and in another decade or so (left) she would help to set a style in footwear with a runaway bestselling record.

Walkin'

Meanwhile, my marriage to Tommy Sands was a happy one. We were two kids, traveling around, having a good time. In trying to build a serious, lasting career following his initial success as a teenage idol of the fifties, Tommy worked hard. He had a solid nightclub act put together by his manager, Ted Wick, and arranger, Don Costa. He was also beginning to get some movie roles. Our future looked bright. I was content to move with him rather than seriously pursue my own career at that point. In 1960, with President Kennedy newly installed in the White House, we had moved to New York, to our own new pad, a one-room apartment on East Fifty-fifth Street. Marty and Dolly furnished it for us. Tommy enrolled in Lee Strasberg's classes at the Actors Studio.

We spent wonderful evenings at Strasberg's home. One night there was a famous guest and she caused me to realize that, like everyone else, I had tended to believe every myth and fable about celebrities. Instead of the brassy, breezy, sexy, empty-headed blonde, I found Marilyn Monroe to be wonderfully sweet— softer, more casual, and prettier than I had expected. A lesson learned.

We spent a lot of time with my grandparents. One night we took them to Patsy's restaurant for dinner and then to a Broadway show. When we came out of the theatre we couldn't find a cab to take Marty and Dolly home. The traffic was awful. My grandfather, who had asthma, became ill from the exhaust fumes. Grandma yelled at him for forgetting his "trumpet"—the atomizer spray that opened his bronchial tubes. He couldn't breathe. His asthma was so bad that she often had to give him an adrenaline injection to ease an attack. But she had not carried one with her. The same thing had happened to him not long before when he carried a piece of furniture from the elevator to our one-room apartment. I felt guilty and stupid for not having hired a car.

We had been in New York about a year when it became known that the Russians were placing missiles in Cuba. One afternoon my dad, after receiving a tip from the White House, called from Palm Springs. He was cryptic: "Chicken, book reservations . . . pack a bag. Watch the President tonight . . . be ready to leave as soon as he's finished. I'll have Bob (the driver) pick you up." Though he didn't tell me until later, my father knew that J.F.K. was about to announce the Cuban blockade. He had been told by a Kennedy aide to get his kids out of town because "if they have missiles aimed at Washington, you can bet they'll hit New York at the same time." I didn't have to know the reason because I knew that if Dad made that kind of a call, we should get out.

Back in L.A. Dad showed all of us—Mom, Tina, Frankie, Tommy, and me —a map of deserted airstrips in the United States that had been built for use during World War II. He told us to put up supplies: bottled water, canned food, flashlights, blankets, and a radio. He would let us know when it was time to move. If his dreaded call came, the plan was for us to put the supplies in our cars and drive to Palm Springs. We'd go to the safest airstrip, and then to others if necessary. Dad believed in being prepared: "What is the *worst* that can happen [in a given situation] and how will we deal with it?" A plan would avoid panic and chaos.

Luckily, no one in the nation had to put plans in action. But the missile crisis had brought Tommy and me back to L.A., and we decided to stay. We put a down payment on a house and settled in. Tommy still recorded for Capitol, and was doing well in films.

When Dad started Reprise I asked him to let me try my hand at a single. He talked to his chief executive, Mo Ostin, and Mo said he didn't want any rock and roll records. I said that rock was here to stay but I agreed to do a novelty record like Annette Funicello. Mo said okay and put me together with Annette's producer, Tutti Camaratta.

My record was called "Cufflinks and a Tie Clip" (talk about novelty!). It was backed with an R & B (rhythm and blues) song called "Not Just Your Friend." The first time I heard the record on the radio I was in the car listening to my favorite station, KCMJ, which featured mostly black artists. The deejay said, "Here's Frank Sinatra's daughter's first effort." I was so startled to hear my R & B song played on this station and so thrilled to hear myself on the radio, I drove straight to KCMJ and got the disc jockey's autograph (talk about young).

My producer, Tutti Camaratta, picked another novelty song, "Like I Do," for the second single and we struck marinara. The record went to number one in Italy, Japan, and many other countries, but didn't even get *played* in the United States. My boss, Dad, was very pleased that his kid was making money, though not very much, for his new label. I assured him that one day I'd give Reprise its first number one in the U.S.—if they'd lift the moratorium on rock.

Tommy and I found a brand-new house up in the hills. It was a little more spacious and had a perfect bedroom for a nursery. I was looking forward to starting our family; Tommy said he was too. But when we were about to move into our new house he became frightened of the responsibility of children—he was only twenty-seven and though he was successful, he had not yet proved himself to himself.

Tommy sought advice from a therapist. Between them, the decision was made to end our marriage. They didn't ask me or tell me about it. We spent the few days before Easter of 1964 at the Sands Hotel. When we returned, Tommy unpacked, then repacked his suitcase and hid it in the closet. He didn't want to spoil Easter Sunday for everybody, but the day after Easter he dressed and we

Mr. and Mrs. Tommy Sands during the filming of Darryl F. Zanuck's The Longest Day, *Caen, France.*

started to chat, as we usually did, about our plans for that day. I thought it was odd that he was wearing a suit and tie, but I figured maybe he had a lunch date or something. He opened the sliding closet door and pulled out his suitcase and stood there, looking at me, trying to say something. I know how difficult it was for him, because he is a kind person who would never intentionally hurt anyone —especially me. Finally he spoke. "I'm going away . . . I want you to get a divorce right away. I want you to get on with your life . . . you'll be better off without me . . ." and the next thing I knew, before I could *hear* what he had said, he was gone. I recovered enough to run to the garage, but even though I banged on the car, he kept going.

I knew he wasn't coming back; Tommy didn't go in for grandstand plays. If he hadn't kept going he wouldn't have been able to try leaving again—it took too much out of him. Of course, I didn't know how right he was about our relationship; I was still looking at my life and our marriage as though they were on a Cinemascope screen.

I walked back into the house and called my mother. I said, "Mom, Tommy's gone and he isn't coming back . . . I'm all right now, but I don't know how long I will be. Please come get me." I sat in the living room for a while and I didn't cry. I was still in my nightie and, realizing this, I walked into the bedroom to dress. I saw our rumpled bed and fell apart. My mother took me to her home.

I had been working in a movie with my Dad, Deborah Kerr, and Dean Martin. It was called (sorry 'bout this) *Marriage on the Rocks.* My first day back on the picture Naomi, the hairdresser, was trying to make me look presentable. I heard my Dad's voice from outside the makeup room. The sound of his voice triggered a spilling out of all the pent-up sadness (I was trying to be brave) and I broke down—hard. Naomi got me through it. She splashed my face with cold water and discreetly called in Shotgun Britton, the makeup man. Shotgun patched me up so Dad wouldn't know about my tears. If he had known, he would have stopped filming and sent me home.

I asked for only token alimony—one dollar a year for five years. My mother was worried: "You can't move into the new house. You don't have the money for the mortgage." I said, "I know that. I have to borrow some from you. But I'll pay you back." And I did. Very quickly.

When Reprise moved to Warner Brothers, Mo Ostin put me with producer Jimmy Bowen, saying, "This girl has had hit records all over the world. Let's get her one here." Jimmy's roots were country and he didn't quite know what to do with Sinatra's daughter. We both tried very hard to cut a commercial record. But, though we did some interesting sides like Cole Porter's "True Love" (with an ominous rhythm feel), we didn't make magic.

Jimmy was friends with Barton Lee Hazlewood, Duane Eddy's producer. Duane had become a big record seller. Lee told Jimmy he knew how to record me and then made a deal with Mo. I was just about to be dropped from the label. Mo didn't want to spend money on another Nancy Sinatra session, but Lee played him a song and said he would get me a chart record the first time out. Mo said he'd give Frank's kid one more chance.

I was still staying with my mother. Jimmy brought Lee to her house. My father was there for a visit and he sat in the living room, reading the paper, while Jimmy, Lee, arranger Billy Strange, and I met in the bar. Lee strummed his guitar and sang the songs he wanted me to record. I especially liked a song that had only two verses and asked him if he could write a third verse. He said,

Breaking each other up is a way of life with Sinatra & Co. Here, with a piece of electrician's black tape across his upper lip, Sinatra undoes Dean Martin, when they were supposed to be shooting a straight scene. (See back of book commentary on movie **Marriage on the Rocks.***)*

"That's really not a girl's song. I sing it myself onstage." But he said he would write a third verse.

When they left, my dad said, "The song with the two verses is the best." Sure, he'd been *reading.*

While Lee worked on a third verse for that song, we recorded "So Long, Babe." It looked like a hit—and then it was, landing on the charts at about the same time as another "Babe" song, Sonny and Cher's "I Got You, Babe." I repaid my mother (as much as anyone can ever repay a mother) and things began looking up.

So, Mo Ostin signed Sinatra's daughter to a second contract with Reprise. This was not an act of charity; it is important to capitalize quickly on a success. With "So Long, Babe" on the charts and selling, I had now, like any performer, an edge in getting another record made and onto the lists. Still, although it's easier, it's harder. Now you have to try for a *smash* hit, not settle for any lesser ambition.

So it was vital that my second session with Hazlewood, arranger Billy Strange, and engineer Eddie Brackett be fruitful. Not to follow up "So Long, Babe" with another entry that made the charts would have been suicidal in such a highly competitive business. I'd probably not get another shot as good. We recorded "The City Never Sleeps at Night." And the B side was the song my dad liked, the one with two verses. Lee had added a middle verse.

The band was recorded first. (In this new technical era, the band and the singer no longer perform together in the studio: the band track is laid down first, then the singer listens and sings and in this way the voice track is added.) Billy Strange had done two solid charts that were country-rock ("rockabilly"). When I played them at home later, I called Hazlewood and said, "Listen, Barton, release the B-side track as it is. Don't even bother with a vocal—that track is a *smash.*" I sat there in my new house on Betty Lane, thinking of my date to record tomorrow, with what I felt was a hit track in my lap and butterflies in my tummy. If this record happened to become big, it would be because of that track.

We were ready to do the overdubbing at United Recorders Studio B. I asked Lee how I should sing the songs. He said, "Like a fourteen-year-old girl in love with a forty-year-old man." I didn't know what he was talking about.

Lee and Eddie "fattened" my voice with a tape reverberation technique —in essence the same principle used in the slap-back echo effect on Elvis's voice on "Heartbreak Hotel"—only much less. It worked fine except I was still singing like Nancy NiceLady. Lee hit the talk-back switch in the booth and his deep voice blew my ears off. "For chrissake, you were a married woman, Nasty, you're not a virgin anymore. Let's do one for the truck drivers." This was shocking to a somewhat sheltered girl like Sinatra's daughter. "Say something tough at the end of this one," Lee ordered. *"Bite the words."*

I did. I bit.

I still believed the B side should be the A side and I announced it bitingly to everybody as I strutted out of the studio with my new nasty image. I played the tape for Dad and he agreed. Late that night, Lee called me at home and said, "Nasty, this is Barton. We're going with 'Boots.'"

I knew what this record had. It does happen—you actually *feel* a hit. I had been recording for almost six years without such a feeling. I just knew we had a hit.

I had promised my dad the first number one for his label. I was, in fact, off

The "Boots" team in a recording session. Composer-producer Lee Hazlewood (head in hands), Billy Strange, arranger-conductor (bearded), the author-singer (bootless).

by one record. Old friend Dean Martin's "Everybody Loves Somebody Sometime" was the first. "These Boots Are Made for Walking" was the second. "Boots" reached number one in three weeks, a rate unheard of then. The Beatles' "I Wanna Hold Your Hand," soon afterward, was the only record to do the same thing. That's how big "Boots" was. "Boots" and I won three Grammy nominations (losing to Barry Sadler's "The Ballad of the Green Berets," a song about the Vietnam war).

Lee said, "Your name could have been Nancy *Jones* and 'Boots' would have been a smash." And I said, thanking him again, that without him my name might have been Nancy Jones.

God Bless the Child

My father was so proud and happy. He'd call me up and say, "Hello, star." Or, "Hiya, record seller." By the time "Boots" had topped the charts he was introducing himself to his audiences as "Nancy's father." I was proud, too, because I owed it to him; he had put his faith in me and had been such a good sport about my quitting school. I presented to him my gold album. The plaque read, "Thank you, Daddy."

home soon." And he grabbed my hand so tightly that the doctors had to pry his fingers open to get me out. The doctors were grinning. One said, "That's the first response we've had from him at all." The man was in a coma and they had thought he wasn't able to hear.

For months afterward I couldn't talk about it at all. When the military air transport got us back to San Francisco at about 2 A.M., we were told there were no flights to L.A. until eight o'clock. I was suddenly frightened, drained; everything from the trip was now coming apart inside me. I called my father and said, "Daddy, please send the plane. I want to come home."

To this day, I can't watch anything about Vietnam—the sights are just too painful. I cannot talk about the sights, sounds or smells of war. I have only feelings—no words. But I do run into guys all the time who say, "Thank you."

"What do you mean, 'Thank you?'"

"I saw you in Vietnam," a man will say, "and it really made me feel good."

That makes *me* feel good.

By the time of the Vietnam tour, my brother, who had done his own USO tour there, was established as the third singing Sinatra. He had started, a few years before, with Sam Donahue and "The Tommy Dorsey Band," and he was making great strides. When Frankie Jr. and company opened at the Royal Box in New York's Americana Hotel, a lot of Frank Sr.'s friends were there. Jack E. Leonard, Toots Shor, Jackie Cleason, Earl Wilson and Joe E. Lewis led the applause. *Newsweek* magazine noted that "Gleason stayed through two shows and was so overcome he had to cry a little. When young Frank sang 'Someday My Happy Arms Will Find You,' Lewis wept too. 'One of the greatest lines of all times,' the comedian blubbered. 'He's talking about a bottle of scotch.'"

Comparing Sr. and Jr., *Newsweek* said: "Dad had a leaner and hungrier look . . . Frank Jr. sings pleasantly and his voice has a color reminiscent of his father's . . ." In noting the difference between the 1940s and the 1960s audiences, *Newsweek* added: "When Daddy sang, teenagers swooned and squealed. When Frank Jr. sang last week, middle-aged women looked maternal and the men at their sides bawled into their booze."

The reviews were good, albeit sentimental. "There isn't one of us who doesn't wish him good luck and perhaps a climb to stardom" (Louis Sobol). Or not quite unbarbed: "A tribute to his mother" (Earl Wilson).

"I'm so nervous," muttered FS to a *Life* reporter, "this is killing me." Recovering, he said, "He sounds just like his old man. As a matter of fact, the kid sings *better* than I did at that age."

With two of his kids launched and the third, Tina, on her way to an acting career, Frank Sinatra was proud. So was I. In fact, soon he would be working for me. Royal Crown Cola gave me a hefty budget for my own TV special. FS Sr., FS Jr., Dean Martin, and Sammy Davis, Jr., agreed to be my guests. I'll never forget those guys coming through for me like that. I called it "Movin' With Nancy" and because I wanted a fast-moving, sharply edited, documentary-style show (not unlike today's commercials and videos), I decided to use film rather than tape. (Tape is flat and ugly.) I wanted one person and no one else to produce it. Jack Haley, Jr., was doing a lot of TV. I asked if he would be interested. Haley was with David Wolper's company and didn't feel like rocking the boat. Unless . . . "I'll do it if you let me direct it, too." "Deal," I said. I asked other friends to help. Tom Mankiewicz to write, David Winters to choreograph, Bill Schwartz and

A television Special, "Movin' with Nancy," was sponsored by Royal Crown Cola, who put up something like a half million dollars. Given the fact that her father, Sammy Davis, Jr., and Dean Martin worked for scale (minimum money), she still managed to spend the entire amount and wound up with nothing, another testimony to the Sinatra urge for quality in every aspect of production. Martin missed his own daughter's singing debut, Sammy missed an engagement at Tahoe, and Nancy missed the opportunity to prove herself a shrewd businesswoman. But the special won an Emmy.

Frank Bueno to produce for my Boots Enterprises, Sally and Jack Hanson (Jax) for the costumes. And of course, Billy Strange to do the score. Lee Hazlewood and I did "Jackson" and "Some Velvet Morning."

Jack Haley and I figured that Dean's work would take about an hour and a half. We started at 8 P.M., but the special effects got complicated. Dean's own daughter was making her singing debut at a little club at ten o'clock that night. He missed it. He was incredibly generous to me. He never complained. He had to keep going back to the trailers and waiting for the next setup. It just took so much time. And he came over to me about two o'clock in the morning and said, "You know, there's nobody else in the world that I would have done this for." And I put my arms around him and started to cry and I said, "I'm *really* sorry. I know you wanted to get out of here and I'm so sorry."

The day we were to film Sammy's number, we rented a Winnebago motor home for him and stocked it with his favorite wine and food and magazines. Unassuming Sam, realizing that nobody else in the crew had a place to go, never used the trailer, opting for forty winks in the back seat of his car. Everybody else used it. What a guy.

I told Haley and Mankiewicz not to write any dialogue for FS and me. I didn't want to take a lot of his time. We'd film him in a recording studio, the natural place for him to sing, and it came off beautifully. Pop sailed through it, was grateful for the considerate way we handled his segment. (The editing on the sound-track album later was less than marvelous, with the tempo changing during his "Younger Than Springtime" but, forgiving father that he is, he never mentioned it.)

One lesson I failed to learn. He had taught me to accept credit where it is due. Why? Because it helps you to get more work. But I never had myself listed as executive producer, which I was. That sort of thing wasn't done in those days by many women (we were still "girls") and none of my advisers suggested it. It was my feminine mistake, pun intended, and not the last one.

The night of the press preview of "Movin' With Nancy" at Chasen's Restaurant, it seemed as if *everybody* came. The cast, crew, staff, friends, family and some honest, legit journalists. Nobody except the people closest to it knew what the show was like because, like a movie, it had been done in pieces over a three-week period. We floored them. Everybody cheered and laughed and applauded. My father embraced me with shining eyes. He didn't have to say a word. His tears were eloquent.

Jack Haley won an Emmy.

I made movies, too—*Speedway* with Elvis Presley, and Roger Corman's *The Wild Angels*, with Peter Fonda, Bruce Dern, Diane Ladd, Gayle Hunnicutt, Michael J. Pollard, and a young dialogue director, Peter Bogdanovich. I was horribly miscast and out of my league among such splendid actors. Peter took me under his wing but even enfolded, it was clear that Bette Davis and Hepburn had no successor. In both 1967 and 1968, the motion picture exhibitors' organization chose me as the Top Female Box Office Personality, a title which came in spite of the minor fact that I was awful. Accidentally, I had shown up in (a) an Elvis movie and (b) what turned out to be a cult movie.

Then came the chance I'd been hoping for. Bill Miller, entertainment director of the new International Hotel in Las Vegas, offered me a three-week engagement in the 2,000-seat showroom—following Barbra Streisand and Elvis. I said yes, elated and real scared. I had never performed in a nightclub before. I had done fair dates and movies and a lot of TV, but this was the big

August 1969. By happy accident, the three singing Sinatras all played Vegas at the same time. Nancy at the International, Frank Sinatra at Caesars Palace, and Frank Jr. at the Frontier. After marquees blazed with this momentary monopoly, young Frankie hosted a vast, cheerful buffet/breakfast for the three bands, crews, and guests of the singing Sinatras who, as before, had the world on a string.

CHAPTER FOURTEEN
TRANSITION

The Age of Aquarius

It was an age of sorts, of Cassius Clay, the Beatles, the Pill, of Woodstock, minis, Baez, Dylan, of the hip and the hippies, the Mets, the moon, of tuning out and turning on. Of Black Power, Flower Power, and, in his own way, a continuing surge—for a time—of Sinatra Power. Reflecting in the sixties on his work, he said:

"I think I get an audience involved personally in a song—because I'm involved. It's not something I do deliberately. I can't help myself. If the song is a lament at the loss of love, I get an ache in my gut. I feel the loss myself and I cry out the loneliness, the hurt, and the pain . . . Being an eighteen-karat manic-depressive and having lived a life of violent emotional contradictions, I have an overacute capacity for sadness as well as elation."

He reflected, as others were doing, on religion: "I have a respect for life— in any form. I believe in nature, in the birds, the sea, the sky, in everything I can see or that there is *real* evidence for. If these things are what you mean by God, then I believe in God. But I don't believe in a personal God to whom I look for comfort or for a natural on the next roll of the dice. I'm not unmindful of man's seeming need for faith; I'm for *anything* that gets you through the night, be it prayer, tranquilizers, or a bottle of Jack Daniels. But to me religion is a deeply personal thing in which man and God go it alone together, without the witch doctor in the middle. The witch doctor tries to convince us that we have to ask God for help, to spell out to him what we need, even to bribe him with prayer or cash on the line. Well, I believe that God *knows* what each of us wants and needs. It's not necessary for us to make it to church on Sunday to reach him. You can find Him anyplace . . .

"There are things about organized religion which I resent. Christ is revered as the Prince of Peace, but more blood has been shed in his name than any other figure in history . . . I'm for anything and everything that bodes love and consideration for my fellow man. But when lip service to some mysterious

*"As I approach the
    prime of my life
I find I have the
    time of my life . . ."*

deity permits bestiality on Wednesday and absolution on Sunday—cash me out."

It was an age of love—love-ins and live-ins and slogans about making love, not war.

Shortly before my recording success, my father fell in love—hard. In 1965 Frank Sinatra was fifty years old, I was twenty-five, the new woman he loved was twenty, and my father wanted to marry her. I did a lot of soul-searching about it. I thought that perhaps I had failed to be the daughter I wanted to be, and that perhaps he needed me more than I realized. I thought he might be afraid of slipping over into middle age, and had reached out to Mia Farrow to save him. I questioned and worried and wondered but there was no need to. I should have known better.

As I began to spend time with Mia and Pop—dinners, baseball games—I realized how good for him she was. She called him "Charlie Brown" and he called her "my Mia." Although Mia wasn't into material things or extravagances, Sinatra presented her with a light yellow Thunderbird—"to match your hair"—and she wrote poems for him. They were romantic. The Swinger and the Flower Child. They were good together.

FS had so much bachelor rowdiness in his life with Dean and Sam and his other pals that he needed Mia's gentleness. And Mia needed someone to lean on, to help her mature.

Mia came from a big family. Her father was the director John Farrow; her mother, the actress Maureen O'Sullivan. I once asked Mia's "mum" what it was like to be Sinatra's mother-in-law.

Maureen O'Sullivan: "The thing that impressed me most about your father was, I suppose, his 'correctness of life.' Everyone, everything had its place and was treated accordingly. He answered the telephone himself, read each letter he received, and dictated an answer—knew what was going to be for dinner (and ordered it, often . . .). Every person, every thing, seemed to have its own niche in his plan . . . I was his mother-in-law and was treated accordingly. That is to say, with respect and kindness. In fact, it was quite funny because sometimes I would make a joke not quite in the mother-in-law context and his face would freeze into disapproval even though the joke was fairly harmless. So I learned not to do that. It worked the other way, too. When Mia and I were his guests at Palm Springs just before they got married, the telephone rang and Frank answered. The call was from some nosy newspaperman who had somehow got his number and wanted to know if we were there. 'How did you get this number?' demanded Frank, and he added as an afterthought, 'Don't call back, dammit.' He hung up the phone and looked at me sort of conscience-stricken. 'I'm sorry, Maureen.' I said that under the circumstances his language could have been stronger.

"Besides being an organized person, your father is a man of flair and sensitivity. We were high above the clouds in his Lear Jet on the way to New York. Mia was, as she always is, too thin, and your father was trying to coax her into eating. 'Have some dessert.' Hidden behind the cake was a little box with this lovely engagement ring. Such a dear way of doing things."

Mia didn't like crowds, but she accompanied Dad on the road and sat in the audience where he could sing to her. Many times Tina and I would sit with her, and Dad would introduce "my daughter Tina, my daughter Nancy, and my Mia."

In the hotel suite the three of us, Tina, Mia, and I, hung out in our

She called him "Charlie Brown," he called her "my Mia"; This Roddy McDowall photograph is a personal, private, unpublished one, given out by the couple as a Christmas gift to loved ones.

pajamas—Mia in her fuzzy slippers—until late in the day. Then, getting ready for showtime was fun. While Dad hit the steam room and dressed with the guys, we borrowed each other's clothes and makeup and shared a lot of laughs. It was like a dorm.

In Los Angeles, they bought a house in Bel Air and Mia, with decorator Laura Mako, created a cozy, romantic home with lots of dark wood and bright fabrics. The Old English house reflected Mia's love for the traditional. She had a little loft where she could think and read. They were very proud when they took me on the first tour. It was a party house, too. We had good times in the yellow, white, and chocolate brown bar.

They also spent a lot of time in Palm Springs. Adding on to his house there, Dad put in a tennis court, another two-bedroom bungalow, and projection/game room. Also a separate four-bedroom dwelling with a big living room/kitchen area, which he named the Christmas Tree House because of the big pine trees in front of it, and because it looked so out of place, a beautiful white house with dark green shutters and a shingled roof, straight out of old Connecticut, sitting in the middle of his desert property.

Tina, Frankie, and I loved the Christmas Tree House. It became our house, the kids' house. With all these new additions, the compound now slept twenty-two people, and it was full to capacity much of the time.

Freddie Brisson: "Frank's a giver by nature . . . He'd invited twenty-two friends to spend from December 18 until after New Year's with him. My wife Roz [Russell] and I drove down and spent a couple of days cleaning up the mess the workmen had left behind—Frank loves all that; he's up early in the morning, tearing around, supervising everything—and then we went into town to buy what was still needed for the house. Every one of Frank's guest bedrooms has two dressing rooms and two baths, so a man and his wife don't have to drip on each other. And all these baths and dressing rooms required stocking.

"In the village, we helped Frank pick out glasses and soap dishes, toothbrush holders and wastebaskets and makeup mirrors. If you visit the Innkeeper, you want for nothing. A whirlpool bath in your tub. Your medicine cabinet filled with cotton balls and eye pads and mouthwash and shaving tackle. Shower caps in your bureau drawers, bathing suits in your closet. There is also an old railroad freight car turned into a communal sauna and gym.

"After the more practical purchases had been effected, Frank decided the new guesthouse needed some paintings on the walls. The three of us walked into a store, and Frank was checking out the merchandise when the salesman, who had done a double-take, came rushing over. 'Mr. Sinatra, can I help you?' 'How many paintings have you got here?' asked Frank. 'I don't know,' said the man. Frank walked along a little further, admiring the pictures. 'I'll take 'em all,' he said. 'What?' said the salesman. 'I'll take 'em all.'

"That afternoon, when the delivery man arrived at the Sinatra spread with a truckful of art, Frank put him to work. 'You're gonna help hang 'em,' he said. And, for about four hours, Frank, Rosalind and I, along with the man off the truck, hung pictures in the new guesthouse. By the time the other guests arrived, every ashtray and potted plant, book and magazine Frank had acquired for the new cottage was in place."

The Innkeeper, indeed. His attention to detail and to desires can be remarkable.

Writer/director Garson Kanin: "I was at one of Frank's great Christmas/ New Year's holiday bashes down at the place at Palm Springs . . . one of the big sessions. Bennett Cerf was there, and the Leland Haywards, and the Arthur Hornblows. Of course, it's well known that he's the single greatest host since Perle Mesta. He got up at five o'clock every morning and he worked like a goddamned Yankee innkeeper all day to see that everybody had the right number of toothpicks. One day we went over to the golf club to have lunch, and my wife Ruth [Gordon] ordered a hamburger, and she said to the waiter, 'Could I have a slice of raw onion?' And Frank looked at her, quite astonished, and he said, 'You like raw onions?' And Ruth said, 'Yes, sometimes, on a hamburger, I'll have a slice of onion.' And Frank says, 'The onion they have here is no good. This is just onion. You gotta have Maui onions if you're gonna have a hamburger.' So Ruth said, 'What's a Maui onion?' And he said, 'You don't know what a Maui onion is?' And she says, 'I've never heard of such a thing.' 'For crying out loud,' he said. So he got up from the table and left.

"Late that afternoon, Mia said she wanted to take us for a drive to show us some part of the desert. We got into Mia's car and we drove for about fifteen miles and we were listening to the news on the radio. And the announcer said, 'Well, if you happen to like Maui onions, it's a good thing to know Frank Sinatra, because one of his guests expressed a desire to have some and Mr. Sinatra has phoned to Hawaii and the pilot of flight number such and such is going to deliver these onions to Los Angeles.' And the next day at lunch, we ate Maui onions. And they were the greatest onions that anybody ever had."

He is the perfect host. It's not often that a guest one-ups him, but it did happen at least once. Composer Leslie Bricusse and his four-year-old son Adam were invited to Palm Springs for a four-day weekend. As Bricusse recalled it:

"Adam received his best-behavior speech from me attentively, and with a couple of well-timed 'Yes, Daddys,' made me think everything was going to be all right. When we arrived and he was introduced to Frank, Adam pronounced 'Franksinatra' as though it were one word, and persisted in this throughout his stay. I remember wondering to myself for a fleeting moment whether I had misled Adam to believe that Franksinatra was a place, rather than a person. 'We're going to Frank Sinatra for the weekend,' I had said.

"Adam also met Jilly, who was down there, and together, Frank and Jilly spent the first hour attempting to corrupt Adam's impeccable four-year-old British accent into broad Brooklynese, by teaching him choice phrases like, 'I'm wit youse, baby,' and 'Who are dese bums?'—which received Adam's enthusiastic cooperation and lasting admiration.

"There was an atmosphere of rare tension in the usually relaxed household that weekend, due to the fact that the World Series was on television early each morning, and had developed into a protracted cliff-hanger. Despite the lateness of the nights before—movies in the Great Hall until either the last of us fell asleep or Frank threatened to show *Lady in Cement* to make us all go to bed —Frank, Jilly, and I would religiously make it to the sofa facing Channel Four in the Chinese Room each morning in time for the first pitch of the new game. We would stare blankly and unspeaking until either hot coffee or a good play sparked us to life.

"Adam, who had usually been up for hours before we surfaced, would have breakfasted and explored the estate with another new-found friend, Frank's black houseman, who for Adam was the real king of the place, because it was he who fed Adam and played all sorts of games with him—and when you're four years old, that's it!

"Three super new friends. Very flattering for a small boy—and perhaps a bit confusing, too . . . On the third morning, in the middle of the crucial seventh game, Adam wandered into the room to see us. He was frowning. 'Where's Franksinatra?' he asked. Nobody spoke. 'I've lost Franksinatra,' announced Adam. Frank responded. 'Hey, Adam, you bum,' he said. 'I'm Frank Sinatra.' Adam shook his head. 'No, not you,' he said. 'The black one.'"

Mia and her Charlie Brown had their problems, too, and after a year and a half of marriage, I heard that they had separated. Knowing Dad was in trouble, I went to Miami where he was doing a movie.

My dad was sad. He had that empty feeling and soon we were talking about the time, just before he'd married Mia, when he'd said, "I don't know, maybe we'll only have a couple of years together. She's so young . . . But we have to try . . ." Now he was hurting, but he said it would be harder for Mia to mend because of her age. "When you get to be my age," he said, "you've built a wall around yourself. You don't hurt as much as you used to."

Wall or no wall, my father hurt like hell. Just like everybody else.

The following summer FS was taping a TV special. I went to the studio to watch the "dress." The dress rehearsal went very well and, as always, it was taped, so that there would be editing options in case a few flaws slipped through during the taping of the final performance.

I was in Dad's dressing room when he came off the set. His friend Jilly took him aside and told him that Mickey Rudin, his lawyer, had called and that everything was over. He meant that Mia and Mickey had completed the final divorce proceedings in Nicaragua. Daddy asked Don Costa if the dress re-

Living well is the best revenge. With his friend, "the Chinaman," Yul Brynner, by the pool at the FS compound in Palm Springs. Brynner was once introduced on an opening night by Sinatra as one of three Oscar winners in the audience (with Burt Lancaster and Rod Steiger). Brynner signaled frantically to FS, holding up four fingers, but Sinatra only looked puzzled. After the show FS asked Brynner what all the semaphoring was about. "There were not three Oscar winners in the room," said Brynner, "but four." "No," said Sinatra, saddened that he had failed to introduce a person. "Who else?" "You Charlie."

hearsal had gone well for the orchestra. Then he looked around at the rest of us, took a beat, and said, "Let's go with the dress rehearsal. I can't do it again now." It was as if somebody had turned out the lights in his eyes.

Their marriage was finished but my friendship with Mia was not. We had managed to survive, to become good friends, in part because of our love for Frank Sinatra. I never had the feeling that I *had* to like her because she was my father's wife; I liked Mia for herself and for the way Dad had been when he was with her.

After they split up, she sought solace in India, with Maharishi Mahesh Yogi, guru for The Beatles. Then Mia put her pain into a brilliant performance in *Rosemary's Baby*.

(Overleaf) In Palm Springs, Sinatra deals with Ringo, one of the—by current count—seven dogs and four cats in residence, rescued from the pound. FS finds homes for them, mainly his own.

215

218

Mia's best qualities were always right up front. Today I love her for those same qualities: gentleness, intelligence, humor, and a very quiet strength. She is my friend, and we still have long talks—about the old days, about Pop, and, of course, about our children; she has seven and wants two more. She still has no interest in material things. Her life is full of love and work.

Almost twenty years after she had been Mrs. Frank Sinatra, Mia kept a promise to me. She wrote:

"When I think of the times we were alone together (my favorite times) it sounds too sentimental . . . crossword puzzles . . . spaghetti sauce . . . TV in bed . . . our puppies . . . walks . . . breakfasts . . . all those orange things . . . his incredible sweetness . . . *the purity of his feelings* . . . his smile . . .

"Looking back, I think that for us, our ages finally mattered. I was too ill at ease with his remoteness and unable to fathom his complexities. Though I knew how much he needed it, given my real immaturity I could not, I was not capable of being enough of a friend, however much I wanted to be. We had a great amount of love between us but we lacked understanding in everyday life as well as of the major, deeper themes. Today he is still a part of me. I think of him often and wish him the very best because he deserves it and, of course, because I love him."

The promise? This book is the result of a conversation with Mia, Dad, and the publisher Bennett Cerf. We were having a quiet dinner at Trader Vic's in Beverly Hills one night shortly after the wedding, and the new Mrs. S expressed her sorrow over all of the nastiness in the press—the comparing of ages, and the "Mama Mia" jokes. Dad remarked, "I wonder when the next book will be out and we'll have to go through it all over again . . ." Bennett said, *"You'd* better write a book about your father, Nancy, and tell the true story—once and for all. Think seriously about it. You have a responsibility."

Mia seconded that. Dad said nothing. But I knew by the look on his face that I would write a book—*this* book. Mia promised to help—and she has.

Guess Who

By the time their divorce came through, Frank Sinatra was no longer working at the Sands. The Copa Room was so small and the big Circus Maximus at Caesars Palace offered him opportunity to reach more people and earn a bigger salary. He took it.

Caesars Palace must have added ten rooms every time FS appeared there. The place always seemed to be under construction—and I have a hunch the appearances of FS paid for it all. The marquee occasionally read "GUESS WHO"; this finally evolved to a simple: "HE'S HERE." Nothing else needed to be said. The waiters, the bellmen, the guests, the whole place took on ten thousand volts of energy with each new FS appearance. They called him "the Noblest Roman of Them All" and said so on the medallions they had made for the guests. He packed every show, sometimes to the distress of the Las Vegas Fire Department, whose inspectors were constantly moving people out of aisles and off stairways. And the bedlam spilled over to the other hotels. When FS was in town, the whole town felt it.

My second Las Vegas appearance was at Caesars. The Blossoms and the

The Chairman and the Count. One of the great collaborations were those hours when Frank Sinatra, jazz singer, met up with Count Basie, bandleader. Basie was the pianist with the lightest touch and the biggest band sound in captivity. During one of their tours, says the author, "Dad's trunks, containing his music, were delayed. He asked Bill Basie how much show time he could fill. Basie looked at his watch and replied calmly, 'Let's see now, it's 6 P.M. on Sunday night. I think I can play until late Tuesday afternoon.'"

As Sinatra faced fifty, he said: "One thing I'd like to do if I can find the time is a long series of one-nighters, all over the country. I'd take an orchestra, like Basie, and a few other performers— comics, what have you . . . I'd like to go into a town and just sing for an hour or two, concert- style. It would be fun, and might even help the cause of good, solid jazz." Indeed, that is just what he has been doing for years (though sadly, of late, without the Count).

Osmonds, who had appeared with me at the International, joined up again. We added a chorus line of twelve guys and the show, which Hugh Lambert pro- duced and directed, was hailed by the critics and audiences. We were literally the talk of the town for a time. It was impossible to get a reservation. The house record was smashed.

Following this record-breaking engagement, Caesars offered me a fine, fat, long-term contract. My manager and attorneys were working out the details when my father called with what I think of as a This-is-what-really-happened call.

He had followed me into Caesars with his own show and a few nights after it opened, he got the impression that someone was being unfairly treated in the casino. So he went to the office of one of the bosses, Sandy Waterman, who —after some harsh words—pulled out a gun. Jilly and a security guard got the gun away from him but my father was furious. He told me that he was leaving Caesars "for good."

I was as angry as he was. You argue, sometimes somebody swings—but guns? *Never.*

My father could have been killed. So I killed the deal. I told my manager to forget the multimillion-dollar seven-year contract. I would not play Caesars again either.

As it worked out, over the next several seasons I ended up bouncing from one hotel to another for engagements, and GUESS WHO was back working at Caesars within a year.

Ah, well. I had made the choice of my own free will. If I had gone to him, he would gladly have helped to get me reinstated. But I didn't even tell him about it until fourteen years later, from the stage during our final Caesars Palace show.

Another incident in the sixties suggests our family loyalty. FS had a lovely vacation home overlooking Acapulco Bay, sharing it with us and with friends. One morning we were ready to go to the airport—Mom, Tina, Frankie, and I— to meet FS. We had our visas and luggage and were moving toward the door when my phone rang.

"Chicken," he said, "I can't go dere."

"Why not, Daddy?"

He had been called by a local man named Raoul, who looked after the place for us, and warned that they wouldn't let Sinatra through customs. "But you and the others can go on without me." He explained that he didn't under- stand it all, but Raoul said something about a clerk in the government, some- where, who didn't like our movie *Marriage on the Rocks*, and an official had given an order: Do not let Sinatra back into Mexico.

I said, "I'm in that movie too. If they don't want you, they don't want me either." Dad didn't want our vacation spoiled, but I insisted again that his fight was our fight.

I was angry. My dad had done much charity work in Mexico. During 1961 and '62 he went there twice, each time at his own expense, taking his band and entourage there for the sole purpose of doing benefit performances for Mexican charities. Now some bureaucrat was telling him he couldn't come to visit his own house.

The brouhaha turned out to be an annoying inconvenience. Indeed, as it developed, the Mexican government had not banned FS from the country, although for a long while the petty bureaucrat made it seem so. The minor official based his whole "case" on a couple of scenes in *Marriage on the Rocks,* in one of which an actor says, "Don't drink the water"; in the other there was a reference to quickie marriages and divorces. It was so stupid. And the embarrassment the situation caused my family, especially my father, was hurtful, humiliating, unnecessary.

Nineteen sixty-eight was a presidential election year. During the primaries, though my heart was with Bobby Kennedy once he entered the race because he had promised to end the war, I didn't campaign publicly for him, because of my father's relationship with the administration.

In Miami Beach Dad and I watched as President Lyndon Johnson gave a television talk. This was the startling "I shall not seek nor will I accept the nomination . . ." speech. Afterward, we spoke, as we had before, about the war, politics, possibilities.

My father believed strongly in Hubert Humphrey. He felt he should run. I said, "He must address the issue of Vietnam." "I agree," Dad said. "But he won't as long as he is Johnson's Vice-President. He will not embarrass L.B.J. by denouncing the war." I couldn't abide this—I had seen that atrocious war and I knew it had to end. My father knew it, too. He also knew that Hubert Humphrey felt the same way. If Humphrey had told the American people then how much he hated that goddamned war, he would have won the election. But he waited too long.

When Bobby was killed our nation was shredded. We had all taken too much. Nobody could be indifferent anymore to the outcome.

For a while after the assassination, Frank Sinatra, though still campaigning for the Vice-President, was quiet. We didn't discuss it any longer. I joined his team. I went all out for Humphrey. Traveling for show business and on Democratic Party business was a strain but we all had to do something. I was in Chicago for the Democratic Convention in '68. My father called and told me to stay in my hotel—there was going to be trouble. I was so tired I thought, "To hell with it," and got out of town.

Dad also campaigned hard for H.H.H. He helped him with his TV presentations. Gave him lessons about the camera. We did private fund-raising rallies, public rallies, luncheons, dinners, big shows. When it was over, and we had lost by so little, Dad became quiet again. In 1969 our candidate wrote me about his friend.

Hubert H. Humphrey: "My first recollection of your father was during the time of Roosevelt. I recall the good work he did on behalf of racial equality and fair employment practices. I recall how he went to the schools and talked to the young people about all forms of prejudice and intolerance. Your dad was a hero to these kids and he took this powerful message right to them—touching both their hearts and minds. I am convinced that this early dedication and activity personified by your father helped create the political climate that made possible the passage of the civil rights legislation in the 1960s. Thousands and thousands of boys and girls in the 1940s who have become parents and mature citizens in the 1960s had their eyes opened for the first time to the evils of prejudice by your dad . . ."

Hubert recalled the time in 1968 when he and my father went to the White House one night, very late. They went in the back entrance and up in the elevator to find the President in a characteristic posture for receiving visitors. He was in his bedroom, flat on his stomach, having a rubdown. He looked up and said, "Hiya, Frank. What have you and Hubert been conspiring to do tonight?"

What they had been conspiring to do was a series of concerts in Watts, an almost war-torn ghetto in Los Angeles, the proceeds of which would be used for voter registration, to help implement the Voting Rights Act of 1965.

"What I recall most about your father . . . is his great concern for the country, and particularly for black Americans who have been so long denied an equal opportunity . . . He is a solid, devoted American liberal in the tradition of Roosevelt and Truman, Kennedy and Johnson, and—if I can be immodest—myself."

Grandpa

The year of trouble and turmoil was not over. Two months after the sad election defeat of Hubert Humphrey, in January 1969, I was hosting a Kraft Music Hall Special at NBC Studio 8H in New York when my Dad and Jilly walked in. I was surprised. I hadn't expected them. I raced over with my usual enthusiasm. "Daddy, I'm so happy to see you. What are you doing here?" I was hugging and kissing and smiling, and then realized that he wasn't smiling. His eyes were red and tired. He said simply, "Please call your grandfather."

He gave me the phone number of a hospital, which I called, but Marty, who was being examined by the doctor, said, "I'll call you back." When he did, I couldn't come to the phone at that moment because I was undressed, getting body makeup. I didn't know then how important it would have been to find a way to take that call.

By the time I was able to call him again, Grandpa was too ill to talk. Dad rushed him to the most famous heart surgeon in America, Dr. Michael De Bakey in Houston, Texas. But Grandpa was beyond help. "Despite all our efforts to improve his condition over the next five days in order to perform an operation for his aneurysm of the aorta," Dr. De Bakey later informed me, "he unfortunately became progressively worse."

The asthma that had plagued my grandfather all his life had developed into emphysema. So, to compound his heart problem, his lungs were failing. Dr. De Bakey told me that in all the years he'd spent watching people deal with their parents' grave illnesses, he had never seen anything like my father's devotion. He was moved by such concern, and especially by the unashamed displays of affection and "tender love."

For five agonizing days my father watched his father die. Each time he entered the room he said, "Hello, Dad," and kissed him. And he kissed him each time he had to leave the room. In between, he held Grandpa's hand. He caressed his face and he wiped his mouth. They had always been openly affectionate, men of few words, understanding each other easily.

To lose your father out of your sight, to lose him on an operating table or in an accident, that must be wrenching enough. But to be at his side, holding his hand, hearing him gasp for air . . . To watch him die. I don't know . . . I just don't know and cannot imagine the magnitude of that grief or the torture for both men. I don't know what they went through individually. But they went through it together. I just know that this was the latest loss for the man called Sinatra. The man I call Dad had lost the man he called Dad.

FS: "My father was a darling man, a quiet man . . . a lonely man, and shy . . . Oh, but he was a lovely, lovely man. I adored him. In some ways, the greatest man I ever knew in my life."

LIFE

Sinatra Says Good-by and Amen

A farewell to 30 very good years

JUNE 25 • 1971 • 50¢

CHAPTER FIFTEEN
ONE MORE FOR THE ROAD

In 1971 he decided to step out of the spotlight. He has "capped a career," as Life *put it, "that included 58 films, 100 albums, and nearly 2,000 individual recordings." And more. "I'm tired," he told Tommy Thompson. "It's been a helluva 35 years. I always sang a tough book, you know . . . It used to wring me out." His father's death meant a change of life and attitude, as well. He wanted to at least "pause to think things over," said his friend Rosalind Russell, "to be without pressure for the first time in his active life."*

Like many Americans, my father had been silently strong through the assassinations of J.F.K. and Bobby and Martin Luther King, Jr. He had taken the loss of Mia, and Hubert Humphrey's defeat. But when his father died, something snapped.

Grandpa's funeral was a nightmare. My grandparents were living in Fort Lee, but Hoboken and Jersey City also honored Marty's memory. At the mortuary chapel, Dad, Mom, Frankie, Tina, and I stood by the casket for hours, shaking hands and thanking people for coming to pay their respects. I don't know how it happened, but after that, somehow we ended up in a bizarre receiving line. The people, most of them elderly, were so touching. They seemed to *need* to tell Marty's boy how sorry they were. Dad couldn't take it. He walked back to the more private part of the chapel. The rest of us took turns out front. Dolly was quiet. My mother had been looking after Grandma. She had shopped for a mourning veil and made sure Dolly was dressed comfortably each day.

The requiem mass was painless, all things considered, but the drive to the cemetery was not. Grandma had chosen a grave in another town and every person in the area who knew Marty was in the cortege. The side streets were guarded by fire trucks, black-and-white Dalmatians, and uniformed firemen who stood at attention when the hearse passed. As nice as they were, the townspeople caused a traffic jam that took hours to clear. When we finally reached the cemetery, Dad was upset with Grandma's bad judgment. Dolly liked a good funeral and her husband had to have the best—but she hadn't realized that their friends and neighbors, augmented by Dad's fans and interested bystanders, would turn the funeral into a circus.

At the gravesite there was bedlam. So many people. Thank God for Jilly Rizzo and Dad's good friend Danny Schwartz. They were all over the place trying to maintain order. Our priest, Father Robert Perella, was conducting the

burial ceremony and offering up prayers when Dolly tried to throw herself on Marty's coffin. "Hurry up, Bob. *Hurry up,*" my dad said, as he and Danny and Jilly pulled Grandma back. Father Bob raced through the holy water and incense and started the final prayer. Grandma was wailing, "Marty, Marty, don't leave me." Dad again said, "Hurry up, will ya, Bob?" and Father Bob jumped to an Amen and we placed flowers on the coffin and managed to get Dolly into the car. Jilly and Danny had figured out a different route back to Fort Lee. There had been no time for a decent service, a proper goodbye.

Less than a year later, Dolly moved Marty's body back to Fort Lee and, eventually, to Palm Springs.

Back at Grandma's house, Uncle Vince, who had lived with Marty and Dolly for over fifty years, and others brought out food. About sixty of us went to the basement bar where Marty used to make his famous banana daiquiris, and where all the framed photographs on the walls reflected the rich, full life of the Sinatras. It was a sad night, but Daddy found comfort in his family and close friends. Soon afterward, he began building a house for Grandma on his property in Palm Springs. And he began considerable soul-searching.

Politically, his alliances had begun to change. This was a time of protest from the Left against the flag, remember. He was still a registered Democrat, and his liberal views still held in most areas (including the controversial question of terminating a pregnancy, which he believed should be up to the individual woman and her situation). Ronald Reagan, an old friend, welcomed his support in the 1970 campaign for reelection as California's governor.

Frank Sinatra, Jr.: "Pop came out for him, but advised him to move a little more to the middle of the road." This support did not sit well with Tina, who is assertively liberal today as Daddy once was (and in reality still is, if the right man is running).

Hugh Lambert and I made plans for Dad's fifty-fifth birthday. We had been making other plans as well. We had fallen in love. Since we worked so well together, we thought we would make a good team offstage too. And since Daddy liked to *give* presents on his birthday, I decided he should give me to Hugh. He did.

Our wedding was held in a beautiful small church in Cathedral City, California, a church normally filled on Sunday afternoons by the area's Mexican families. They had come to church as usual this Sunday but found it closed and were milling about outside when my father drove up with Jilly and my brother.

Frank Jr.: "These people were in their white dresses, carrying their little flowers, standing there, most of them speaking no English, and Pop wanted to know what was going on. 'We closed the church after masses today just for the wedding party,' one of the priests said. And the color came up in Pop's face, and he said, 'You closed *their* church? To *them?*' He said, 'Open up the doors, let 'em all in. Don't keep them out of their church.' "

They came in and helped celebrate my wedding. I loved it.

I'm not sure my father was overawed by the solemnity of the ceremony. During the proceedings, Dad said later, he couldn't take his eyes off Hugh's shoes when we were kneeling at the altar. Because they were brand-new, the soles were a pretty beige color and without a scratch, like a little boy's party shoes. Pop said he wanted to take a crayon and print *L* and *R* on them for left and right.

Dad hosted the wedding celebration at his house in Palm Springs. My

sister caught my bouquet (I threw it right to her) and Uncle Ruby caught my garter (he had to fight Leo Durocher for it). Hugh's mother, Mae, turned out to be some kind of match for Pop. She hung out at the bar with him and the guys until six o'clock in the morning. It had been a beautiful day. But painful, too, because my grandpa wasn't there.

I felt closer to my dad after he "gave me away" than I ever had before. He seemed a little more introspective, but at the same time more relaxed. He bought a piece of property in the mountains above Palm Springs, not too far from where Frankie had gone to school, and planned to build a house where all of us could get away from the heat and the smog. He also bought back his hillside home in Los Angeles. He sold his lovely Grosvenor Square flat in London and his East Seventy-second Street, New York, apartment and reestablished headquarters at the Waldorf Towers. He was beginning to plan for the future and I felt very much a part of it.

Between nightclub engagements, Hugh and I spent a lot of time with Dad in Palm Springs, and my relationships with both my men were thriving. I felt safe and secure. Mom and Dad were together a good deal, and with Grandma living "next door," we were really a family again. It was a peaceful time. Dad's trips away seemed like disruptions—to all of us.

For a long time he had been saying, "Will somebody please get me the hell off the road?" He was tired and sick of the traveling. So it didn't surprise me when he informed us that on March 21, 1971, he would formally announce his retirement. He said that although he'd enjoyed the exciting three decades of work, there had been "little room or opportunity for reflection, reading, self-examination, and that need, which every thinking man has, for a fallow period, a long pause in which to seek a better understanding of changes occurring in the world."

Now he was fifty-five. A good time to pause and think. To think about the changes in the world at large and in *his* world—especially the loss of his father, about his own priorities, and his own mortality.

He went out on top. On April 15 Sinatra received one of the highest honors bestowed by his peers—a special Oscar, the Jean Hersholt Humanitarian Award, presented by the Motion Picture Academy of Arts and Sciences. Then on June 14, for his final appearance, he was the headline performer at a Los Angeles benefit for the Motion Picture and Television Relief Fund. A stream of stars—Jack Benny, Sammy Davis, Don Rickles, Bob Hope, Barbra Streisand—preceded him onstage. Daddy sat in his dressing room with the writer Thomas Thompson. "He was nervous," Thompson reported. "He had carefully orchestrated this finale and being the most meticulous of men, he wanted it played with style and grace. He took the typewritten list of the fourteen songs he would sing and he looked at it over and over again. He threw it down on the table and began doodling. His felt pen created a house, then he filled it with black strokes, covering the windows and doors as if no one lived there anymore . . ."

He took a look back at the days he sang for cigarettes in Jersey: "So here I am tonight forty years later, going out the same way I came in—singing for nothing." He took exception to reports that he was retiring because of his health: "My health is spectacular. In fact, it's never been better. That's why those goddamn rumors burn me. It shows the irresponsibility of the American press." Before going on, he took some kidding from Don Rickles: "You're gonna be great out there, Frank. People love pity, Frank."

"Is there anybody," Thompson wondered, "whose voice does for him

what his has done for us, all of us over thirty, all of us who recollect Sinatra drifting over from the phonograph in the corner of the living room, the fire low, the wine spent, Sinatra murmuring reassurances. Sinatra, every man's advocate in seduction. Sinatra, every man's ally in romantic defeat."

He was introduced onstage by Roz Russell and I can still hear her distinctive voice: "This assignment is not a happy one for me. Our friend has made a decision. His decision is not one we particularly like, because we like him. He's worked long and hard for us for thirty years with his head and his voice and especially his heart. But it's time to put back the Kleenex and stifle the sob, for we still have the man, we still have the blue eyes, those wonderful blue eyes, that smile; for one last time we have the man, the greatest entertainer in the twentieth century."

He said, "Might as well begin at the beginning." And then he sang "All Or Nothing At All." "I've Got You Under My Skin." "I'll Never Smile Again." "The Lady Is a Tramp." "Ol' Man River." Then his frequent closer, "My Way." And everybody offered up the loud applause with which they would honor the end of his career.

Except the world's greatest entertainer, the master tugger of heart-strings, did one more—a rousing "That's Life."

Again, the applause to usher out his era. But with the clear call for encores, perhaps for never-ending encores, and in the tradition of respecting the audience, the song, the composer, the lyricist, the arranger, he did one last piece of work.

Thomas Thompson: "He had built his career, he said softly, on saloon songs. He would end quietly on such a song. He slipped from his words into 'Angel Eyes,' surely a song for the short hours. He ordered the stage dressed in darkness, a pin spot picking out his profile in silhouette. He lit a cigarette in midsentence and its smoke enveloped him. He came to the last line. 'Excuse me while I . . . disappear.' And he was gone.

"It was," wrote Thompson—and I most emphatically agree—"the single most stunning moment I have ever witnessed on a stage."

After thirty years, he did a final thirty minutes. He did a predictable encore, then an unexpected one. His art, fame, fortune, the legend, and even many of the facts, were in the record books.

Dear Nancy —
It Was
a thrill working
with you. We
must do it again
real soon.
Bye!
the Former Super Star

CHAPTER SIXTEEN
OL' BLUE EYES

Time Out

Shortly before retiring, Dad had realized a dream: the Anthony Martin Sinatra Medical Education Center in Palm Springs, for which he had raised the funds. In its dedication, he evoked the memory of Marty, his late father.

FS: "He's here [he said, pointing to his head] and here [pointing to his heart] and this splendid structure is my dad's kind of dream, just as it is yours and mine. I remember a line in a childhood prayer that said, 'Send me blessed dreams and let them all come true.' "

Well, Pop, your dream has come true.

The governor of California spoke, too, and added to the thought of dreams. He said that two parents once invested their dreams in their son.

Ronald Reagan: "They saw the dream come true, beyond anything they could have hoped. Then the son gave it back to them. Frank, you're living proof that life does begin when you begin to serve."

The tears turned to laughter when Dr. Dan Kaplan made Dad an honorary staff member of the hospital. The gesture was probably unnecessary, Dr. Kaplan observed, because "Frank's been operating for years."

Dad had worked hard for Reagan, too, and that was part of his political change of focus. Though retired, and still a registered Democrat, he followed more strongly than ever his practice of voting for the man, the candidate, not the party. Richard Nixon's announced policies made more sense to Sinatra than George McGovern's so it followed that Nixon was his man in the 1972 presidential race. He was drawn to Mr. Nixon in part because "in the early sixties, President Kennedy had advocated recognition of Red China in his book *Strategy of Peace.*" For years, FS had felt that the United Nations was remiss in their stand on the issue.

FS: "I don't happen to think you can kick 800,000,000 Chinese under the rug and simply pretend that they don't exist. Because they do. If the UN is to be

But now the days are short,
I'm in the autumn of the year.
And now I think of my life as
vintage wine
from fine old kegs.
From the brim to the dregs,
it poured sweet and clear,
It was a very good year . . .

The "Former SuperStar" inscribed this grizzled portrait for his daughter Nancy as he moved into what would be a restless retirement.

truly representative, then it must accept *all* the nations of the world. If it doesn't represent the *united* nations of the world, then what the hell have you got? Not democracy—and certainly not world government."

He wasn't out of sympathy with the aims of the antiwar movement and he was only half joking when he spoke to the growing role of women and their possible use of an ultimatum: "If all the women in the world would say to their men, 'Forget *it* until you get rid of all the weapons,' there wouldn't be any more war."

Dad's support of Nixon did not sit so well with all of the members of his family, especially with the McGovernites among us.

Tina: "He came out publicly one afternoon—I think it was a Friday. The report said, 'Frank Sinatra endorses Richard Nixon'—and I hit the roof! This is where he and I *are* alike. And I called him on the phone and I said, 'Goddamn it, I've been working for George McGovern for six months—I haven't swayed twenty voters and you just probably swayed two million.' He said, 'That's the way it goes, kid. Are you angry?' I said, 'I'm very angry!' He said, 'You work in your way, I'll work in mine. That's politics—it's a free country.' I said, 'I'm really upset.' He said, 'Why don't you get in your car and come down here?' So I drove down to Palm Springs. I was loaded for bear and he was ready to take me on, and we had it out and he said, 'Whatever it is you believe in, fight for it. And do the best you can—and be as effective as you can—but I came out for *my* man and if I swayed voters, I swayed voters, but I have to go public too.'

"He's said to me many times, 'The older you get, the more conservative you get.' He's still the street kid, but he's in a society that—well, some of his friends are so stuffy, but he likes it. It's a place, a standing in life that he, I think, wanted to attain."

Tina didn't stop. She fought for it. "Agnew was at the Palm Springs house for a party, and I was running around getting voters to register for the '72 election. Every time I'd land a Democrat, I'd shout, 'Got one!' And Agnew would laugh.

"During Watergate I'd get on Daddy about Nixon. He'd say, 'Nobody's perfect.' He has loyalties. That lawyer, Charles Colson, who went to jail because of Watergate, and Vice President Agnew—he remained friendly with all of them. He loves underdogs; he is crazy about the guy who needs help."

He is. And he will defend anyone who has made a mistake. His attitude is this: He's made mistakes. We've all made mistakes. The President of the United States is a human being and can make mistakes.

Richard Nixon: "Among the characteristics which impress me about Frank are his unfailing loyalty to his friends whether they are up or down, his refusal to be anybody but himself as distinguished from other celebrities who can not resist putting on airs, and his unfailing candor and honesty in dealing with the media."

Frank Sinatra was a man of privilege in 1972, a man in favor with power brokers from the President on down. And yet he felt an underdog himself. The reason was by then familiar: another probe into his "ties to crime," this one by a congressional investigating committee. "He is the most investigated American performer," Pete Hamill later wrote, "since John Wilkes Booth." Why had he been summoned before the congressional committee? It had to do with an investment in a racetrack.

Attorney Mickey Rudin: "The facts of the matter were that it was a minor investment. Evidence developed that they were trying to use your father's

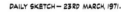

"SURE I'VE RETIRED—
BUT I STILL LIKE YOU GUYS AROUND
IN CASE I FEEL LIKE A SING IN THE BATH"

name to promote the track. Even before there was any knowledge that the racetrack involved persons that the newspapers would refer to as Mafia, and the fact that there was evidence of attempted bribery of the Massachusetts governor, a plan was made for the return of the investment, and withdrawal from that investment. The money was returned. The file in that matter was turned over to the FBI by us, before any request was made for the file but in anticipation that something might go wrong. In other words, *we* went to the law enforcement authorities and told them of our involvement before anybody could raise questions as to that involvement."

Nevertheless, Frank Sinatra was called before the committee, a travesty that resulted in no evidence that he'd done anything wrong and personal apologies to him from at least two congressmen. FS delighted in one comment only: that of the person who said, succinctly, "Frank Sinatra has been the victim of printer's ink." This time, at last, Dad protested publicly. In an article published in the July 24, 1972, New York *Times,* he wrote:

"At one minute after 11, on the morning of July 18, I walked into a large hearing room in the Cannon Office Building in Washington to testify before a group called the Select Committee on Crime. The halls were packed with visitors; the rows behind me were sold out. And every member of the Congressional committee was present, an event which I'm told does not happen too often.

"The details of what happened that day have already appeared: the tedious questioning about a brief investment I made in a minor league race track ten long years ago; whether or not I knew or had met certain characters alleged to be in the crime business; whether I had ever been an officer of the Berkshire Downs race track, etc. With my lawyer providing some details that had been lost in the passage of time, I answered all questions to the best of my ability. Assuming that the committee even needed the information, it was apparent to most people there that the whole matter could have been resolved in the privacy of a lawyer's office, without all the attendant hoopla.

"But there are some larger questions raised by that appearance that have something to say to all of us. The most important is the rights of a private citizen in this country when faced with the huge machine of the central Government. In theory, Congressional investigating committees are fact-finding devices which are supposed to lead to legislation. In practice, as we learned during the ugly era of Joe McCarthy, they can become star chambers in which facts are confused with rumor, gossip and innuendo, and where reputations and character can be demolished in front of the largest possible audiences.

"In my case, a convicted murderer was allowed to throw my name around with abandon, while the TV, cameras rolled on. His vicious little fantasy was sent into millions of American homes, including my own. Sure, I was given a chance to refute it, but as we have all come to know, the *accusation often remains longer in the public mind than the defense.* In any case, an American citizen, no matter how famous or how obscure, should not be placed in the position of defending himself before baseless charges, and no Congressional committee should become a forum for gutter hearsay that would not be admissible in a court of law.

"Over the years I have acquired a certain fame and celebrity, and that is one reason why so much gossip and speculation goes on about me. It happens to a lot of stars. But it is complicated in my case because my name ends in a vowel. There is a form of bigotry abroad in this land which allows otherwise decent people, including many liberals, to believe the most scurrilous tales if they are connected to an Italian-American name. They seem to need the lurid fantasy; they want to believe that if an entertainer is introduced to someone in a nightclub, they become intimate friends forever. But it is one thing to watch a fantasy for a couple of hours on a movie screen and then go home. It is quite another thing when the fantasies are projected on real, live human beings, because it doesn't say 'the end' when they are finished. Those human beings have to go on living with their friends, family and business associates in the real world.

"We might call this the politics of fantasy. Sitting at that table the other day, I wondered whether it was any accident that I had been called down to Washington during an election year, a year in which Congressmen have difficulty getting their names into the newspapers because of the tremendous concentration on the race for the Presidency. It certainly seemed that way.

"And I wondered if the people out there in America knew how dangerous the whole proceeding was. My privacy had been robbed from me, I had lost hours of my life, I was being forced to defend myself in a place that was not even a court of law. It wasn't just a question of them getting off my back; it was a question of them getting off everyone's back. If this sort of thing could happen to me, it could happen to anyone, including those who cannot defend themselves properly. I would hope that a lot of Americans would begin to ask their representatives, in the Government and in the media, to start separating fantasy from reality, and to bring this sort of nonsense to an end once and for all."

Nice 'n' Easy

Despite the strength of his statement, it wouldn't end, of course. But I was proud of him for speaking out.

And, retired or not, he still went out—and began to do some traveling, this time for fun. At times we were able to share the fun; at times it was something else. One of his trips was to Biarritz. He invited my mother, Hugh, and me to join him, after he had been there for a few weeks. Quickly we got our passports and vaccinations and packed. We were ready to leave on the 9 A.M. flight to New York and then on to Nice, where Dad and Jilly were to meet us. At that point, the phone rang.

"Hi, Chicken."

"Hi, Dad."

"You all ready to leave?"

"Yep."

I knew what was coming. He had been on the Riviera for a few weeks and I sensed that he would be getting restless. He said quietly:

"I wish I were coming the other way."

"Why don't you?" I said. And he did. So much for traveling.

Oddly, it was President Nixon who was indirectly responsible, at least in part, for Sinatra's slow but sure reentry as a performer. The Nixon campaign brought him onstage. On October 20, 1972, for example, FS sang at a Young Voters for Nixon rally in Chicago. This was the first time he had sung in public since his retirement and he did "My Kind of Town (Chicago is)," picking the right tune, as usual, for the right time and place.

I've been a puppet, a pauper,
a pirate, a poet,
a pawn and a king
I've been up and down
and over and out
and I know one thing.
Each time I find myself
flat on my face,
I pick myself up and get back
in the race—

An appearance on November 1, 1972, raised $6.5 million in bond pledges for the state of Israel. In March '73 he received an award from the Thomas A. Dooley Foundation, and in April he appeared at the White House. This time it was the President who drew the criticism.

President Nixon wrote to me, January 30, 1984, that: "My most vivid memory is of that occasion when he sang at the White House after the dinner we gave for the President of Italy. When it was announced that he would sing, some of the critics wrote to me, objecting that because of his 'background' [there it is again] he should not have been invited. I thought this was nonsense and responded in that vein . . .

"I felt that he was one of the nation's outstanding performing artists and that our guest from Italy could not feel more complimented than to have him perform on that occasion."

Mr. Nixon said that he considered it one of his best decisions. And I wondered who some of the "critics" were. Apparently they had not read the New York *Times* on Dad's "politics of fantasy," or perhaps they were under a rock when members of Congress apologized to him.

But, criticism or not, slowly and inexorably Frank Sinatra was moving back to work. He'd had some time to relax, he began to miss what had been for so long at the core of his life, and eventually he agreed to go along with the requests made in the more than thirty thousand letters he had received, many, according to his secretary, Lilian Peloso, begging him to "at least make an album again."

He recorded an album that contained, among other songs, "Send in the Clowns," "Winners," and "Let Me Try Again." There had been a great deal of discussion in our family about the title for the album and when I learned his list of songs, I suggested that he call the album *Let Me Try Again.*

He looked at me with that deep stare as if to say, "Will you get outta here with that corny stuff." Then he said, "I've already got the title."

I said, "What? What?" He told me.

I *hated* it. I said, "You're kidding. That's awful."

Awful or not, his choice prevailed. The album—and then a November 1973 television special—was called *Ol' Blue Eyes Is Back.* This phrase became part of the American folk culture, which shows how wrong I was about it!

Hugh did the choreography and staging for the television event. Gene Kelly was Dad's special guest star. Tina and I talked for days about what to wear. The audience invited to the taping was jeweled, black-tie and glamorous—a Who's Who of Hollywood, a guest list that could unnerve even the most seasoned performers. "Uncle" Gene and Pop (who had just been named "Entertainer of the Century" by the songwriters of America) were visibly excited and nervous. But the audience loved their whimsical "Can't Do That Anymore" and Dad's singing and Gene's dancing on "Nice 'n' Easy." Aside from the newer album cuts, Dad reprised "I Get a Kick Out of You," "I've Got You Under My

The two guys in sailor suits were re-united again for the TV special that welcomed back "Ol' Blue Eyes." "The audiences loved Uncle Gene's dancing on 'Nice 'n' Easy,'" writes the author, "and Dad's singing 'I Get a Kick Out of You,'"—although there were problems with the voice.

You simply can't forget her, the moment you have met her, your heart will wear her picture like a frame. Tina, Tina, nobody quite like Tina. That's the little lady's name...

Tina, in some ways as outspoken as her father, shares several other traits—the temper; a streak of solid gold stubbornness; an independence; and what she calls a tendency to "control and create."

Tina (her wedding day) recalls FS's reaction when her niece was born. "Dad and [promoter-producer] Jerry Weintraub were in New York. As the sun came up, they said, 'That's it, no more drinking, no more late hours,' they'd start to take care of themselves. They went that evening to a seafood restaurant and Dad got a call from Hugh. Nancy had just given birth to A.J. Dad came back to the table and said, 'That's it,' that's the end of being on the wagon, and they had drinks, whereupon Dad ordered thirty thousand clams. Jerry said, 'You can't do that,' and Dad said, 'Yes, I can. I'm a grandfather and I want thirty thousand clams.' The headwaiter asked coolly, 'How would you like them served?' and Dad said, 'In bowls, a hundred at a time.'"

The two celebrants went through hundreds before they gave up and went on to other revels.

Skin," "Street of Dreams," "Here's That Rainy Day," and many other Sinatra standards.

The show was a hit but Dad said later, "When I haven't sung for a while, my reed gets rusty." There were, indeed, problems with his voice.

He told me, "If you don't sing all the time, when you go back it's a whole new voice. No bottom; you gotta pound on it for a while."

Robert Merrill: "After a two-year retirement, the vocal cords and the muscles don't respond right away. He realized that. So he called me—he was coming to New York for ten one-nighters in a row. And he was worried that his voice wouldn't hold out. He has a great ear and he knew his singing wasn't really right. He told me his problem. I said, 'Yes, I heard it.' He said, 'Can we meet? I'd like you to listen to me sing.'

"We met at his hotel, the Waldorf Towers. He sang for me and I gave him exercises—scales—to do to relax his throat. When you're in trouble and you're tired, you tighten your throat to get *some* sound out—and that makes you even more tired.

"See, the trick of singing well is to have the throat open, relaxed. Let the voice come through into the resonating cavities. What he was doing was keeping the voice down. He thought he was making big sounds, but he wasn't. You *try* to make big sounds, you're forcing it. You have to let it flow.

"He knew this, but he'd been away. It's like getting out of a sickbed and trying to walk right away. Your muscles are tired. You have to practice and vocalize. He understood it and he did the exercises and he did his ten performances with no problems. Then he went on TV and talked about the trouble he'd had and said, 'I have a great teacher—Bob Merrill.' Well, I'm *not* a teacher professionally, and suddenly I started getting calls from all sorts of people who wanted to study with me."

Hugh and I continued to spend a lot of time in Palm Springs, the warmth of family increased by the glow of carrying my first baby. Christmas Eve, 1973, we finished our late show at the Sahara in Las Vegas, then boarded the plane at 2:30 A.M. We headed to Palm Springs, tired and hoping that Angel, the gardener, would be at the airport to pick us up. Arriving, we saw a small crowd on the runway: Mom, Tina, Frankie, assorted friends and a mariachi band led by Guess Who singing "Jingle Bells."

The house was ablaze with Christmas lights outside and in. It was beautiful. We sat by the big fireplace and had hot toddies and sandwiches until 6 A.M.

After a big brunch on Christmas Day, Grandma's birthday, we prepared for a trip to the house in the mountains. As we left I said, "Where's Grandma?"

"She doesn't want to come," said Dad. "And I don't know what to do with her when she gets like that."

Hugh and I walked to Grandma's. "I'm not going up that goddamn mountain," she said; "I don't care if it is my birthday and Christmas."

We pleaded, not wanting to leave her alone, but she had made up her mind. Since the Christmas/birthday dinner was planned for the Mountain House and all the presents were already there, under the tree, we had to go without the birthday girl. We were quite accustomed to those little wars between Dad and Dolly—but still, it was hard leaving her.

The Mountain House was glorious. It was cold, with just enough snow up there to give us a white Christmas. We exchanged gifts, had a simple dinner, and relaxed by the fire until it was time for Hughie and me to return to Las Vegas.

We made it to Vegas for our eight o'clock show Christmas night, exhausted but full of memories to last a lifetime. For me, the most vivid, even now, is that of my parents' glowing faces as they sang "Jingle Bells."

In early 1974, Frank Sinatra gave still another gift. He gave his other daughter away. Tina married record mogul Wes Farrell in Dad's penthouse apartment at Caesar's Palace. As they walked down the aisle, Tina felt what we all know as familiar panic—unless you are feeling it for the first time. "Oh, my God," she whispered.

"What's wrong?" FS said.

Tina just answered, "Oh, Daddy."

Knowing her anxiety, he broke the tension by whispering back, "Don't worry, Pigeon, you can always get a divorce."

It worked and Tina laughed her way to the altar, serious as she was.

My first daughter, Angela Jennifer, was born on May 22, 1974. Ol' Blue Eyes met Baby Blue Eyes at Cedars of Lebanon Hospital in Los Angeles. When he held her in his arms for the brief moment they would allow him, I knew we had given him the greatest possible gift. He had given me life, and now I had added to his.

My father's name is on records, films, buildings, hospital wings, orphanages, TV shows, books. And yet, until my first child was born he had no real link to the future.

Frank Sinatra: "I said a silent prayer that the world would be as good to this little angel as it's been for me. I guess what makes me the happiest about all this, of course, is that our little beauty was born safely and well, and that her mother, my own Nancy with the laughing face, is so well and happy. And I wouldn't be telling the whole truth if I didn't admit all this gives a little tug at my own heart strings to think that my mother, little A.J.'s great-grandmother, is alive and in great shape and so thrilled by all this . . ."

Then he changed the tempo. "All I ask is that Nancy never let the child grow up and see *The Kissing Bandit*. I've been trying to change my name ever since. As a matter of fact, the picture was so bad that on leaving the theatre, I made a citizen's arrest of the cashier."

By then he was, as you can see, back in form, wisecracking his way to the top once more, a top he had somehow never vacated. He was playing once more to overflow crowds at Caesar's and his high spirits overflowed, just as he was overjoyed by his granddaughter. From the stage, he raised a toast to the brand-new A.J., saying, "I wish her a hundred times the fun I've had—and one hundred times as many guys as I've had broads."

Some grandfather.

But he was as serious, devoted, and concerned a grandparent as one could want in those hopelessly wholesale sweepstakes of human love.

He was working Caesar's on his first Father's Day as a grandfather and Hugh and I decided to surprise him with a visit. We commandeered Dad's Lear, and with nanny Mary Bryson in tow, flew to Las Vegas, planted A.J. in her bassinet outside the door to his suite, rang the bell, and hid around the corner.

He opened the door to find his three-week-old grandchild—a bundle of dark hair, elfin blue eyes, and flailing arms—cooing up at him. I suspect he had never heard a sweeter song. He scooped her up and held her close.

Then he called out to everyone—his staff and musicians who occupied the rooms up and down the corridor—to come and meet her.

Eventually, even her parents were allowed in.

You make me feel so young, you make me feel like spring has sprung . . .

Hugh and Nancy Lambert, FS and baby A.J.

CHAPTER SEVENTEEN
THE CHAMP

e was back at work. In July 1974 he did a second tour of Australia, once again an episode marred by problems with the press, some generated by them, others self-induced. After the long flight to get there—Australia is not just around the corner—he was tired and chose to avoid the mob scene at the airport. A number of reporters took offense and were unnecessarily cruel the next day. FS answered their remarks with a few choice ones of his own from the stage and what amounted to an international incident was generated.

This brought a harsh reaction from certain Australian unions who refused to work on his concerts, and others who refused to service his airplane. The scrappy exchange was blown completely out of proportion—and the tour was almost blown with it.

Dad's attorney, Mickey Rudin, negotiated a truce and a final concert was televised nationally, for the people who hadn't gotten a chance to see him live.

To his audience, Sinatra said with his own blend of sincerity and breeziness, "I like coming here and I like the people. I love your attitude, I love the booze, and the beer, and everything else. I like the way the country is going and it's a swinging place." Peace.

Back in the U.S.A. he was not looking for new problems, new challenges, or new worlds to conquer. His promoter, Jerry Weintraub, however, had an idea.

Weintraub: "He wasn't too keen on doing TV. He didn't want to rehearse, he didn't want to bother with it. I went to Vegas to meet with him, and I went up to his suite and we had a cup of coffee. He said, 'What do you want, pal?' I said, 'I want you to do a TV special.' He said, 'Aw, I don't want to do a TV special.' 'Come on,' I said. 'We'll do it live from Madison Square Garden and we'll call it "The Main Event." And we'll make it like a boxing ring. We'll get Howard Cosell to do the announcing. [That's what did it. Dad loves Cosell.] You are the main event, you're the greatest singer in the world, you'll be the main

I've sung with the best, and I've had it all.
I've gone from neighborhood saloons to Carnegie Hall.
And the experience I have to say was grand.
But I couldn't have made it without them—
here's to the band . . .

event.' He said, 'I like it. Do it.'

"We put the thing together and we went into New York and we had 350 technicians working on that show. I was producing it, and I was over at the Garden and Frank never came over. I had all these people and it was a live show and we were doing an album and we were going to broadcast around the world as well. So it was not a little thing that we were doing here. And I called him at the hotel and said I needed the lineup of songs. But he kept stalling me.

"Finally I got a call from his secretary and she gave me a bunch of songs. And they're none of his songs. No 'Chicago,' no 'My Way.' Nothing. None of his stuff. I said, 'My God. I gotta talk to him.' So I run over to his hotel, walk into the suite, and he's sitting in his bathrobe reading the newspaper. I said, 'Frank, what are you doing?' He said, 'I wanted to see ya, I figured it was the only way to get you over here.' Then he gives me his songs, his regular lineup. And he says to me, 'I'll see ya over there. What time we starting?' I said, 'Nine o'clock we're on the air live, round the world.' He said, 'Great, I'll be there. Don't worry about it.' "

Jerry worried: "Twenty till nine, his limousine pulls up. He gets out of the car, and he walks backstage, and he says to me, 'Pal, you don't look too good.' I said, 'We got a lot of work to do, you know, I'm in a panic.' And he said to me, 'Who's gonna put up a card when we got five minutes to go, so I can start "My Way"? Put him in a red shirt so I can see him.'

"We start the show, and we're walking down the aisle and we get to the curtain where his music is supposed to start, and he turned to me and he said, 'Jerry, you look white as a sheet.' I said, 'I'm scared to death.' And he looked up and he pinched my cheek, and he said to me, 'Don't worry about it, pal. You got me into this, and I'm gonna get you out of it.' "

With more than twenty thousand people inside the arena and a second live audience stretching from Nova Scotia to Rio de Janeiro, he put on a landmark performance.

Producer George Schlatter: "Frank himself is an event. He's more than a singer, more than a person. There is that energy he exudes. Plus, he's always prepared and always on time. I've known him many years and I've never known him to be late. Always early. In a town where late is a way of life.

"We did a TV show with him and John Denver. I put together the longest medley I had ever done, which was a look back musically at the career of FS. Behind Frank and John there were three huge screens, all intertwined with projectors—his whole career projected on these screens. And in front of him there were guys from the Harry James band on one side, the Tommy Dorsey band on the other side, the Nelson Riddle orchestra in the center, and Basie in front. A hundred musicians. And top to bottom, it was a fourteen-minute medley. I said, 'We're going to do this in one take, and I want it rehearsed. I want the band here at twelve o'clock, ready to rehearse. Frank's not on call till one, but I want to know everybody's there.'

"They're all there and we get the sound balanced, and at twelve-thirty Frank walks in—half an hour early—and says, 'How long am I gonna have to wait?' And I said, 'Nelson?' And Nelson played the medley. And Frank said, 'That sounds pretty good.' I said, 'Would you like to sing that once?' He said, 'Yeah, of course I'd like to sing it once.' So he and John sang the medley. And Frank said, 'What are we gonna do now?' I said, 'Well, you don't need it, but John needs to rehearse it again, 'cause these are new songs to him.' And so they ran through this medley again, and Frank says to me, 'Well, what time do we do

"Here's to the Band." He had, as the lyric says, sung with the best, and had it all, but all was never enough. These lines from Tennessee Williams, says Nancy, sum it up: "It is only in his work that an artist can find reality and satisfaction, for the actual world is less intense than the world of his invention and consequently his life, without recourse to violent disorder, does not seem very substantial. The right condition for him is that in which his work is not only convenient but unavoidable."

There were times,
*   I'm sure you knew,*
when I bit off more
*   than I could chew.*
But through it all,
*   when there was doubt,*
I ate it up, and spit it out.
The record shows I took the blows,
and did it my way . . .

Dad in his Dracula outfit (right), October 13, 1974. The man does a little show at Madison Square Garden called, simply enough, "The Main Event"; television carried the performance worldwide and, as sure as the sun succeeds the stars, an album followed.

this?' I said, 'The audience is coming at seven o'clock.' He said, 'Damn. What do you think, why don't we do it at six?' I said, 'Hey, that sounds good to me.' He said, 'No, really.' So we went around and we got an audience together. And now we're ready to go. And you've got to understand, there's one hundred musicians onstage and three projectors and seven cameras and a fourteen-minute medley of songs, some of which John Denver didn't really know.

"So Frank comes out of the dressing room about five till six, and he says, 'How late are we gonna be?' I said, 'We're gonna start at six o'clock Mr. Sinatra.' And he says, 'Okay.' Now we get up there and Weintraub says to me, 'This is it, one take.' And I say, 'Absolutely.' I know how Frank hates to rehearse and how he hates to do more than one take.

"He starts singing and it was great. But in the middle of the medley, your father hits a clam you could drive a truck through. Really blows a note. He may have only hit six in his life, but this was number one or two of the six. The rest of the medley is great and when we go downstairs, everybody tells him, 'That was great, that was great.' I was standing there and I didn't say anything. He said, 'What do you think?' I said, 'I loved almost all of it.' He said, 'Did you hear it?' I said, 'Yeah.' He says, 'Are you telling me you want to do it again?' I said, 'I'm telling you, *you* want to do it again.' So he looks at me, and he can look at you longer in a few seconds than anybody in the world, 'cause those big blue eyes go right through you like two laser beams. And he looked at me for what seemed, oh, three and a half years, and everybody kinda backed up like there was gonna be a shootout. 'Cause he's not crazy about retakes. He says, 'I'll give you four bars on either side.' I said, 'Deal.' He knew where it was, what it was, sang it again, and that was the best note he ever hit in his whole life. He got to the end of the four bars and said, 'Good night, everybody,' and he was in the car and gone while they were still applauding.

"He's one of our national treasures. Anywhere you go in the world, when you talk about America they know Coca-Cola, they know the Statue of Liberty, they know Sinatra. And yet, with all of that, there is an innocence to him. There is an innocence in his fierce loyalties. An innocence in his sense of what is right. A boyish naughtiness. I think when he's all alone, he's about nine years old. There's a childlike quality in this man. He loves cherry bombs. He loves birthdays. He loves Christmas. He's patriotic.

"And he loves to laugh. That man *loves* to laugh. I went down to his place in Palm Springs to go horseback riding. And I rode out across the desert. And I was looking good. Damn, I had on a cowboy suit and a cowboy hat, and I was looking *good.* We got back to the barn and up to the rail, and I fell off the horse. So I made everyone promise, 'Let's not tell the big guy.' Well, by the time we got back to the house, he knew it. And he still calls me 'Hopalong'! So you never want to let him catch you at anything, 'cause he will stay on you."

The laughs and the high life were tamer for Frank Sinatra in the seventies than in previous decades. But only in comparison to the kind of expectations Tina once described: "One year I flew to meet him in Monte Carlo. On the plane he had said, 'I've a *big surprise* for you!' As I was coming into Nice from Munich, all these fireworks were going off. It was so elaborate. I looked out the window and I said, 'Oh, my God! When he throws a surprise, he really throws a surprise!'

"It was Bastille Day. I didn't know it until I got off the plane. I said, 'Did you do that?' He said, 'No, I think the French did it. Two hundred years ago.' "

There were still sillinesses in the seventies. Tina: "I can't tell you about

"A portrait is often a revelation to the painter as well as to the sitter. When I finished Frank's portrait, I found I had painted a man withdrawn into himself, thinking private thoughts. It is not the face of an extrovert; that face appears when the music and the fun start and he bares himself in song . . . never all of himself, but enough to captivate several generations and still remain an enigma to them and, perhaps, himself."　　　　*—Paul Clemens*

the night he set off the cherry bombs in the lobby of this hotel in Paris and the concierge nearly had a heart attack. I *can't* tell you about that." There were still manic impulses. Publisher Bennett Cerf: "A boisterous and happy party at Bill Styron's house in Martha's Vineyard ended with Frank and Bill trying persistently to get Fidel Castro via long distance to protest the fact that they couldn't seem to get decent Cuban cigars in New England any longer." And there were still wild trips.

Golf champion Ken Venturi: "In the middle seventies, I lived in Palm Springs and Francis and I were almost inseparable. One day he said, 'Would you like to go to Chicago? I have to perform there on New Year's Eve.' Sure. So he said, 'Why don't we take a train?' He rented some private cars on a train from San Bernardino to Chicago and a bunch of us get ready to go. I pick up a couple of brakeman outfits—the scarfs, the overalls, the oilcans, the whole thing—and some other props and I stash them away. You're going to be on the train for two days you might as well have something to do.

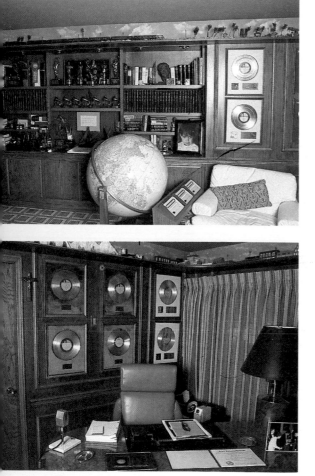

The private man's private places. Office, Palm Springs, full of golden records, pictures, globe, and memories, mostly golden.

"We meet at Francis's house and we go in two limousines from Palm Springs to San Bernardino. We arrive at San Bernardino about an hour early, so we go into a bar—there's a fellow playing pool with a couple of hookers—and we ordered a round of drinks. The drinks came and there was one short. The girl who took the order was about six foot tall, about 190, and Pat Henry said to her, 'Excuse me, but you forgot this gentleman's drink.' And he was pointing at Francis. She said, 'What did you have?' And Francis said, 'Gin and tonic.' She said, 'You're not fooling me now, you guys?' She looked under the table to make sure we hadn't hidden one, then she said to Francis, 'Are you kidding me?' He said, 'No, I'm serious! I didn't get one.' She said, 'Well, you look like an all-right guy. I'll take it *this* time, but don't try this trick again!'

"We get on the train and we ride through the night. In the morning Pat Henry and I put on the brakeman outfits I bought. The train makes a stop—'for about fifteen minutes,' the conductor said—and Pat and I go outside. We're on this track, surrounded by homes. Pat and I get into an argument and we're talking in a broken Italian: 'Hey, what you gonna do-a with this-a train?' And so on, down the line. We began to shout. People began to open up their shades. We had oilcans and Pat says, 'Is that a good-a oil you're using?' And I said, 'It's-a the best oil you can-a have for this-a train.' He says, 'Let me see.' I had filled it with Coca-Cola and I squirted it in his mouth. He rattles it around in his mouth a little bit, then swallows it and then he goes, 'Yeah, that's-a good oil—you can-a use this.' So we go up and down the train, oiling the wheels and every now and then we squirt a little bit of it in our mouths and wash it around and knock it down and the people are staring at us. What's going on?

"In Albuquerque we stop at the train station and there are a bunch of Indians with headdresses and the whole thing. Everybody except Francis is off to one side of the car, looking out the window. So I ran in and got this arrow I'd made, which you could stick around your head. I whispered to Francis, 'Put this on your head and sit there and don't say anything.' He does. Everybody was still looking out the other side and I said, 'We've got to get the hell out of here! These people look dangerous.' Pat Henry says, 'You've got to be kidding—dangerous. I mean, there's nothing . . .' I said, 'Don't kid *me* about dangerous. Turn around!' And there Francis was, with the arrow in his head."

Another day, in Palm Springs, they were playing charades. Ken Venturi: "You'd have a certain amount of time to get the title and then a timekeeper who says, 'Time's up!' Well, he was trying to give us a clue for a song title when his

Dear Francis Albert Who said Barber Shop Quartets were passé? Ronald Reagan

Dear Frank, in appreciation of our friendship. Gerald R. Ford

Best wishes, Jimmy Carter

Dear Frank— all this lacks is our top White House crooner. With you in it—what a great quintet— [signature]

In a valuable photograph, four Presidents inscribe best wishes to citizen Sinatra.

date, Barbara Marx, said, 'Time's up!' He said, 'Time can't be up!' She said, 'Time is up.' He said no, she said yes. He then proceeded to say how well he knew the time and that she was wrong and now we thought our game of charades is almost over. So she had this clock in her hand—a nice little antique clock—she showed it to him and said, '*This* is why you're wrong.' And he said, 'I'll show ya about the clock!' And he picked up the clock and he threw it across the room and it hits the door and shatters. And now there is a complete silence and no one knows what to do. And I jumped up and I said, 'I got it!' And they said, 'You got what?' And I said, 'I got the title!' So he says to me, 'What do you mean?' I said, ' "As Time Goes By." ' "

The mixture of fun and games, tension and relaxation continued and nothing much seemed to have changed. Concerts in New York with Count Basie and Ella Fitzgerald. The London Palladium with Basie and Sarah Vaughan, where there were 350,000 orders for the 15,000 available tickets. FS gave 140 performances in 105 days during 1975.

In 1976 the Friars Club chose him as "Top Box Office Name of the Century" and not only colleagues but colleges began to recognize him. He accepted the Scopus Award of the American Friends of Hebrew University in Israel and an honorary Doctor of Humane Letters designation from the University of Nevada. This hardworking, self-educated dropout (he was always reading in spare moments) from the Hoboken school system called Dolly with the news from Nevada, saying, "Ma, I graduated today."

The quiet, personal good deeds multiplied. In Honolulu he went to

Overleaf: Super Granddad walks with A. J. Lambert, his year-and-a-half-old associate, to his chartered plane, which he is surely ready to give her.

Fly me to the moon and let me play among the stars. Let me see what spring is like on Jupiter or Mars. In other words, hold my hand . . .

dinner with his friend Buck Buchwach, the newspaperman, and said, "I hear you've been having trouble with your heart."

"Yep, but I've been feeling okay for the past few months and I'm working full time at the newspaper."

"Never mind," my father said. "Here's what you're going to do. Clean up whatever you have to at the office, then hop a plane to Houston and see Dr. De Bakey. I'll phone. He'll be expecting you."

Buck Buchwach: "Dr. De Bakey . . . Because of his backlog of patients at that time, one was lucky to get an appointment after six months. I arrived at the Houston hospital in the afternoon and that night—after an angiogram examination—Dr. De Bakey told me I was probably going to die in less than two years if I didn't have a coronary bypass operation. The next morning he operated. I had a tougher time than predicted, but after a double bypass and ten days in intensive care, I was moved to a private room for a remaining ten days in the hospital . . . Frank called the nurses daily to check on my condition. Then he sent my brother Lew and his wife Sylvia in a private twin-jet to pick up my wife and me at the Houston airport. He didn't want me subjected to any possible delays or problems with commercial aircraft, so had us flown directly to Portland, Oregon, where I recuperated for four weeks at my brother's home.

"Every single day I was in Portland I received a phone call in the early afternoon from Frank, wherever he was, inquiring about my condition, kidding me, boosting my spirits, massaging my ego, and transmitting as much encouragement as anyone ever got over a phone line . . . I was scared. I thought I was going to die. Those calls were life-restoring doses, far more effective than any prescription. . . .

"Now, ten years after that dinner with Frank Sinatra in Honolulu, I am happy, healthy, working a full schedule at the newspaper, and enjoying my widely scattered seven children to the fullest—all because in 1974 The Man ordered me to get a medical checkup and then made sure I survived.

"I never had a friend who asked so little and gave so much of himself."

There were, in the midst of all this, melancholy moments for Frank Sinatra in those mid-seventies. Late one winter night, after dropping off a date, he was in his limousine with the writer Pete Hamill.

"You have to go home?"

Hamill said no.

"And so for more than an hour," Hamill wrote, "on this rainy night in New York, we drove around the empty streets.

" 'It's sure changed, this town,' he said. . . .

" 'Ah, well,' I said. 'Babe Ruth doesn't play for the Yankees anymore.'

" 'And the Paramount's an office building,' he said. 'Stop. I'm gonna cry.' "

They drove on.

". . . 'You like people and they die on you. I go to too many goddamned funerals these days. And women,' he said, exhaling and chuckling again, 'I don't know what the hell to make of them. Do you?'

" 'Every day I know less,' I said.

" 'Maybe that's what it's all about,' he said. 'Maybe all that happens is you get older and you know less.' "

CHAPTER EIGHTEEN
GRANDMA'S MOUNTAIN

On St. Patrick's Day, March 17, 1976, I had my second child, a perfect little girl, Amanda Katherine. She was a delight; I looked awful.

All my life I'd been chemically, metabolically, like my father—a skinny adolescent and, in my twenties, even skinnier, prompting one clever critic to compare me—unfavorably, I think—to a cadaver. Now I couldn't lose weight.

It was as if I had invented the post-partum blues. My doctor, confronting my earlier skinniness and anxiety, had always told me not to worry. As I stuffed myself with mashed potatoes and milkshakes, he'd say: "You'll see. After you have babies, your body will change." It had changed, all right. But while my physical problem would be solved quickly, I was about to confront an emotional crisis that would take a lot longer to work out.

And what I have to write now should be seen in that light, as the first reactions of a temporarily emotionally unstable young woman.

My sister had told me that Dad and his friend Barbara Marx were in a serious relationship, perhaps even engaged. I didn't believe her. Barbara wasn't Daddy's type. What's more, when I went to Palm Springs for Easter, Mom was there with us and Barbara, who had lived in Palm Springs for years with her third husband, Zeppo, was nowhere around. Also, the last time Mom had come down to Dad's, she and I had gone over to Barbara's for margaritas. How could Barbara and Dad be seriously involved?

Easter in Palm Springs was lovely—a much-needed vacation for me, I had so much help with my babies—and I enjoyed seeing them in the arms of their grandparents.

Dolly cracked me up one night. She loved to slip me a little cash when she could, and always insisted on putting the money in my hand. One night she folded up some bills and put them in two-year-old A.J.'s hand and then she did the same thing with her infant great-granddaughter. Amanda Kate couldn't grasp the money, but Dolly managed to hold it against her tiny palm long

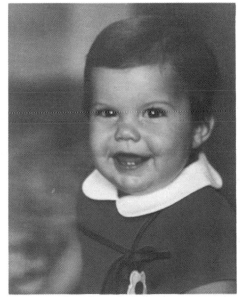

His mother loved this portrait (opposite page) by photographer Frank Sinatra of her granddaughter and great-granddaughters. Nancy Sinatra holds A.J. (left) and Amanda. His mother liked to bestow sentimental gifts on the girls, mostly green, fresh, and folded, from her purse. Above, Amanda Lambert, "A.K.," new arrival.

When Grandma wasn't spending money on the kids, she liked to make it at the track. AJ seems so serious, in the bright light of Dolly's beaming smile, that she must have been thinking about the odds.

enough to say, "Here, baby. Here's your first present from your great-grandma." Dolly believed in simple, basic things—like cash.

Good Friday was typically quiet, with a visit to church. Holy Saturday was spent at the pool, with Dad taking pictures of his daughter and granddaughters. Easter Sunday was lovely. Dolly was so proud. We *were* a fabulous family. My parents looked so right together. I saw a glimpse of that happy ending.

Frank Sinatra married Barbara Marx on July 11, 1976. I cried for a week before the wedding. Because I knew this was It. Again, my instincts ran the reel off its sprockets. My Hollywood kid's fantasy feelings of happy trails into the sunset were wrong. No chance now for him and my mother to get together and grow old together, spend the rest of their lives together—which I think we'd all been hoping for, including my mother. That hurt more than anything. It was finally and forever over, and my mother would have to come to grips with it.

Barbara and Dad were married at Sunnylands, the lovely Rancho Mirage estate of Walter H. Annenberg, publisher of *TV Guide* and former Ambassador to the Court of St. James's. Just before the ceremony, Daddy called Tina and me aside. He didn't take us out of the room, but just to one corner. He said, "I want you to know that I've thought this out very carefully. I thought a lot about Mother, and I know this is the right decision. This marriage is the way to go. This is the best thing for me."

I felt terrible. Still, just the fact that he was getting married was a relief. In the years since he'd been divorced from Mia, I'd felt a certain amount of responsibility whenever he was alone a lot—you know, as if there were something I should be doing that I wasn't doing. And I didn't want to be his wife. Tina didn't want to be his wife. But with parents, you worry if they're alone.

There were amusing moments at the wedding. They exchanged rings, and cars too (Barbara bought Dad a Jaguar and he bought her a Rolls-Royce), and when the judge asked the bride if she took the groom for richer or poorer, Dad announced, "Richer, richer." But my eyes just glazed over. I would look at life through that glaze for a long time to come. I kept thinking about my mother.

We were expected to stay the night, so we did. But left quickly the next day.

For the month of August, Grandma invited me and the children to La Jolla, where she always spent the summer. We played on the beach, and from our rented apartment, just below Dolly's, we could see the seals cavorting on the big rocks out in the ocean. Dolly spent her days at the track in Del Mar. When she had a winner, she would press winnings into her great-granddaughters' tiny hands.

FS and Barbara visited us one day on their way back from Newport Beach where Dad had done a photo session with his old friend John Wayne. They looked happy—Barbara blond and pink, Dad tanned and smiling, his blue eyes bright. I was moved to tell them so. I was happy for them. And as we waved goodbye, I felt—my whole being felt it—that my Dad was really gone.

Dolly felt it, too. We sat with the children and watched the birds that were nesting on the patio. I looked out at the sea and asked Grandma if we could spend the whole summer with her next year. She sighed, just the way Daddy does, and said, "I won't be here next summer."

"Why not?" I asked. "You hate the desert heat, you love the track. Why wouldn't you rather be here?"

She said matter-of-factly, "I won't be anywhere."

I sort of laughed it off: "Oh, c'mon, Gram."

But Dolly was serious. She said, "I'm tired, Baby . . . I miss Marty."

We saw her next at her birthday dinner on Christmas night. She, like her only son, was a December child.

On January 6, Dad opened once again at Caesar's Palace. He flew to Las Vegas early in the day with a group of friends from Palm Springs. Grandma and her friend Anne Carbone were supposed to have gone with Dad, but—and this was so unlike her—Grandma didn't feel like it. She said she wanted to go later. She said she would come to the Showroom directly from the airport.

When Dad left, a coming storm was already sweeping Los Angeles. Clouds and fog had darkened the pass and were coming in over the desert valley. That's when Grandma went on her odd errand. She had asked Dad to give her the few pieces of jewelry she kept in his safe, and now she wanted to put them in her deposit box at the bank. As if moved by some strange premonition, she ran that errand and a couple of others. Then she went home to dress.

Dolly was meticulous—again, like her son. Her hair was groomed at all times. I never saw her with curlers or pin curls. Once in a while I saw a clip holding an already carefully designed wave, but that was all. She had small hairpieces which augmented the upswept curls on her crown. She wore one this day. Her maid, Maria, watched her put it on.

Grandma bathed and splashed on her favorite White Shoulders cologne, she dressed in her black brocade and a pair of those funny little boots of hers. When my record "Boots" was climbing the charts, she used to say it was because of *her* boots. She had the boots made to order because the high tops helped to control a chronic swelling in her ankles.

Grandma did all the things she always did when she was going out, but she took a longer time to do them.

She packed her rosary, her white lace handkerchief with the *N* on it, an extra pair of glasses, some breath mints, her allowance check, her money purse, her tiny religious medals, some small bobby pins and her compact in her black ostrich double-strapped handbag. Concerned about the time, Maria asked her if she needed help. Maria had not seen "Mrs. S." like this before. Grandma was never late.

By the time she had buttoned her black broadtail coat and wrapped her kerchief around her head, the sky was black. It was the worst storm in years. Dolly was one hour late for the chartered plane that was to take her to Vegas.

She said goodbye to Maria, then told her to remember that "if anything happens to me, everything goes to my grandson." She got in the car with Anne.

Our gardener, Angel, a dear, gentle man who has been part of our family for twenty-five years, drove them to the steps of the jet. Grandma said to Angel, "Remember, everything goes to my grandson."

I know how difficult it was for her to climb those steps. According to her doctor, she was only weeks away from needing a walker.

The plane taxied down runway three-zero and waited for clearance. Visibility was not good, with a low cloud cover on the ground. When they were airborne, visibility was almost zero. It was to be instruments all the way. They could see little from the starting end of the runway.

The Palm Springs airport lies in the Coachella Valley, at a point where two mountain ranges come together forming a V, or a pass. Looking toward L.A., Mount San Jacinto is on the left and Mount San Gorgonio is on the right. To fly to L.A. from runway three-zero, a plane proceeds due west, or left, heading

At Sunnylands, the Annenberg estate in Rancho Mirage, Barbara Marx and Frank Sinatra are married. Nancy is open about her sentiments at the time: "I cried for a week before the wedding."

The helicopters went to search. But Dolly Sinatra seemed to have known that her flight would have no earthly end.

for the pass. To fly to Las Vegas, however, the plane would have to turn northeast, or right, almost immediately and climb above 12,000 feet.

At 5:50 P.M. my mom phoned me. Mickey Rudin had called her to report that Grandma's plane was overdue. It had left Palm Springs at 5 P.M., due in Las Vegas at 5:20. There had been no communication with it since 5:02.

We all knew it was over. We all hoped for a miracle.

Frank Sinatra did his opening show that night. I know he did it for his mother.

The morning after the plane disappeared my dad summoned Frankie, Tina, and me. Hugh and I drove down. We kept the car radio and a second portable radio tuned to the local news stations, hoping to hear of that miracle. We went past the turnoff to the Rialto Airport at the foot of the San Bernardino Mountains. I couldn't take my eyes off those mountains. They were on our left and a little ahead of us for a while as we drove south and east. They were majestic, covered with the whitest, heaviest snowfall I had ever seen up there. It was always a little eerie, looking up at snow-covered mountains from a temperature of 80 and 90 degrees in the sunshine; this time it was awesome.

I remember crying a lot on that drive and saying things like, "Maybe they were able to land," and, "Maybe they're freezing up there." I remember needing my mother and missing my children. But mostly I remember a feeling I had never had before—as if I might explode, as if my body might blow apart. I think now that it was panic.

My brother was about thirty minutes ahead of us and had stopped at the rescue command center at the Rialto Airport. He spoke to a few of the volunteers and some reporters who were waiting for word. There was none. Mickey Rudin and Jilly, who had flown into Rialto by helicopter, rode with Frankie to Palm Springs and slept all the way. They were exhausted; they had been up all night, trying to help.

When Hugh and I got to Palm Springs, we walked into a private mass being said by Father Geimer in Dad's living room. Dad was sitting in a chair, reading his missal. I sat down quickly and waited for some sort of calm to come, but none did. Everything seemed to be in slow motion. We were in a capsule—sort of floating.

After mass, Dad and I held onto each other. I said, "Daddy, I don't know how to help you." And he said, "Just be here." I felt safe in his arms, my cheek resting on his soft beige pullover. He asked why I hadn't brought the children. I told him I'd thought I should leave them home because, at two and a half and ten months old, they were very normal, very noisy. He just said, "Oh, okay."

Hugh and I looked at each other, understanding. The next day, Hugh went to Los Angeles and came back with the girls. I realized later, as I held them, that we *needed* their noises and smells and energy. Their mere presence gave us faith: they were still so fresh from God. I felt that same "safe" feeling with them in my arms.

There was no word about the plane. My brother spent most of the time in his room in the Christmas Tree House. My sister and I just sat or roamed around. People came by but didn't stay. An endless chain of sad, worried faces.

Angel and his son came. The boy, Ruben, had just come from the mountain where he had been searching for "Mama." His clothes were still soaked from the snow and he was crying. He broke my heart.

In desperation, Tina and I spoke by phone with the famous psychic Peter Hurkos. He promised to concentrate on the problem and call back.

Dad went up in a helicopter to help in the search. He found nothing. I was grateful for that.

The second night I sat with him in front of the fire. I asked what rescuers do when they find a plane down. I asked rather general questions, but he sensed my need and answered in specifics. He told me that if there are no survivors, they try to identify body parts and put them into separate bags. He told me carefully, but thoroughly, what the procedure is and how it is done. I wondered if he had asked someone the same thing that day. There was an odd comfort in hearing such matter-of-fact details.

By the third day we were all accepting the inevitable, I think, but as we admitted later, each had his own private bit of hope.

Peter Hurkos phoned with a description of the location of the wreckage. I'll never forget that scene. Dad, Jilly, Tina, all of us leaning on the bar, studying the map, with wide-open eyes, and ears hanging on Peter's every word trying to pinpoint the spot on our map. He said the reason it hadn't been spotted was that it had not gone straight but had made a quick, sharp left turn. Was this our miracle? I conjured up a picture of Grandma, Anne, and two pilots huddled together trying to keep warm. I mean, okay, they made a crash landing, they're injured, but they're alive.

Nothing useful came of the Hurkos calls but it was something to do.

We went to bed without any resolution. We were saddened about the pilots, too. They were not just pilots but human beings, with frailties, abilities, families. I thanked God for my children—for the continuity of life.

At about 11:30 P.M. the intercom buzzed in our room. Barbara's voice said, "They found it."

It's amazing what hope can do for the human face and what the absence of hope does to the same face. I'll never forget coming from my room and seeing my father's face.

The wreckage had been located just yards away from where Dad had been up in the chopper the day before. In the last couple of seconds the pilots must have seen the mountain because they pulled back on the stick to try to avoid the crash. They broke off treetops before they hit. The plane had split in two—the nose was shattered. The fuselage was pretty much intact.

The pilots' bodies disintegrated on impact. There was nothing left of them to be put into body bags. "Grandma was found strapped in her seat," Mickey said. I forced myself to believe that.

I kept thinking, "Somebody should go and look at the remains—make sure." "Mickey's going," someone said. "Jilly's going," someone else said later. As it turned out, nobody went. Nobody could face up to it.

A subsequent investigation and lawsuit disclosed that a controller at the Palm Springs airport had used confusing language which could have caused the pilot to think that he should maintain his current altitude and heading. Because of other air traffic in the area, he was required to keep to a 9,000-foot altitude. When he finally received clearance to increase his altitude, it was too late. With these problems and poor visibility, the little plane had gone almost straight into the mountain at full takeoff speed. The liability was divided approximately equally between the controller and the pilot, who had the final responsibility to know the airport and the surrounding terrain.

After the investigation, I was given Grandma's black double-strapped handbag, bent and twisted out of shape. But it wasn't burned. I still have it. And

Natalie Catherine Garavente Sinatra.

the few things she had so carefully put into it as she was dressing that day were unharmed.

Always, when somebody he loved died, Daddy needed to be alone for a while. Nobody could comfort him. But this time it was different. He needed us with him. The images of his mother blown to bits or twisted and broken or whatever happens in a plane crash must have almost destroyed him. The suddenness of it—alive one instant, not sick; dead the next—that's not the way you expect people to die. He had hired the plane for her. I'm sure he must have carried a lot of guilt about that. And Anne, Dolly's good friend from New Jersey, Dr. Carbone's wife: Dad had known her practically all his life.

Substantively and symbolically, it was a crucial loss. They'd fought through his childhood and continued to do so to her dying day. But I believe that to counter her steel will, he'd developed his own. To prove her wrong when she belittled his choice of career. He'd transcended the fame any American entertainer had ever achieved. Their friction first had shaped him; then, I think, had remained to the end a litmus test of the grit in his bones. It helped keep him at the top of his game.

There had been security for him in Grandma's strength and a sense of worth in being able to take care of her. Now, there was a gap. A vast void of love and reliance and responsibility. And he was closer now, with both parents gone, to running out of his own seasons.

Daddy doesn't talk much about his boyhood anymore. He used to, when Grandma was alive. And a lot of laughter has gone from his life. Yet there must still be solace somehow in looking up at the mountain—so much more beautiful and lasting a memorial than any graveyard—and some peaceful feeling to live in the shadow of Grandma's mountain.

*At his mother's funeral,
January 12, 1977*

Grand Marshall FS and Barbara, 1980 Tournament of Roses Parade.

CHAPTER NINETEEN
THE BEST IS YET TO COME

That's Life

or a number of years I had trouble adjusting to Dad's marriage. Although I felt relieved about his not living alone anymore, I had other, ambivalent feelings. Dad used to shower us with gifts all the time and that stopped. All of his gifting was to his new wife. This sounds selfish. It wasn't the gifts; it was what they meant. It wasn't the lack of presents: it was the lack of his presence. When you tend to show love by giving presents and they stop, well, what is there to think?

I felt I was losing him. He had begun a new life with a new family. His home, our home, was newly decorated and foreign. I felt uneasy and almost unwelcome. No more hanging out till the wee hours, reminiscing. No more laughs about the old days. I sensed the distance between us growing and, after trying various methods to narrow the gap, with no success, I found myself reaching out with the most basic, direct approach: "Dad, what's wrong? You don't hug me anymore."

He said, "Oh, I'm sorry, really, there's nothing wrong. Maybe I've just been thoughtless. You should have told me before."

So simple, so easy.

I got over thinking that the love had stopped, but there were other questions. I couldn't quite come to grips with the fact that his expressive love for my mother had not led to remarriage. Finally, I resolved that his affection for her was genuine, and would continue forever. But it had taken time for me to understand its depths and its limits.

I grew to understand something about myself, too, which made me feel ashamed. Barbara had a grown son, Bob. With Ava and Mia, there had been no other children. There was some talk about adopting him and my father was introducing him as "our son." My concern was that giving him the family name would be wrong, for him, for us. After all the "Mamma Mia" jokes, what would they do with the sudden appearance of a Bobby Sinatra? I couldn't help feeling

that to be a Sinatra kid, you had to pay your dues; had to go through the tough times with the business and the press and the personal crises. To be a Sinatra, you needed a history that carried a mix of pain and prominence. A bit second rate of me, perhaps; everyone has troubles, but someone just can't step in and take over. It doesn't work. Candidly speaking, I was not concerned about the sharing of wealth (that doesn't interest me) but of our name.

I had always been protective. The Sinatra name helps or hurts, depending on who you're talking to. Nobody feels halfhearted about a Sinatra. When people began smoking marijuana at a party at Sharon Tate's house in the pot-busting sixties, even though fifty or sixty of Hollywood's biggest celebrities were there, a police raid would cause the Sinatra name to loom largest in the headlines. So I left. I was always leaving situations that could bring mud raining down on the family. Not that I'm an innocent—just a realist about some things. Dad is, too. He and Jilly have an expression: "I can't go there." (Or, as Jilly pronounces

it, "I can't go dere.") Danger. Violation of law. Not a place for a Sinatra to be.
You can't go dere. That was one of the prices you paid for being a Sinatra, for
being a Sinatra kid. So now—with newcomers in the family fold—I was having
some trouble accepting them.

This was *my problem*—*my* own invention. Something I had to work
through. And both Dad and Barbara helped me, Dad, by being patient and
loving, and Barbara by saying, "Just because we are now part of the same family
doesn't mean we have to like each other all the time. It's okay."

Barbara didn't have it easy either. Coming into a very close family of
adults, she had a few walls to knock down and a few minds to open, yet she was
understanding. She asked about my mother often, with a genuine interest.

As I was trying to adjust to Dad's marriage, he was busy working around
the world. The street-smart kid had become drawing-room smart, his international stature crystallized. At London's Royal Albert Hall in March 1977, with
Princess Margaret and Ava Gardner in the audience, he gave a memorable
concert in behalf of the National Society for the Prevention of Cruelty, to
Children. His popularity in London was so great, a group of his British fans
started a movement to rename the Royal Albert Hall, the Francis Albert Hall.
At Hebrew University in Jerusalem in April, 1978, he dedicated the Frank
Sinatra International Student Center (funds he raised had built the center). At
the foot of the pyramids in Eygpt in 1979, he gave an open-air concert that
raised more than half a million dollars for Mrs. Anwar Sadat's several charities.

That year, 1979, was a new mix of triumphs and sorrows. His first new
album in five years, *Trilogy*, was released and was judged to be "historic" by the
renowned critic Leonard Feather. But 1979 was also the year that Dad's dear
friend Irwin Rubinstein—Uncle Ruby of Ruby's Dunes restaurant in Palm
Springs—died.

Frank Sinatra, Jr.: "It was Thanksgiving weekend. Pop called the cemetery in Palm Springs and the guy in charge said, 'My gravediggers are off until
next Tuesday.' And my father said to this man, 'You never buried somebody who
was Jewish? You have no knowledge of the fact that tradition dictates that when
a man dies, you have the wailing that evening and he's buried by sunset of the
day after his death?' Pop says, 'You're not familiar with the tradition of this that
goes back to the time of Abraham? You're going to break tradition?' Pop says, 'I
will pay the extra wages—overtime, double hours, triple, golden hours, plati-
num hours, whatever you want to call it.' Well, the guy that ran the cemetery
didn't budge. My old man got off the phone and said, 'I'm going to go over there
and punch that sonofabitch right in his nose and if *he's* too old, I'll punch his *son*
in the nose!' He said the last jokingly. But I said:

" 'Pop, let's cool off.'

"He said, 'The man was like a father to me.' Ruby was; in the eulogy Pop
delivered he called Ruby 'a warm feast in a cold forest.' He said, 'Here's a
tradition that's gone on now for forty-three hundred years and this guy wants to
quote me holiday regulations all of a sudden.' And he couldn't believe it, you
know—it bugged him so much. The principle of the thing."

Principle. Tradition. Truth. Sinatra's secret code. He's not famous for it,
but he has come out fighting for fairness frequently, mostly for others, occasionally for himself.

As Tommy Thompson, himself a great reporter, observed, some reporters insisted that wherever FS went, a wall of "goons" and bodyguards strong-
armed a passageway. It is true that crowds make walking difficult and some-

times can be unintentionally dangerous. Thompson saw one newspaper photograph that identified two sturdy men as Sinatra's "bodyguards." Thompson knew that they were actually two of his long-time musicians, one piano player, one guitarist. "Some bodyguards," said FS. "They get drunk every night. They can't look after their own bodies, much less mine."

I Could Write a Book

Sinatra's troubles with the press—most often with columnists who care less for the truth than for the dirt—go back a long time and, sadly, continue. The song title "Stormy Weather" could describe his relations with some of the press. Back in the forties, a gossip columnist said that FS had "laundered money," i.e., been a courier for Lucky Luciano. In fact, FS had been in Havana on a short vacation and Luciano was in a casino there with his entourage and they had exchanged greetings, not cash. Elements in the press, at that time right-wing, who had earlier accused Sinatra of being a Communist sympathizer now accused him of mob connections. He was incensed, and when he encountered the columnist who had started the Havana rumors afterward at Ciro's, an exchange that involved the writer calling FS a "greasy wop" led FS to knock him down.

But much of the time he didn't, or couldn't, fight back. And the increasing anger people saw was the result of having to bury it, not get it out, not get it right.

Dad's first film in the 1960s was to have been based on William Bradford Huie's *The Execution of Private Slovik,* the true story of the only American soldier executed for desertion in World War II. Albert Maltz, the man who wrote *The House I Live In,* was hired by FS to adapt Huie's book for the screen. The press jumped all over Sinatra for hiring Maltz who, like other victims of the house Un-American Activities Committee, had spent months in a deferral road camp for refusing to answer questions. The Hollywood community, like Washington, was shaken by "McCarthyism." And even though the Senate eventually censured McCarthy, some of his victims' careers were destroyed.

Frank Sinatra's passions run deep and his fight for what has come to be called human rights is among his most intense. He wanted to fight this thing about Maltz. He contemplated taking out advertisements in the newspapers, listing the titles of fine films that had been written by blacklisted writers, using —as they had to, in order to work—assumed names. He could have asked Maltz to use another name but he felt that many Americans believed as he did that McCarthyism was unfair and he refused to go that route. He could not, in the end, fight for Maltz's rights or his own right to hire whomever he pleased because of his friendship with and ties to the then Senator John Kennedy.

A characteristic story ran in the Los Angeles *Herald-Examiner.* SINATRA HIRES MALTZ. Subhead: "Writer Figured in Red Probe." Maltz was said to be "identified as a communist in Congressional hearings," and was thus branded a member of "The Hollywood Ten," who had refused to name names. "Sinatra refused to say why he had defied the Hollywood agreement against hiring Communists," and was one of only three prominent Hollywood figures to do so (the others, Stanley Kramer and Otto Preminger). "Sinatra is known to be a strong supporter of John F. Kennedy," the paper added. The New York *Times* said that Sinatra had considered keeping the hiring secret until after the forth-

Arriving for dinner one night at Patsy's, a favorite New York restaurant, he was informed— cautiously—that the upstairs dining room was packed solid with Yankees, victorious over the Dodgers. FS said, "Good. Tell them the British are coming." He encountered Bucky Dent, who stood speechless. "Kid, you cost me a lot of money," he said. "But you played a great game." To Lou Pinella: "You're Barbara's favorite . . . she says you're 'cute.'" To Mickey Rivers: "Man, you have got to be the kookiest cat in the outfield." To Billy Martin: "You did a great job in managing these monkeys to victory."

As the restaurant's proprietors, Sal and Joseph, wrote Nancy: "We all know your father's a winner. But he's also a good loser. He treated them to dinner."

coming Democratic National Convention, given the prospects for the nomination of Senator Kennedy. Also, there was the friendship of FS and Peter Lawford, the actor who was married to one of the candidate's sisters.

Asked about these connections, Sinatra said: "I make movies and I don't ask the advice of John F. Kennedy. And he does not ask my advice on how to vote in the Senate."

Nevertheless, he decided to scrap the picture. He chose not to go ahead, he said, because of the reaction of "my family, my friends, and the American public." I was confused. I knew that his family was with him, and many of his friends, too. I also knew that he had refused to let newspaper stories influence him in the past. This wasn't like him. I didn't know why until much later. He had declined to cite his concern about J.F.K. as the real reason.

Even as I was concluding this book, the problem surfaced again. In Washington, D.C., during the time of rehearsals for the 1985 Inaugural Gala, the Washington *Post* published an editorial called "The Rat Pack." It again dragged out the same old stuff, including the painful thing about J.F.K. staying at Bing's. FS, who had worked for months putting together the show for the President and Mrs. Reagan and the nation—without recompense, of course—was crushed. Then, after the personal hurt, he became furious. Because this was not only humiliating to him; it might embarrass the Reagans.

Knowing the truth, they, typically, stood by their friend. So did the Vice-President. When asked by reporters about the incident, Bush said, "Leave him alone. Just leave him alone!" *(That* didn't get on television.)

My father finally snapped at one television interviewer, but speaking to *all* the disreputable ones, said, "You're dead. You're all dead." Meaning not a threat but "You simply don't exist for me anymore." (That *did* go on television.)

It started me thinking again about the way some people abuse the First Amendment, which is precious and vital, and whether there is any possible way to cause careless reporters, reckless "journalists," et al., to become more responsible. Doctors answer to the AMA, lawyers to the ABA. TV has its Standards and Practices, films have M.P.A.A. and its rating system. The press answers to no one. Is there no code of ethics, no board of the best in journalism, to halt the cruelties, the harassment, the lies? At least let them be held accountable to each other. People like my family and yours could be protected without diminishing the First Amendment. And perhaps others will not have to spend a lifetime trying to undo the damage caused them by innuendo and irresponsibility.

In 1981 Sinatra applied for a gaming license in Nevada, and this time he had important facts read into the record. Here is how he brought that about:

—First, he exercised his rights under the Freedom of Information Act and had the government disclose all their files on "Frank Sinatra."

—He then turned these files over to the state of Nevada. In the past, the FBI had refused to turn over their files. (Part of their refusal was probably motivated by their knowledge that there was nothing incriminatory in them.)

—The FBI files indicated that my father had been investigated endlessly, for thirty years. (The early FBI files had him listed as a "Communist" because he appeared at a rally with Mrs. Eleanor Roosevelt, and because he sang "The House I Live In.")

—The files disclosed that there was no evidence of Mafia membership, Mafia affiliation, or doing business with the Mafia.

—The FBI files also showed that the stories about Sinatra and members of the Mafia had come out originally as rumors printed in newspaper articles—

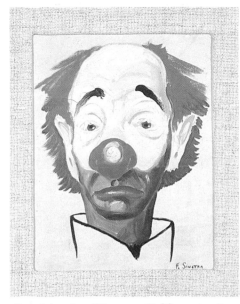

Send in the Clowns. *Self portrait by Sinatra. Once he wrote a note to Nancy:*

"Chicken—a thought,

"Strange, but I feel the world we live in demands that we be turned out in a pattern that resembles, in fact, is, a facsimile of itself. And those of us who roll with the punches, who grin, who dare to wear foolish clown faces, who defy the system—well, we do it. And bully for us!

"Of course, there are those who do not. And the reason I think is that (and I say this with some sadness) those uptight, locked-in people who resent and despise us, who fear us and are bewildered . . . will one day come to realize that we possess rare and magical secrets. And more—love.

"Therefore, I am beginning to think that a few (I hope many) are wondering if maybe there might be value to a firefly, or an instant-long Roman candle.

"Keep the faith,
Dad"

Gregory Peck, FS, and Cary Grant aboard the Fabergé jet.

Greg, Cary, Frank— in Flight

Two letters from two close friends who know—and understand

Gregory Peck: "A while back I finished work on a movie in Rome. . . . Veronique and I stayed at the studio long enough to say thanks and goodbye to the Italian crew. This involved a lot of hugging and kissing among grown men. We then ran for the train that would take us on an overnight journey to Menton, near Monte Carlo. There we were to join the Sinatras, Morton Downeys, and a few other pals for a restful weekend . . .

"In the morning we were awakened by the porter at 7 A.M. . . . I lay in my berth eyeing four very large suitcases, wondering how I would wrestle them out the window of the wagons-lits onto the station platform. There would be no baggage handlers at 8 A.M., and the platform was a hundred yards long. My sacroiliac was out of whack. I commenced grumbling to Veronique, blaming her for the uncaring, hostile attitude of the French toward visitors, especially Americans, etc., etc.

"We knew that our friends, who have been known to keep late hours, would not be meeting us at that hour. The train pauses in Menton for only three minutes. I hopped out . . . Veronique and the porter shoved the four monster bags out the window to me. My lower back collapsed. It felt like it had been injected with a massive dose of Tabasco sauce. Veronique nipped off the train just in time. As we watched the train pull away, I saw, far down the platform, a baggage wagon coming . . . the man behind it in khaki overalls and a navy blue cap covered with gold braid. The other stranded passengers

rumors which were *reported* as rumors, but were subsequently reported and reported and reported again until they were "facts."

At the conclusion of the hearing, Frank Sinatra was given a license.

He had generally tried to take the position of No Comment, or, as he would put it, "Look, I'm not going to deny every piece of crap that comes along. I'm not going to *dignify* them with a response."

At various times, because of his loyalty to others or declining to dignify his attackers, he had sometimes lashed back, but most often he had subdued his feelings. I had learned, as he had long since, that to most columnists it's not news that my father can be a nice guy or that my brother is a decent kid. The many benefactions didn't start to come out until late in life. Without a newspaper or a TV station at his command, the only forum open to him, he thought, was his microphone. So he used it to vent some of his anger, sometimes humorously, sometimes viciously. He reached only a few thousand people, whereas the liars reached millions through their media. But it was a healthy outlet for him. And for those of us who shared and understood his plight, each little jab he struck was significant and understandable. Though some remarks were not in good taste, I saw the set-to as a David vs. Goliath kind of thing, a mighty blow by a man some saw as mighty himself but who was, in dueling with the coarser members of the press, a little guy against a giant.

Not everyone agreed. One day his old friend Peter Pitchess, former Sheriff of Los Angeles County, took my father aside before a nightclub performance. "Now look, Francis, you've reached a certain stage; you're a grown man, a mature man. You don't want to go around fighting the press like you have in the past. Just ignore them. You're too dignified a man now, and your stature is such—let them say what the hell they want."

Sinatra said, "What are you driving at?"

"Well," Peter said, "I hear that the other day you called [so-and-so] a 'two-dollar whore.'" He named a syndicated columnist who regularly attacks FS.

"Yeah, I did."

stood by in shock as Sinatra wheeled our bags out. Could it be an American astronaut who looked like Frank Sinatra?

". . . I don't know anyone else who does things like that all the time. First comes the impulse, then the follow-through. It is typical Sinatra behavior.

"You have to like a man like that. He is colorful. He is generous. He shows his feelings. I have known him since 1942. He is the friend I would call if I needed help in an emergency. I don't discuss Frank with the press. An interviewer asked me recently to explain our friendship. 'Frank is so volatile,' he said, 'and you are so laid-back, Frank is a Republican, and you are a Democrat.' 'And the interview is over,' I said."

Cary Grant: "My dear Nancy:

"It delighted me to be asked to write about your father for your book. My rather more objective viewpoint could hardly be the same as that held by his daughter. Still, I hope that in many ways our opinions will meld.

". . . is a unique man. Utterly without hypocrisy. Bluntly yet loyally opinionated. Unaffected and, to me, uncomplex despite everything written. It's almost frightening to some, to be faced with honesty. Frank fascinates the curious: the writers who try to analyze an enigma that is not an enigma; perhaps hoping to discover those qualities responsible for the man's personal appeal. Well, I think I know the quality. It's truth. Simple truth. Without artifice. I remember reading somewhere that in a world of lies a truth seems like a lie.

"Forty years ago, coming out of the old Astor Hotel on Broadway, I'd been buttonholed by a casual acquaintance who, while I was trying to recollect his name, suddenly went into a tirade about a young man who was blocking the sidewalk, impeding progress, showing off, stopping traffic. The inequity of my acquaintance's remarks touched off a chain of thought that has persisted in me ever since. That young man, who eventually became your father, was merely trying to walk from his car to the Paramount's performer's entrance.

He had not blocked the sidewalk . . . the crowd had. They were responsible for blocking the sidewalk in their efforts to touch him, photograph him, pull at him for autographs or other unfathomable reasons.

"It has become customary to accept the behavior of certain people toward celebrities. But why should a publicized person cause special excitement? The reason evades me. Why is it not sufficient to see and enjoy the performance of a great entertainer or athlete and then leave him or her alone? Why invade privacy? . . . It's extraordinary how many uninvited people find it necessary to make personal remarks, occasionally uncivil, to a celebrity. What prompts them? Is it their need for attention? . . . This is the constant plight of your father . . . I, at least, spent most of my working days in the comparative security of a studio, whereas your father works before huge live audiences throughout the world, surrounded by people of all kinds . . .

"It's a sad paradox that the people whose acquaintance one would most like to make are the people least likely to introduce themselves. Yet I've been approached by strangers, while sitting quietly reading, captive in a commercial airliner, and been forced to listen to incredible anecdotes about notables—exaggerated yarns gleaned from already exaggerated gossip columns—written by second-class writers who may never have met the persons about whom they write so knowingly. I've often read innuendos or implications about myself that were so blatantly wrong that I was staggered by the writer's imagination. It astonished me (and I bet it astonished your father also) to learn that according to recent biographies, Errol Flynn was a Nazi spy, Tyrone Power a homosexual, and Joan Crawford a harridan who beat her daughter with a wire clothes hanger. Ridiculous. The victimized dead cannot defend themselves. Though the fabrications are refuted by others close to them, the damage has been done. I've already conditioned my wife and daughter to expect the biographical worst . . .

"Such 'biographers' are seldom

fastidious in research. Your father, in reverse tribute to the adulation accorded him, also has been the subject of unbounded envy . . .

"I remember a comedian who, after speaking admiringly of Frank Sinatra to his psychiatrist, was told that Mr. Sinatra was a very very sick man who earned fabulous amounts of money and stayed up all night indulging in wine, women, and song. To which the comedian meekly replied that he wished he could be as sick, if only for a week or two. Well, the average man after finishing his work at 5 P.M. usually has a drink, a meal, and then relaxes for another four, five, or often six hours; Frank finishes work around midnight and then relaxes for a similar length of time—and what better way to relax than in the company of cheerful theatrical friends among whom are often some very attractive people?

"I've read more nonsense about Frank Sinatra than possibly anyone else in our time. Indulge me a little more, Nancy. I've read that he loses his temper, becomes pugnacious and irritable. Yet I've been with him on countless occasions and seen no evidence even of annoyance; altho', as I've said, I have often wondered how he managed to contain himself. If Frank loses his temper, it must be that he has been severely provoked.

"He's been cussed and discussed. Few people can be aware of the demands made upon the man—the incessant requests for appearances at benefits, for interviews; demands from old, and new, associates; and the resultant anger and frustration of those he cannot possibly oblige. Yet I know of no entertainer whose generosity to people in need is greater.

"I doubt if anyone reading this could keep his or her temper if subjected to similar harassments.

"When I was younger, it was all I could do sometimes, after a long day, to keep from flying apart and yelling to the heavens.

"Still, no one enjoys his audience more. Nor they him.

"This letter, dearest Nancy, must remind you of that worn-out excuse that if I'd had more time, I'd have written a shorter, less repetitive letter.

"Happiest thoughts and love . . ."

Peter, not one for mincing words himself, said, "You know it's a mistake, goddamn it! You're making a first-class jerk out of yourself because you're just setting yourself up for those bastards."

"Peter," my father said, "you're right. By God, you are right. I'm gonna apologize."

So Peter Pitchess and his party went to their table at ringside. After the opening act, Sinatra was announced and came out on the stage. He sang for a while, then on his break he looked around and said, sorrowfully but strongly, to some of the audience, "You know, I have an apology to make." The timing was perfect. Dead silence. "Yes, I want to apologize because I once called [so-and-so] a two-dollar whore. I must apologize. She's only a one-dollar whore."

A few years later Peter and his wife went on a trip to Africa with my father and Barbara. As they went into the place where Dad was to sing, Barbara took Sheriff Pitchess aside and said, "For God's *sake*, Peter, don't ask him to apologize to anybody."

Sometimes, if Dad's feuding with the press from the stage and says something wicked, someone in the audience shouts, "Don't do that." Then he'll get serious: "Hey! They can write anything they want about me, about you, about anybody, and you have no way to get even. There's no way to answer back. Well, this is my way to get back. This is my forum."

Despite the stinging sharpness of his counterattacks, there have been times when I thought FS was too restrained—patient to the point of frustration. As in the situation of the gunslinger with the fastest draw, the newest kid reporter in town is always looking to make a name, force a showdown, challenge the old man. Sinatra's friends understand this.

Robert Merrill: "I remember being backstage at the Met before he performed a concert there. He had a lot of press there and he handled everyone beautifully. Then one girl from a local station put a microphone in front of his face. She said, 'Mr. Sinatra'—he was very nice to her, very pleasant—'What are *you* doing at the Metropolitan? What could you *do* at the Metropolitan?' Now, I held Francis's hand, you know. I sort of wanted to hold him back, but he was very pleasant. 'Well,' he said, 'I do a little singing and I dance and I do comedy and I juggle.' And she said, 'Come on, now! Do *you* belong in the Metropolitan?' She was insulting him, hurting him, trying to get something controversial. She was trying to pick a fight. He was very nice. Very controlled. But *I* wasn't. *I* got angry! I grabbed the mike, and her, and shoved her off."

Gregory Peck: "Recently an interviewer asked me to explain my friendship with Frank. 'Frank is so volatile,' the interviewer said, 'and you are so laid back. Frank is a Republican, and you are a Democrat, and . . .'

" 'And the interview is over,' I said."

There are occasions, few enough but worthwhile, when Sinatra, despite the number of times they've laid down the gauntlet, does not fire back. Talking to an Associated Press dinner, he mellowed, at least for the moment:

FS: "I want to thank you for the privilege of appearing here. I think it only fitting that I be invited to speak to a gathering of newspapermen, considering the marvelous relationship I have always had with the press. I believe that in certain quarters of the Hearst empire, I am known as the Eichmann of song . . .

"Now, many of you have heard that I have in the past been harmful and brutal to members of the Fourth Estate. These are lies, vicious rumors started by a few distinguished reporters I happened to run down with my car . . ."

I want to wake up in a city that doesn't sleep to find I'm king of the hill, top of the heap. These little town blues are melting away I'm gonna make a brand-new start of it in old New York. If I can make it there, I'll make it anywhere. It's up to you New York, New York . . .

Goin' Out of My Head

Whatever my father's fortunes, mine were not exactly wonderful by the end of the seventies. My finances were tight and I had to get back to work. We were supposedly a two-career family. While Hugh had gone into TV development at Warner Brothers, I hadn't had any career except the monumental one of motherhood for six years.

I had sold millions of records worldwide, I'd had gold records, big hits, and then had stopped in midgallop, to have and raise my children. Now A.J. and Amanda were old enough to understand that people have to work for a living, so I had a nice talk with them and tried to break back into the recording industry. I had great trouble getting a label to sign me, because Bette Midler's famous line from one of the Grammy Award shows honoring recording artists is true: "Welcome to the Grammies, where you're only as good as your last two minutes and forty-five seconds."

In the years that I had been away, the turnover had been astounding. All the wonderful, creative people who had built the labels earlier had ridden off into the sunset somewhere, and twenty-five-year-old whiz kids were running corporations, and passing around cocaine during meetings. They remembered my records from *when they were kids.* That was scary. ("Gee, when I was fifteen, 'Boots' was my favorite song.") I was already over the hill.

Finally, old friend Jimmy Bowen put me together with Mel Tillis at RCA. Mel and I did some duets in Nashville which became hits on the country charts. But I wasn't back. So, in 1982, I asked my father for help.

He said, "Go on tour with me for a year and let's see what happens." What he intended, was for me to rebuild my career with his help, then go off on my own again, which was extremely generous of him.

On tour (Las Vegas, Lake Tahoe, Atlantic City, the opening of the renovated Universal Amphitheater in L.A.) I had to learn again what I had known so well about communicating with FS: the shortest distance between two points is a straight talk. But for a time, I couldn't bring myself to do that. Then circumstances forced my hand.

The Frank Sinatra Show at that time consisted of FS, The Man; Charlie Callas, the comedian; and Nancy Sinatra, what they used to call the girl singer. Because two vocalists back-to-back didn't seem a good idea, the plan was that I would open, Charlie would follow, and my father, of course, was the feature. Now, opening a show if you're a comic is one thing: if the audience is restless or noisy or hasn't settled down, you have the tools to fight back and to get laughs. He can joke with them, fuss with them. People being seated during your act can feed the act. But when I opened, there was the usual bedlam that occurs whenever FS is the star on the bill. I'd be up there, trying to get Dad's show off to a rousing start, up there and into my second and third songs, and the waiters in the Circus Maximus at Caesar's still would be rattling trays, while others would be showing people to their seats, and guests would be skirmishing at the rope, trying to get seats at all . . .

Attempting to sing in the midst of this chaos is tough enough. And one of the cardinal rules on stage is to make the audience comfortable. Part of my responsibility was to keep the spotlights off the people who were late because they are usually already embarrassed about walking into the middle of a singer's act. So, each show, I tried to "help" these folks by moving to the opposite side of

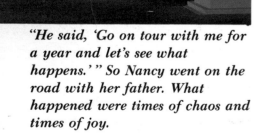

"He said, 'Go on tour with me for a year and let's see what happens.'" So Nancy went on the road with her father. What happened were times of chaos and times of joy.

the stage from them and the spotlight operators automatically followed me, keeping the latecomers from becoming part of the show. This technique worked fairly well until one night when there were five empty tables at the start —each of which sat twenty people.

Funny? The guys in the band flashed me "uh-oh" looks as I started to panic. People started working their way down the long, skinny tables stage right. I ambled stage left, singing, "Well, I think I'm goin' out of my head . . ." and there was another group of a dozen more. Back over to the right. More people. I went to center stage—and more people. I had *no* place to go to get the spotlights off these people. ". . . I think I'm goin' out of my head . . . over you-oo-ooo . . . over you-oo . . ."

After the show I had a chat with Angelo, the maître d', who ran the showroom. He promised to help me. And indeed, for the next few shows, everything was okay. Then the same things began to happen. I went to Angelo and said, "I'm on time. You be on time, and everything will be fine." He said, "You know how it is, Nancy—they're gambling or having dinner in another room and, because they're high rollers, they wait till Frank comes on. Or I'll get a call from the pit to hold ringside for a big spender from Japan . . . you know how it is. I've got to do it."

I said, "I don't care how much money you lose, Angelo, we have to open this show properly."

The next night, the entertainment director, Alan Margolies, was backstage and I explained the problem. He said, "I'll take care of it. It's absolutely wrong." So everything was fine for a few shows. Then—BAM!—I was sharing the stage with 150 people again.

Meantime, on all business and professional matters, FS and I had been talking through other people: secretaries, conductors, sound men. I had been receiving messages like, "This is too long." "Cut this." "Change that." "Do it this way." "Put another song here." The directions had come one at a time, so it was no big deal. Then came the last straw. After a particularly harrowing dodge-the-people game the night before and an emotional call from my daughter Amanda, who missed me, Dad's Gal Friday—dear, adorable Dorothy Uhlemann —called. She said, "Nance, everybody's cutting two or three minutes tonight so your dad can get out in time to see Robert Goulet."

That's it! I thought. *I've already cut down to twenty minutes! If I don't talk at all, I've got five songs. Twenty minutes! When I was doing my own shows, twenty minutes was my warm-up. No. I will not cut to seventeen minutes. It'll look like he's doing me a crummy favor. A throwaway. I won't. I won't. I won't.*

Silent tantrum over, I called my husband and ranted aloud. "Hugh, I can't stand it anymore. I'm opening for a comic. They won't get the people in and nobody's helping me. He's cut me from twenty-eight minutes to twenty and now he expects me to cut another song so he can get off early to see (excuse me, Bob) Robert f——g Goulet. My father is an insensitive person and I can't deal with him anymore."

Hugh said, "Tell him."

Hugh's logic really made me mad sometimes.

The phone rang. Dorothy said, "Your dad wants to talk to you." I thought, *Oh, shit!* I knew if I heard his voice, I'd just spill it all out. I've always done that. Too late.

"Hi ya, shortie. How ya . . ."

"The great moments were when he'd bring me back for an extra bow, sharing the tumultuous applause that greeted his sudden appearance on stage. These would be wonderful gestures for any performer who wasn't his kid . . . but for <u>me</u> . . ."

"I CAN'T STAND IT ANYMORE! I can't deal with middlemen, I'm not getting any communication from you. I don't know if what I'm doing is wrong, good, bad, indifferent, stinking, rotten, terrific. You never *tell* me anything. I can't get anybody to seat the people before I come out. I spend half of my time on stage dodging waiters and people who are late! *Yech!*"

He said, "Why didn't you tell me?" (Goddamn logic again!)

"Because I didn't want to bug you and I didn't want to go over anybody's head."

He said, *"You* know me well enough to know that if you're doing something I don't like, I'm going to tell you."

"No," I said, "you haven't told me—you've been telling the sound man, who's been telling me."

"That doesn't mean I don't like what you're doing. It means that we're juggling for time. We have a long show."

I said, "Then juggle more with Charlie and leave me alone!"

"If I haven't told you you're doing a good job, I'm sorry," he said. "You know how I am: I *expect* the people I hire to do good work. If they don't, they don't work for me. You're working for me, you're doing a good job."

I said, "Why didn't you tell me? I need to hear it from *you.*"

He said, "Will you stop it? You're being childish!"

"I *am* your child. I'm not just your opening act."

That quieted him. And me. He said, "Well, let's take one thing at a time. First of all, you don't have to cut anything tonight. We'll be a few minutes late for Robert Goulet, it doesn't matter."

I said, "Thank you."

And he said, "Secondly, I will take care of this business of people not being seated on time. We won't start until they're seated. That'll teach the management. They want the show to go on on time. They want the showroom emptied on time so they can get the people into the casino. If they don't get the showroom filled on time, we won't start on time, and the audience won't get out on time. And they'll figure it out and they'll learn."

And that was it. No problems after that—not in Vegas, not in Atlantic City, not anywhere. I could have saved myself a big headache by going to FS in the first place.

He knew that whatever my problems, my underlying concern was for him, because I was working for him, I was opening the show for him, and if I didn't do it right, then—as Hugh says—"There goes the third act!" If something in a play gets botched up in the first act, it's like dominoes. It's the same in a nightclub or a concert—if something goes wrong with the opening act, the second and third acts struggle to make up for the problems in front.

In the end, none of the specific "problems" mattered. I couldn't handle them it seems, because, though I wished otherwise, I found I could not exist without my family. I needed to be with my children. My priorities had dramatically changed.

That night, the night of our talk, Daddy was there when I went *on* stage, and he was there when I came *off* stage. And he said, "You were wonderful." He put his arms around me and said, at last, "Good job."

The Medal of Freedom, awarded to Frank Sinatra in 1985—his nation's highest civilian award.

FS and the loyal friend who (like several others) is always there, Jilly Rizzo. All dressed up with someplace to go: the wedding of Princess Caroline of Monaco.

The grandfatherly one in action.

FS: "I'm not old enough to understand adults, but I think I know enough to understand kids. And I think if we can get the kids together, maybe we'll be able to keep them together when they get to be adults."

Wrote poet Amanda Lambert (age 8):

"MY GRANDPA—Francis Albert Sinatra

"My grandpa, Frank Sinatra, is a very well-known singer, for most of his albums like, 'L.A. Is My Lady,' 'High Sosiety,' and 'New yorkNew york.' But I think that he is the best grandpa in the whole wide world!!!
"My mother, Nancy Sinatra, is a well-known singer to, but one thing my grandpa liked best was . . . . KIDS!!! Yep, always loved kids!
"By and by my grandpa became more and more famous! But 'OL' BLUE EYES' will always be my grandpa! . . . . And I love him to!!!!!!!!"

In 1983 when FS received the Kennedy Center Award for Lifetime Achievement, the President and Mrs. Reagan greet their friends, Amanda and A. J. Lambert, Frank, Barbara, and Nancy Sinatra.

Opposite: Various portraits by artists of note. (Top) Dong Kingman. (Center) Norman Rockwell. (Bottom) Sculptor Robert Berks: "He said: 'When I give replicas of this away, it will be the nearest thing I can give them of me . . . the way I feel . . . pain and joy at the same time.'"

Mr. Anonymous

eing on the road with FS wasn't all work, fussing, misunderstandings. One night we went out and overindulged: Dad, Charlie, Dorothy, a whole gang. It was terrific fun. Dad laughed so hard at Charlie's antics, he fell right off his chair. Literally. "How come we don't have more nights like that?" I said the next day. "Well, you know," he said, "we can't do that all the time anymore."

He had been doing serious work in the eighties—staging the 1981 Inaugural Gala for President Ronald Reagan, doing an extraordinary concert in Brazil—and he was about to win a lucrative contract at the Golden Nugget in Las Vegas and Atlantic City. His professional verve was there—the timing, the delivery, the taste, the expert use of the microphone to augment and bring out the best his voice could give. But the style had changed.

He no longer smoked. He said, "Smoking is stupid." Just stopped, cold turkey, one day. After forty years of Lucky Strikes. He did not often drink— occasionally a vodka and soda or a Jack Daniel's with water and ice, which I

276

rarely saw him finish. "He's more conscious of mortality," Tina said one day. I nodded in agreement. "He's calmed down. In fact, he's gotten quite dull," she joked.

In his sixties, pushing toward seventy, he reflected more than ever the old-fashioned values that always had been in his roots. Receiving one of the most significant tributes of his life—the Kennedy Center Honors for Lifetime Achievement—he invited the family to Washington, D.C., to share the occasion. There was to be a dinner presided over by the Secretary of State, a White House reception hosted by the President and Nancy, and a distinguished presentation of the awards at the Kennedy Center. Barbara, her son Bob, Hugh, Tina, Frankie, and I were invited to all the events.

The man my now-single sister had been going with for more than two years was excluded from the state dinner because of the limited seating. Tina was furious. If Robert couldn't go, she said, she wouldn't. She'd be at the other ceremonies, but not that one.

It was a clash of the two strongest Sinatra wills. For weeks before, they didn't speak. The night of the dinner, right before getting dressed, I went to my father's hotel suite. Barbara was sitting there. Now Barbara has heavy responsibilities. She is on call twenty-four hours a day. She must be perfectly groomed. Her hair must be great from the time she gets up in the morning. She must always be in the correct fashions. She must know the protocol of seating people, how to plan menus. Because they travel in glittering circles, meeting presidents, popes, princes, kings, queens. ("Why are these people his friends?" cracked television star Merv Griffin at the fiftieth Inaugural Gala. "Because they need somebody to look up to, too, just like you and me.")

Barbara handles all that beautifully.

She had learned a lot about us, as we had about her. And she had become a strong, supportive, and protective ally. So she said to me, "Do you think there's a chance that your sister will change her mind and come tonight? Because I could still make the phone call, have Dorothy arrange for her place at the table." I said, "No way. Knowing Tina, she only brought one dress." Barbara said, "You know, your father doesn't ask very much of you kids. Wouldn't you think that your sister could do this?" I said, "Look, she has her reasons and she's strong enough to stand up to him. I'm not going to get in the way of this. I'm really not." But then I said, "She's been going with Robert for a long time. I really think that not inviting him is kind of strange." "Well . . ." Barbara said, "they're not married." I said, "Barbara, give me a break! They're not married!" "Well," she said, "that's the way your father thinks."

I know. He is in many ways an old-fashioned man. That's why he's had so many marriages. Because he would not just *live* with anybody. It goes against the grain. Whatever he may have carried from his childhood, it is still there.

There are still flashes and sparks of the other life—like the baseball game in Atlantic City at three o'clock in the morning between players in sweatshirts reading "Ol' Blue Eyes" (Dad's team) and "Ol' Red Eyes" (Dean's team). "The game was called," said Dean, "on account of light." But sometimes at reunions with Sammy and Dean, it was mostly the reminiscences that were raucous. Reminiscences about the time, for example, when Sammy cussed out Sinatra at the Sands.

Sammy Davis, Jr.: "This was back when I could *really* drink. I called Frank everything. They all tried to stop me—Jack Entratter, Carl Cohen—but I

wouldn't let them. 'Aw, get away from me.' Finally, somebody got me to bed and the next morning one of the guys who worked for me said, 'Well, I don't know whether I should start packing now—or wait awhile.' I said, 'What are you talking about?' He said, 'Do you know what you did last night?' And then he told me. I got up and said, 'Well, I got to face it. I got to face Dean, got to face Frank.'

"In those days we'd always meet in Frank's suite when we woke up—have a little taste, a little coffee. No matter how late we stayed up, by ten or eleven—I'm talking about nonworking days—Frank would be up, be reading the paper in his robe, his pajamas. And that's when the day would start. So I walked over there and I ran into one of Dean's guys and he said, 'Oh boy. Oooh!' Now I *know* I'm in it up to here.

"I went into the suite and said, 'Good morning. I understand I made a fool of myself last night. I would like . . .' Frank interrupted me. 'Don't you want a cup of coffee or something?' 'Maybe a cup of coffee,' I said. And I went to the coffee, and I was shaking—the tortures of the damned, because whatever they were going to do to me couldn't be as bad as what I was thinking. Frank waited until everybody left and I'm sitting there and I said, 'Frank, I'm sorry.' And he said, 'Look, we've all done exactly what you did last night, but if you can't handle it, don't do it. Now, what are we going to do today?'

"Just trims all the fat and sweat away. Best piece of advice I ever received."

The shortest distance between two points . . .

If the style during the personal hours was changing, the style onstage still had enormous impact. And the response had its impact on Sinatra. When he went to do the concert in Rio, he encountered a reaction like nothing he had ever seen—not at the Paramount, not with Dorsey, the television specials, in Vegas. This was its own special encounter.

FS: "I had never been to Rio. My records had been popular there for years, going back to when F.D.R. was President, when they received our broadcasts. I had been all over the world but for some reason, never to Brazil.

"You know, there was an expression they used down there. When a young man was courting a young woman, and things would get pretty far along, and the girl would put on the heat about doing something about marriage, the young man would stall them with, 'When Frank Sinatra comes to Brazil . . .'

"Well, when we did get there, a lot of weddings and babies date from about that time.

"The day of the concert, it was raining. I kept looking out the window all day, wondering whether it would let up. But it kept on coming down. Not a light rain; a real downpour. And, do you know, the people started taking their seats at eight o'clock in the morning and they kept coming in, sitting there all day in the rain.

"When we got to the stadium at night for the concert, it was still raining—and I had never seen a place as big as Maracana. It was a soccer stadium, of course, and there were 275,000 people in it. It was immense. They had a huge center stage with six wings, all miked, and while I sang, I had to keep running from one wing to another to each mike, until I was out of breath. But before that, there was a long walk to the stage and when I got there, and picked up the

The immense soccer stadium in Rio, Maracana, was the setting for a special experience—a gift from the heavens, a lyric sung by the crowd, and a kiss by a bandit.

first mike, the rain stopped. At that instant.

"Everybody gasped.

"I looked up to the sky, toward heaven, and I said, 'Thank You.' They dissolved. Brazilians are a religious people, you know . . .

"The concert went well and I was in the midst of singing a song I know as well as my hand when I lost the lyric. Just blew it. Nothing. I had been singing "Strangers in the Night" and when I stopped and couldn't remember how it went, the whole stadium started to sing it for me—*in English.*

"I was touched . . .

"Near the end of the program, I heard a pounding noise and turned around and there was this mountain of a guy, running at me. I thought, Okay, this is it. But he ran up to me and kissed me (on the cheek) and then ran off.

"I learned later that in Brazil they have this guy who's called the Kissing Bandit or something like that and he kisses everybody, had kissed the Pope's shoe, and so on . . .

"And then, when I finished the last song, did the encore, I put the mike down. And the rain started again."

By 1983, Dad's whole crowd had calmed down. When they gathered, it was more often for a tribute than for tumult. On December 11, 1983, for example, Cary Grant, Milton Berle, Danny Thomas, and many more headliners attended the Variety Club All Star Party for Frank Sinatra, honoring his music and humanitarian works. We listened to Richard Burton movingly acknowledge the man called "Mr. Anonymous." With words written by Paul Keyes, Burton said, "Frank is a giant. Among the givers of the world, he stands tallest. He has more than paid rent for the space he occupies on this planet, forged as he is from legendary loyalty and compassion carefully hidden . . . Other than himself, there is no one who knows the magnitude of his generosity."

Burton spoke of the many people who had received "unexpected envelopes . . . special delivery answers to their prayers . . ." He told of "those awakened by late night phone calls which solved their problems, only on condition that they share your covenant of secrecy . . ." And of "those who were surprised by signed checks with amounts not filled in . . . Those performers down on their luck, who suddenly landed that role they never expected, and still don't know whom to thank."

I looked across the table, as best I could, to see a matching mist of tears in

Choreographer-dancer Twyla Tharp recently produced a stunningly successful dance number, set to songs by Sinatra. From Nancy Sinatra's interview with Tharp:

T.T.: . . . [I wanted] access to all that sentiment and emotion . . . as well as all those things societally we attach to those songs. There's a certain morality and a certain kind of period, so that [they]serve as a set, almost a visual set for the piece.
N.S.: You said something earlier about depth of information?
T.T.: Those songs mean more than music. They stand for whole generations. And his career is extraordinary in spanning [them] . . .

N.S.: How did you pick the songs?

T.T.: I listened to everything I could get hold of. One had to be the narrative of the piece. I see it as a statement about one long developing relationship, danced by different couples. It also had to make sense musically, so that it wouldn't be an affront to his ear or my ear or anyone's ear. The songs are: "Softly, As I Leave You"; "Strangers in the Night"; "One for My Baby"; then the first "My Way," which was early and aggressive; and "Something Stupid," the only one I think of as specifically humorous; and then "All the Way"; "Forget Domani"; "That's Life"; and then the last "My Way," which is later and much more mellow . . . I've always heard the sentiment of that song differently, not as a selfish statement but in context, as the only way people can relate to one another . . . Unless an individual in a relationship can do it "their way" and "theirs" is also their partner's way, it doesn't work . . .

I've listened to those songs by now thousands of times and they still have resonance and meaning. I feel he's given so much to the culture and his songs mean so much to so many people that it's a privilege . . . to say nothing of the fact that the genuine emotion he recorded into these songs keeps itself alive time after time.

You know, I sit in my dressing room and listen to those songs coming through the squawk box and they still move me.

N.S.: Did you feel you knew him before you met him?

T.T.: I can't lie. I felt I knew him intimately. When we met, I asked, "How'd you learn to sing so big?" And he had a simple and appropriate answer, "I like to sing." Which makes sense because singing is obviously something he understands in a fundamental way. It is something that is really in him to do.

N.S.: That's for damn sure.

T.T.: Those songs mean a lot to me, too, and I'm happy to share with people anything I may understand about them. Which is one of the reasons why the dance piece is so popular. Audiences love it. They have a great time and they're happy. What more can you ask for? They're happy and they're moved. And they recognize things in themselves. That means a community of spirit. And that's what I think theater should be.

my father's eyes, as much at Burton's eloquent delivery as anything else, I think.

With the secrecy eroding, the good works had now become part of his legend.

So much, in the end, blurs into an unfinished portrait. Not everything can be understood about the person at the core of a personality. To even begin to reach that core, it is important to know, for example, that Frank Sinatra is often an uncomfortable man.

The director Richard Brooks, for one, has perceived this. He has known Frank Sinatra as an "extremely private individual who has had to live his life as a totally public individual." He sees Sinatra as a man with a compelling need to be free, caught in the claustrophobia of celebrity. Paul Clemens, chosen to paint his portrait several years ago, never forgot Dad's first reaction: "I like it, but— you know—something bothers me about the eyes." The eyes were looking straight ahead. "Do you think you'd like them better averted?" Paul said. Sinatra said yes.

So outgoing, yet also so withdrawn. His personality flows from a clash between extremes, a clash that stretches back to the little boy assertive enough to run away to Cousin Buddy's or track down the doctor who attended his birth and troubled enough to bury himself beneath the covers and cry. When Frank Sinatra flails out, he is dealing as much with inner demons as with outer irritants. Remember the man aggressively placing phone calls to Ava in Spain and collapsing from martinis to hide from the pain. Consider, as critical to his life, the disappointments, the disillusionments. Now and then, I wonder if, as some people believe, the camera can steal the soul, what can an audience of 200,000 or twenty million or a hundred times that do?

The fears, the needs, that make him sensitive to slights also produce the sensitivity that enables his songs to touch souls.

"There are women who hand him flowers on stage and at the end of his shows," Richard Brooks said. "Most of them are not looking for romance with him. They are thanking him for some memory they've had in their lives. You can see it in their eyes. They would like him to know that he's made them *feel* something—probably something very deep and very good. They're not there so they can say, 'I touched Frank Sinatra.' It's not that they touched Frank Sinatra. It's that somewhere, somehow, Frank Sinatra touched them."

In a critical review of a recent (1984) album, John Swenson noted "Sinatra's overwhelming interpretation of 'New York, New York,'" pointing out that "people who wouldn't set foot on Manhattan Island invest quarter after quarter to hear Frank extolling its virtues around the globe."

Or take this thoughtful comment in *Newsday*, 1984, by an astute journalist, a writer's writer and peerless American observer:

Murray Kempton: "When I hear Frank Sinatra, I have no basis for assuming that his particular lonely heart has learned its lesson, but, for the moment, every fiber of my being believes it has."

This capacity to reach people sustains him, reassures him that not only his recordings, but the human impact of his songs, will endure. "What motivates him most," Garson Kanin thinks, "is a driving need to communicate. You can hear that when you listen to his singing. I said to him once, 'Frank, what is your real, overall ambition in life? In the long view, what would you like to really feel that you've accomplished?' And he thought for quite a while and then he said,

'Well, I think my real ambition is to pass on to others what I know.' "

Dad primarily meant about music, but there is more. He has wisdom. You can't put anything over on him because he knows where you're coming from every minute of the day: he's been there, he knows every emotion. "You know," he told Kanin, "it took me a long, long time to learn what I now know, and I don't want that to die with me. I'd like to pass that on to younger people."

He dislikes this kind of analysis, but, again, I consider his near-death at birth, the dousing in cold water that brought a stillborn baby alive, the event that has most shaped his life. "He was born fighting," someone once said, "because he was born dying." And the prevailing fight that has been with his own mortality. It is a fight that has stiffened as his parents died, and as the roster of good friends dwindles. He recently attached a gym to his bedroom and now, as well as swimming, he works out regularly. After more than sixty years, he had the forceps scars of his birth removed from his face and neck. Since Grandma's death, he has actively returned to the church, attending mass every Sunday and sometimes during the week. He is a little insecure with aging and afraid of dying. He is, then, like you and me, hopelessly, helplessly, happily human.

The ceremonies at the Kennedy Center honored his lifetime in the arts. It was an acknowledgment—"There is not the remotest possibility," said Gene Kelly, who introduced him, "that he will have a successor"—but it was also a summation of his nearly seventy years. And looking up at Sinatra sitting in the presidential box, I kept thinking, "He looks older. God, he suddenly looks older. He didn't look this old at the White House two hours ago." Every time I turned to look, he seemed to have aged another ten years. He was shrinking.

Much later, on another occasion when we were alone, I said, because I sensed what that temporary aging was about, "You know, I hope you don't let phrases like 'Lifetime Achievement Award' and things like that get you down. You realize that you're only sixty-nine years old." He said, *"Only* sixty-nine. I'm going to be seventy. How much time could I possibly have left?" "At *least* twenty-five years," I said. "You know, Grandma would still be alive today. You have longevity in your family. You can live to be a hundred and six. What was the report on your last physical checkup? The doctor said you had the body of a thirty-five-year-old. All you have to do is keep getting those checkups. You're *healthy!"*

Usually, to such remarks he had said something like, "Oh, yeah. I'm fine, don't worry about me, kid," and sloughed it off. This time he was quiet. He listened, quietly listened.

I said, "I don't think you should let those things get to you."

He laughed softly and gently. "Well, what am I going to be doing when I'm ninety-five?"

"I really don't know. Maybe writing or teaching. Maybe painting. But I know you're going to be doing something creative."

And he said, "Well, yeah, maybe."

"I guarantee it," I said, "if you continue to take care of yourself. You're not smoking, you're hardly drinking. What can go wrong as long as you take care of yourself?"

And I said to my daddy, "That's the best present you can give me. You take care of you for me, and I'll take care of me for you. Because you—healthy and happy—are all I want."

Please, God.

. . . You'd never know it,
but Buddy, I'm a kind of poet
and I've gotta lotta things to say.
And when I'm gloomy,
you simply gotta listen to me,
until it's talked away . . .

ENCORE

". . . The nightingale pierces his bosom with a thorn when he sings his song . . ."

The music of Frank Sinatra sings our joys, our sorrows and our silences. His voice goes on filling our hearts as well as our ears and is likely to go on doing so for a long time. He sings of love and loneliness, of exultant life and of still, small hours sadness, and in some curious way, the holy spirit moves and abides in him, I think. He sings as he operates, with spirit, not fear; with energy, not ennui. In his soul, way down deep, is a force, an energy that motivates him, guides him, and separates him from himself, making him and his work bigger than his life. It is this force that enables him to survive the decades; this energy that has helped him to find a measure of eternity before his body tires of the journey.

Sinatra has received much. This is, in part, because he has given much. And also because he has driven so hard, so far and so fast. He is a little crazy because, as it is said, "The overly concerned and sincere drive themselves crazy."

He has been driven by ambition, by ego, by inextinguishable talent and by gentleness, a force that can be almost violent, a love that is surpassing.

I've tried to put a spotlight not just on the pleasures but on the problems, not just on the bright or the dark but into the interesting shadows. (He likes recording late at night. "The later the better. My voice was not meant for daytime use.") I hope that you have learned a little more about this man, Sinatra, from my own personal, privileged, biased, loving, indeed peculiar perspective. What have *I* learned? Well, a few facts, to start with, because I had to find them to set them down. And, among other matters, a few more lessons from a man who didn't set out to teach or preach or, for that matter, to become anyone's model:

—That it is important never to stop dreaming of what could and should be. And to encourage others to dream.

—That in an audience's love, which is quite tangible, there is great power and strength for the taking, if one keeps an open heart.

—That a public figure is rarely alone. He seldom has the opportunity to do any private work, to experiment without risk. After a time, everything is an event.

—That if one says, "I am totally good, and I don't do bad things," one is likely to do bad things.

—That there is an attitude that comes with success, an arrogance, that can rob us of innocence.

—That getting older is a gift of life and that every age has its compensations. We have to tune in to what is best about each stage of our lives—find out where we belong—and make the most of it. Some people don't want to see my father on stage at seventy. But, typically, he is teaching us something. He's saying, "It's okay to grow old. Look, if I can do it, you can do it, too. And let's do it together. We've done everything else together. Sure, I'm scared, but I'm not going to give in to it."

As 1985 began, Larry King, a radio talk-show host and *USA Today* columnist, asked him about nostalgia. "I don't have any 'Good-Old-Days' memories," he said. "My whole life is the good old days." Bravo, Pop! We're learning from you again.

He is timely and timeless. His passions are greater and so is his pain. Seeing him hurt is devastating for me because he suffers as violently as he loves. He goes through a sort of carnage of the mind. Dismembered thoughts. A battered heart. A torn, sometimes dislocated, spirit. Inside, the healing is dreadfully slow.

While outside, the grin remains, the sudden flash of smile. The façade. The constant silly jokes.

As I have attempted to put feelings and facts on paper, the words don't look quite right. They seem so inadequate, so much less than I really feel, so much less than they were. If we cannot, in the end, understand him, perhaps he is a phenomenon of life, a force of nature, to be respected more than understood.

Well, as must be pretty apparent by now, my dad is my hero. Not a statue in the park, not just another pretty face without blemishes, not just a black bow tie and black patent leather shoes, always going away. I'm never free of a problem nor do I truly experience a joy until we share it. I need him to know when I'm hurting. I need him to know when I'm happy. I need him to know, to hear me, and in that I am no different from every daughter and, I suppose, son.

My father and I are still as close as can be, still joined at the hip. There is almost nothing within the parameters of a father-daughter relationship that we haven't shared. And yet we have lived our lives in the relentless presence of "the end of things." It is said that the way to love anything is to realize that it might be lost to you. That is a painful way to love a person. That is how I love my father.

In every hello there is a goodbye. In every greeting a farewell. Children who share their parents with the world know this. Sadness in the happiest of times. Emptiness in the fullest moment. And, since fathers and adult daughters don't, can't, spend their lives together, those moments become more precious as the years go by. I have been blessed to have him with me, with us, this long— so very blessed to have shared so much with a unique man and a fine family. When he is gone, when it is "done and done," I won't have to watch his films or play his recordings to remember, I'll carry his blood in my veins, his life's music in my heart and see his immortal soul in the bright, loving eyes of my children.

Nancy Sinatra Lambert
January, 1985

APPLAUSE

Producing this book has been, all things considered, an "interesting" experience—fun, exciting, difficult, painful—a little like having a baby; especially in that it is a surprise, no matter how well we know the parents. From concept to christening finery, this production was blessed by the strength and talent of several parents at conception, to thousands in delivery, and we all paced the floor and shared the labor. During development its sights, sounds and shape, nurtured by the loving care of these people, changed several times.

It was Steve Gelman—former *Life* magazine editor, now West Coast Editor of *TV Guide*—who, almost four years ago, began to shape this book. Steve took a mountain of material (cartons of scrapbooks, clippings, notes, letters, and two tons of photographs) that had been cluttering my life and threatening my sanity, and somehow forced it into the manageable, workable manuscript I used as my foundation when writing the final drafts.

The physical beauty of this book is the result of the dedication and talent of its designer, Irwin Glusker. Irwin, a New Yorker with mighty fine credentials, came into my life in Los Angeles during the late seventies, when he had his first look at my thousands of photos and snaps.

Over the years, he devoted much of his time and energy to this bi-coastal project. Irwin—who was affectionately nicknamed "Mr. Oscar" because my Portuguese housekeeper, Helena, had trouble pronouncing "Glusker"—patiently allowed me to lead him through Frank Sinatra's life in pictures. He created—with the help of Sara Abrams and Kristen Reilly—the first layouts without having read a word of the text. He made the second pass at layouts also without having read a word of the text, which wasn't ready. He was patient and understanding. Irwin is a man of elegance and taste, and this book reflects both.

Alex Gotfryd, Doubleday's Art Director, is a worldly, gentle man. His impeccable sense of style is matched with a care for substance. Working with Irwin and the rest of us on the Sinatra team but never interfering, he deftly guided the graphic aspects of the book—and sometimes more.

Sam Vaughan, Editor-in-Chief and Vice President of Doubleday, put his reputation on the line for me eight years ago when he took me and my dream into his life and made us part of him. Sam had no reason to trust me, let alone spend company dollars on the outcome. But he did—I think in part because, as he told me, "I grew up with Frank Sinatra . . ." And in part because—even though he is brilliant, witty, a dedicated husband, father and grandfather, and on personal terms with heads of state, Presidents, and some of the world's finest writers—he is also a little bit crazy.

Strong, sometimes silent Sam, put this team together, and handled it, with our separate egos, diplomatically and patiently. In the end he not only married all the manuscripts, but contributed some thoughtful words of his own. No Sam? No book!

Anne Rothenberg, daughter of Daniel and Lillian Fitzpatrick, wife of Jim, mother of Katie, Erin, and Danny, brought her experience with the highly regarded *Architectural Digest* and *Life* magazine to the project and it served us well. Annie tracked down photographs, sources, and photographers. She was relentless in her quest for the best, and generous in the giving of herself and her time. She stayed with me in spite of the fact that many times I asked her to do the impossible. For Annie, nothing was impossible and I am a better person for knowing her.

Krisha Fairchild, my assistant and the newest member of our team, in less than one year had my life and this project completely organized. She listened, learned, grew, and contributed with nary a word about the confusion, the long hours, and my tantrums. As a result, this is a better book than it might have been. Her typing skills may be, as she puts it, "a little lacking" but her enthusiasm and ability are not. She is a whiz.

To the wonderful folks on my dad's staff—Susan Reynolds, Elvina Joubert, Lori Thompson, Irving "Sarge" Weiss, and the top troubleshooter, Dorothy "Dot" Uhlemann—I am very, very grateful.

And a thank-you to Ric Ross for giving of his time on various scavenger hunts, for his many hours of research and support. And to Joan Ward, Mr. Vaughan's charming and capable Gal Friday, for her positive attitude, delightful sense of humor, and helpful suggestions all the way through. And to James Moser who, with Joan, helped to keep *Sam* and thus me on track—many thanks. I am no less grateful to those listed below for their contributions toward my dream: Harry Abrams, the staff at the Palm Springs Airport, Michele Weirick Andelson, Bonnie Barton, Alan Berliner, John Bryson, Bennett Cerf, Jim Cohen, Stan Cornyn, Digby Diehl, Allyson Dockray, John Dominis, Jim Edwards, Lynne Faragalli, John Forbess, Linda Hathorn, Connie Mascari, Viola and Pee-Wee Monte, Mo Ostin, Pamela Owens, Lilian Peloso, Richard Peters, Jilly Rizzo, Judith Rose, Wayne Rowe, Scott Sayers, Lee Solters, Phil Stern, Sharon Sweeney, Lena Tabori, Ed Thrasher, Lou Valentino.

One important note. These people are not only talented and caring, but they can keep a secret. Each person who has been directly involved with this project is completely trustworthy, which to me is part of their measure. Security was very important. It would have been a disaster if bits of this book had shown up, out of context, in one of those "rags" at the supermarket checkout.

To the Doubleday people: Nelson Doubleday, Henry Reath, Frank Cermak, Patrick Filley, Belle Blanchard Newton, Bill Barry, Albert Yokum, John T. Sargent, Jr., Chaucy Bennetts, Jackie Everly, Linda Winnard, Marianne Velmans, Adrienne Welles, Kathleen Antrim and the rest of their superb sales, promotion, production, and rights selling team—and to those hundreds whom I may never have the pleasure of meeting—thank you. You have all given my father a priceless gift.

My friends and family—my sister, brother, mother, my husband and my children, just to begin with—*all* our friends and family, have helped to create this book. I am deeply in debt to them, as to friends and fellow performers and colleagues who are the various "voices" of this book. Their names are in the text itself and the value of their contributions will be self-evident.

And finally, to the main voice of the book, in addition to my own: to my father, whose autobiography this has turned out to be, at least in part. He contributed time and energy and *facts* to fill in the gaps, to help set straight misunderstandings or misinformation. He has contributed so much to this book that it is, to a certain extent, *his* book. And we have often indicated this by the simple initials "FS," as he often signs his own letters and notes. After all, he has led the life that made the book possible, impossible, and interesting.

As I hope becomes clear elsewhere, Dad, I love you very much—and wish *you* had kept a diary.

THE ALBUMS

Frank Sinatra and Sy Oliver . . .

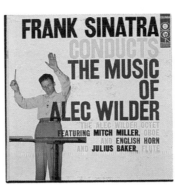

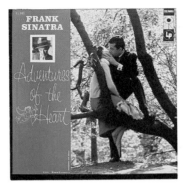

. . . and Axel Stordahl . . .

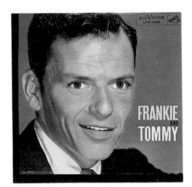

. . . **Nelson Riddle** . . .

. . . **Gordon Jenkins** . . .

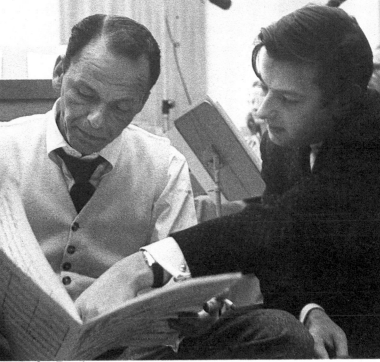

. . . André Previn . . .

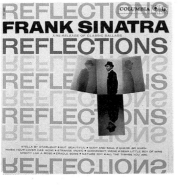

. . . Fred Waring . . .

. . . Neal Hefti . . .

. . . Billy May . . .

. . . **Claus Ogerman** . . .

. . . **Quincy Jones** . . .

. . . **Don Costa** . . .

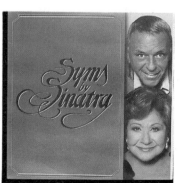

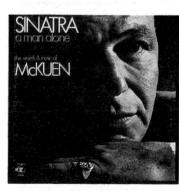

PHIL STERN/GLOBE PHOTOS

THE FILMS

LAS VEGAS NIGHTS (Paramount), 1941

HIGHER AND HIGHER (RKO Radio), 1943

TILL THE CLOUDS ROLL BY (MGM), 1946

SHIP AHOY (MGM), 1942

REVEILLE WITH BEVERLY (Columbia), 1943

STEP LIVELY (RKO Radio), 1944

ANCHORS AWEIGH (MGM), 1945

IT HAPPENED IN BROOKLYN (MGM), 1947

THE MIRACLE OF THE BELLS (RKO), 1948

THE KISSING BANDIT (MGM), 1948

TAKE ME OUT TO THE BALL GAME (MGM), 1949

MEET DANNY WILSON (Univ.–Intl.), 1951

FROM HERE TO ETERNITY (Columbia), 1953

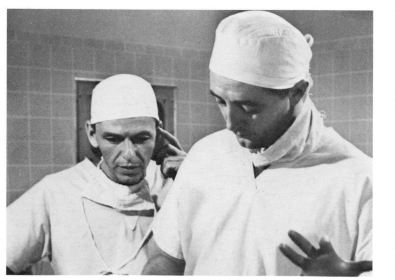

NOT AS A STRANGER (UA), 1955

THE TENDER TRAP (MGM), 1955

ON THE TOWN (MGM), 1949

DOUBLE DYNAMITE (RKO Radio), 1951

SUDDENLY (UA), 1954

YOUNG AT HEART (Warners), 1955

GUYS AND DOLLS (Goldwyn–MGM), 1955

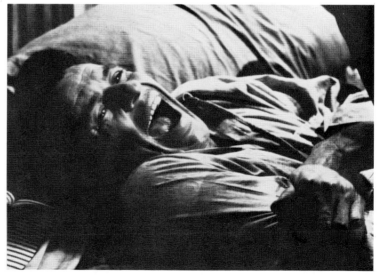

THE MAN WITH THE GOLDEN ARM (UA), 1955

MEET ME IN LAS VEGAS (MGM), 1956

JOHNNY CONCHO (UA), 1956

THE PRIDE AND THE PASSION (UA), 1957

THE JOKER IS WILD (Paramount), 1957

SOME CAME RUNNING (MGM), 1958

A HOLE IN THE HEAD (Capra–UA), 1959

HIGH SOCIETY (MGM), 1956

AROUND THE WORLD IN 80 DAYS (Todd), 1956

PAL JOEY (Columbia), 1957

KINGS GO FORTH (UA), 1958

NEVER SO FEW (MGM), 1959

CAN–CAN (20th Century-Fox), 1960

OCEAN'S ELEVEN (Warners), 1960

PEPE (Columbia), 1960

THE ROAD TO HONG KONG (UA), 1962

THE MANCHURIAN CANDIDATE (UA), 1962

4 FOR TEXAS (Warners), 1964

ROBIN AND THE SEVEN HOODS (Warners), 1964

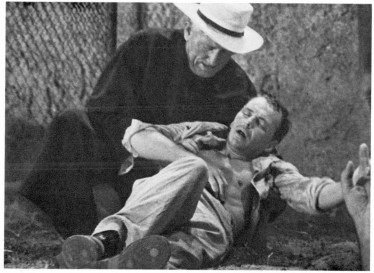

THE DEVIL AT 4 O'CLOCK (Columbia), 1961

SERGEANTS 3 (UA), 1962

COME BLOW YOUR HORN (Paramount), 1963

THE LIST OF ADRIAN MESSENGER (Universal), 1963

NONE BUT THE BRAVE (Warners), 1965

VON RYAN'S EXPRESS (20th Century-Fox), 1965

MARRIAGE ON THE ROCKS (Warners), 1965

CAST A GIANT SHADOW (UA), 1966

THE NAKED RUNNER (Warners), 1967

TONY ROME (20th Century-Fox), 1967

DIRTY DINGUS MAGEE (MGM), 1970

THAT'S ENTERTAINMENT (MGM), 1974

THE OSCAR (Embassy Pictures), 1966

ASSAULT ON A QUEEN (Paramount), 1966

THE DETECTIVE (20th Century-Fox), 1968

LADY IN CEMENT, (20th Century-Fox), 1968

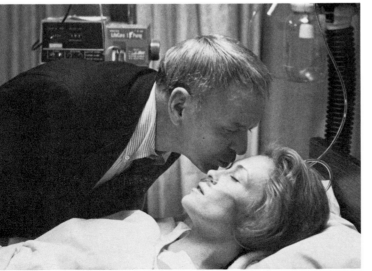
THE FIRST DEADLY SIN (Filmways), 1980

CANNONBALL RUN II (Golden Harvest Films), 1984

THE FACES

H.S.H. Prince Rainier of Monaco, FS, H.S.H. Princess Grace, and
   H.R.H. Princess Sophia of Greece, II.R.II. Prince Juan Carlos of Spain.
FS and Michael Jackson.
FS and Billy Daniels.
Mahalia Jackson and Sidney Poitier.
FS and Col. Tom Parker.

Mary, Babe, Champ, and Dolly Garavente.
FS and John Wayne.
Chester Babcock, a.k.a. Jimmy Van Heusen.
Garson Kanin and Ruth Gordon.

George Burns, Gracie Allen, and FS.
Gene Cherico.
Sarah Vaughan and FS.

Lee and Walter Annenberg and FS.
Jersey Joe Walcott, FS, Rocky Marciano.
The Haleys: Jack, Jack Jr., and Flo.
FS and Richard "Nicky" Conte
Murray Woolf and Gloria Lovell.

Red Skelton.
Duke Ellington and FS.
FS and Princess Grace.
Harry Cohn, Jack Entratter, FS,
   and Kim Novak.
Sammy Cahn, Jule Styne, and FS.

AJ, Buddy Garavente, Nancy, Amanda.
Jimmy Stewart.
Orson Welles, FS, Rags Ragland.
Joe E. Lewis, FS, and Swifty Morgan.
AJ, Amanda, and Bert.

FS and Debbie Reynolds.
Joe DiMaggio and FS.
Toots Shor, and Quentin Reynolds.
Ronnie Flint, Tommy Gallagher, Chasen's.
FS with Peggy Lee.

Rosalind Russell and Harold Gibbons.
FS and Ernie Kovacs.
James Dean and Sammy Davis, Jr.
Joe Parnello.
Eleanor Roosevelt and FS.

Henry Kissinger and FS.
FS and Ms. Lillian Carter.
George "Bullets" Durgom and FS.
Mary Martin and FS.

Tony Bennett.
Dean Martin, Jerry Lewis, FS, ca. 1950.
FS and Harry James.
FS and Mitzi Gaynor.
Lori Thompson.

The Martins and the Sinatras.
FS, Dean Martin, Jerry Lewis, ca. 1980.
Mike Frankovich and FS.
R. J. Wagner, Natalie Wood, and FS.
Simon Wiesenthal and FS.

(same as column 3)
Dean Martin, Ken Lane, and FS.
Jay Richard Kennedy.
FS and Paul Anka.
FS with Patsy and Rose D'Amore.

LaVerne Gunton.
Jack Benny, FS, and Eddie Fisher.
Richard Rodgers and FS.
Guy McElwaine.
Alan King and Harry Belafonte.

Jackie Heller and FS.
Jackie Gleason and Frank Jr.
Danny and Rosemarie Thomas with FS.
Jack Donohue and FS.
Shirley MacLaine and FS.

Rod Steiger and FS.
FS and Rod McKuen.
FS and Luciano Pavarotti.
FS and Emmanuel Lewis.

Lauritz Melchior and FS.
FS and Morton Downey.
George Jacobs.
Robert Weitman and Margie Durante.
The Shah of Iran and FS.

Bobby Burns and FS.
Arturo and Amanda.
Jilly and Adrianna.
Pat DeCicco.
Sonny Burke.

FS and William S. Paley.
FS and Ray Sinatra.
Nat "King" Cole and Sammy.
FS and Kirk Douglas.
FS and Bill "Suntan Charlie" Miller.

FS with Jack Benny, Mary Livingstone.
FS with Veronique and Cecilia Peck.
Tommy Lasorda and FS.
Milton Berle and FS.
FS and Van Johnson.

George Burns and Nancy Sinatra, Sr.
David Tebet and FS.
Nancy Sinatra, Sr., and Harry Kurni
Charlie Turner.

Irwin "Ruby" Rubenstein, Leo Durocher,
   and Bernie "O.J." Frandt.
Martin Gabel and Arlene Francis.
President Roberto Viola and FS.
Alan Ladd and FS.
Frank Capra, Edward G. Robinson.

Juliet Prowse and FS.
Ed Wynn, Ethel Merman.
FS with Kitty and Mervyn LeRoy.
FS and Spencer Tracy.
Ross Hunter and Barbara Stanwyck.

Rosalind Russell and Anne Douglas.
Bob Hope, FS, and Tallulah Bankhead.
FS and Al Jolson.
O. J. Simpson and Sugar Ray Robinson.
FS and Phil Harris.

Nancy and Billy May.
Nancy, Liza Minnelli, and Goldie Hawn.
Jack Warner, Jack Valenti, and FS.
Hank Henry and FS.
Lauren Bacall and FS.

Prime Minister David Ben-Gurion.
Vincente Minnelli and Sam Goldwyn.
Nathan and Linda Golden.
FS with King Hussein and his Queen.
Vito Musso and FS.

FS, Dr. and Mrs. Michael DeBakey.
Marlene Dietrich and FS.
Jilly, Earl Weaver, Leo Durocher.
Paul Clemens.
Tony Mottola.

Anthony Quinn and Tony Curtis.
FS and U Thant.
Tommy Lasorda, FS, Charlie Callas.
FS and Steve McQueen.
Floyd Patterson and FS.

FS and Buddy Hackett.
Brad Dexter and Dick Bakalyan.
Barbara Rush and FS.
Jimmy Durante and Howard Koch.
AJ. Amanda, "Uncle" Lew Wasserman.

FS with David Niven and Bert Allenberg.
FS, Beverly Sills, and Robert Merrill.
Bennett "the Bookmaker" Cerf.
FS, Joe Delaney, and Ed McMahon.
Joey and Sal Scognamillo of Patsy's.

Natalie and Danny Schwartz.
FS and Red Buttons.
FS, Harry S Truman, and George Jessel.
Nancy with Bobby Darin.
FS with Gary Morton and Lucille Ball.

FS and Joe Louis.
FS and Bing Crosby.
FS and Robert Mitchum.
R. J. Wagner, Jilly, and Charlie Callas.
FS and Jack Klugman.

Billie and Henri Giné.
FS and Loel Guinness.
David Janssen and FS.
FS and Don Rickles.
FS and Ray Charles.

Elton John and FS.
Jilly Rizzo and Pat Henry.
Buddy Rich, Johnny Mercer, and FS.
FS and Itzhak Perlman.
FS and Ruth Koch.

Perry Como, FS, Dionne Warwick, George Burns, Queen Elizabeth II, Nancy Reagan.
FS and Mikhail Baryshnikov.
Elvina "Vine" Joubert.
FS and Flip Wilson.
Altovese and Sammy Davis, Jr.

Orson Welles and FS.
Perry Como and FS.
Ella Fitzgerald, Count Basie, and FS.
Rosemary Clooney and FS.

FS and Ingrid Bergman.
Manie Sacks, Paul "Skinny" D'Amato.
FS and Skitch Henderson.
Ruth Cosgrove Berle and FS.
Major Edward Bowes.

FS and Johnny Carson.
FS and Steve Garvey.
FS and Henry Fonda.
AJ, Amanda, Larry "Nifty" Victorson.
FS and Dean Martin with Jack Warner.

Irv Cottler.
Gary Cooper, Jack Benny, Danny Kaye.
Richie Lisella and FS.
Sarge Weiss, Pat and Jim Mahoney.
Edward G. Robinson.

Edie Mayer Goetz and Alfred Hart.
(same as column 6)
FS, Don McGuire, and Hank Sanicola.
FS, George Raft, and James Cagney.
Elizabeth Taylor.

FS and Morris Stoloff.
FS and Claudette Colbert.
FS and Judy Garland.
AJ and Amanda with Bill Stapeley.
FS with Lou Costello and Bud Abbott.

FOR THE RECORD

It seems impossible to write a life the way it is lived and have a cohesive story. Professional or working situations, though lived in concert with the personal everyday happenings, are for the most part intrusive in a narrative. So this section of the book contains the material so vital to the documenting of my father's life, yet difficult to include in the main body of the text. A reference section.

There are many reference books available which deal with FS's career. Some of them are quite accurate. I have tried to correct a few mistakes, to set the record straight, as best I can. This is not intended to be the definitive Sinatra reference book. But my hope is that a student of Dad's life or of American music and films can find it useful—at least as a general outline of his work.

Compiling this section was made easier than I had anticipated because some interested people had already built a foundation. I relied on several sources for production credits, cast lists, reviews, and quotes. Then, for a peek inside, I supplied my own impressions, those of coworkers, and those which my father has shared with me.

My sincere thanks to the following people:

Richard Peters, *The Frank Sinatra Scrapbook*
Gene Ringgold and Clifford McCarty, *The Films of FS*
Albert I. Lonstein, *Sinatra—An Exhaustive Treatise*
Ed O'Brien and Scott Sayers, Jr., *The Sinatra Sessions*
Leonard Maltin, *TV Movies, 1985–86 Edition*

The largest debt of thanks owed here is to businessman Ric Ross, who may be Frank Sinatra's biggest fan. Ric has, as a hobby, spent enormous amounts of time and energy collecting stories, information, and facts about my father's life and work. And he has generously shared it all with me. Where this book is concerned, the old Chinese proverb, "When in doubt, do nothing," was changed to, "When in doubt, ask Ric."

THE YEARS

1915 Birth of Francis Albert Sinatra, Hoboken.
1935 Hoboken Four wins "Major Bowes' Original Amateur Hour."
Movie: Short Subject: Major Bowes Theatre of the Air.
1937
First permanent singing engagement, Rustic Cabin.
1939
Marriage of FS and Nancy Barbato.
First appearance with Harry James, Hippodrome, Baltimore.
First record with James: "Melancholy Mood," "From the Bottom of My Heart" followed by "All or Nothing at All."
1940
First appearance with Tommy Dorsey Band.
First record with Dorsey and Pied Pipers: "The Sky Fell Down."
First child: Nancy Sandra. Born: Jersey City.
First #1 Single: "I'll Never Smile Again."
TOP TEN: "Imagination," "Tradewinds," "Our Love Affair," "We Three," "Stardust."
1941
OUTSTANDING MALE VOCALIST, *Billboard, Downbeat.*
TOP TEN: "Oh Look at Me Now," "Do I Worry," "Dolores," "Everything Happens to Me," "Let's Get Away from It All," "This Love of Mine," "Two in Love."
Movie: *Las Vegas Nights.*
1942
First solo recording, "The Night We Called It a Day," "The Lamplighter's Serenade," "The Song Is You," "Night and Day," Bluebird Records.
Last recording session with Dorsey. Eighty-three songs in two years.

First solo appearance, with Benny Goodman, Paramount Theatre, New York.
#1: "There Are Such Things."
TOP TEN: "There Are Such Things," "Just as Though You Were Here," "Take Me," "Daybreak."
First radio show: "Reflections," CBS.
Movie: *Ship Ahoy.*
1943
First solo nightclub act, Riobomba Club, New York.
Columbia rereleases: "All or Nothing at All."
First Columbia recording session with Alec "The Professor" Wilder, accompanied by the Bobby Tucker Singers: "Close to You," "People Will Say We're in Love," "You'll Never Know."
First solo concert West Coast, Hollywood Bowl.
First appearance Wedgewood Room, Waldorf-Astoria, New York.
Declared 4-F by Army.
TOP TEN: "In the Blue of the Evening," "It Started All Over Again," "All or Nothing at All," "It's Always You," "You'll Never Know," "Close to You," "Sunday, Monday or Always," "People Will Say We're in Love."
Radio: "Your Hit Parade," "The Broadway Bandbox."
Movies: *Higher and Higher, Reveille with Beverly.*
1944
Second child: Franklin Wayne Emanuel. Born: Jersey City. Sinatra family moves to California.
"Columbus Day Riot," Paramount Theatre.
TOP TEN: "I Couldn't Sleep a Wink Last Night," "White Christmas."
Radio: "Your Hit Parade," "The Frank Sinatra Show."
Movie: *Step Lively.*
1945
Civil Rights lectures.
USO tour.
AMERICAN UNITY AWARD.
COMMENDATION: National Conference of Christians and Jews.
COMMENDATION: Bureau of Inter-Cultural Education.
First recording session as conductor.
TOP TEN: "I Dream of You," "Saturday Night," "Dream," "Nancy."
Radio: "Songs by Sinatra," "The Frank Sinatra Show."
Movies: *Anchors Aweigh, The House I Live In.*
1946
OSCAR, *The House I Live In.*
JEFFERSON AWARD, Council Against Intolerance in America.
AMERICA'S FAVORITE MALE SINGER, *Downbeat.*
MOST POPULAR SCREEN STAR, *Modern Screen.*
#1: "Five Minutes More," "The Voice of Frank Sinatra" (LP).
TOP TEN: "Oh What It Seemed to Be," "Day by Day," "They Say It's Wonderful," "The Coffee Song," "White Christmas."
Radio: "Songs by Sinatra."
Movie: *Till the Clouds Roll By.*
1947
ABC Radio Poll: SECOND MOST POPULAR LIVING PERSON (Bing Crosby was first, Pope Pius XII was third!).
"SINATRA DAY," Hoboken.
TOP TEN: "Mam'selle," "Songs by Sinatra" (LP).
Radio: "Songs by Sinatra"; returns to "Your Hit Parade."
Movie: *It Happened in Brooklyn.*
1948
Third child: Christina. Born: Los Angeles.
TOP TEN: "Christmas Songs by Sinatra" (LP).
Radio: "Your Hit Parade."
Movies: *The Miracle of the Bells, The Kissing Bandit.*

1949

HOLLZER MEMORIAL AWARD, Los Angeles Jewish Community.
TOP TEN: "The Hucklebuck."
Radio: "Your Hit Parade," "Light Up Time."
Movies: *Take Me Out to the Ball Game, On the Town.*

1950

TV debut, Bob Hope.
Signs contract with CBS-TV.
First appearance at London Palladium.
TV: "The Frank Sinatra Show."
Radio: "Light Up Time," "Meet Frank Sinatra."

1951

Marriage to Ava Gardner, West Germantown, Pennsylvania.
Radio: "Meet Frank Sinatra."
Movies: *Double Dynamite, Meet Danny Wilson.*

1952

Paramount Theatre, New York.
Final recording session, Columbia.
Screen test: *From Here to Eternity,* Columbia Pictures.

1953

First Capitol recording session: "Lean Baby," "I'm Walking Behind You."
European concert tour.
Radio: "Rocky Fortune," "To Be Perfectly Frank."
Movie: *From Here to Eternity.*

1954

OSCAR, Best Supporting Actor, *From Here to Eternity.*
TOP MALE SINGER, *Billboard.*
MOST POPULAR VOCALIST, *Downbeat.*
SINGER OF THE YEAR, *Metronome.*
#1: "Young at Heart."
TOP TEN: "Three Coins in the Fountain," "Songs for Young Lovers" (LP), "Swing Easy" (LP).
Radio: "To Be Perfectly Frank," "The Frank Sinatra Show."
Movie: *Suddenly.*

1955

First Australian tour.
TV: "Our Town," NBC, with Paul Newman and Eva Marie Saint.
TOP TEN: "Learnin' the Blues," "Love and Marriage," "In the Wee Small Hours" (LP).
Radio: "The Frank Sinatra Show."
Movies: *Young at Heart, Not as a Stranger, The Tender Trap, Guys and Dolls, The Man with the Golden Arm.*

1956

OSCAR NOMINATION, Best Actor, *The Man with the Golden Arm.*
British Cinematography Council: Special Award, *The Man with the Golden Arm.*
THE MUSICIAN'S MUSICIAN, *Metronome.*
TOP TEN: "Hey, Jealous Lover," "Songs for Swingin' Lovers" (LP), "This Is Sinatra" (LP).
Movies: *Meet Me in Las Vegas, Johnny Concho, High Society, Around the World in 80 Days.*

1957

Signs contract ABC-TV.
TOP MALE VOCALIST, *Playboy.*
ALL-AROUND ENTERTAINER OF THE YEAR, *American Weekly.*
MR. PERSONALITY, *Metronome.*
TOP TEN: "Close to You" (LP), "A Swingin' Affair" (LP), "Where Are You?" (LP).
TV: Series of specials.
Movies: *The Pride and the Passion, The Joker Is Wild, Pal Joey.*

1958

Breaks all existing American Nightclub Records, the Fountainebleau, Miami Beach.
ENTERTAINER OF THE YEAR, Al Jolson Award, B'nai B'rith.
TOP MALE VOCALIST, *Playboy.*
#1: "Come Fly with Me" (LP), "Only the Lonely" (LP)—120 weeks!

TOP TEN: "This Is Sinatra, vol. 2."
TV: "The Frank Sinatra Show."
Movies: *Kings Go Forth, Some Came Running.*

1959

LOVE VOICE OF THE CENTURY, New York *Post.*
Australian concert tour.
TOP MALE VOCALIST, *Playboy.*
GRAMMY, Album of the Year, "Come Dance with Me."
GRAMMY, Best Solo Vocal Performance, "Come Dance with Me."
TOP TEN: "Come Dance with Me" (LP), "No One Cares" (LP), "Look to Your Heart" (LP).
Movies: *A Hole in the Head, Never So Few.*

1960

TOP MALE VOCALIST, *Playboy.*
TOP BOX OFFICE STAR OF 1960, Film Exhibitors of America.
ONE OF THE MOST ATTRACTIVE MEN IN THE WORLD, *McCall's.*
FS forms Reprise Records.
#1: "Nice n' Easy" (LP).
TV: Special welcoming Elvis Presley home from the Army.
Movies: *Can-Can, Ocean's Eleven, Pepe.*

1961

Produces President Kennedy's Inaugural Gala.
Tribute to Martin Luther King, Carnegie Hall.
TOP MALE VOCALIST, *Playboy.*
First Reprise album: "Ring-a-Ding-Ding!"
TOP TEN: "Sinatra's Swingin' Session" (LP), "All the Way" (LP), "Ring-a-Ding-Ding" (LP), "Come Swing with Me" (LP), "Sinatra Swings" (LP).
Movie: *The Devil at 4 O'Clock.*

1962

Radio stations begin "Sinatra-thons," "Frank Sinatra Days," etc.
Engagement to Juliet Prowse.
TOP MALE VOCALIST, *Playboy.*
Round the world tour for children's charities:
    SILVER HEART AWARD, Variety Club of Great Britain.
    KEY TO THE CITY, Tokyo.
    Meeting with Israel's David Ben-Gurion.
    ITALIAN STAR OF SOLIDARITY AWARD.
Narrates short film, *Sinatra in Israel,* filmed during tour.
Last Capitol session.
TOP TEN: "Sinatra and Strings" (LP).
Movies: *Sergeants 3, The Road to Hong Kong, The Manchurian Candidate.*

1963

Marty and Dolly Sinatra, fiftieth wedding anniversary.
TOP MALE VOCALIST, *Playboy.*
Merger Reprise Records and Warner Bros. Records Inc.
TOP TEN: "Sinatra-Basie" (LP), "The Concert Sinatra" (LP), "Sinatra's Sinatra" (LP).
Movies: *Come Blow Your Horn, The List of Adrian Messenger.*

1964

Dedication: FRANK SINATRA YOUTH CENTER FOR CHRISTIANS, MOSLEMS, AND JEWS, Nazareth, Israel.
TOP MALE VOCALIST, *Playboy.*
First performance, Sinatra and Basie, Sands Hotel.
TOP TEN: "Days of Wine and Roses," "Moon River and Other Academy Award Winners" (LP).
Movies: *4 for Texas, Robin and the Seven Hoods.*

1965

COMMANDEUR DE LA SANTÉ PUBLIQUE, presented by French President Charles de Gaulle.
TOP MALE VOCALIST, *Playboy.*
MAN OF THE YEAR, Conference of Personal Managers.
Newport Jazz Festival, with Count Basie.
GRAMMY, Album of the Year, "September of My Years."
GRAMMY, Best Solo Vocal Performance, "It Was a Very Good Year."

TOP TEN: "Sinatra 65" (LP), "September of My Years" (LP), "A Man and His Music" (LP).
TV: Documentary on FS, Walter Cronkite, CBS.
TV: Special, "Sinatra: A Man and His Music," CBS.
EMMY AWARD, Outstanding Musical Program, "Sinatra: A Man and His Music."
PEABODY AWARD, Distinguished Achievement in Video Programming, "Sinatra: A Man and His Music."
Movies: *Von Ryan's Express, Marriage on the Rocks, None but the Brave* (directorial debut).

1966
Inaugural Gala, California Governor Edmund G. "Pat" Brown, staged by FS.
Marriage to Mia Farrow, Las Vegas.
TOP MALE VOCALIST, *Playboy.*
GRAMMY, Album of the Year, "Sinatra: A Man and His Music."
GRAMMY, Record of the Year, "Strangers in the Night."
EMMY Nomination, "Sinatra: A Man and His Music, Part 2."
#1: "Strangers in the Night" (single and LP).
TOP TEN: "That's Life " (single and LP), "Sinatra at the Sands" (LP).
Movies: *Cast a Giant Shadow, The Oscar, Assault on a Queen.*

1967
National Chairman, American Italian Anti-Defamation League.
#1: "Something Stupid."
Movies: *The Naked Runner, Tony Rome.*

1968
TOP MALE VOCALIST, *Playboy.*
PLAYBOY HALL OF FAME.
TOP TEN: "My Way" (longest run in British chart history, 120 weeks).
Movies: *The Detective, Lady in Cement.*

1969
HONORARY ALUMNUS, UCLA.
TOP MALE VOCALIST, *Playboy.*

1970
Royal Festival Hall, London, charity concerts with Basie.
Daughter Nancy marries Hugh Lambert (on FS's fifty-fifth birthday).
Movie: *Dirty Dingus Magee.*

1971
Inaugural Gala, California Governor Ronald Reagan.
Dedication: ANTHONY MARTIN SINATRA MEDICAL EDUCATION CENTER, Palm Springs. Funds for center donated by FS.
Announcement of retirement.
Tribute to FS read into Congressional Record, Senator John Tunney
JEAN HERSHOLT HUMANITARIAN AWARD. OSCAR.
DISTINGUISHED SERVICE AWARD, Los Angeles.
Retirement Concert, benefit Motion Picture and Television Relief Fund.

1972
MEDALLION OF VALOR, State of Israel.
HIGHEST ACHIEVEMENT AWARD, Screen Actors Guild.
HUMANITARIAN AWARD, Friars Club.

1973
MAN OF THE YEAR AWARD, March of Dimes.
SPLENDID AMERICAN AWARD, Thomas A. Dooley Foundation.
TV: Special, "Ol' Blue Eyes Is Back," ends retirement.
ENTERTAINER OF THE CENTURY, Songwriters of America.
MAN OF THE YEAR, All-American Collegiate Golf.

1974
Hosts American Film Institute's Salute to James Cagney.
Granddaughter: Angela Jennifer Lambert. Born: Los Angeles.
Japanese tour.
Australian tour.
MAN OF THE YEAR AWARD, from the city of Las Vegas.
TV: "The Main Event," Madison Square Garden.
Movie: *That's Entertainment.*

1975

American and Canadian tour.
European tour.
Broadway, with Basie and Ella Fitzgerald.
London Palladium, with Basie and Sarah Vaughan.
Charity concerts, Jerusalem Center for Arab and Jewish Children.
CECIL B. DeMILLE AWARD, Golden Globes.
Honorary Citizen of Chicago.
FRANK SINATRA CHILD CARE UNIT, St. Jude's Children's Research Center, Memphis, Tennessee.

1976
ENTERTAINER OF THE YEAR, Friars Club.
HONORARY DOCTOR OF HUMANE LETTERS, University of Nevada at Las Vegas.
Daughter Christina marries Wes Farrell.
Granddaughter: Amanda Katherine Lambert. Born: Los Angeles.
Marriage to Barbara Marx, Rancho Mirage.
Muscular Dystrophy Telethon, reunion Dean Martin and Jerry Lewis.
SCOPUS AWARD, American Friends of the Hebrew University of Israel.
JERUSALEM MEDAL, Jerusalem, Israel.
CERTIFICATE OF APPRECIATION, City of New York.
Movie: *That's Entertainment Part II.*

1977
FREEDOM MEDAL, Independence Hall, Philadelphia.
Charity concert, National Society for the Prevention of Cruelty to Children, Royal Albert Hall, London.
CULTURAL AWARD, Israel.
TV movie: *Contract on Cherry Street.*

1978
Dedication, FRANK SINATRA INTERNATIONAL STUDENT CENTER, Mount Scopus Campus, Hebrew University, Jerusalem.
TV: Dean Martin's "Man of the Hour."

1979
PIED PIPER AWARD, American Society of Composers, Authors, and Publishers.
TRUSTEES AWARD, National Academy of Recording Arts and Sciences.
PRIMUM VIVERE ("LIFE FIRST") AWARD, World Mercy Fund.
INTERNATIONAL MAN OF THE YEAR AWARD, presented by President Gerald Ford.
GRAND UFFICIALE DELL' ORDINE AL MERITO DELLA REPUBBLICA ITALIANA, Italy.
Charity concerts, the Pyramids, Cairo, Egypt.
Grand Marshall, Columbus Day Parade, New York.
HUMANITARIAN AWARD, Columbus Citizens Committee, New York.
TV: Fortieth Anniversary in show business, "Sinatra: The *First* Forty Years." Caesar's Palace, Las Vegas.
Benefit, produced by FS for The Memorial Sloan-Kettering Cancer Center, Metropolitan Opera House, New York. First of five (through 1984).
FRANK SINATRA WING, Atlantic City Medical Center, New Jersey.
#1: "Trilogy" (LP) (six Grammy nominations).

1980
Grand Marshall, Tournament of Roses Parade, Pasadena.
Largest live paid audience ever recorded for a solo performer: Maracana Stadium, Rio de Janeiro, Brazil.
"Valentine Love-In" for Palm Springs Desert Hospital.
METROMEDIA CERTIFICATE OF ACHIEVEMENT, Los Angeles Bicentennial.
FIRST MEMBER, Simon Wiesenthal Center Fellows Society.
ENTERTAINER OF THE YEAR, *Atlantic City Magazine.*
JOHNNY MERCER AWARD, Songwriters Hall of Fame.
HUMANITARIAN AWARD, Variety Clubs International.
Royal Festival Hall, Royal Albert Hall, London.
Narrates documentary film, World Mercy Fund, West Africa.
Red Cross Gala, benefit, Monte Carlo, Monaco.
NATIONAL CAMPAIGN CHAIRMAN, National Multiple Sclerosis Society, 1980, 1981, and 1982.

Movie: *The First Deadly Sin.*
1981
Produces and directs Inaugural Gala, President Ronald Reagan.
Daughter Christina marries Richard Cohen.
FRANK SINATRA STUDENT SCHOLARSHIP FUND, Hoboken.
Concerts, Sun City, South Africa.
ORDER OF THE LEOPARD, from President Lucas Mangope of the
Republic of Bophuthatswana—first white person to receive this
honor.
Concerts, Buenos Aires, Argentina, São Paulo, Brazil.
ENTERTAINER OF THE YEAR, *Atlantic City Magazine.*
1982
White House performance for Italian Prime Minister.
Radio City Music Hall, with Luciano Pavarotti, George Shearing.
TV: First Cable TV Special: "Sinatra, Concert for the Americas," in the
Dominican Republic.
Universal Amphitheater, benefits for Jules Stein Eye Institute, Loyola
Marymount University, Motion Picture and Television Relief
Fund.
1983
THE SINATRA FAMILY CHILDREN'S UNIT FOR THE CHRONI-
CALLY ILL, Seattle Children's Orthopedic Hospital. Variety
Clubs.
KENNEDY CENTER HONORS AWARD FOR LIFETIME ACHIEVE-
MENT.
1984
HONORARY DOCTOR OF FINE ARTS, Loyola Marymount, Los
Angeles.
DISTINGUISHED AMERICAN AWARD, Boy Scouts of America.
European tour.
MEDAL OF HONOR FOR SCIENCE AND ART, FIRST CLASS, highest
civilian honor, Vienna, Austria.
Movie: *Cannonball Run II.*
1985
Produces and hosts Inaugural Gala, President Reagan.
DOCTOR OF ENGINEERING, Honoria Causa, Stevens Institute,
Hoboken.
MEDAL OF FREEDOM, May 1985, Washington, D.C.

"MR. ANONYMOUS"

The following is a partial list of charities and causes supported by
my father (and of course, many others) through contributions and benefit
performances.

This is a cross section and not comprehensive, reflecting what I
have been documenting only since 1965. I have not mentioned individuals or individual families because of their right to privacy, and because
Dad does most of these good deeds anonymously and I must respect that.

Friars Clubs, SHARE, Jewish Welfare Fund, WAIF, State of Israel, UCLA,
Italian American Anti-Defamation League, American Civil Liberties
Union, United Jewish Appeal, Neighbors of Watts, Thalians, Southern
Christian Leadership Conference, numerous police departments, Na-
tional Society for the Prevention of Cruelty to Children, St. Jude's Hospi-
tal, Villa Scalabrini, Nos Ostros, Motion Picture Relief Fund, Eisenhower
Medical Center, Easter Seals, Desert Hospital, March of Dimes, Preven-
tion of Blindness, Boys Town, Variety Clubs, Cedars Sinai Hospital,
United Cerebral Palsy, Muscular Dystrophy, B'nai B'rith, College of the
Desert, City of Hope, Lenox Hill Hospital, Hebrew University, Reiss-
Davis Clinic, World Mercy Fund, Atlantic City Medical Center, Children's Diabetes Foundation, The Memorial Sloan-Kettering Cancer Cen-
ter, Multiple Sclerosis Society, Red Cross, Cabrini Medical Center, At-
lanta Task Force, Mental Health and Child Abuse Foundation, Dubenoff
Center, St. John's Hospital, Myasthenia Gravis Foundation, Musicians
Union, Jules Stein Eye Institute, Loyola Marymount University, Motion

Picture and Television Fund, Duke University Children's Hospital,
SPRINT, Retinitis Pigmentosa Foundation, American and International
Heart Associations, Foster Grandparents Plan, BRAVO, Father Ed Mof-
fett of the Marian Medical Mission (Catholic Leprosy Service/Korea).

It would be impossible to calculate how many millions of dollars,
pounds, francs and yen FS has raised for the sick, the hungry, and the
needy of this world in his fifty-year career. The lifetime total must be in
the hundreds of millions. To give one example, in just five concerts for
one charity (The Memorial Sloan-Kettering Cancer Center) he raised
more than $9 million. This money, called the Frank Sinatra Fund, is used
for people who cannot pay for the care they need. Because of him, no one
is refused treatment because of lack of funds.

This is typical of so many other situations which developed out of
his love and concern for people everywhere.

"Love suffers long and is kind—
Love never fails."

St. Paul

THE MOVIES

It is important to me to look closely at the films of Frank Sinatra,
because most of them were good and because in a life so filled with
marvelous music, the impression persists that he is a singer who has also
done a little acting, a song-and-dance man who happened to do a dramatic role now and then. If he had never been a singer, but had done
only romantic, comedy, and dramatic roles, the FS career as an actor
would still be very considerable in itself.

A movie company is like a family. Seeing one another every day
for months and sometimes living together on locations near and far can
bring people as close as can be. The finish of a production—"that's a
wrap"—can mean a dreadful letdown and, worse, for emotional actors, a
separation anxiety.

Each film is a chunk of the people's lives and not to be treated
lightly, no matter what the end result. *Nobody* sets out to make a bad
movie. Everyone has high hopes. Or as Dad put it to me recently, "I
made some pretty good pictures . . . and I tried a few things that
turned out to be mistakes."

MAJOR BOWES' AMATEUR THEATRE OF THE AIR (1935) Biograph
Productions, Inc. An RKO Release. Produced and directed by John H.
Auer.

This was a series of short subjects filmed at Biograph Studios in
New York. It is reported that Dad played a (nonsinging) waiter in his first
one and I know that he was part of a minstrel show in his second. Both
were done when he was with the Hoboken Four.

LAS VEGAS NIGHTS (1941) Paramount. Produced by William LeBaron.
Directed by Ralph Murphy. Screenplay by Ernest Pagano and Harry
Clork. Music direction by Victor Young. Numbers staged by LeRoy Prinz.
Some arrangements by Axel Stordahl. With Constance Moore, Bert
Wheeler, Tommy Dorsey. Dad appeared here as the male vocalist with
Dorsey's band, singing "I'll Never Smile Again." This was his first movie
review by George Simon of *Metronome:* "He sings prettily in an un-
photogenic manner."

SHIP AHOY (1942) MGM. Produced by Jack Cummings. Directed by
Edward Buzzell. Story by Matt Brooks, Bradford Ropes, and Bert Kal-
mar. Screenplay by Harry Clork. Additional material by Harry Kurnitz
and Irving Brecher. Music supervisor and conductor, George Stoll.
Dances directed by Bobby Connolly. With Eleanor Powell, Red Skelton,
Bert Lahr, Virginia O'Brien, The Tommy Dorsey Orchestra (with Frank
Sinatra, Jo Stafford, and Buddy Rich).

Tommy and the band were a little more visible in this one. Dad
sang "The Last Call for Love," and "Poor You."

Variety: "Dorsey's own tromboning, Ziggy Elman's trumpet,
Buddy Rich's drum work, and Frank Sinatra's singing, latter doing 90%

of the vocalizing in the film and doing it well, stands out."

REVEILLE WITH BEVERLY (1943) Columbia. Produced by Sam White. Directed by Charles Barton. Screenplay by Howard J. Green, Jack Henley, and Albert Duffy. Music director, Morris Stoloff. With Ann Miller, William Wright, Dick Purcell, Franklin Pangborn, Larry Parks, Duke Ellington and his orchestra, Count Basie and his orchestra, Bob Crosby, the Mills Brothers. In this one Dad sang the Cole Porter great, "Night and Day."

Although he appeared in the film singing just one number (as did all of the musical guest stars), *Reveille* came out during the time when Dad's popularity was reaching its hysteria status. The press was calling it "Sinatramania" and dubbing him "Sultan of Swoon" and "the Voice that Thrills Millions"—which was eventually shortened to "the Voice."

HIGHER AND HIGHER (1943) RKO. Produced and directed by Tim Whelan. Screenplay by Jay Dratler and Ralph Spence. Based on the play by Joshua Logan and Gladys Hurlbut. Music director, Constantin Bakaleinikoff. Musical arrangements for FS by Axel Stordahl. Vocal arrangements by Ken Darby. With Michele Morgan, Jack Haley, Frank Sinatra, Leon Errol, Marcy McGuire, Victor Borge, Barbara Hale, Mel Torme, Mary Wickes, Dooley Wilson. The songs Dad sang included, "I Couldn't Sleep a Wink Last Night," "The Music Stopped," "You Belong in a Love Song," "I Saw You First," (with Marcy McGuire) and "A Lovely Way to Spend an Evening," both by Jimmy McHugh and Harold Adamson.

Hollywood Citizen News: "He portrays himself so naturally that you catch yourself thinking, 'He can act, too.' "

STEP LIVELY (1944) RKO. Produced by Robert Fellows. Directed by Tim Whelan. Screenplay by Warren Duff and Peter Milne. Based on the play *Room Service* by Allen Boretz and John Murray. Music director, Constantin Bakaleinikoff. FS's musical arrangements by Axel Stordahl. With George Murphy, Adolphe Menjou, Gloria De Haven, Walter Slezak, Eugene Palette, Wally Brown, Alan Carney, Anne Jeffreys, Dorothy Malone. One of Dad's favorite songwriting teams, Sammy Cahn and Jule Styne, wrote his songs, including "Come Out, Come Out, Wherever You Are" and "As Long as There's Music."

The hysteria was still mounting, and never more evident than here, when Dad finally gave and received his very first screen kiss.

Time: "As shuddering exhibitors remember from his first picture, Sinatra's name on the marquee is sufficient to guarantee lipsticky posters on the outside, moaning galleryites within."

ANCHORS AWEIGH (1945) MGM. Produced by Joe Pasternak. Directed in Technicolor by George Sidney. Screenplay by Isobel Lennart. Music supervised and conducted by George Stoll. FS's musical arrangements by Axel Stordahl. Dances created by Gene Kelly. With Kathryn Grayson, Gene Kelly, Jose Iturbi, Dean Stockwell, Pamela Britton, Rags Ragland. Songs by Sammy Cahn and Jule Styne include "What Makes the Sunset?" "The Charm of You," "I Begged Her," and "I Fall in Love Too Easily." "Lullaby" ("Wiegenlied") by Johannes Brahms.

Thalia Bell, *Motion Picture Herald:* "All the world knows Frank Sinatra can sing; now it turns out that he can act, too. His characterization of Kelly's shipmate is delightful."

Anchors Aweigh was rated the year's best picture in an anniversary poll by *Screen Guide.*

THE HOUSE I LIVE IN (1945) RKO. Produced by Frank Ross. Directed by Mervyn LeRoy. Original screenplay by Albert Maltz. Musical director Axel Stordahl. The song Dad sings in the opening scene is "If You Are but a Dream," but the inspiration here comes from the song, "The House I Live In," by Earl Robinson and Lewis Allan. He sings it to the gang of boys in the alley after he has given them some insight into the nature of intolerance.

This film was Dad's idea. He got the talent to donate their time. He arranged for the proceeds to go to youth-oriented charities. And he did all this to get some important things said to people who might not otherwise want to listen. It won an Oscar.

Cue: ". . . a film that packs more power, punch and solid substance than most of the features ground each year out of Hollywood. The picture's message is Tolerance. . . . Mr. Sinatra takes his popularity seriously. More, he attempts to do something constructive with it."

TILL THE CLOUDS ROLL BY (1946) MGM. Produced by Arthur Freed. Directed by Richard Whorf. Screenplay by Myles Connolly and Jean Holloway. Adapted by George Wells. Story by Guy Bolton. Music supervised and conducted by Lennie Hayton. Orchestrations by Conrad Salinger. With June Allyson, Lucille Bremer, Judy Garland, Kathryn Grayson, Van Heflin, Lena Horne, Van Johnson, Angela Lansbury, Tony Martin, Virginia O'Brien, Dinah Shore, Robert Walker, Gower Champion, Cyd Charisse.

This film is the life story of Jerome Kern and serves as a showcase for many of his songs. "Look for the Silver Lining," "Why Was I Born?," "Can't Help Loving That Man." The one Dad sings is L. B. Mayer's favorite, "Ol' Man River."

IT HAPPENED IN BROOKLYN (1947) MGM. Produced by Jack Cummings. Directed by Richard Whorf. Screenplay by Isobel Lennart. Musical supervision, direction, and incidental score, Johnny Green. Orchestrations by Ted Duncan, with FS's vocal orchestrations by Axel Stordahl. Piano solos by André Previn. Songs by Sammy Cahn and Jule Styne, "Brooklyn Bridge," "I Believe," "Time After Time," "The Song's Gotta Come from the Heart," and "It's the Same Old Dream." Staging and direction of musical numbers by Jack Donohue. With Kathryn Grayson, Peter Lawford, Jimmy Durante, Gloria Grahame.

This is a "soldier coming home from the war" plot and they have a lot of laughs with it.

Newsweek: "Sinatra becomes a smoother performer every time out."

THE MIRACLE OF THE BELLS (1948) RKO. Produced by Jesse L. Lasky and Walter MacEwen. Directed by Irving Pichel. Screenplay by Ben Hecht and Quentin Reynolds. Music by Leigh Harline. With Fred MacMurray, Alida Valli, Lee J. Cobb. Since he was playing a priest, Dad sang an a cappella "Ever Homeward" by Kasimierz Lubomirski, Jule Styne, and Sammy Cahn.

FS: "The quickies I made for RKO before signing with MGM were never meant to be anything much, and 'Miracle Of The Bells', in which I had my first nonmusical acting part, turned out less well than we had hoped."

THE KISSING BANDIT (1948) MGM. Produced by Joe Pasternak. Directed by Laslo Benedek. Screenplay by Isobel Lennart and John Briard Harding. Music supervised and conducted by George Stoll. Dance director, Stanley Donen. With Kathryn Grayson, J. Carrol Naish, Mildred Natwick, Mikhail Rasumny, Billy Gilbert, Sono Osato, Ricardo Montalban, Ann Miller, and Cyd Charisse. Some of the songs are "Senorita," "Siesta," "If I Steal a Kiss," and "What's Wrong with Me?"

I remember visiting Dad on the set during the filming of *Bandit*. He wore the most beautiful costume, beaded and embroidered. I thought he was the handsomest man in the whole world!

My father may make jokes about this movie and equate sitting through it to a sinister form of torture, but I think it's adorable. And some of the critics liked it too.

TAKE ME OUT TO THE BALL GAME (1949) MGM. Produced by Arthur Freed. Directed by the incomparable Busby Berkeley. Story by Gene Kelly and Stanley Donen. Screenplay by Harry Tugend and George Wells. Musical supervision and conduction by Adolph Deutsch. Dances directed by Gene Kelly and Stanley Donen. With Esther Williams, Gene Kelly, Betty Garrett, Edward Arnold, Jules Munshin. Songs, "Yes, Indeedy," "O'Brien to Ryan to Goldberg," "The Right Girl for Me," "The Hat My Father Wore," "It's Fate, Baby, It's Fate" by Roger Edens, Betty Comden, and Adolph Green. "Strictly U.S.A." by Roger Edens. And of course "Take Me Out to the Ball Game" by Albert von Tilzer and

Jack Norworth.

During the filming of *Ball Game,* Uncle Gene confided in me how shocked he was by my skinny father's idea of a good lunch: a Coca-Cola and a Mars bar!

ON THE TOWN (1949) MGM. Produced by Arthur Freed. Directed by Gene Kelly and Stanley Donen. (This codirecting credit, Gene's first, was quite a feat in those days and was an indicator of how aware the studio was of his unique genius.) Screenplay by Adolph Green and Betty Comden, based on their play which was inspired by an idea by Jerome Robbins. Music supervised and conducted by Lennie Hayton.

Leonard Bernstein! Comden and Green! Roger Edens! Great names—great score! With Gene Kelly, Betty Garrett, Ann Miller, Jules Munshin, Vera-Ellen, Florence Bates, Alice Pearce, George Meader.

Dad remembers how Gene Kelly and Stanley Donen fought MGM's long-standing "Shoot it on the lot" policy. *On The Town* was actually filmed on location in New York. That may not seem unusual today—but back then it was quite an accomplishment. It was a risk and a big investment that paid off. According to *Motion Picture Daily,* "Never before has any motion picture grossed as much on any one day in any theater anywhere." I don't know anyone who doesn't like this movie!

DOUBLE DYNAMITE (1951) RKO. Produced by Irving Cummings, Jr. Directed by Irving Cummings, Jr. Based on a Leo Rosten story. Screenplay by Melville Shavelson. Music by Leigh Harline. Songs by Jule Styne and Sammy Cahn include "Kisses and Tears" and "It's Only Money." With Jane Russell, Groucho Marx, Don McGuire. Sexy Jane's name in this movie is "Mibs Goodhug!"

Cue: "Sinatra and Marx do yeoman comedy labors, and Miss Russell seems nicely type-cast."

MEET DANNY WILSON (1951) Universal International. Produced by Leonard Goldstein. Directed by Joseph Pevney. Screenplay by Don McGuire. Based on a story by Harold Robbins. Music director, Joseph Gershenson. With Shelley Winters, Alex Nichol, Raymond Burr. There were some great songs in this one, "She's Funny That Way," "You're a Sweetheart," "All of Me," "I've Got a Crush on You."

Dad called *Danny Wilson* "the first role I could ever get my teeth into."

Variety: "Title role is tailor-made for Sinatra and he plays it to the hilt with an off-hand charm that displays the various facets of his personality."

FROM HERE TO ETERNITY (1953) Columbia. Novel by James Jones. Produced by Buddy Adler. Directed by Fred Zinnemann. Screenplay by Daniel Taradash. Music supervised and conducted by Morris Stoloff. Background music, George Duning. With Burt Lancaster, Montgomery Clift, Deborah Kerr, Donna Reed, Ernest Borgnine, Jack Warden. Song: "Re-enlistment Blues" by James Jones, Fred Karger, and Robert Wells. *Eternity* won eight Oscars: Best Picture. Best Direction. Screenplay. Cinematography (Burnett Guffey). Film Editing (William Lyon). Sound (John P. Livadary, head of department). Supporting Actress (Donna Reed). Supporting Actor (Frank Sinatra).

The story takes place at Schofield Barracks, Honolulu, in the Summer of 1941 and tracks the lives of a group of soldiers and their ladies through the bombing of Pearl Harbor.

Ernest Borgnine was, in his words, "a starving actor in New York," resigned to trying to get a job with the post office, when he got his big break—the part of Fatso Judson, the sergeant who kills Sinatra's corporal Maggio, in *Eternity.*

Ernest Borgnine: "I went to work the first day and as luck would have it, my first scene was with Frank Sinatra and I'm dying inside, because here was the man who sang "Nancy" (I named my daughter because of that song). My idol, my everything. I loved him in everything he ever did. And I said, 'How can I, a mere nothing, come on here?' . . . but I knew I had to play this part as the meanest s.o.b. that ever existed, otherwise the part won't play. So I was out there pounding the piano and everything else, and we started this scene. I'm looking around and I see

Frank Sinatra dancing with this girl. And I see Montgomery Clift over with somebody else. And over standing on the side were Deborah Kerr and Burt Lancaster talking to Fred Zinnemann. I was just engulfed with stars. And I'm just shaking, you know. And Fred suddenly looked up and said, 'Okay, begin the scene!' So we started. I'm playing the piano and it came to the point where Frank says, 'Come on, why don't you stop this banging on the piano, will ya? Give us a chance with our music.' And I stood up to say my first line. I said, 'Listen, you little wop.' He looked up at me, and as he looked up at me, he broke out into a smile and he said, 'My God, he's ten feet tall!' Do you know, the whole thing just collapsed.

"His laughter broke the tension. It was so marvelous. I've never forgotten Frank for that. He was the most wonderful guy to work with that you ever saw in your life. He knew how I must have felt, you know. And because of it, he took the time to break that tension. That's something that I have done with everybody that I've ever worked with since. I break the ice for the other people. And I think it's nice, because it reverberated all down the line."

Long after *From Here to Eternity* was filmed, Ernie was making the movie, *Marty,* for which he won an Oscar. He says, "I was brought to location up in the Bronx. As I got out of the car, I walked over toward Delbert Mann and Paddy Chayefsky, the director and writer. I said, 'Hi, how are you?' And I heard a voice behind me say, 'Hey, there's that son of a bitch killed Frank Sinatra.' I turned and looked over my shoulder, and there was a bunch of boys standing there. I thought nothing of it. I walked over and changed my clothes, got my script, and started walking along the pavement, talking to myself, saying some lines, getting ready for the night's shooting. There was a tap on my shoulder. I turned, and it was this bunch of fellas. They said, 'Hey, are you the guy killed Frank Sinatra?' And I said, 'Yeah.' Well, some guy in the back spoke up in Italian and said, 'I think we ought to beat the hell out of him.' I understand Italian, being of Italian descent myself, and in Italian I said, 'Wait a minute fellas, it happened to be in a picture, and we happen to be good friends. If you want to start something, I'll take you on, but one at a time.' And one of the guys said, 'You're Italian?' I said, 'Yeah.' 'Well why the hell didn't you say so!' And from then on they brought all sorts of pizzas and wine and everything else. But the guy in the back still insisted that I shouldn't have killed Frank Sinatra."

SUDDENLY (1954) A Libra Production. United Artists. Produced by Robert Bassler. Directed by Lewis Allen. With Sterling Hayden, Nancy Gates, James Gleason, Kim Charney, Christopher Dark, Paul Frees.

This is a story of terrorism. FS plays John Baron, a calculating killer whose gang takes a family hostage in a town called Suddenly and uses their house above the railroad tracks as a lookout. His plan is to shoot the President of the United States as his train goes by. A near-classic, this is a gripping story, and one of Dad's best performances. The black-and-white film was made from an original screenplay by Richard Sale. Sale based the story on President Eisenhower's train trips to and from Palm Springs.

Newsweek: "As an assassin in the piece, Sinatra superbly refutes the idea that the straight-role potentialities which earned an Academy Award for him in *From Here to Eternity* were one-shot stuff."

YOUNG AT HEART (1955) An Arwin Production. Warner Brothers. Produced by Henry Blanke. Directed by Gordon Douglas. A remake of a John Garfield film. Based on "Sister Act," a story by Fannie Hurst. The Garfield screenplay, *Four Daughters,* was written by Julius J. Epstein and Lenore Coffee. It was adapted for this film by Liam O'Brien. With Doris Day, Gig Young, Ethel Barrymore.

FS plays Barney Sloane, a down-and-out song writer who falls in love with Laurie Tuttle (Doris). Doris and Dad hadn't worked together since "Your Hit Parade" in 1949. *Young at Heart* was a warm and sentimental movie. The songs were special. Besides the title song, there are "She's Funny That Way," "Someone to Watch Over Me," and "One For My Baby."

NOT AS A STRANGER (1955) Stanley Kramer Production. United Artists. Produced and directed by Stanley Kramer. With Olivia de Havilland, Robert Mitchum, Gloria Grahame, Broderick Crawford and

Charles Bickford, Lee Marvin, Lon Chaney. Based on Morton Thompson novel. Screenplay by Edna and Edward Anhalt. This black-and-white movie about young doctors has some mighty fine performances. There is one hysterical scene of FS playing intern Alfred Boone—imitating their teacher (Broderick Crawford) in front of the rest of the interns. With a German accent, he is performing fake surgery on a fake cadaver. He gets caught.

One scene in *Not as a Stranger* has giant Mitchum fighting frail Frank in their room. After finishing the filming, Bob said of his friend, "The only man in town I'd be afraid to fight is Frank Sinatra. I might knock him down, but he'd keep getting up until one of us was dead."

THE TENDER TRAP (1955) MGM. Produced by Lawrence Weingarten. Director Charles Walters. Screenplay by Julius J. Epstein from the play by Max Shulman and Robert Paul Smith. With Debbie Reynolds, David Wayne, Celeste Holm, Jarma Lewis, Lola Albright, Carolyn Jones. Music by Jeff Alexander. Title song by Sammy Cahn and Jimmy Van Heusen.

In my opinion, FS and Debbie should have made more movies together. They were a good team. They were funny and romantic. It's too bad nobody saw the potential. We might have had Powell and Loy, Tracy and Hepburn, Bogart and Bacall—and Sinatra and Reynolds. They didn't do any more movies together, but they are still friends.

Debbie Reynolds: "When we were doing *The Tender Trap* together, he took me under his wing. I was only 23. It was during the filming that Eddie [Fisher] and I announced our engagement. Frank took me to lunch. He was very serious. He tried to advise me on my first step toward marriage. He said, 'You know, Debbie, your life may be very difficult if you marry a singer. It is not the individual necessarily, it's the singer's way of life. You have to think very hard about this, Debbie. Please give this very deep and serious thought.' I didn't . . . and I should have!"

GUYS AND DOLLS (1955) A Samuel Goldwyn Production. MGM. Producer Sam Goldwyn. Director Joseph L. Mankiewicz. Screenplay by Mankiewicz, based on Damon Runyon's "The Idyll of Miss Sarah Brown." Marlon Brando, Jean Simmons, Vivian Blaine. The musical comedy with book by Jo Swirling and Abe Burrows has one of the finest scores ever written—Frank Loesser wrote it. My dad feels the movie casting was wrong except for the original Broadway players: Vivian Blaine, Stubby Kayo, B. S. Pully, and Sheldon Leonard, etc. FS remembers being thrilled by the opening song of the Broadway show, "Fugue for Tinhorns" ("I got the horse right here, his name is Paul Revere . . .") as performed by Kaye, Silver, and Danny Layton. Other monuments from that moment: "If I Were a Bell," "Sue Me," "Sit Down, You're Rocking the Boat," and "Luck Be a Lady."

THE MAN WITH THE GOLDEN ARM (1955) A Carlyle Production. United Artists. Produced and directed by Otto Preminger. With Eleanor Parker, Kim Novak, Arnold Stang, and Darren McGavin. Nelson Algren's novel was adapted by Walter Newman and Lewis Meltzer. The Elmer Bernstein score is without question one of the finest in movie history. Even the sound track album cover is a classic. Shorty Rogers's jazz sets the scenes and documents the time.

This was an avant-garde, black-and-white gem with only one flaw. The entire film was shot on a soundstage with a few exteriors on the RKO back lot. Location shooting might have been better. On the other hand, the tightness of the sets gives the production a surrealistic, miniature feeling. The title, by the way, refers to Frankie Machine's card-dealing talent—not the fact that he is a drummer or that he shoots heroin. Most people cite the cold-turkey withdrawal scene as *the* scene here. My favorite is the one in the jail cell when Machine, watching a screaming junkie, relives his own horror. My father's face is frightening, not pretty here. It's quite an amazing change.

MEET ME IN LAS VEGAS (1956) MGM. Produced by Joe Pasternak. Directed by Roy Rowland. Screenplay by Isobel Lennart. Starring Dan Dailey, Cyd Charisse, and Jerry Colonna. FS did cameo role at the Sands.

JOHNNY CONCHO (1956) A Kent Production. United Artists. Produced by Frank Sinatra. Cowritten by the director Don McGuire and David P. Harmon, based on Harmon's story "The Man Who Owned the Town." A bunch of the boys—Sinatra, McGuire, Riddle, Sanicola—got together to make a cowboy movie. Cast: FS, Keenan Wynn, William Conrad, and Phyllis Kirk.

HIGH SOCIETY (1956) MGM. With Bing Crosby, Grace Kelly, and Celeste Holm. Once again Dad teamed with director Charles Walters (*The Tender Trap*) with excellent results. This is John Patrick's adaptation of Philip Barry's *The Philadelphia Story* with a swell Cole Porter score. A reminder of the good old days at MGM. The A-team: Johnny Green, William Tuttle, Helen Rose, Sidney Guilaroff—great names from Hollywood's heyday.

The groaner and the crooner played the Cary Grant/Jimmy Stewart roles (from the film *The Philadelphia Story)* and there was a tangible feeling of affection and mutual respect in all their scenes. The Bing-Frank duet "Well, Did You Evah?" was the highlight of the movie.

Grace Kelly: "I'd always longed to do a musical and, of course, working with Bing and Frank was simply marvelous. They create a certain excitement and are two very strong personalities. So it was fascinating for me to be in the middle—watching the tennis match go back and forth from one to the other with tremendous wit and humor—each one trying to outdo the other. . . . Frank and I did two numbers, 'You're Sensational' and 'Mind If I Make Love to You.' He has an endearing sweetness and charm. . . ."

On the set of *High Society*, Frank and Bing were nicknamed "Dexedrine" and "Nembutal." "Dexedrine" because of Pop's high energy level, and "Nembutal" because of Bing's laid-back approach.

AROUND THE WORLD IN 80 DAYS (1956) A Michael Todd Production. United Artists. Todd-AO. Directed by Michael Anderson. Starring David Niven, Cantinflas, Shirley MacLaine, and Robert Newton. Dad's honky-tonk "Piano Player" cameo in *Around the World in 80 Days* is a gem. He has his back to the camera during the entire sequence, is literally part of the atmosphere, until the scene ends and the camera moves in. With typical Sinatra humor he simply turns and looks over his shoulder—cigarette dangling from his lips—and grins. No dialogue. Perfect.

Marlene Dietrich also appears in this scene and she called Sinatra: "The gentlest man I have ever known, the Mercedes-Benz of men."

THE PRIDE AND THE PASSION (1957) A Stanley Kramer Production. United Artists. Produced and directed once again by Stanley Kramer *(Not As a Stranger).* Screenplay by Edna and Edward Anhalt, based on the novel by C. S. Forester called *The Gun.* With Cary Grant, Sophia Loren, Theodore Bikel, Joan Wengraf, Jay Novello.

Sophia Loren: "It *[The Pride and the Passion]* was my first contact with the American world. I was at the start of my career and the mere thought of having to appear before this idol made me tremble like a leaf. During the shooting period we did not see much of each other because I used to go to bed very early. One day some journalists asked him to say in just two words what he thought of me and it was then, when he answered in a humorous and at the same time comical way, 'She's the mostest,' that I realized how different he really is from what one would think at first. I did not know English very well at the time, but I thought the expression he used was magnificent. I was honestly struck and I shall never forget it, especially as coming from Frank Sinatra it had the immediate effect of making me feel at ease with the American world, with everybody. He could not have found a kinder or more friendly way of doing it and I shall never stop being grateful to him for it."

THE JOKER IS WILD (1957) An A.M.B.L. Production. Paramount. Directed by Charles Vidor. Screenplay by Oscar Saul. Book by Art Cohn. Frank Sinatra portrays his friend, comic Joe E. Lewis. The other stars were Mitzi Gaynor, Jeanne Crain, and Eddie Albert. With Beverly Garland, Jackie Coogan, and Leonard Graves. Notable names were involved throughout: Hal Pereira, Wally Westmore, Edith Head, Sam Briskin (producer), Vista-Vision, and Sophie Tucker.

This project was near and dear to all of us—we treasured Joe E. He was a fighter who won against great odds and Pop played the hell out of the role. As Joe E. said, "Frankie enjoyed playing my life more than I enjoyed living it."

Joe started out as a singer and the songs in the movie were great, "I Cried for You," "Chicago ("Chicago, That Toddlin' Town . . ."), "If I Could Be with You." "All the Way," written by Cahn and Van Heusen, won one Academy Award. Joe E. and FS had worked nightclubs together. At one point, Joe wrote later, "We were together for eight or ten weeks, left Miami Beach together, went to the Sands, lived together in Palm Springs, then at his home in Beverly Hills, every minute a laugh, a ball. Finally, Frank had a picture commitment and couldn't stay out with me until all hours. When I left, Frank found a note on his pillow: 'Dear F . . . I can't stand this constant bickering . . . Goodbye, Joe E.' "

My dad remembers a plane trip with him that was a supreme fiasco. They flew from Miami to L.A. in a Martin 404, a prop plane, and forgot to stock the bar. FS: "I calmed Joe and said we'd buy a bottle when we stopped for fuel. The first stop was Tennessee—a 'dry' state. The second stop was at 4 A.M. Everything closed. That's the way it went, ten hours, crosscountry, without a drink. I never heard the *end* of it."

PAL JOEY (1957) An Essex-George Sidney Production. Columbia. Directed by George Sidney, one of Dad's first "teachers." Dorothy Kingsley did the screenplay based on John O'Hara's musical comedy. The Rodgers and Hart score is . . . Well, the titles say it all: "The Lady Is a Tramp," "A Small Hotel," "I Could Write a Book," "Bewitched," "I Didn't Know What Time It Was," and more. Amazing. With Rita Hayworth and Kim Novak. And more famous Hollywood names: Morris Stoloff, George Duning, Nelson Riddle, Fred Karger, Henri Jaffa, Jean Louis, Ben Lane, Harold Lipstein, Hermes Pan. What a team!

The role of Joey Evans was originated on Broadway by Gene Kelly, and the fact that Dad played it on the screen enhanced their friendship, contrary to what such a situation might imply. Rita and Kim were perhaps Hollywood's most beautiful bookends.

George Sidney: "About billing, Frank was smart enough to say, put Rita first, and then me, and then Kim. Because here we had the big star, Rita, and then we had the new one coming up, Kim, and Frank between the two . . . and every man in the world, whether he'd like to admit it or not, he says, 'Gee, I would like to be that fella. . . .' What a sandwich!

"We were standing in front of Columbia Studios, and a fella came by—somebody who had been somebody—and we talked to him for a second, and then he went. And Frank said to me, 'You know, no one's gonna ever say: "That used to be Frank Sinatra." ' "

KINGS GO FORTH (1958) A Frank Ross-Eton Production. United Artists. Produced by Frank Ross (The House I Live In). Directed by Delmer Daves. The screenplay by Merle Miller was based on Joe David Brown's book. Natalie Wood is Monique, Tony Curtis is Sgt. Britt Harris, and FS is Lt. Sam Loggins. Original music by Elmer Bernstein features some great names in jazz: Pete Condoli, Mel Lewis, Richie Kamuca, Red Norvo, Jimmy Weible, and Red Wooten. About U.S. soldiers fighting and playing in the south of France. Natalie plays the daughter of a black father and a white mother. Sam loves Monique but Monique loves Britt who turns out to be a bigot.

FS: "I took this part as a performer, not as a lecturer on racial problems. When it comes to bigotry, though, I think that the intellectual can be twice as dangerous as the person with no education. The uneducated man can be taught he is wrong. But the intellectual will rationalise . . . I think most people who have any kind of common sense and think fairly will not go out of the theatre and start race riots. As for the bigots, they'll scream at anything."

SOME CAME RUNNING (1958) MGM. Produced by Sol Siegel. Vincente Minnelli directed the John Patrick/Arthur Sheekman script. FS went home to MGM for this Cinemascope picture which was his first with Dean Martin and Shirley MacLaine. Also Martha Hyer, Arthur Kennedy,

Nancy Gates. The original novel was written by *From Here to Eternity* author, James Jones. Once again, music by Elmer Bernstein.

My father so loves Shirley MacLaine's performance that he screens it regularly for guests in his home. He points out to everyone the scene in the schoolroom: The camera does not move—close shot on Shirley. As she speaks her lines, she softly, quietly *dissolves*. No tricks. No edits. Just pure feeling and talent—exquisitely done.

A HOLE IN THE HEAD (1959) A Sincap Production, United Artists. Produced and directed by the one and only Frank Capra and written by Arnold Schulman from his play. Edward G. Robinson, Eleanor Parker, Thelma Ritter, Carolyn Jones, and the great Keenan Wynn. Frank's son is played by Eddie Hodges and together they perform the Oscar-winning "High Hopes" which became JFK's theme song. "All My Tomorrows" is another beauty by Van Heusen and Cahn. Nelson Riddle did the rest. This is one of my favorite Sinatra movies. It makes me laugh and it makes me cry.

NEVER SO FEW (1959) A Canterbury Production. MGM. Edmund Grainger (Sands of Iwo Jima, The Flying Leathernecks) producer and John Sturges director. With Peter Lawford, Gina Lollobrigida, Steve McQueen, Paul Henreid, Charles Bronson, Brian Donlevy, Dean Jones, Richard Johnson. The Tom T. Chamales book which was adapted by Millard Kaufman made a pretty strong impact.

Dad had seen Steve McQueen on TV and suggested to Sturges that he get McQueen for this movie. They had a terrific time. In compensation for the long, on-location shooting (in Burma, Ceylon, and Thailand), Frank and Steve played a few pranks to while away the time. The funniest, according to FS, was when a policeman was asking Dad to stop clowning around with cherry bombs. Steve crept up behind the guy and set three off right between his feet. My Dad said "His hat blew right off his head—that McQueen was *really* crazy." It seems FS finally met his match.

When McQueen wanted to do his own stunts in *Never So Few*, he was stopped because as Dad put it, "That was a big no-no at MGM. But they worked something out and he did them all. He was *crazy.*"

Guy McElwaine, who is now head of Columbia Pictures, was Dad's public relations representative then. He remembered when Steve McQueen's craziness almost got him in bad trouble. It seems one of McQueen's firecrackers somehow found its way into the pants of a member of the crew, a grip.

Guy McElwaine: "This guy was huge. And he was angry. He yelled at McQueen, 'I don't care who you are, I'm gonna punch you.'

"Your father jumped in between them, looked up at the big guy, and said, 'I'm gonna save your life—I'm gonna let you fight *me*—because if you fight *him*, he'll kill you!' The man said, 'I have no fight with you, Mr. Sinatra.' Frank said, 'Then you have no fight.' "

CAN-CAN (1960) A Suffolk-Cummings Production. 20th Century-Fox. Directed by Walter Lang. Screenplay by Charles Lederer and Dorothy Kingsley. William Daniels, Hermes Pan, Irene Sharaff, Ben Nye. With Shirley MacLaine, Maurice Chevalier, Louis Jourdan, and Juliet Prowse. Cole Porter's songs, arranged and conducted by Nelson Riddle: "I Love Paris," "C'est Magnifique," "It's All Right with Me," "Montmartre," "Let's Do It," and more.

When Nikita Khrushchev visited the United States he was entertained by the cast of *Can-Can*. They performed the "Can-Can" dance number which Khrushchev later called "immoral." *Newsweek* magazine reported that the advance ticket sales were bigger than those for *Ben Hur*, saying that, ". . . being condemned by Khrushchev may be an even bigger commercial asset than being banned in Boston."

OCEAN'S ELEVEN (1960) A Dorchester Production. Warner Brothers. Produced and directed by Lewis Milestone. A Nelson Riddle score. Songs by Cahn and Van Heusen. Screenplay by Harry Brown and Charles Lederer. Story by George Clayton Johnson and Jack Golden Russell. With Dean Martin, Sammy Davis, Jr., Peter Lawford, Joey Bishop, Angie Dickinson, Richard Conte, Cesar Romero, Patrice Wymore, Henry Silva,

Buddy Lester, Akim Tamiroff, Hank Henry, Red Norvo, and cameos by Red Skelton, George Raft, and Shirley MacLaine.

Of the "Summit" movies, my father said, ". . . of course they're not great movies. No one could claim that . . . We're not setting out to make *Hamlet* or *Gone with the Wind* . . . We gotta make pictures the people enjoy. Entertainment."

PEPE (1960) A G.S.-Posa Films International Production. Columbia. Produced and directed by George Sidney. Cantinflas, Dan Dailey, Shirley Jones. FS did a cameo "guest star" appearance in a Las Vegas casino sequence.

THE DEVIL AT 4 O'CLOCK (1961) A Columbia Picture. Directed by Mervyn Le Roy. With Spencer Tracy, Kerwin Mathews, Jean Pierre Aumont, Barbara Luna. Music by George Duning. Special Effects by Willis Cook. The title comes from a proverb, "It is hard for a man to be brave when he knows he is going to meet the devil at four o'clock."

Dad called Tracy the "Grey Fox." He said, "I learned a lot from him, everybody did." Of FS, the Grey Fox said, "Nobody at Metro ever had the financial power Frank Sinatra has today. *The Devil at 4 O'Clock* was a Sinatra picture. Sinatra was the star. Although we worked very differently, he knew what he wanted and there were no fireworks, though some people said there would be."

It was during the run of *Devil* that Dad organized and produced the Gala for President Kennedy.

SERGEANTS 3 (1962) An Essex-Claude Production. United Artists. Directed by John Sturges. Produced by Frank Sinatra. Executive producer, Howard W. Koch. Music by Billy May. With Dean Martin, Sammy Davis, Jr., Peter Lawford, Joey Bishop, Henry Silva, Ruta Lee, Buddy Lester, Hank Henry, Phil Crosby. This is the Gunga Din story with American Indians.

Dad did his own stunts, even the one where he is dragged under a wagon while Dean was inside it trying desperately to stay there! Dad said he didn't mind the dragging, but what really bothered him was the way Dean kept stomping on his fingers as he was thrown back and forth.

ROAD TO HONG KONG (1962) A Melnor Films Production. United Artists. With Bob Hope, Bing Crosby, Dorothy Lamour. FS and Dean did cameos—as visitors from another planet.

THE MANCHURIAN CANDIDATE (1962) An M. C. Production. United Artists. An absolutely flawless gem of a movie that must be seen. It is, however, not for dummies. You have to think when you watch this one. John Frankenheimer's best. A fine George Axelrod screenplay, based on Richard Condon's novel. With Laurence Harvey, Janet Leigh, Angela Lansbury, Henry Silva, James Gregory, Leslie Parrish, John McGiver, Kligh Dhiegh, Whit Bissell, Richard LePore, Nicky Blair.

Frankenheimer's use of the hand-held camera adds to the bizarre feel of this movie. Angela Lansbury is devastating. This is first-rate, and everybody is good. This is one of those rare times when everything worked.

FS: "I'm more excited about this part than any other part I've played. I'm saying things in this script that I've never had to speak on the screen before. Never had to speak at all for that matter. Long, wild speeches."

Said the writer and co-producer, George Axelrod: "I thought it would be terrific to have that marvelous, beat-up Sinatra face giving forth long, incongruous speeches.

"During the filming of the karate scene, with Henry Silva, FS accidentally broke a dining table with his hand and managed to break his finger, too. Nobody knew about the broken finger until after the scene was finished because FS just kept on."

COME BLOW YOUR HORN (1963) An Essex-Tandem Production. Paramount. Produced by Norman Lear and Bud Yorkin. Directed by Bud Yorkin. Screenplay by Norman Lear. Based on a play by Neil Simon and his brother. Music composed and conducted by Nelson Riddle. Good title song by Cahn and Van Heusen. With Lee J. Cobb, Molly Picon, Barbara

Rush, Jill St. John, and Tony Bill.

When Lee J. Cobb (who plays FS's father here—a domineering artificial fruit manufacturer) suffered a heart attack in 1955, Dad frequently visited him in the hospital.

Lee J. Cobb: "In his typical, unsentimental fashion, Frank moved into my life . . . flooded me with books, flowers, delicacies. He kept telling me what fine acting I still had ahead of me and discussed plans for me to direct one of his future films."

THE LIST OF ADRIAN MESSENGER (1963) A Joel Production. Universal. Directed by John Huston. With George C. Scott, and Dana Wynters. Cameos by Tony Curtis, Kirk Douglas, Burt Lancaster, Robert Mitchum, and Frank Sinatra. Dad was one of the disguised guest stars, playing a gypsy stableman. Everyone in the cast and crew was sworn to keep the secret identities a secret. We even had trouble finding a production still where Dad was unmasked. But I knew. He was the one wearing the Sinatra family crest ring.

4 FOR TEXAS (1964) A Sam Company Production. Warner Brothers. Produced and directed by Robert Aldrich. Music composed and conducted by Nelson Riddle. Title song by Cahn and Van Heusen. With Dean Martin, Anita Ekberg, Ursula Andress, Charles Bronson, Victor Buono. Special guest stars—the Three Stooges, who gave Dad and Dean a run for their money.

Dad tells the story of a well-choreographed fight scene where Dean forgot to duck. He took a Sinatra hook and rode it to the floor. Dad's concern for Dean was short-lived, though. Before he could reach down to help his friend to his feet, he felt Dean's teeth gnawing at his ankle!

ROBIN AND THE SEVEN HOODS (1964) A P-C Production. Warner Brothers. Produced by Frank Sinatra. Executive producer, Howard W. Koch. Directed by Gordon Douglas. Screenplay by David R. Schwartz. Music composed and conducted by Nelson Riddle. Songs: "Style," "Mr. Booze," "Don't Be a Do-Badder," and the classic "My Kind of Town." With FS as Robbo, Dean as Little John, Sammy as Will (Scarlet), Barbara Rush as Marian, Peter Falk as Guy Gisborne, Edward G. Robinson as Big Jim, and Summit newcomer Bing Crosby as Allen A. Dale.

Bing: "I just took the part for a lark. I thought, Gee, it will be fun working with those guys—we'll have a lot of laughs. But it came right at the time of Jack Kennedy's assassination. Then there were a lot of delays. And our coordination fell apart."

This satire on Robin Hood amplified the already growing notion that the Summit members were becoming, in some odd, wacky way, folk heroes. Journalist John McLain: "They certainly are liberal to a fault, insanely generous and public-spirited. They are a crazy and wonderful part of America."

NONE BUT THE BRAVE (1965) An Artanis Production. Warner Brothers. Produced and directed by Frank Sinatra. Executive producer Howard W. Koch. Screenplay by John Twist and Katsuya Susaki. Music by John Williams. With Clint Walker, Tommy Sands, Brad Dexter, Tony Bill, Tatsuya Mihashi, Takeshi Kato, Sammy Jackson, Richard Balkalyan, Rafer Johnson, and Dick Sinatra (son of Dad's cousin, bandleader Ray Sinatra).

FS: *"None but the Brave* is an anti-war story that deals with a group of Americans and a group of Japanese stranded together on a Pacific island during the war. I have tried to show that when men do not *have* to fight there is a community of interests."

There was to be another kind of fight during the filming. On Sunday, May 10, Tommy (Sands) and Dick Balkalyan and I went sightseeing in Honolulu. When we got back to our hotel, Tommy's friend Earl Finch was waiting for us. His face was ashen. "There's been an accident. Your father is okay, but he wants to see you right away." We drove to the airport where Dad's pilot, Don Lieto, was waiting, the engines running on the chartered Cessna. On the short flight to Lihue, Don told us what had happened.

FS, Jilly, Howard and Ruth Koch, and some of the cast were relaxing in Dad's house on the private beach across the highway from the

Cocoa Palms Hotel. When Ruth announced that she wanted to go for a swim, Dad went along. He had been warned about the treacherous undertow, and he didn't want her to go in alone. Although Ruth was staying close to shore, a large wave struck her and the undertow was so strong she was instantly swept out about seventy-five yards. Dad went out after her. Just then a second wave brought *her* back close to shore, and its undertow pulled *him* out about two hundred yards. Dad is a strong swimmer, but he couldn't fight his way back in.

Meanwhile, Ruth yelled to the people inside the house for help. They raced to the beach. Actor Brad Dexter swam out to Dad, Howard Koch swam to the aid of his wife, and Jilly—knowing that if FS was in trouble the water must be bad—tried to find a boat. There was none. In all, my father fought the surf for thirty-five minutes. "In another five minutes he would have been gone," said Fire Lieutenant George Keawe, who took part in the rescue. "His face was turning blue." Keawe had been summoned by the Cocoa Palms Hotel after Jilly called for help.

A neighbor, Alfred O. Giles, having heard the shouts, plunged into the waves with his surfboard. According to the L.A. *Herald Examiner:* "Two other men, County Supervisor Louis Gonsalves and Harold Jim, swam to Sinatra from the main beach. They said Sinatra, although a good swimmer, appeared to be losing his fight with the undertow. Mrs. Koch was holding her own. By the time the firemen arrived, Gonsalves had reached Sinatra and had helped the singer to Giles' surfboard. One of the firemen swam out and brought Mrs. Koch back to shore. However, the ordeal for Sinatra and his rescuers was not over yet. With the singer clinging to the board, Gonsalves and Giles were pushed back to sea time and again by the high surf as they attempted to bring him to shore. Keawe plunged into the surf, tossed a rope to the rescuers and managed to pull them to the beach. Sinatra was put on a stretcher and carried to the house. 'He was exhausted,' an attending physician said, 'but otherwise, his condition is satisfactory.'"

When I got to the house Dad was in his bed. He looked very pale. We went right to the basics. I said, "How are you doing?" He said, "I'm hungry." I said, "How about some peppers and eggs?" He said, "Okay." I made sure the peppers were cooked soft the way he liked them. We had pepper and egg sandwiches and watched TV together until he fell asleep. I wanted to ask him many questions, but I didn't. I wanted to tell him how much I loved him, but I didn't have to.

VON RYAN'S EXPRESS (1965) A P-R Production. 20th Century-Fox. Produced by Saul David. Directed by Mark Robson. Screenplay by Wendell Mayes and Joseph Landon, based on the novel by David Westheimer. Music by Jerry Goldsmith. With Trevor Howard, Raffaella Carra, Brad Dexter, Sergio Fantoni, Edward Mulhare, John Leyland, Wolfgang Preiss, James Brolin, Richard Balkalyan, Michael Romanoff.

The novel ends with escaped prisoners of war riding off into Switzerland on a highjacked train. The shooting script followed Westheimer's story, but my father didn't agree. The ending was fine for the book, but not for the movie. If Von Ryan rode happily off into the Swiss sunset, on a train he had never wanted to steal in the first place, the emotionally involved theater audiences would throw rocks at the screen. One other important point to FS was that the hero, Colonel Ryan, in the course of the escape, was forced to kill a young woman. Dad felt that to let Ryan off the hook on that score was against the unwritten laws of moviemaking. The argument over the ending ensued throughout the filming.

Richard Zanuck, who was president of Fox, and his father, Darryl, were interested in the possibility of a sequel (Westheimer wrote one) and if Ryan were killed that would be impossible. Ryan (FS) and Major Fincham (Trevor Howard) could be wounded by the Germans and fall on the tracks as the train pulls away. The final shot would reveal the two lying on the ground looking at each other as shiny, black German boots surround them. Dad said "wrong" and held fast, knowing he was right.

My father's respect for Darryl Zanuck ran deep. Of the three top studio chiefs—Goldwyn, L. B. Mayer, and Zanuck—FS had always felt that Goldwyn put his money where his mouth was, L.B. had the best roster and organization, but Zanuck was the best qualified. Darryl knew movies well. He wrote them, he produced them, he directed them, he edited them—he *knew* them.

When Dickie Zanuck discussed the ending of *Von Ryan's* with his father, the elder Zanuck, though still convinced the movie should reflect the novel, deferred to his son. It was tricky. The success of the movie at the box office was riding on the final scene. The younger Zanuck put his reputation on the line and agreed to go with Sinatra.

The result was a perfect ending to a fine movie. As the train pulls away from the last confrontation, Ryan runs after it on the tracks. The Nazis close in behind him as he desperately races for the train. Fincham extends his hand, reaching out to pull Ryan aboard. Shots ring out. Ryan, shot in the back, lies dying on the tracks as the train moves on to freedom without him.

MARRIAGE ON THE ROCKS (1965) An A-C Production. Warner Brothers. Produced by cinematographer William H. Daniels. Directed by Jack Donohue. Screenplay by Cy Howard. Music by Nelson Riddle. With Dean Martin, Deborah Kerr, Cesar Romero, Hermione Baddeley, Tony Bill, John McGiver, Davey Davison, Michel Petit, and Nancy Sinatra.

As a child I had visited Dad's movie sets often. When my husband Tommy made *None but the Brave* with FS, I enjoyed the weeks on location. At last, with *Marriage on the Rocks,* I was able to actually be in a movie with my father and to observe firsthand the working FS.

It was a good, sharp, learning experience. The on-set atmosphere was energetic and smart, with a no-nonsense (except for an occasional lapse by FS or Dean) feeling. Jack Donohue, with a slew of credits (including most of the "I Love Lucy" TV shows) under his belt, helmed the production easily. I had the good fortune to meet and work with some of the biggest names on the old Warner Brothers team: Costume designer Walter Plunkett, makeup supervisor Gordon Bau, and hairstylist Jean Burt Reilly.

I had done a "beach movie" called *The Ghost in the Invisible Bikini* for A.I.P., and *For Those Who Think Young* for Howard Koch at Paramount, so I was not a total newcomer. I knew about "action" and "cut" and "marks." But I was still *very* nervous. And, of course, I felt the added pressure of wanting my dad to be proud of me. We had several scenes together and he was helpful, rehearsing with me and giving me suggestions. I must admit, I found the scenes we weren't in together much easier to do. I'd love to have another opportunity to work with Dad now, to see if I would be more relaxed, and perhaps, better. But father-daughter scripts don't come along too often.

CAST A GIANT SHADOW (1966) A Mirisch-Llenroc-Batjac Production. United Artists. Produced and directed by Melville Shavelson. Screenplay by Melville Shavelson. Based on a novel by Ted Berkman. Music by Elmer Bernstein. With Kirk Douglas, Senta Berger, Angie Dickinson. Yul Brynner, John Wayne, and FS did guest star roles.

THE OSCAR (1966) A Greene-Rouse Production. Embassy Pictures. Produced by Clarence Greene. Executive producer Joseph E. Levine. Directed by Russell Rouse. Screenplay by Harlan Ellison, Russell Rouse, and Clarence Greene. Based on Richard Sale's novel. With Stephen Boyd, Elke Sommer, Milton Berle, Eleanor Parker, Joseph Cotton, Jill St. John, Tony Bennett. Cameos by Merle Oberon, Bob Hope, Frank Sinatra, and Nancy Sinatra, as guests at the Academy Awards presentation ceremonies.

ASSAULT ON A QUEEN (1966) A Sinatra Enterprises—Seven Arts Production. Paramount. Produced by William Goetz. Directed by Jack Donohue. Screenplay by Rod Serling. Novel by Jack Finney. Music by Duke Ellington. With Virni Lisi, Tony Franciosa, Richard Conte, Alf Kjellin, and Errol John. An off-the-wall story about some crazies trying to rob R.M.S. *Queen Mary.*

THE NAKED RUNNER (1967) A Sinatra Enterprises Production. Warner Brothers. Produced by Brad Dexter. Directed by Sidney J. Furie. Screenplay by Stanley Mann. Novel by Francis Clifford. Music by Harry Sukman. With Peter Vaughan, Derrin Nesbitt, Nadia Gray, Toby Robins, and Inger Stratton.

Some critics didn't like this one. I did. Sidney Furie *(The Ipcress File)* and FS work in a similar, quiet way. Some critics called it dull. I call it understated, subtle. People don't have to chew the scenery to show energy and power.

TONY ROME (1967) An Arcola-Millfield Production. 20th Century-Fox. Produced by Aaron Rosenberg. Directed by Gordon Douglas. Screenplay by Richard L. Breen. Novel, *Miami Mayhem*, by Marvin H. Albert. Music by Billy May. Songs by Billy May and Randy Newman. Title song by Lee Hazlewood, sung by Nancy Sinatra. With Jill St. John, Richard Conte, Gena Rowlands, Sue Lyon, Simon Oakland, Jeffrey Lynn, Lloyd Bochner.

My recordings were becoming hits in the U.S. and around the world. During this period I was asked to do three title songs. One was for my own movie, *The Last of the Secret Agents*, another was for the James Bond movie *You Only Live Twice*, and the third was for *Tony Rome*. I was very honored.

THE DETECTIVE (1968) An Arcola-Millfield Production. 20th Century-Fox. Produced by Aaron Rosenberg. Directed by Gordon Douglas. Screenplay by Abby Mann. With Lee Remick, Ralph Meeker, Jack Klugman, Horace McMahon, Tony Musante, and Robert Duvall. *I love this movie!* Pop at his best. Vintage Sinatra.

LADY IN CEMENT (1968) An Arcola-Millfield Production. 20th Century-Fox. The sequel to *Tony Rome*. Produced by Aaron Rosenberg. Directed by Gordon Douglas. Screenplay by Marvin H. Albert and Jack Guss. Music composed and directed by Hugo Montenegro. Orchestrations by Billy May. With Raquel Welch, Dan Blocker, Richard Conte, Martin Gabel, Lainie Kazan, Pat Henry.

Gordon Douglas: "I had been continually rehearsing a scene with a young actress, who had little experience and understandably was nervous. Frank, who was to be in the scene later, had the sensitivity to see it. He knew his being around would only make her more nervous so he disappeared to the back of the set. We continued to rehearse and she continued to gain confidence and became more relaxed. I was still concerned how the shooting of this scene would come across. Frank came over to me and said, 'Relax, she'll be fine.' And to top it all off, he did a little prophesying. 'She's also going to be a big star.' I guess maybe I lacked a little sensitivity because at that time I could not see it. But I'm sure that actress, who goes by the name of Raquel Welch, will forgive me."

Raquel Welch: "I think Frank is suspicious of most women. He thinks they only go for him because of who he is. That's why he likes Nancy, his first wife. She knew him when he was nothing, and he trusts her absolutely."

DIRTY DINGUS MAGEE (1970) MGM. Produced and directed by Burt Kennedy. Screenplay by Tom and Frank Waldman and Joseph Heller. Based on David Markson's novel *The Ballad of Dingus Magee*. Music by Jeff Alexander. Additional music by Billy Strange. Title song by Mike Curb. With George Kennedy, Anne Jackson, Lois Nettleton, Jack Elam, and John Dehner.

FS in longjohns in Yerkey's Hole, New Mexico, circa 1880. He needed this silliness after Grandpa died.

THAT'S ENTERTAINMENT (1974) MGM. Producer/director Jack Haley, Jr.'s masterpiece. With Fred Astaire, Bing Crosby, Gene Kelly, Peter Lawford, Liza Minnelli, Donald O'Connor, Debbie Reynolds, Mickey Rooney, Frank Sinatra, James Stewart, Elizabeth Taylor. FS hosts a segment, and his MGM films are well represented.

THAT'S ENTERTAINMENT PART II (1976) MGM. Produced by Daniel Melnick. Directed by Gene Kelly. Hosted by Fred Astaire and Gene Kelly. The clips of Dad in *Part II* are from *Anchors Aweigh, Till the Clouds Roll By, High Society, The Tender Trap*, and *It Happened in Brooklyn.*

CONTRACT ON CHERRY STREET (1977) An Artanis Production. Columbia. Made for Television. Directed by William A. Graham. With Harry Guardino, Martin Balsam, Henry Silva, Verna Bloom, Michael Nouri, and Martin Gabel.

Critic Leonard Maltin: "Sinatra's first TV-movie has him well cast as a NYC police officer who takes on organized crime in his own fashion after his partner is gunned down. Aces to this fine thriller." Adapted by Edward Anhalt from Philip Rosenberg's book.

THE FIRST DEADLY SIN (1980) Filmways. Produced by George Pappas and Mark Shanker. Directed by Brian G. Hutton. Novel and screenplay by Lawrence Sanders. Music by Gordon Jenkins. With Faye Dunaway, David Dukes, Brenda Vaccaro, Martin Gabel, James Whitmore. My father was so excited about this one. He had been away from feature movie-making for ten years and hadn't had a good role since *The Detective* in '68. This was a good one and the few scenes with FS and Faye Dunaway, his dying wife, are touching. They are shown in their apartment and the relationship is evidenced—visually and audibly—by the kind of music they like, the decor, the bed, the books . . . A lesson in moviemaking here. Begin with a good book. (As with *Eternity, Joker, Candidate* and *Von Ryan's.)*

CANNONBALL RUN II (1984) Golden Harvest Films. Produced by Albert Ruddy. Directed by Hal Needham. With Burt Reynolds, Dom De Luise, Shirley MacLaine, Marilu Henner. Many guest stars, including Dean and Sammy, who reprised their *Cannonball Run* roles. FS flew to Tucson, spent one night, and worked only four hours. He would have done more if they had asked him to. Sammy had initially asked him if he would do a bit in the movie because, after years of searching, nobody had come up with a story for another Summit movie. *Cannonball II* would unite them on film again.

THE ALBUMS

My father has been recording for almost fifty years. In order to cover a half century of product without writing a second book, I have had to make some difficult choices.

The albums released by Columbia and RCA, though they are very fine, are composed of singles that he recorded while under contract to each label. They were subsequently gathered together and released as albums. The producers for RCA were Harry Meyerson and Leonard Joy. For Columbia, Bill Richards and Mitchell Ayers.

There are also several albums on various labels that are collections of "V Discs." These were studio recordings Dad made for the U.S. Government's Overseas Victory Disc Program between 1943 and 1949.

I have chosen to deal with only the work Dad did on the Capitol and Reprise labels. These discs are all albums, in the fullest sense of the word. All of them, even the compilations, were conceived, arranged, and produced as cohesive units, with a lot of input from Dad.

THE CAPITOL YEARS—

SWING EASY (1953) Ten-inch LP. Producer, Voyle Gilmore. Arranger, Nelson Riddle. "Just One of Those Things," "I'm Gonna Sit Right Down and Write Myself a Letter," "Sunday," "Wrap Your Troubles in Dreams," "Taking a Chance on Love," "Jeepers Creepers," "Get Happy," "All of Me." Pop's first LP and still one of the best. *Billboard* announced the results of its disc jockey poll. Favorite male singer? Frank Sinatra. Favorite album? *Swing Easy.*

SONGS FOR YOUNG LOVERS (1954) Ten-inch LP. Producer, Voyle Gilmore. Arrangers, Nelson Riddle, George Siravo. "My Funny Valentine," "The Girl Next Door," "A Foggy Day," "Like Someone in Love," "I Get a Kick Out of You," "Little Girl Blue," "They Can't Take That Away from Me," "Violets for Your Furs." A *slam dunk* album!

IN THE WEE SMALL HOURS (1955) Producer, Voyle Gilmore. Arranger, Nelson Riddle. "In the Wee Small Hours of the Morning," "Mood

Indigo," "Glad to Be Unhappy," "I Get Along Without You Very Well," "Deep in a Dream," "I See Your Face Before Me," "Can't We Be Friends," "When Your Lover Has Gone," "What Is This Thing Called Love," "Last Night When We Were Young," "I'll Be Around," "Ill Wind," "It Never Entered My Mind," "Dancing on the Ceiling," "I'll Never Be the Same," "This Love of Mine" (co-written by FS).

This is my favorite Sinatra album. It doesn't reach the depth of despair of "Only the Lonely" or "A Man Alone" . . . but then, maybe that's why I love it so. The album notes. "Standing in front of the mike with his hands nearly always jammed into his pockets, his shoulders hunched a little forward, he sang. And as he sang, he created the loneliest early-morning mood in the world."

SONGS FOR SWINGIN' LOVERS (1956) Producer, Voyle Gilmore. Arranger, Nelson Riddle. "You Make Me Feel So Young," "It Happened in Monterey," "You're Getting to Be a Habit with Me," "You Brought a New Kind of Love to Me," "Too Marvelous For Words," "Old Devil Moon," "Pennies from Heaven," "Love Is Here to Stay," "I've Got You Under My Skin," "I Thought About You," "We'll Be Together Again," "Makin' Whoopee," "Swingin' Down the Lane," "Anything Goes," "How About You."

One of the reasons these early theme albums worked out so well, aside from the creative content, is they had a lot of songs. Today, there are sometimes only six or eight per album—"Swingin' Lovers" had *fifteen!*

HIGH SOCIETY (1956) Music and lyrics by Cole Porter. Music supervised and adapted by Johnny Green and Saul Chaplin. Orchestration by Conrad Salinger, Nelson Riddle, and Skip Martin. "High Society Calypso," "Little One," "Who Wants to Be a Millionaire?" "True Love," "You're Sensational," "I Love You, Samantha," "Now You Has Jazz," "Well Did You Evah?" "Mind If I Make Love to You?" Louis Armstrong and his band swing their way through two of the numbers, and Bing Crosby, Grace Kelly (in her first musical), and Celeste Holm join Dad on this sound track album from their film.

TONE POEMS OF COLOR (1957) Conducted by Frank Sinatra. Lyrics based on poems by Norman Sickel. FS selected eight of the finest contemporary composers and commissioned each to write a new composition based on the mood of a color, a mood well established for them by Norman Sickel's poems. Victor Young wrote "White" and "Black." Gordon Jenkins, "Green." Billy May, "Purple." Jeff Alexander, "Yellow" and "Brown." Alec Wilder did "Gray" and "Blue." Nelson Riddle wrote "Gold" and "Orange." Elmer Bernstein wrote "Silver." And the young André Previn did "Red."

From the liner notes: "Here, under the skilled baton of Frank Sinatra, a symphony orchestra performs twelve exciting new compositions, vividly reflecting a rainbow-hued range of mood and character . . . In his direction of the orchestra Frank Sinatra adds a brilliant new dimension to his stature."

THIS IS SINATRA (1957) Producer, Voyle Gilmore. Arranger, Nelson Riddle. "I've Got the World on a String," "Three Coins in the Fountain," "Love and Marriage," "From Here to Eternity," "South of the Border," "Rain (Falling from the Skies)," "The Gal That Got Away," "Young at Heart," "Learnin' the Blues," "My One and Only Love," "The Tender Trap," "Don't Worry 'Bout Me."

CLOSE TO YOU (1957) Producer, Voyle Gilmore. Arranger, Nelson Riddle. Featuring the Hollywood String Quartet. "Close to You," "P.S. I Love You," "Love Locked Out," "Everything Happens to Me," "It's Easy to Remember," "Don't Like Goodbyes," "With Every Breath I Take," "Blame It on My Youth," "It Could Happen to You," "I've Had My Moments," "I Couldn't Sleep a Wink Last Night," "The End of a Love Affair."

This distinguished chamber group helped Dad and Nelson play a joke on the Capitol executives. They recorded an extra song on April 5, 1956. It had been written for FS by Jimmy Van Heusen and Johnny Burke

who—besides writing classics—often wrote nonsensical stuff for Bing's "Flop Parade" feature on his radio show.

They left the poignantly orchestrated song on the demo of the album. It went out to the big brass, who all promptly proclaimed it "beautiful!"

They would have released the album in its entirety if Pop hadn't intervened. He took the song off the album, proclaiming the bosses "dense!" This is how the "beautiful" ballad goes:

I used to sit by my fireplace
And dream about you.
But now that won't do.
There's a flaw in my flue.

Your lovely face in my fireplace
Was all that I saw.
But now it won't draw.
My flue has a flaw.

From every beautiful ember a memory arose.
Now I try to remember and smoke gets in my nose.
It's not as sweet by the unit-heat
To dream about you.
So darling, adieu.
There's a flaw in my flue.

A SWINGIN' AFFAIR! (1957) Producer, Voyle Gilmore. Arranger, Nelson Riddle. "Night and Day," "I Wish I Were in Love Again," "No One Ever Tells You," "I Got Plenty O' Nuttin'," "I Guess I'll Have to Change My Plan," "Nice Work If You Can Get It," "Stars Fell on Alabama," "I Won't Dance," "The Lonesome Road," "At Long Last Love," "You'd Be So Nice to Come Home To," "I Got It Bad and That Ain't Good," "From This Moment On," "If I Had You," "Oh! Look at Me Now."

A JOLLY CHRISTMAS FROM FRANK SINATRA (1957) Producer, Voyle Gilmore. Arranger, Gordon Jenkins. With The Ralph Brewster Singers. This is quite simply the best Christmas album ever made—by anyone anywhere to this day.

PAL JOEY (1957) Arranger, Nelson Riddle. Music by Richard Rodgers, lyrics by Lorenz Hart. Music supervised and conducted by Morris Stoloff. Adaptation by George Duning and Nelson Riddle. "There's a Small Hotel," "Bewitched," "Do It the Hard Way," "Plant You Now, Dig You Later," "You Mustn't Kick It Around," "That Terrific Rainbow," "I Didn't Know What Time It Was," "The Lady Is a Tramp," "Strip Number," "Dream Sequence," "My Funny Valentine," "I Could Write a Book," "Main Title," "Great Big Town," "Zip."

WHERE ARE YOU? (1958) Producer, Dave Cavanaugh. Arranger, Gordon Jenkins. "Where Are You?" "The Night We Called It a Day," "I Cover the Waterfront," "Maybe You'll Be There," "Laura," "Lonely Town," "Autumn Leaves," "I'm a Fool to Want You" (co-written by FS), "I Think of You," "Where Is the One," "There's No You," "Baby, Won't You Please Come Home."

The Sinatra/Jenkins coupling is a killer. Ballads of longing with deeply romantic orchestrations. Irresistibly sweet.

COME FLY WITH ME (1958) Producer, Voyle Gilmore. Arranger, Billy May. Pop's first *stereo* album. "Come Fly with Me," "Around the World," "Isle of Capri," "Moonlight in Vermont," "Autumn in New York," "On the Road to Mandalay" (words by Rudyard Kipling), "Let's Get Away from It All," "April in Paris," "London by Night," "Brazil," "Blue Hawaii," "It's Nice to Go Trav'ling . . . But It's Oh So Nice to Come Home."

This first Sinatra/May effort was not to have been first. Earlier, when FS wanted Billy for the singles "South of the Border" and "My Lean Baby," Billy was touring with his band. But, the ex-trumpet player May told me, he gave permission for Nelson Riddle to write the charts in the Billy May style.

Later, for a Smothers Brothers show, Billy returned the favor for

Nelson.

THIS IS SINATRA, VOL. 2 (1958) Various producers. Arranger, Nelson Riddle. "Hey! Jealous Lover," "Everybody Loves Somebody," "Something Wonderful Happens in Summer," "Half as Lovely Twice as True," "You're Cheating Yourself," "You'll Always Be the One I Love," "You Forgot All the Words," "How Little We Know," "Time After Time," "Crazy Love," "Wait for Me," "If You Are but a Dream," "So Long, My Love," "It's the Same Old Dream," "I Believe," "Put Your Dreams Away," which had become Dad's theme song in the 1940s. He asked Ruth Lowe, who wrote "I'll Never Smile Again" to compose it for him. She, Stephen Weiss, and Paul Mann came through.

(FRANK SINATRA SINGS FOR) ONLY THE LONELY (1958) Producer, Dave Cavanaugh. Arranger, Nelson Riddle. "Only the Lonely," "Angel Eyes," "What's New," "It's a Lonesome Old Town," "Willow Weep for Me," "Goodbye," "Blues in the Night," "Guess I'll Hang My Tears Out to Dry," "Ebb Tide," "Spring Is Here," "Gone with the Wind," "One for My Baby." The title song features Dad's friend, composer Harry Sukman, at the piano.

In a time of nothing but brilliance, how does one album outshine the others? I don't know. It seems to be a personal thing, like knowing exactly where you were, and who you were with when you first heard a particular song. This album, it seems, is the one people are remembering today. (Linda Ronstadt loved it so much, she fashioned a whole new career direction based on it and had Nelson do the charts for her last two albums.)

Sammy Cahn and James Van Heusen, who composed the title song, wrote about FS and loneliness: "The Frank Sinatra we know and have known (and hardly know) is an artist with as many forms and patterns as can be found in a child's kaleidoscope . . . a Sinatra singing a hymn of loneliness could very well be the real Sinatra."

COME DANCE WITH ME (1959) Producer, Dave Cavanaugh. Arrangers: Billy May and Heinie Beau. "Come Dance with Me," "Something's Gotta Give," "Just in Time," "Dancing in the Dark," "Too Close for Comfort," "I Could Have Danced All Night," "Saturday Night," "Day In-Day Out," "Cheek to Cheek," "Baubles, Bangles, and Beads," "The Song Is You," "The Last Dance."

All brass, reeds, and rhythm. Great album. Great cover.

LOOK TO YOUR HEART (1959) Produced by Voyle Gilmore with Lee Gillette and Dave Dexter, Jr. Arranged by Nelson Riddle. A collection of recordings from 1953 through 1955, including the singles: "Anytime, Anywhere," "When I Stop Loving You," "I Could Have Told You," and "Same Old Saturday Night." Plus the title song from the film *Not as a Stranger* and three songs from the TV production of *Our Town:* "Look to Your Heart," "The Impatient Years," and "Our Town" (I don't know why "Love and Marriage" was excluded). Also: "If I Had Three Wishes" and the exciting "I'm Gonna Live till I Die" with Ray Anthony.

NO ONE CARES (1959) Producer, Dave Cavanaugh. Arranger, Gordon Jenkins. "When No One Cares," "A Cottage for Sale," "Stormy Weather," "Where Do You Go," "I Don't Stand a Ghost of a Chance with You," "Here's That Rainy Day" (one of Dad's favorite songs, written by Johnny Burke and James Van Heusen), "I Can't Get Started," "Why Try to Change Me Now," "Just Friends," "I'll Never Smile Again," "None but the Lonely Heart."

The liner notes on *No One Cares* were written by Ralph J. Gleason, editor of *Jazz* magazine and syndicated columnist, whose "Rhythm Section" appeared in many newspapers across the country. Heading into the 1960s after a decade of incomparable Sinatra albums, Gleason wrote:

"It is as certain a truth that Frank Sinatra is the greatest ballad singer of his generation as that Charlie Parker was a musical genius, Frank Lloyd Wright an architectural poet and Joe DiMaggio, hitting a ball, a thing of classic beauty.

"Sinatra can take lyrics that are in themselves banal, lyrics that are trite and sometimes even slight enough to be silly, and yet he can make them live and breathe and communicate emotion. . . . Note, for instance the way in which he sings the verse to a song. Verses never have the impact that the chorus has. Yet, when he sings them, they take on new life, set the stage for the mood and the message of the song."

CAN-CAN (1960) Music arranged and conducted by Nelson Riddle. Songs by Cole Porter. Sound track from the movie. "Entr' acte," "It's All Right with Me," "Come Along with Me," "Live and Let Live," "You Do Something to Me," "Let's Do It," "I Love Paris," "Montmartre," "C'est Magnifique," "Can-Can." And what FS calls "the saddest song ever written"—"It Was Just One of Those Things."

NICE 'N' EASY (1960) Producer, Dave Cavanaugh. Arranger, Nelson Riddle. "Nice 'N' Easy," "That Old Feeling," "How Deep Is the Ocean," "I've Got a Crush on You," "You Go to My Head," "Fools Rush In," "Nevertheless," "She's Funny That Way," "Try a Little Tenderness," "Embraceable You," "Mam'selle," "Dream," by Dad's favorite lyricist, Johnny Mercer.

SINATRA'S SWINGIN' SESSION (1960) Produced by Dave Cavanaugh. Arranged by Nelson Riddle. "When You're Smiling," "Blue Moon," "S'posin'," "It All Depends on You," "It's Only a Paper Moon," "My Blue Heaven," "Should I," "September in the Rain," "Always," "I Can't Believe That You're in Love with Me," "I Concentrate on You," "You Do Something to Me." A fat album with up to thirty-four musicians.

ALL THE WAY (1960) Produced by Dave Cavanaugh and Voyle Gilmore. Arranged by Nelson Riddle. A collection of hit singles and movie songs recorded from 1957 through 1960. "All the Way," "High Hopes" from *A Hole in the Head,* "Talk to Me," "French Foreign Legion," "To Love and Be Loved," "River, Stay Away from My Door," "Witchcraft," "It's Over, It's Over, It's Over," "Ol' MacDonald (Had a Farm)," "This Was My Love," "All My Tomorrows," the theme from *A Hole in the Head.*

COME SWING WITH ME! (1961) Producer, Dave Cavanaugh. Arrangers, Billy May and Heinie Beau. "Day by Day," "Sentimental Journey," "Almost Like Being in Love," "Five Minutes More," "American Beauty Rose," "Yes Indeed!" "On the Sunny Side of the Street," "Don't Take Your Love from Me," "That Old Black Magic," "Lover," "Paper Doll," "I've Heard That Song Before."

Billy May did some fine stuff here with eight trumpets, four French horns, a tuba, six trombones, two bass trombones, rhythm, percussion, and a harp. From the liner notes: "Working from this unusual instrumentation, Billy has split the brass into sections which answer or echo each other, and come through with backing in the same class as Frank's singing."

FS had moved from Capitol to his own label, Reprise, by 1961. Capitol continued to release his work. So did RCA Victor and Columbia, so many albums overlap each other.

Since this is not the definitive Sinatra reference, I will not mention the overlapping albums or the reissues. Instead I will move on to the Reprise collection now.

REPRISE RECORDS

I have discussed at length in the text the reasons why it was so important to Dad to form his own recording company, to record on his own label. In 1961 Dad asked Morris "Mo" Ostin, who was with Verve Records, to head the Reprise team. With the addition of executive Jay Lasker, promotions men Ernie Farrell and Sammy Laine and art director Merle Shore, they were on their way.

On December 19 and 20, 1961, FS and jazz arranger Johnny Mandel recorded the first Reprise album, *Ring-a-Ding-Ding.* It turned to gold. With the next two albums, Reprise was introducing the quality of product that would live up to its motto, "To play and play again."

My coverage of the Reprise albums is more personal, because I was grown up when they came out and more personally involved with them.

The teams, the times, the songs—especially the songs—made some of the 1960s albums classics. This is how Frank Sinatra chooses his songs for an album:

FS: "It depends on whether I'm recording a single or an album. If I find a song I like, I'll record it as a single. For an album, I like to keep all the songs in the same genre—swing, love songs, etc. Once I decide what type of music I want for the album, I make up a list of song titles I'd like to record, and my associates (arranger, etc.) suggest songs. When we actually get down to the point where arrangements have to be done, I go through the list again and pick out eight to ten songs and go with them."

Producer Sonny Burke explained how the arranger is chosen:

Burke: "Assuming the songs are picked, Frank himself has extremely definite ideas on the kind of music he wants to hear behind himself. He very often will suggest the arranger he wants. Also, he'll save a song for another project when a more appropriate arranger will be working. But most often, the arranger has been chosen automatically at the same time the project itself is decided upon."

Dad works hard in preparation for a recording session. If he hasn't sung for a while, he starts warming up a couple of weeks prior to the date with a daily vocal workout which includes exercises and rehearsing of the songs to be recorded. His pianist/conductor, who is "on call," accompanies him. It is during this phase that one is likely to hear some funny sounds from the famous throat, followed by a comment like, "I think I swallowed a shot glass," or "Anybody got an old reed?" (Lately he has wondered why, contrary to the normal lowering of a voice that is growing older, his is stronger in its *upper* register.)

Burke: "He trains for a recording session like a fighter would for a championship fight. When he comes in to a session, he's ready for work."

Here is a look at some of that work—that *ton* of work.

RING-A-DING-DING (1961) Producer, Felix Slatkin. Arranger, Johnny Mandel. "A Foggy Day," "A Fine Romance," "Be Careful, It's My Heart," "Let's Face the Music and Dance." And more. From the liner notes: "A good musician sings on his instrument. Sinatra sings as though he were a strong, mellow horn. . . . Who else could come on as intimate and soft as he does and yet remain as absolutely masculine as Rocky Marciano?"

SWING ALONG WITH ME (1962) Retitled **SINATRA SWINGS** because of a Capitol Records' injunction. They felt the original title was too close to their FS album called *Come Swing with Me*. Producer, Neal Hefti. Arranger, Billy May. Billy's wit, his great humor runs rampant, especially in "Moonlight on the Ganges" and "Granada." "Don't Cry Joe," "Don't Be That Way," and "Have You Met Miss Jones" are neat. "Curse of an Aching Heart" is the song the Hoboken Four sang in 1935.

I REMEMBER TOMMY (1962) Producer, Neal Hefti. Arranger, Sy Oliver. "I'm Getting Sentimental Over You," "Imagination," "Without a Song," "I'll Be Seeing You," "Polka Dots and Moonbeams," "The One I Love," and several others, all favorites from Dad's days with the Tommy Dorsey Band.

FS: "I really think it has some of the best work I've ever done. I feel sentimental over Dorsey . . . I tried to sing the songs as he used to play them on his trombone."

SINATRA AND STRINGS (1962) Producers, Neal Hefti and Skip Martin. Arranger, Don Costa. This album opened up a whole new era. The orchestra got bigger. Pop wanted that lush string sound. This is a mini-concert album. "All or Nothing at All," "Night and Day," "It Might as Well Be Spring," "Yesterdays."

For me, the outstanding cut here is "Come Rain or Come Shine." I was on tour with Dad in 1983 when Don Costa died. I remembered the last time I saw him. I sat on his lap in the wings at Caesar's while we watched Dad (for the umpteenth time) do "Come Rain or Come Shine" which is one of his favorite songs. And Don, who was in a melancholy mood, said, "That's still the best chart I ever wrote."

SINATRA AND SWINGIN' BRASS (1962) Producer, Chuck Sagle. Arranger, Neal Hefti. "Goody, Goody," "Love Is Just Around the Corner,"

"Pick Yourself Up," "Tangerine," and "Don'cha Go 'Way Mad" (with ten "babys" in succession and trombones playing the same pulsing note for sixteen bars). FS left the choice of songs to Hefti for the most part. Dad wanted to have a whole new sound and feel—more jazz. "I Get a Kick Out of You" was recorded at a much faster tempo than he performs it on stage with the same chart. On this album, FS once again reminds us of the importance of words.

FS: "The hardest thing is to pick the songs that mean something, and even when the words don't mean much, to sing them in such a way that they seem to."

SINATRA SINGS GREAT SONGS FROM GREAT BRITAIN (1962) Producer, Alan Freeman. Arranger, Brian Farnum. "London By Night," "We'll Meet Again." Recorded in Bayswater and not released in the United States, this album contains some beautiful ballads. "A Nightingale Sang in Berkeley Square" is my favorite.

FRANK SINATRA CONDUCTS MUSIC FROM PICTURES AND PLAYS (1962) Dad picked up the baton again to conduct some of the great songs which had originally come from plays and movie scores. "All the Way," "Affair to Remember," "Moon River," "Exodus," "I've Grown Accustomed to Her Face," "The Girl that I Marry," "If Ever I Would Leave You," and more. Produced by composer-arranger Harry Sukman.

ALL ALONE (1962) Producer, Neal Hefti. Arranger, Gordon Jenkins. "Remember," "The Song Is Ended," "Together," "What'll I Do?" "Oh How I Miss You Tonight" . . . If you have this album and haven't thought about it for a long time, play it now—it's one of the best.

Dad and I were sitting at the bar one night listening to a "Sinatra-thon" on the radio. The DJ introduced "What'll I Do?" He said, "This is for the dark times . . . the short hours." My Father listened to himself for a while ("What'll I do with just a photograph to tell my troubles to . . .") and he said, "That was tough to do. I couldn't do that anymore. It takes great control."

When you listen to "When I Lost You," remember that the day it was recorded, my dad had just been a pallbearer for his friend Ernie Kovacs. January 15, 1962.

SINATRA AND BASIE (1963) Producer, Neal Hefti. Arranger, Neal Hefti. This album is subtitled "A Historic Musical First," and that, it was. "Pennies From Heaven," "Please Be Kind," "I Won't Dance."

Robin Douglas-Home: "Both (have) definite techniques; when Sinatra touches a song, it never subsequently sounds right sung by anyone else; when Basie touches a piano keyboard, the sound tells you those fingers could belong to only one man . . ."

Neal Hefti's name doesn't appear on the album because he wanted equal billing with Sinatra and Basie or no billing at all. My dad disagreed with Neal. Bill Basie was the star here.

In the middle of the October 22 recording date, everything *stopped*. A TV was hooked up so everybody could watch Frank, Jr. in his first guest appearance on *The Jack Benny Program*. Dad was so proud he sent Uncle Jack a wire that read, "Thanks, Jack. Frankie's Father."

THE CONCERT SINATRA (1963) Producer, Chuck Sagle. Arranger, Nelson Riddle. A classic. Side A: "I Have Dreamed" . . . "My Heart Stood Still" . . . "Lost in the Stars" . . . "Ol' Man River." Side B: "You'll Never Walk Alone" . . . "Bewitched" . . . "This Nearly Was Mine" . . . "Soliloquy." Some of the most powerful songs in American popular music—eloquently performed, exquisitely presented. Nelson had been writing for FS at Reprise from the first. For example: the singles "Tina" and "The Second Time Around." But, still under contract to Capitol, his name could not appear on Reprise labels—until this one.

This was recorded on Stage 7 at the Samuel Goldwyn Studios in order to capture the best possible sound. You don't need an echo chamber; this stage acts as an echo chamber—and experts say that its natural reverberation characteristics are splendid.

MUSICAL REPERTORY THEATRE (1963) Produced by Sonny Burke.

My father conceived and produced this collection of four albums of music from popular stage shows. He had new arrangements written, and he put together a company of guest stars—singers and actors. When he was recording these albums, Dad told me, "This is how Broadway shows should sound." It's fabulous stuff into which Dad *et cie* put a lot of care and energy.

FINIAN'S RAINBOW Harburg and Lane. Arrangers: Bill Loose, Warren Barker, Gene Puerling, Nathan Van Cleave, Jerry Fielding, Nelson Riddle, George Rhodes, Ralph Smale, Skip Martin, and Marty Paich. Performed by: The Hi-Lo's, Rosemary Clooney, Dean Martin, Bing Crosby, Debbie Reynolds, FS, Sammy Davis, Jr., Lou Monte, The Mary Kaye Trio, The McGuire Sisters, and Clark Dennis. Among the songs are: "How Are Things in Glocca Morra?" "If This Isn't Love," "Old Devil Moon," and "Necessity."

GUYS AND DOLLS Frank Loesser. Arrangers: Billy May, Bill Loose, Skip Martin, Nelson Riddle, Jerry Fielding, Nathan Van Cleave, and Warren Barker. Performers: FS, Bing Crosby, Dean Martin, Jo Stafford, The McGuire Sisters, Dinah Shore, Debbie Reynolds, Clark Dennis, Allan Sherman, and Sammy Davis, Jr.

KISS ME KATE Cole Porter. Arrangers: George Duning, Warren Barker, Gene Puerling, Billy May, Nelson Riddle, Skip Martin, George Rhodes, Herb Spencer, and Jerry Fielding. Performers: The Hi-Lo's, Jo Stafford, FS, Dean, Sammy, Johnny Prophet, Phyllis McGuire, Lou Monte, Dinah Shore, Keely Smith. Among the songs are "Why Can't You Behave," "Too Darn Hot," "So in Love," and "Always True to You (in my fashion)."

SOUTH PACIFIC Rodgers and Hammerstein. Arrangers: Nathan Van Cleave, Skip Martin, Billy May, Nelson Riddle, Bill Loose, Marty Paich, Warren Barker, and Gene Puerling. Performers: The McGuire Sisters, Jo Stafford, FS, Keely Smith, Bing Crosby, Sammy Davis, Jr., Dinah Shore, The Hi-Lo's, Debbie Reynolds, and Rosemary Clooney.

SINATRA'S SINATRA (1963) Producer, Sonny Burke. Arranger, Nelson Riddle. The book *Picasso's Picasso* inspired the title. Twelve rerecorded FS favorites, including "Young at Heart," "In the Wee Small Hours of the Morning," "I've Got You Under My Skin," and "Nancy" with an updated lyric. This was Pop's first four-track album.

FRANK SINATRA SINGS DAYS OF WINE AND ROSES, MOON RIVER, AND OTHER ACADEMY AWARD WINNERS (1964) Producer, Sonny Burke. Arranged and conducted by Nelson Riddle. "The Way You Look Tonight," "Three Coins in the Fountain," "Secret Love," "Love Is a Many-Splendored Thing," "All the Way."

Most of Frank Sinatra's recording was done at Studio One of Western Recorders and Studios A and B at United Recorders, one block away, on Sunset Blvd. in Hollywood.

Reprise moved to Warner Bros. Records. There was now a new team: Mike Maitland, Joe Smith, Ed Thrasher, Stan Cornyn.

In 1964 Bing Crosby joined the Reprise crooners. He told the press, "Let's face it, Sinatra is a King. He's a very sharp operator, a keen record chief and has a keen appreciation of what the public wants. I'm happy to be associated with him after all these years."

AMERICA, I HEAR YOU SINGING (1964) Producer, Sonny Burke. Frank Sinatra, Bing Crosby, Fred Waring and the Pennsylvanians. Sonny Burke gathered several arrangers for this flag-waver. I remember being excited about hearing this album and racing to Dad's as soon as I could. I expected him to play it for me, in sequence. But he had the tape cued up to "The Hills of Home," which was done a capella by the Pennsylvanians. "Wait 'til you hear this, Chicken, you're gonna fall down." I did. By the way, Pop redid "The House I Live In." This one's even better than the first because his voice is stronger.

I love my father's patriotism. I love the fact that he is so open and honest about his feelings for and about our nation. This beautiful album is an example of his deep love and respect for the U.S.A.

IT MIGHT AS WELL BE SWING (1964) Producer, Sonny Burke. Arranger, Quincy Jones. The second set for Sinatra and Basie, augmented by strings. "The Best Is Yet to Come," "I Can't Stop Loving You," "I Wish You Love," "Fly Me to the Moon."

Quincy Jones: "I remember when I arranged the album for your Dad and Basie. We worked out at Warner Brothers. Frank was in a bungalow, and next door was Dean's dressing room. Your Dad put me in there to write the arrangements. I stayed in one weekend, working. I fell asleep about seven o'clock on Monday morning. At about eight o'clock there was a knock on the door. And it was your Dad in an army uniform, saying, 'How do you like your eggs?' I'll never forget that. It was like waking up in a dream, Sinatra asking me, 'How do you like your eggs, Q?' "

Q wrote some of his best arrangements for this album. Beautiful stuff. My favorite is "The Best Is Yet to Come," but Neil Armstrong, Buzz Aldrin, and Mike Collins didn't agree with me. They liked Pop, Bill, and Quincy's "Fly Me to the Moon" so much they took it with them aboard Apollo XI on July 16, 1969. One of the great thrills of our lives was hearing Pop singing to us—from outer space via Mission Control!

For the speed with which it all worked, Q admired Dad's concentration and Basie's economy. He also felt the Basie band was a cohesive group that couldn't be touched by a studio band. Each time he wrote an arrangement they liked, "they just took it from there." They added a distinctive personality to the score.

Quincy explained why he hired extra horn players for the album. "By having extra men in reserve we don't have to disturb a singer's groove. There are times when a singer who is building a groove and building a picture on a song might have to stop and wait until the blood comes back into the trumpet players' lips."

About Basie and Sinatra, Jones noted that both have "the remarkable ability to eliminate the negative." And about my father, Q said, "So far as I can put the essence of Frank into words, I'd say that he just makes everything work. He makes everything fit."

ROBIN AND THE SEVEN HOODS (1964) Producer, Sonny Burke. Arranger, Nelson Riddle. "My Kind of Town, Chicago Is . . ." From the movie's sound track.

SOFTLY AS I LEAVE YOU (1964) Arranged by Ernie Freeman, Nelson Riddle, and Billy May. Producer Jimmy Bowen started to nudge Pop toward the pop singles charts with a new approach. "Somewhere in Your Heart," "Tell Her You Love Her Each Day," "When Somebody Loves You." Ernie Freeman gave him another new sound—a little bit square—nice.

TWELVE SONGS OF CHRISTMAS (1964) Producer, Sonny Burke. Arrangers, Nelson Riddle, Dick Reynolds, Jack Halloran, Harry Betts. Dad, Bing, and Fred Waring and his Pennsylvanians got together and gave the world a beautiful Christmas package.

SEPTEMBER OF MY YEARS (1965) Producer, Sonny Burke. Arranger, Gordon Jenkins. This album won three Grammy Awards. A classic. In honor of Dad's fiftieth birthday and his acceptance of, and sadness about, middle age. "Don't Wait Too Long," "The Man in the Looking Glass," "It Gets Lonely Early," "How Old Am I," "September Song," "This Is All I Ask."

This album marks the first time I ever thought about what life would be like for me without my father. I knew it was a special theme created by specialists for a special occasion, and as much as I loved it, it was painful to listen to. I realized then that if something happened to him I wouldn't be able to listen to his records anymore—I couldn't—at least not for a very, very long time. "And let the music play as long as there's a song to sing . . . and I will stay younger than spring."

SINATRA '65 (1965) Various producers. Arranger, Nelson Riddle. This is a compilation of singles and miscellaneous songs from sessions scattered throughout the early sixties. "I've Never Been in Love Before," "When Somebody Loves You," "You Brought a New Kind of Love," "Luck Be a Lady," and others.

MY KIND OF BROADWAY (1965) Producer, Sonny Burke. Arrangers, Billy May, Nelson Riddle, Torrie Zito. An album of songs from successful Broadway shows. "Golden Moment," "Luck Be a Lady," "Hello Dolly!" "They Can't Take That Away from Me," "Nice Work If You Can Get It," and "Without a Song" among others.

A MAN AND HIS MUSIC (1965) Produced by Sonny Burke. If you can afford only one Sinatra album, this is it. Narrated and sung by FS. It is an anthology, a musical biography—thirty-one songs and one comedy sketch. *The* arrangers are here: Riddle, Jenkins, May, Costa, Oliver, Mandel, Freeman.

STRANGERS IN THE NIGHT (1966) Produced by Sonny Burke. Arranged by Ernie Freeman and Nelson Riddle. "Summer Wind," "Call Me," "On a Clear Day," "Downtown." Mixed in with some standards like "All or Nothing at All," "My Baby Just Cares for Me," and "The Most Beautiful Girl in the World."

Jimmy Bowen's nudging paid off. The album was Number One on the charts, and the single won two Grammys as "Best Solo Vocal" and "Record of the Year"—and Dad didn't even like the damn song!

MOONLIGHT SINATRA (1966) Produced by Sonny Burke. Arranged by Nelson Riddle. All moon songs. My favorites, "I Wished on the Moon," "The Moon Was Yellow," and "Moonlight Becomes You." My brother's favorite, "The Moon Got in My Eyes."

SINATRA AT THE SANDS (1966) Producer, Sonny Burke. Conducted and arranged by Quincy Jones and Billy Byers. Dad's very first "live" recording. Four sides of prime Basie-Sinatra tunes . . . twenty songs, two monologues, and a cup of tea. Some of the twenty were: "Come Fly with Me," "I've Got a Crush on You," "I've Got You Under My Skin," "The Shadow of Your Smile," "One for My Baby." (And that's just one side!) "Fly Me to the Moon," "You Make Me Feel So Young," "It Was a Very Good Year," "Where or When," "Angel Eyes," "My Kind of Town."

THAT'S LIFE (1966) Produced by Jimmy Bowen. Arranged and conducted by Ernie Freeman. As the album's subtitle puts it, "My, My, That's Life, An Assemblage of Songs Which Say Much, And to Many, by Frank Sinatra." "I Will Wait for You," "Somewhere My Love," "What Now My Love," "You're Gonna Hear from Me," and more. Great title song. ". . . Each time I find myself flat on my face . . . I pick myself up and get back in the race . . . that's life . . ."

FRANCIS ALBERT SINATRA & ANTONIO CARLOS JOBIM (1967) Produced by Sonny Burke. Music of Antonio Carlos Jobim, arranged by Claus Ogerman. An American, a Brazilian and a German created a *beautiful* album. "Dindi" (pronounced JinJee). "Quiet Nights of Quiet Stars," "Meditation," "How Insensitive," "Once I Loved." This is the most romantic sound in the world and my favorite music.

Stan Cornyn reported that at the sessions, Ogerman, "tiptoed about . . . ridding every song of clicks, bings, bips, all things sharp. Seemed like the whole idea was to out-hush each other." My dad said, "I haven't sung so softly since I had the laryngitis." Cornyn added, "If he sang any softer, he'd have to be lying on his back." A trombone player who had put his felt hat across his horn to muffle the sound, said after hitting a clam, "If I blow any softer, it'll hafta come out the back of my neck."

I would be remiss if I didn't mention Jobim's lovely vocals on four of the songs. Cornyn describes "Tone" (Dad's nickname for Antonio) as a ". . . slight and tousled boy-man, speaking softly while about him rushes a world too fast. Antonio, troubled not by the clamor in the world. Troubled more by the whisperings in his heart."

FRANK SINATRA (1967) Produced by Jimmy Bowen. With some new arrangers for Dad, H. B. Barnun and Billy Strange. Plus Claus Ogerman, Ernie Freeman, and Gordon Jenkins. A mixed bag: "The World We Knew," "This Town," "Born Free." And "Something Stupid," with yours truly.

FRANCIS A., EDWARD K. (1968) Produced by Sonny Burke. Arranged by Billy May. Features Duke's band with superstars intact. Recorded on Pop's birthday. "Sunny," "I Like the Sunrise," "Poor Butterfly." By the way, the "A" is for Albert, and the "K" is for Kennedy.

Stan Cornyn's liner notes paint a vivid image of the session. Duke is zoot-suited. He sets up, precisely, his "cafeteria": Cokes, cigarettes, Kleenex, ice, towel. Pop is dressed in suit, vest, and tie. "Where's the extrumpet player?" In lumbers Billy May dressed for the occasion in faded khakis and his best tennis shoes. Alto-sax player Johnny Hodges and FS reminisce about "Indian Summer." Frank remembered having to sing it in Jack Leonard's key back in the Dorsey days when Tommy refused to transpose it. And how, "My eyeballs would fall out every time on the top note." Then they'd do a take, this time the song is in Frank's key. Johnny Hodges does a solo so hypnotizing that Pop almost forgets to sing. When you hear it, listen for his delayed reentry.

Cornyn: "They hear back their music. Sinatra's eyes, when his song is happening, they also happen. And Duke, during playback, strutting. Playback finished, they turn to one another. 'Elegant record, Francis.' Francis' reply, 'Always glad to hear that about that kind of carrying on.' "

FRANK SINATRA'S GREATEST HITS (1968) Various producers. Arranged by many of his favorites, old and new. "Strangers in the Night," "That's Life," "It Was a Very Good Year," "Something Stupid," "Somewhere in Your Heart," "The World We Knew," "Softly as I Leave You." On the cover you can see the Sinatra family crest ring, which we all wear.

THE SINATRA FAMILY WISH YOU A MERRY CHRISTMAS (1968) Produced by Sonny Burke. Arranged by Nelson Riddle. Vocal arrangements by Jimmy Joyce, with the Jimmy Joyce singers. One of the most enjoyable experiences of my life. From shooting the cover to hearing the songs on the radio. Tina was scared, "in a coma," as she approached the mike for her solo. Dad joked, "You got one take, kid." We did "The Twelve Days of Christmas" as reworded by Sammy Cahn. That year Frankie and Tina and I gave Dad *every* gift that was mentioned in the lyric—including "six games of Scrabble, five iv'ry combs, four meerschaum pipes, three golf clubs, two silken scarves . . . and a most lovely lavender tie." By the way, "It's Such a Lonely Time of Year" was an antiwar (Vietnam) song.

CYCLES (1968) Produced by Don Costa. Arranged by Don Costa. This, in my opinion, is the closest Don and Dad came to capturing the sound of the day. I would have chosen *some* different songs, but others, "Little Green Apples," "By the Time I Get to Phoenix," and especially the title song are so nice. ("Wait By the Fire," which is listed on the front cover, does not appear in the album.) "Cycles," the song, was rerecorded in New York and I had the great pleasure of "producing" it at my dad's request, so that "Don can be in the room with me." What an honor. Of course I had by then proven myself by selling a lot of records of my own. But the fact that Dad trusted me—that meant more than my gold records.

From Hal Halverstadt's notes: "Like the great American Buffalo, the Sinatra brand of recording is diminishing. Times were when [you] could be turned on by the spontaneous combustion of a singer and band grooving together. Now, more often than not, the scene is four or five young men and a weary engineer valiantly battling their eight and twelve track equipment. Laying down instrumental tracks, then vocals, combining them, perhaps adding horns, maybe deleting strings, mixing, re-mixing, sometimes coming back only to decide to start from scratch. All of which can result in some earthshaking music. But what's even more special, to the spectator, the speed, utter professionalism, finesse, and genuine excitement of a Sinatra session . . ."

MY WAY (1969) Produced by Don Costa and Sonny Burke. Arranged by Don Costa. The title song was co-written in French by François and Revaux. When Dad first played it for me at Caesar's Palace in its original version, we thought it would be an important piece of material. Paul Anka wrote the English lyric and you know the rest. Dad was, at fifty-four, young enough to sing the almost morbid words, "And now, the end is near, and so I face the final curtain . . ." without it depressing him (and me). Now, sixteen years later, I don't like to hear it anymore. I'd rather listen to "Mrs. Robinson" or "All My Tomorrows." I love Ed Thrasher's photos and presentation here.

A MAN ALONE (1969) Produced by Sonny Burke. Arranged by Don Costa. Music and lyrics written for FS by poet Rod McKuen. This album is a good example of what happens when the writer *knows* his man.

McKuen: "I could relate to him because, even though he had been married three times and had three children, he was a loner."

Dad was in a state of flux when he and Rod worked on this project. He and Mia had parted. His father was ill. He was troubled and lonely. He removed "Happy Birthday Me" from the collection because it was, as Rod puts it, "so right on the mark," too painful. Because of the emotional time, *A Man Alone* took longer than most to be completed. But Dad worked hard, perhaps harder than ever before, to make it what it is.

"Frank was one hour early to each session so we could go over the material again. I'd never seen him do that before," Rod told me. FS relied heavily on his friend's judgment. "How's the tempo, Rod?" He never changed the running order—he left it exactly the way it was the first time McKuen played him the demo.

Rod and I agree that "I've Been to Town" and "Love's Been Good to Me" are great and that "Empty Is" is brilliant, but the writer says there's no way to pick *one* favorite because the album plays as a one-piece unit.

McKuen: "I would like to point out that your dad was given the latitude for some acting on this album—he is a fine actor."

FS: "Real singing is acting. I sang so well because I felt the lyrics here and here and here [head, heart, guts]. Whatever the man was trying to say in the song—I'd been there and back. I *knew* what it was all about."

WATERTOWN (1969) Produced by Charlie Calello. Written by Bob Gaudio for Dad. About Watertown, New York. Bob Gaudio: "It was designed to be a TV special. A story of a small town and a guy's trials and tribulations. It lost the impact and turned out to be an album that not too many people understood."

SINATRA AND COMPANY* (1970) Produced by Sonny Burke and Don Costa. The * is attached to some powerful names: Antonio Carlos Jobim, Don Costa, and Eumir Deodato. Each side of this album was produced and arranged independently. "Wave," arranged by Eumir Deodato, is perhaps one of Pop's technically best.

FRANK SINATRA'S GREATEST HITS, VOL. II (1971) Various producers and arrangers. "My Way," "A Man Alone," "Cycles," "Goin' Out of My Head," "Something," "The September of My Years." This album came out during Dad's brief retirement, with the advance promotionals expressing the wish that ". . . one can view this album as a look back before going forward . . . hoping it is the portent of future albums that will combine to give us *Greatest Hits Vol. III.*"

OL' BLUE EYES IS BACK (1973) Producer, Don Costa. Arrangers, Gordon Jenkins and Don Costa. "You Will Be My Music," "You're So Right," "Winners," "Nobody Wins," "Send in the Clowns," "Dream Away," "Let Me Try Again," "There Used to Be a Ballpark," "Noah."

Back to incredible Stage 7 at Goldwyn Studios, with Costa at the controls and Jenkins wielding the baton—the A team. My father, now fatherless, had taken two years off after Grandpa died.

Stan Cornyn: "As if anticipating the questions and knowing there's no thunder roll of an answer to give if he's asked why he's doing this [recording again], he lays out the answer to everyone's most tiresome question and says, 'I just figured I'd do some work. No fun trying to hit a golf ball at eight at night.' . . . A record exec whispers how he wants to 'go on the road with this album and compare him to . . . to Lincoln.' Gordon Jenkins asks, 'Where did the baritone go?' And the baritone goes to his microphone . . . He sings with his hands on top of the music stand, holding firm on the music stand, trying hard. . . . He sings and it's

the voice that brings it all back and you realize that not one—isn't it curious?—not one other voice so clear and clean in all the years has come along, not one other. He is still, no contest, the best this world knows . . . He is, to his audience, as he sings, a real and enduring value, a firm handhold in a very slippery, very anonymous world. . . ."

And the world welcomed Ol' Blue Eyes back.

SOME NICE THINGS I'VE MISSED (1974) Reprise. Produced by Don Costa, Jimmy Bowen, and Sonny Burke. "You Turned My World Around," "Sweet Caroline," "The Summer Knows," "If," "You Are the Sunshine of My Life," "What Are You Doing the Rest of Your Life?" "Tie a Yellow Ribbon Round the Old Oak Tree," and more.

"The Summer Knows" and "If" were a study in contrasts. The first was done in eighteen takes (So much for one-take Sinatra. That's for movies; for albums, he has done as many as twenty-five or thirty . . .). "If" was done in two. It would have been done in one except that FS noticed some "sand" in it. Not enough of the gravel-quality "to sell to a dealer," he said, "but I think we need another one."

I was with Mom and Hugh in Palm Springs waiting out the last two weeks of a difficult pregnancy when Dad recorded this album. John Brady described the end of one session: "He said goodnight to some of the soft, pretty ladies, and to Father O'Connell [Grandma's priest] . . . 'Say a couple of small prayers for my Nancy, OK?' said the singer. 'I'm gonna be a granddad, you know.' "

THE MAIN EVENT (1974) Produced by Don Costa. Featuring Howard Cosell. "The Lady Is a Tramp," "I Get a Kick Out of You," "Let Me Try Again," "Autumn in New York," "I've Got You Under My Skin," "Bad, Bad Leroy Brown," "Angel Eyes," "You Are the Sunshine of My Life," "The House I Live In," "My Kind of Town," "My Way."

This is the sound track from the televised concert at Madison Square Garden. With Woody Herman and the Young Thundering Herd.

TRILOGY (1980) Reprise. Produced by Sonny Burke (it was his idea). Engineer, Lee Herschberg. Album designer, Saul Bass.

From the liner notes called "Odyssey to Trilogy," beautifully written by David McClintick:

"Twenty years into the rock era, Sinatra felt more intimidated than ever by the increasingly complex musical marketplace. He was gripped by doubt about what to record and about the nature of the contemporary audience for his records. . . . It was a struggle that only superior artists endure. A lesser man under similar circumstances would have had no dilemma; he would have recorded nothing. But Sinatra was determined to move forward, to seek and find songs and musical concepts through which he could fulfill the still sizeable potential of his art. . . ."

RECORD ONE—THE PAST Collectables of the Early Years. Arranged and conducted by Billy May. "The Song Is You," "But Not for Me," "I Had the Craziest Dream," "It Had to Be You," "Let's Face the Music and Dance," "Street of Dreams," "My Shining Hour," "All of You," "More Than You Know," "They All Laughed."

(Los Angeles—September, 1979)

David McClintick: "Outside the recording studio on Sunset Boulevard the temperature hovers just under 90 degrees. Brush and forest fires are sprinkling soot on this seedy and vaguely menacing stretch of Hollywood from a sky that has turned from beige to rust to black as the sun has set. It is a Nathanael West sort of evening, and thus is a perfect foil for the magical contrast one finds inside the studio. For inside, it is unmistakably a Mabel Mercer sort of evening. Frank Sinatra, Billy May, a twelve-voice choir and a fifty-five piece orchestra are making a record of 'My Shining Hour,' an extraordinary song composed for the Fred Astaire film 'The Sky's the Limit' in 1948."

"I can't believe we never got to this one—I've been wanting to do it for 35 years," says Sinatra . . . who then recalls that one of his classics, "One For My Baby," is from the same Harold Arlen-Johnny Mercer score . . . Mabel Mercer has kept "My Shining Hour" alive through the years almost single-handedly.

"... On these sooty September evenings Sinatra is rerecording several renditions that he and May had completed two months earlier and that seemed perfectly acceptable then. But after listening repeatedly to cassettes of the July recordings, Sinatra decided he could do better. He changed a few keys, slowed a few tempos, and generally gained further internal command of the songs . . ."

RECORD TWO—THE PRESENT Some Very Good Years. Arranged and conducted by Don Costa. "You and Me," "Just the Way You Are," "Something" (arranged by Nelson Riddle), "MacArthur Park," "Theme from New York, New York," "Summer Me, Winter Me," "Song Sung Blue," "For the Good Times" (with guest star Eileen Farrell), "Love Me Tender," "That's What God Looks Like."

(New York City—August 1979)

McClintick: "In a cavernous CBS studio on East 30th Street, Sinatra is going about the risky business of recording songs that other performers, with styles completely different from his, have made famous. Framed by sound partitions, he stands behind a microphone and music stand facing Don Costa, who is perched on a podium surrounded by 50 musicians. 'Ready, Frank?' asks Sonny Burke from behind a cloud of cigarette smoke in the control room.

" 'I've been ready since I was twelve.'

". . . At the end of the third evening in New York, after hearing the last playback of the session, Sinatra walks back into the studio from the control room and is momentarily startled by a prolonged standing ovation from the fifty instrumentalists and sixteen singers. He has never been more deeply moved by applause. These aren't groupies outside a stage door, after all. They are fellow professionals in the intimidating confines of a recording studio who are grateful for the opportunity to have helped him create joy. And there is another dimension. Many of these musicians weren't yet born when Sinatra began making records in 1939. A few weren't born when he made *From Here to Eternity*. For a man who occasionally worries about appealing to young people, it is nice to be assured in such a touching way that his concern is baseless."

RECORD THREE—THE FUTURE Reflections on the Future in Three Tenses. Composed, arranged, and conducted by Gordon Jenkins. 154 musicians.

(The Shrine Auditorium, Los Angeles—December 1979)

McClintick: "It is difficult to conceive of a more daunting assignment for a composer than being asked to write a suite of music about the future. The possibilities are so vast that whatever approach the composer chooses inevitably will be criticized by others who would have chosen a different approach. 'Reflections on the Future' is no exception to this dilemma and is certain to become one of Sinatra's most controversial recordings. Some will say it is his finest hour. Others will say that certain of its lyrics are too personal. There can be no question, however, that 'Future' includes the most stirring and imaginative music and lyrics that Gordon Jenkins has ever written. The work sweeps across the attitudinal and emotional terrain from sage cynicism, to humor, to vulnerability, to childlike wonder. It explores not only dreams like world peace and space travel but also some of Sinatra's most private musings about his own future and, implicitly, about his past. . . ."

During Christmastime of 1979, the family heard the rough tapes of *Trilogy* in Palm Springs. Four-year-old A. J. and not quite three-year-old Amanda snuggled with their "Pop-Pop." Frankie and Tina and I paced the floor of the Great Hall, unable to sit still. We laughed and cried and shared this unequaled gift of talent and music. It was an evening that lingers.

Though each record stands on its own, the way to listen to *Trilogy* is all at once, in one sitting.

SHE SHOT ME DOWN (1981) Produced by Don Costa. Arranged by Gordon Jenkins, Don Costa, and Nelson Riddle. "Good Thing Going," "Hey Look, No Crying," "Thanks for the Memory," "A Long Night," "Bang Bang (My Baby Shot Me Down)," "Monday Morning Quarterback," "South—to a Warmer Place," "I Loved Her," "The Gal That Got Away"/"It Never Entered My Mind" (medley).

This album nearly recaptured the magic of the earlier theme albums. "Band Bang," "Monday Morning Quarterback," "The Gal That Got Away," and Alec Wilder's "I Loved Her" are outstanding.

SINATRA AND SYMS (1983) Produced by Frank Sinatra and Don Costa. Arranged by Don Costa (and Vinnie Falcone). For the brilliant song-stylist Sylvia Syms this collaboration was "the culmination of a dream" which began in the early 1940s when she and FS met on Fifty-second Street. They had both gone to hear Billie Holiday in one of the many small clubs, and "Lady Day" introduced them to each other. She took the aspiring Sylvia, and Frank, who had just joined Tommy Dorsey's band, across the street to see Mabel Mercer.

Sylvia Syms: "Mabel was not a great singer, but she had a way with words and phrasing that was unique. 'Lady,' whose talent was just the opposite, had an animal instinct about Mabel, and enjoyed bringing people to listen to her."

My father admired Holiday and Mercer, and both he and Sylvia were influenced by them.

Dad produced and conducted this album for "Buddha," as he calls Syms. Don Costa had a heart attack just before the recording sessions began. These were the last arrangements Don wrote.

Sylvia said that as a conductor, "your Papa put phrasing into my mouth that had never occurred to me—and it became incredibly simple. He is the greatest delineator of words. I sit and watch him even now, as a performer watching another performer, not believing the lessons I'm learning."

L.A. IS MY LADY (1984) Producer/Conductor, Quincy Delight Jones. Featuring George Benson, Lionel Hampton, Bobby James, Ray Brown, Steve Gadd, Joe Newman, and Urbie Green. Recorded and mixed by Phil Ramone. "L.A. Is My Lady," "Teach Me Tonight," "It's All Right with Me," "Mack the Knife," "If I Should Lose You," "Stormy Weather," "A Hundred Years from Today," "How Do You Keep the Music Playing?" "The Best of Everything," and my favorite, "After You've Gone"—Frank Foster's chart is a screamer. Check out the trumpet's last note. It's a high A. The voice of Mack the Knife was done by bassist Major "Mule" Holley.

"Q" did a nifty thing; he put FS with some new (to him) and slightly off-the-wall extremely talented arrangers: Sam Nestico, Frank Foster. Plus Torrie Zito and Joe Parnello (Pop's conductor). The title song was arranged by Dave Matthews, Jerry Hey, Torrie Zito, and Quincy—who also co-wrote the song with his wife Peggy Lipton, and Alan and Marilyn Bergman.

This project was a real family affair, and a true labor of love for Quincy—who is probably the sweetest man this side of heaven. I asked "Q" to tell me about the making of *L.A. Is My Lady*.

Quincy Jones: "It's been a long time since I worked like this ['live' sessions] 'cause I go with 24 tracks, overdubbing this, stacking that—and it takes you three weeks a tune.

"It started when The Man came into my office at ten minutes after two, came straight in, opened his briefcase and took out his songs. When he walked out at four o'clock we had rehearsed, set twelve keys, and routined ten songs. An hour and fifty minutes—there's not too many singers who can do that!

"When we recorded at A&M in New York, I called the orchestra for three hours before. We rehearsed and set the balance. He came in at seven o'clock and so help me God, at eight twenty-eight he went home. We had done *four* songs.

"The musicians . . . when they saw how quickly he recorded, they freaked out. But I knew after twenty-three years of working with him that the best thing to do was to have all of our stuff together, because many times Frank gives a great take and the orchestra hasn't even started yet. They can't catch up with him.

"Frank told me that night, 'I can't believe that for forty-five years I've been coming in, wasting my time, listening to a trumpet player ask an alto sax player, "Do you have a G-natural in bar 59?" ' He said, 'This is wonderful!'

"All he had to do was call a number and we'd go straight to the first take. The musicians were like groupies, they were just listening to every note he sang."

In answer to my question, "Why has Dad survived where others haven't?" "Q" said, "God can't waste his time giving everybody something unique or original, so he just picked a few people. He picked a Louis Armstrong, he picked a Duke Ellington, he picked a Frank Sinatra, he picked a Michael Jackson. There's very few people who get *that*. You're talking about big stuff now. . . . And on top of it, Frank took the gift and developed it to its ultimate.

"He knows when to do his homework too. And he picks the right songs. Taste is one of the key words. Taste and style . . . I mean, the way he phrases . . . It freaks me, Nancy."

I would like to take one last look back at the rich legacy of the recorded Sinatra through the words of the articulate critic, Charles Champlin:

"Frank Sinatra is almost beyond challenge as the preeminent American entertainer of his times.

"His admirers now span all the age groups. But I suspect that the heart (and soul) of his audience consists of those of us who go all the way back with him, back to the near anonymity of the Dorsey days . . . and the swoonings and the wall-to-wall lapels.

"And what remains unique about Sinatra is the way in which his own seasons have continued to match those of his audience. The surpassingly romantic and idealistic early Sinatra, I mean, was just right for our young years. He provided the soundtrack for our most optimistic dreams.

"Then, after a period in which it could be said that he and we were all preoccupied, there was suddenly a new Sinatra. The unmatched gifts of timing and phrasing and the respect for the lyrics were unchanged or had become richer. But there was something else, a new maturity.

"The romantic idealism had been tempered with bittersweet wisdom, which did not, however, go all the way to cynicism. The same lyrics to the same songs now had some new, wry overtones. . . .

"Still later, in what I think of as the 'September of My Years'

period, a new mood crept into Sinatra's work, a mellow nostalgia for all the pleasures which life had provided along with the cinders in the eye and the loves who went away, a deeper wisdom, a warmer appreciation for present and remembered joys. . . .

"To listen to Sinatra today is to be reminded all over again that, among the things which are true about him, one is that he holds title to more of our musical memories than anyone else. Also, that if he is made to seem like the last angry man from time to time, what he really is in a special sense is the last passionate man. The emotions he conveys may or may not be, in the nature of things, complex, but they are powerful and persistent and widely-shared. . . .

"With Sinatra there is always a special awareness that the private man, the private experience, has infused the material with a further range of meaning and overtone. And there is always that remarkable sense of the inseparability of his own history and our own, the way in which, from the beginning, his cycles have, in different magnitudes, confirmed our own.

"But what is most extraordinary is that, these many seasons later, Mr. Sinatra is still providing the soundtracks of our very best moments."

My wish is that someday, someone like Charles Champlin will write similar words about someone else. But I can't help wondering who will continue the tradition of the big band "live" music?

What will happen when "live" sessions disappear completely? What will happen to the Billy Mays, the Riddles, the Costas of tomorrow? Will this fabulous music be relegated to the level of nostalgia? That would be a terrible tragedy.

We must try to keep some of the traditions alive. We all have a responsibility to the children of this and other nations to grow musically as well as in recording techniques.

And looking to the past won't make us old-fashioned or dated. If we use the richness of the past in conjunction with the new, it will only make us a little wiser—and just maybe, a whole lot better.

"How do you keep the music playing . . .
How do you make it last . . ."

PHOTO CREDITS

306   H.S.H. Prince Rainier of Monaco, FS, H.S.H. Princess Grace, and H.R.H. Princess Sophia of Greece, H.R.H. Prince Juan Carlos of Spain. Photo by Lukomoski.

FS and Michael Jackson. Photo by Ed Thrasher, courtesy of Warner Bros. Records.

Mahalia Jackson and Sidney Poitier. Photo by Phil Stern/Globe Photos.

FS and Col. Tom Parker. From the collection of Col. Tom Parker.

George Burns, Gracie Allen, and FS. Photo by Ted Allan.

Jersey Joe Walcott, FS, and Rocky Marciano. Photo by Bill Mark.

307   Red Skelton. Photo courtesy of Las Vegas News Bureau.

Duke Ellington and FS. Courtesy of Reprise Records.

Harry Cohn, Jack Entratter, FS, and Kim Novak. Photo courtesy of Las Vegas News Bureau.

Jimmy Stewart. Photo by Alan Berliner.

Joe E. Lewis, FS, and Swifty Morgan. Photo by Bill Mark.

FS and Debbie Reynolds. Photo by Peter C. Borsari.

FS and Ernie Kovacs. Photo by Coburn, Jr.

James Dean and Sammy Davis, Jr. Photo by Jerry Holscher.

Eleanor Roosevelt and FS. Photo by Bill Mark.

308   FS and Ms. Lillian Carter. Photo by Sam Siegel.

George "Bullets" Durgom and FS. Photo by Edward Ozern.

Mary Martin and FS. Photo by Carl Y. Iri.

FS, Dean Martin, Jerry Lewis, ca. 1980. Photo by George Aquino, Studio 6.

FS and Harry James. Photo by Sam Siegel.

The Martins and the Sinatras. Photo by Martin Mills/Globe Photos.

R. J. Wagner, Natalie Wood, and FS. Photo by Murray Garrett—Studio Five.

Simon Wiesenthal and FS. Photo by Art Waldinger/Tru Dimension Co.

FS and Paul Anka. Photo by Sam Siegel.

FS with Patsy and Rose D'Amore. Photo by Bill Mark.

309   Richard Rodgers and FS. Photo by Leo Rosenthal.

Guy McElwaine. Photo by Peter C. Borsari.

Danny and Rosemarie Thomas with FS. Photo copyright © David Sutton.

Alan King and Harry Belafonte. Photo by Bill Mark.

Jackie Heller and FS. Photo by John Dominis, _Life_ magazine, copyright © Time Inc.

Rod Steiger and FS. Photo copyright © David Sutton.

FS and Rod McKuen. Photo courtesy of Reprise Records.

FS and Emmanuel Lewis. Photo by The White House.

Lauritz Melchior and FS. Photo by CBS Photos.

310   FS and Ray Sinatra. Photo by S/Sgt. Mowbray.

Nat "King" Cole and Sammy. Photo by Jerry Holscher.

FS with Jack Benny and Mary Livingstone. Photo by Ed Braslaff, CBS Photos.

Tommy Lasorda and FS. Photo by Nate Cutler/Globe Photos.

Milton Berle and FS. Photo by Pictorial Parade.

David Tebet and FS. Photo by Sam Siegel.

311   Irwin "Ruby" Rubenstein, Leo Durocher, and Bernie "O.J." Frandt. Photo by Milt Jones.

Alan Ladd and FS. Photo by Pictorial Parade.

Juliet Prowse and FS. Photo by John Hamilton/Globe Photos.

FS with Kitty and Mervyn LeRoy. Photo copyright © David Sutton.

FS and Spencer Tracy. Photo by B.C. Mittleman.

312   FS and Prime Minister David Ben-Gurion. Photo by David Rubinger.

Nathan and Linda Golden. Photo by Lee Salem.

Paul Clemens. Photo by Jack Howard.

Anthony Quinn and Tony Curtis. Photo by Bill Mark.

FS and U Thant. Photo by Leo Rosenthal.

313   FS with Joe Delaney and Ed McMahon. Photo courtesy of Las Vegas Convention Center.

Red Buttons and FS. Photo by Sam Siegel.

David Janssen and FS. Photo copyright © David Sutton.

314   Elton John and FS. Photo by The White House.

Buddy Rich, Johnny Mercer, and FS. Photo by Edward Ozern.

FS and Itzhak Perlman. Photo by Sam Siegel.

FS and Mikhail Baryshnikov. Photo by The White House.

FS and Flip Wilson. Photo by Sam Siegel.

Altovese and Sammy Davis, Jr. From the collection of Sammy Davis, Jr.

Orson Welles and FS. Photo by Ted Allan.

Perry Como and FS. Photo by _Movieland_ magazine.

Ruth Cosgrove Berle and FS. Photo by Sam Siegel.

315   FS and Henry Fonda. Photo by Jack Harris.

FS and Steve Garvey. Photo by Gamma/Liaison.

Gary Cooper, FS, Jack Benny, and Danny Kaye. Photo by Ted Allan.

FS and Claudette Colbert. Photo by Sal Coco.

_326–34_   _Album Commentary credits:_

327   "There's a Flaw in My Flue": words by Johnny Burke, music by James Van Heusen. Copyright © 1958 by Burke & Van Heusen, Inc. Copyright assigned to Bourne Co. and Dorsey Brothers, Inc. All rights reserved. Used by permission.

331   Liner notes courtesy of Stan Corwyn, Reprise Records.

332–33   Liner notes courtesy of David McClintick and Bristol Productions, Inc.

334   Liner notes copyright © Charles Champlin.

Final photo by Phil Stern/Globe Photos.

THE VOICES

If to know a man's friends is to know the man, if a man can be judged by the company he keeps, then Frank Sinatra is truly a rich, rich man. The response from friends to my requests were immensely rewarding; in some aspects, overwhelming. Many of the stories and anecdotes unfortunately did not—could not—find their way into this manuscript. There simply wasn't room. (As my editor likes to say, save them for the next one.) But I did want to mention the people who took the time to respond to letters, phone calls, interviews.

My deep, great gratitude goes out to each person listed here. Though some were only echoes or whispers that softly guided my thoughts, these are the voices of this book:

Spiro T. Agnew
Bernie Allen
Steve Allen
Walter Annenberg
Joseph Apone
Fred Astaire

Pearl Bailey
Dick Balkalyan
Tony Bennett
Jack Benny
Robert Berks
Milton Berle
Ruth Berle
Irving Berlin
Jim Bishop
Joey Bishop
Nicky Blair
Ernest Borgnine
John Brady
Leslie Bricusse
Frederick Brisson
Cubby Broccoli
Richard Brooks
Edmund G. Brown
Yul Brynner
Buck Buchwach
Sonny Burke
George Burns
Richard Burton

Herb Caen
James Cagney
Sammy Cahn
Jimmy Cannon
Al Capp
Frank Capra
Bennett Cerf
Charles Champlin
Maurice Chevalier
James Clavell
Paul Clemens
Lee J. Cobb
Betty Comden
Perry Como
Richard Condon
Norman Corwin
Stan Corwyn
Walter Cronkite
Bing Crosby

James Darren
Sammy Davis, Jr.
Doris Day
Dr. Michael DeBakey
Armand Deutsch
Angie Dickinson
Digby Diehl
Marlene Dietrich

Jack Donohue
Gorden Douglas
Kirk Douglas
James F. Downey
Morton Downey
George Doyle
Don Drysdale
Peter Duchin
"Bullets" Durgom
Leo Durocher

Jack Entratter

Vinnie Falcone
Maureen O'Sullivan Farrow
Mia Farrow
Henry Fonda
John Forbess
Gerald Ford
Glen Ford
Dore Freeman

Martin Gabel
Buddy Garaventi
Ava Gardner
Frank Garrick
Mickey Glass
Jackie Gleason
Ralph Gleason
Edie Mayer Goetz
Nathan Golden
Barry Goldwater
Frances Goldwyn
Ruth Gordon
Freeman Gosden
Cary Grant
Hank Greenspun
Harry Guardino
Lowell Guiness
Alec Guinness

Buddy Hackett
Pete Hamill
Phil Harris
Hugh Hefner
Pat Henry
Katharine Hepburn
Paul Hirsch
Celeste Holm
Robin Douglas-Home
J. Edgar Hoover
Lena Horne
Trevor Howard
Hubert H. Humphrey

Harry James
Gordon Jenkins
Antonio Carlos Jobim
Mrs. Lyndon Johnson

Quincy Jones
Matty Jordan

E. J. Kahn
Garson Kanin
Danny Kaye
Sheldon Keller
Gene Kelly
Grace Kelly
Murray Kempton
Jay Richard Kennedy
Paul Keyes
Alan King
Dong Kingman
Dorothy Kirsten
Howard and Ruth Koch
Leon Krohn

Hugh Lambert
Burt Lancaster
Ken Lane
Jo LaSorda
Tommy LaSorda
Peter Lawford
Peggy Lee
Jack Leonard
Jack E. Leonard
Mervyn LeRoy
Jerry Lewis
Joe E. Lewis
John Lindsay
Joshua Logan
Albert Lonstcin
Sophia Loren

Clifford McCarty
Dick McClintick
Guy McElwaine
Rod McKuen
Shirley MacLaine
Ed McMahon
Leonard Maltin
Dorothy Manners
Abe Marovitz
Dean Martin
Rene Martinez
Billy May
Aileen Mehle
Robert Merrill
Bill Miller
Liza Minnelli
Robert Mitchum
Tony Mottola

Leroy Neiman
Charlotte Ford Niarchos
Richard Nixon
Louis Nizer
Kim Novak

Ed O'Brien
Mo Ostin

William S. Paley
Lilli Palmer
Colonel Tom Parker
Eleanor Parker
"Patsy's" (Sal and Joseph Scognamillo)
Luciano Pavarotti
Gregory Peck
Richard Peters
Peter Pitchess
Sidney Poitier

Nancy Reagan

Lee Remick
Debbie Reynolds
Tony Riccio
Buddy Rich
Don Rickles
Nelson Riddle
Gene Ringgold
Jilly Rizzo
Edward G. Robinson
Richard Rodgers
Michael Romanoff
Mickey Rooney
David Rose
Ric Ross
Leo Rosten
Benny Rubin
Milton Rudin
Herman Rush
Rosalind Russell

Pierre Salinger
Scott Sayers
George Schlatter
Harry Schuchman
George Sidney
Phil Silvers
George Simon
Frank Sinatra, Jr.
Nancy Sinatra, Sr.
Tina Sinatra
Stephen Sondheim
Johnnie Spotts
Jo Stafford
Barbara Stanwyck
George Stevens, Jr.
James Stewart
Elsa Stoloff
Morris Stoloff
Bill Stout
Jule Styne
Harry Sukman
Sylvia Syms

Fred Tamburro
Elizabeth Taylor
David Tebet
Twyla Tharp
Danny Thomas
Thomas Thompson
Spencer Tracy
John Tredy

Dorothy Uhlemann

James Van Heusen
Sarah Vaughan
Miguel Aleman Velasco
Ken Venturi
Mort Viner

Robert Wagner
Jack Warner
Dionne Warwick
Lew Wasserman
David Wayne
John Wayne
Jerry Weintraub
Irving "Sarge" Weiss
Sam Weiss
Robert Weitman
Raquel Welch
Orson Welles

Richard Zanuck

. . . AND FRANCIS ALBERT SINATRA.